PHILIP HOWARD

*Fame preparing a monument to Cardinal Norfolk.*

# PHILIP HOWARD

## CARDINAL PROTECTOR OF ENGLAND

*Godfrey Anstruther, OP*

Edited by Gerard Skinner

*with a foreword by Prof. Judith Champ*

GRACEWING

First published in England in 2020
by
Gracewing
2 Southern Avenue
Leominster
Herefordshire HR6 0QF
United Kingdom
www.gracewing.co.uk

*All rights reserved*

No part of this publication may be reproduced,
stored in a retrieval system, or transmitted in any
form or by any means, electronic, mechanical,
photocopying, recording or otherwise,
without the written permission of the publisher.

© 2020, The Trustees of the English Province of the Order of Preachers

The rights of the Trustees of the English Province of
the Order of Preachers to be identified as the author
of this work have been asserted in accordance
with the Copyright, Designs and Patents Act 1988.

The publishers have no responsibility
for the persistence or accuracy of URLs for websites
referred to in this publication, and do not guarantee
that any content on such websites is, or will remain,
accurate or appropriate.

ISBN 978 085244 953 0

Typeset by Word and Page, Chester, UK

Cover design by Bernardita Peña Hurtado

# Contents

| | |
|---|---|
| Foreword by Prof. Judith Champ | vii |
| Acknowledgements | ix |
| Abbreviations | x |
| Introduction | xi |
| 1. The Adventures of Philip | 1 |
| 2. Prior of Bornhem | 19 |
| 3. Grand Almoner | 47 |
| 4. Bishop Elect | 73 |
| 5. The Gathering Storm | 105 |
| 6. The Red Hat | 141 |
| 7. Cardinal in Curia | 157 |
| 8. Protector of England | 181 |
| 9. The King's Servant | 209 |
| 10. Eclipse | 231 |
| 11. Closing Years | 255 |
| Index | 295 |

# Illustrations

Cover. Andrea Casali (1705–84), painted posthumously c. 1750. Cardinal Philip Howard [Cardinal Norfolk].
© Arundel Estates

Frontispiece. Fame preparing a monument to Cardinal Norfolk. © Arundel Estates

*following p. 156:*

1. Engraving of Cardinal Howard

2. *Bue arrostito*, the roasting ox, stuffed with lambs and fowls, provided by Cardinal Howard for the people of Rome to celebrate the birth of a son to James II and Mary of Modena in 1688. Engraving by van Westernon, 1688. © Arundel Estates

3. The Church and Convent of Santa Sabina, Rome. Engraving by Giuseppe Vasi, 1756, from his publication *Delle Magnificenze di Roma Antica e Moderna, Libro Settimo*

4. Martyrs' Chapel, Venerable English College.
© Lawrence Lew

# FOREWORD

## FR GODFREY ANSTRUTHER, OP (1903–1988)

For any historian of English Catholicism since the Reformation, the name 'Anstruther' is synonymous with the four volumes of *Seminary Priests 1558–1800* (1968–77), which give a brief sketch of the three thousand or so Catholic priests who ministered in the shadowy and often dangerous world of Recusant Catholicism. These volumes, written by Fr Godfrey Anstruther, OP, have become the *vade mecum* of historians of the period. They are not, as their author recognized, the last word, but they have become, as he hoped, a starting point for countless academic and personal research projects.

When I began historical research as a doctoral student in the late 1970s, and attended my first Catholic Record Society annual conference, Anstruther was a name on a library bookshelf. It was impossible to be overawed by the eminent Dominican. He had a mischievous glint in his eye and a ready chuckle. As a thirteen-year-old nephew of a star of the music hall, George Lupino, he confided in Fr Bede Jarrett, OP, that he was uncertain whether he was called to be a priest or a clown. 'Why not be both?' was the response!

This set his approach to life. At the same conference, I was cajoled into skipping the formal proceedings to watch the Headingley Test Match on TV, at which Geoffrey Boycott made his hundredth Test Match century. Not only did I learn a great deal about cricket, but was fed comic vignettes of Dominican life, morsels of advice about historical sources, and suggestions about my own juvenile research.

We became firm friends for the last decade of his life, and I was aware, as were other friends and fellow Dominicans, of his continued disappointment that he was unable to find a publisher willing to take on his biography of the seventeenth-century English Dominican Cardinal, Philip Howard.

In 1994, the Venerable English College in Rome was to mark the fourth centenary of the death of Cardinal William Allen, the originator of the English seminaries in exile. I was delighted to remind the college authorities that it was also the third centenary of the death of Philip Howard, Cardinal Protector of England, whose Roman residence forms the core of the present English College buildings.

A double commemoration ensued, and I had hopes of achieving posthumous publication of Anstruther's life of Howard. The English Dominican archives had moved around, and by 1994, they were housed in Edinburgh. I was dismayed to discover that Anstruther's complete typescript could not be found. Only a few chapters, shorn of references, had apparently survived, which I was able to use for a paper delivered at the English College in Rome and published in *New Blackfriars*.

Many years later, the Dominican archives were given a safe home by Abbot Geoffrey Scott, OSB, at Douai Abbey, Berkshire. At some point before they were transferred from Edinburgh someone was able to reconstruct the whole of Anstruther's life of Philip Howard. This sixty-year-old manuscript is now edited and published by Fr Gerard Skinner, and is a major contribution to scholarship in the religious and political complexities of seventeenth-century England.

From 1955, Anstruther lived at the Dominican headquarters at Santa Sabina in Rome, and worked at the Dominican Historical Institute, and as spiritual director in the English College. This gave him the opportunity to explore exhaustively the Vatican and Dominican archives in Rome, and to find sources in London and Oxford and as far afield as Belgium and Spain. Howard's own papers were mostly lost. The research skills honed in those Roman years alerted Anstruther to the rich possibilities of the unconsidered fragments in archives, which would later shape his approach to *The Seminary Priests*.

It is a delight to Fr Godfrey's surviving friends and admirers that his life of Philip Howard has been rescued from oblivion and published. The gratitude owed to Fr Gerard Skinner for completing this task is not only from those of us who knew Godfrey Anstruther. Howard is a significant and largely unknown figure, whose career offers historians a valuable key to the complex interaction of religion and politics in seventeenth-century England. This is long delayed, but an important contribution to our understanding.

Professor Judith Champ
All Souls' Day, 2019

# Acknowledgements

I would like to record my sincere thanks to His Grace the Duke of Norfolk, William Loschert Esq. and the Trustees of the English Dominican Province, without whose support the publication of this biography would not have been possible. I am also most grateful to Professor Judith Champ for writing the Foreword and for her encouragement in bringing Fr Anstruther's work to print. I would also like to thank the following for their assistance: Abbot Geoffrey Scott, OSB, the Rev'd Dr Richard Finn, OP, the Rev'd Lawrence Lew, OP, the Rev'd Dr Aidan Nichols, OP, the Rev'd Alexander Balzanella, the Rev'd Dr Bruce Burbidge, Jess Farr-Cox, Michael Hodges, Craig Irving, the Rev'd Paul Keane, the Rev'd Dr Michael Lang, Paula Lopes McDermid, Dr John Martin Robinson, the Rev'd James McAuley, the Rev'd Nicholas Schofield, Professor Maurice Whitehead and Mgr Dr Philip Whitmore.

Fr Gerard Skinner<br>Editor

# Abbreviations

| | |
|---|---|
| AAW | Archives of the Archdiocese of Westminster |
| AB | Archives générales du Royaume de Belgique. Brussels |
| Agen | Correspondence of the Clergy Agent in Rome. AAW, XXXIII |
| AFOP | Archivum Fratrum Ordinis Praedicatorum, Romae 1930– |
| AGOP | Archivum Generale Ordinis Praedicatorum, Santa Sabina, Rome |
| AP | Archives of the S. Congregation of Propaganda, Rome |
| AV | Archivio Vaticano |
| AVCAU | Archives of the Venerable English College, Rome |
| Avvisi | Newsletters (mostly manuscript) in AV |
| B | Barberini Latin manuscripts, in BV |
| BL | British Library |
| Bod. | Bodleian Library, Oxford |
| BV | Biblioteca Vaticana |
| Cal.SP | Calendar of State Papers |
| Carte | Carte manuscripts in Bod. |
| CRS | Publications of the Catholic Record Society |
| *Dominicana* | *Dominicana*. CRS, XXV |
| HMC | Historical Manuscripts Commission |
| Med. | Arch.Mediceo, in Arch.di Stato, Florence |
| *MOPH* | *Monumenta Ordinis Praedicatorum Historica*, Romae, 1896– |
| NF | Nunziatura di Fiandra, in AV |
| NI | Nunziatura d'Inghilterra, in AV |
| Nunz.Div. | Nunziature Diverse, in AV |
| Nunz.Fr. | Nunziatura di Francia, in AV |
| OB | Archives of the Old Brotherhood, in AAW, A32 |
| Reg. | Registers of the Masters General, OP. AGOP, series IV |
| SB | Segreteria dei Brevi, Vatican |
| Sim. | Archivo General de Simancas |
| SP.29 | State Papers Charles II, in TNA |
| SP.85 | State Papers, Italian, in TNA |
| SP.101 | Newsletter, in TNA |
| Stuart | HMC, Stuart Papers, The National Archives |
| TNA | The National Archives (formerly Public Record Office), London |
| Vat.Lat. | Vatican Latin manuscripts, in BV |

# Introduction

It was originally intended that this book should be a sequel to *A Hundred Homeless Years*[1] and continue the history of the English Dominican province for another half-century with Cardinal Howard as the central figure. It soon became evident that such a plan would do justice neither to Howard nor to the English province. Howard's influence and importance was far wider than his career as a Dominican, and once a cardinal he ceased to be the central figure in the story of his brethren.

There was another reason. The biography of one who lived so long ago is dependent on such documents as chance has preserved, and chance has not been kind to Howard. Of his correspondence with his brethren, with his nuns and with his personal friends all too little remains; of his battles and official correspondence there is an embarrassing abundance. Howard himself is largely responsible for this, as he destroyed his papers before his death. Had they survived it would have been possible to produce a more balanced, and I believe a more engaging, portrait. All too occasionally we get a glimpse of a warm-hearted and unassuming religious. A gaity and puckish humour peeps out of the rare family letters that remain.

On the other hand an account of his public life is important, for the story of the church in England in his days is still largely an uncharted sea. A hundred years ago when the broad outline of our history was established once and for all by Tierney and Lingard, these controversies were still too recent and too much alive to be treated dispassionately and one half of the story remained inaccessible in the Roman archives. The dissentions amongst the clergy, the problems surrounding the appointment of a bishop, the ravages of Jansenism and Gallicanism, the supposed intransigence of Rome, the controversies over the oath of allegiance and many kindred subjects cannot be justly appraised till all the surviving material is published. This book is no more than a small contribution. It is the life of Howard, not a history of the church. It gives only the correspondence that concerns him, and it has been judged better to omit certain questions altogether rather than treat them cursorily.

The standard *Life of Cardinal Howard* by Raymond Palmer, OP, was published as long ago as 1867. Based for the most part on unpublished documents in the archives of the province, it is still an important work, but it suffers from certain inevitable shortcomings. In 1867 the history of the English Dominicans was virtually unrecorded, and Palmer found it necessary to devote almost a third of his book to introductory matter concerning the order in general and the English province in particular. The rest of the book is interlarded with biographical details of the brethren, valuable in themselves but a constant distraction in the narrative. I am fortunately not faced with these problems. The story of the province has been told more than once, and the biographical details are now easily accessible in Fr Walter Gumbley's *Obituary Notices*.[2] There are other defects in Palmer's book that make it inadequate for modern needs. When he wrote, it was not customary for works intended for the general reader to give references to sources. Also, he relied largely on the Latin *Annals of Bornhem*, compiled in 1719 with the help of a Flemish manuscript now lost. Although extremely valuable it is not strictly contemporaneous and not entirely reliable. He published his *Life* before his visit to Rome in 1881 which furnished him with so much new data from the archives of the Master General. Many sources, including the Vatican, were then inaccessible, and much has since been published, particularly the volume of *Dominicans* by the Catholic Record Society, that renders the task of a modern biographer as much easier.

In *A Hundred Homeless Years* I have told the story of Howard's early struggles, in the setting of his family and his brethren. In order that this biography may be complete in itself I have had to tell that story again, though much more briefly and in a way more in keeping with the rest of the book. I have tried to sketch the outlines of the much-tried novice against a background of cardinalatial purple, resplendent if somewhat sullied.

I am indebted to the officials and staffs of libraries and archives too numerous to name. I owe a particular debt of gratitude to their Eminences Cardinals Agagianian, Prefect of Propaganda, and W. Godfrey, Archbishop of Westminster, for permission to use so much material from the private archives under their charge.

Godfrey Anstruther, OP
Santa Sabina, Rome

## Notes

1. G. Anstruther, *A Hundred Homeless Years: English Dominicans 1558–1658*, London, 1958.
2. W. Gumbley, *Obituary Notices of the English Dominicans, 1558–1952*, London, 1955.

1

## *The Adventures of Philip*

I

IN 1629, WHEN OUR STORY BEGINS, the afterglow of the Elizabethan age had faded. Elizabeth had been dead twenty-six years, and of the great names that survived her, Robert Cecil had died in 1612, Shakespeare and Beaumont in 1616, Raleigh in 1618, William Byrd in 1623 and Francis Bacon in 1626. Of the Elizabethan legal world only the aged Edward Coke remained; of the poets, Donne, Drayton and Ben Jonson were still alive, but their best work belonged to a more congenial age. As for the Catholic minority, the great promise of Campion and Southwell had been cut short by the hangman. Persons had died in 1610, though John Gerard, who ought to have died a hundred times, had still another eight years to live. These great figures of the Elizabethan stage were to have few successors of the same vintage. There was of course Milton, who was just beginning to write, but by and large, literature and life were becoming colourless, and soured by Puritanism. In June 1628, in the skies above Oxfordshire had been seen mounted warriors in battle array; folks had heard the roll of drums, the clash of steel on steel and the shrieks of the smitten. A river in Gloucestershire was seen at times to run blood-red.[1] These wonders had been natural enough in the world of Puck and Peaseblossom; they could not long survive in that of Mr Worldy-Wise and Comus. It was the beginning of the scientific age. Harvey had published his treatise on the circulation of the blood in this same 1628, and Thomas Browne was already busy with his experiments. Abroad Descartes, whose name was to dominate philosophy, had just retired to Holland.

The long-suffering Catholics fared no better than the rest. There were many men of culture among their gentry and clergy; there were still priests zealous enough to die for their faith. But there is scarcely a name that is generally known, and nobody who showed outstanding gifts of leadership when a leader was desperately needed.

It was into this age of transition that Philip Howard was born, on 21 September 1629, at Arundel House in the Strand, the London mansion of his family. He was the third son of Henry Frederick Howard (who used the courtesy title of Lord Mowbray and Maltravers) and grandson of Thomas, Earl of Arundel, widely known as a virtuoso and art-collector. Through his father, Philip inherited the blood of the Norfolks, though the title of Duke of Norfolk had been lost by attainder in 1572 and was not to be revived till 1660. Through his mother, Elizabeth daughter of Esmé Stuart d'Aubigny, 3rd Duke of Lennox, Philip could claim relationship with the royal house of Stuart. His great-grandfather, Esmé, 1st Duke of Lennox, was first cousin of Henry Darnley, who married Mary, Queen of Scots. Thus Charles I, then reigning, and Philip's mother were third cousins. Through the d'Aubignys Philip was also related to the kings of France.

The Norfolk Howards had a persistent, though not unbroken tradition of loyalty to the Old Religion. Philip's great-grandfather, St Philip Howard (after whom he was presumably named) had died for this faith in the Tower under sentence of death in 1595. Then in 1616 Thomas Earl of Arundel had publicly renounced his faith, though he was looked upon by his friends rather as a wayward Catholic than a convinced Protestant. Thomas's wife, Alethea Talbot, remained ever a staunch papist, and so apparently did her children: but in spite of this Philip and his two elder brothers were baptized and educated as Protestants.

There are no facts preserved concerning Philip's early years. The first mention of him is on 4 July 1640 when he was nearly eleven. With his two elder brothers Thomas and Henry he was entered at St John's College, Cambridge, and put under the personal supervision of the President, Dr Richard Baylie,[2] who was soon to be removed and imprisoned by the parliamentarians for his loyalty to the king. Their university career was destined to last only a few months. By the middle of 1641 civil war was imminent and many families fled abroad or sent their children there. In August the earl was deputed to escort the queen mother, Marie de Medici to the Continent at the end of her long visit to her daughter, Queen Henrietta Maria. He took this opportunity of removing his wife, his younger son Viscount Stafford and his three eldest grandsons from the dangers that threatened the country. The boys were sent to school at Utrecht and their grandmother, after a stay at Cologne with the queen mother, settled in Antwerp, where she was joined by the earl in February 1642.

Some time in this year Henry and Philip (there is no evidence as to Thomas) were received into the Catholic Church. In the spring of 1644 the earl set out for France and Italy with Thomas and Philip. Henry may have travelled with them, for by April 1645 he was in Rome, as the guest of Cardinal Francesco Barberini.[3] The others remained in northern Italy and in April 1645 were in Milan. Philip went sightseeing with a servant named John Burbury and asked him to make enquiries for an English-speaking priest, as he wished to make his Easter confession. They were directed to the Franciscans where there was an Irish priest. By one of those chances that determine our destinies it happened that this priest was away and they were referred to the Dominican convent of S. Eustorgio, where the regent of studies was an Irishman named John Baptist Hacket. Thus Philip made his first contact with the Dominican order. Fr Hacket and the young boy took to each other at once. Philip returned on Easter Sunday (16 April) to make his communion and stayed for what was more than a monastic breakfast. They met several times during the following days and Fr Hacket was not over-reticent in singing the praises of his order. He said he would like to see him a Cardinal. When Philip returned to his grandfather, then at Piacenza, he made the most momentous decision of his life, but he kept it to himself.[4] The sequel is best told in what is his earliest extant letter, written to the Dominican Master General:

> I give notice to your most reverend paternity that I returned from Venice to Piacenza with my grandfather on the 8th of this month, whence I left for Milan. I left there for Cremona with Fr Regent on the 21st, travelling in secret so as not to be molested, and this morning Fr Prior has given me the holy habit of our glorious St Dominic, thanks be to God and to your paternity, to whom I am perpetually obliged. I hope by God's grace to bring forth that fruit in religion which my vocation and state demand. Cremona, 28th June 1645.[5]

He also wrote to his grandfather but the letter has not survived. What has survived is an Italian version of a letter of the same date written to the earl by Fr Hacket, and couched in the following terms:

*Philip Howard*

> The proverb says that everyone will draw water to his own mill, and that is what I have done to mine in the person of your excellency's nephew, called in the world Mr Philip Howard. He confided to me that for a long time he had cherished a desire to become a religious, and I advised him to join my own order of St Dominic for many reasons. He entered this morning here in Cremona with supreme satisfaction to all the fathers, by express permission of the Master General, changing his name from Philip to Thomas in memory of that great doctor of Aquino, who, like your nephew, was a nobleman by birth. I hope that this boy will be a worthy follower of him and that one day he will do honour to the church of God and to his order. He is very happy and we too are delighted with such an acquisition. Your excellency must not be upset by this decision of the lad made without your knowledge, as it is the divine will. Nor have you any occasion to complain of me, for I have had no other intention than to serve you, as now I attend your commands, kissing your hands. Cremona, 28 June 1645.[6]

The earl received this news with consternation and bitter resentment. He at once mobilized all the power of his prestige and of his many influential friends in a single-minded endeavour to retrieve his beloved grandson from the clutches of the Dominicans. It must have seemed a fairly simple task. It was an age when almost anything could be done by the patronage of great names. The pope, Innocent X, was said to be completely under the thumb of his sister-in-law, the notorious Donna Olimpia, who, if suitably rewarded, could obtain any favour from him. Then there were the mighty Barberini brothers, who were not likely to jeopardize their friendship with the first peer of England by sponsoring the cause of a boy scarcely old enough to know his own mind. Moreover the Barberinis were deadly enemies of Tomaso Turco, the Dominican Master General, and the fate of this boy was soon caught in the web of ecclesiastical politics. These must be described in some details if his chances are to be rightly assessed.

II

The order which Philip had decided to join was just emerging from one of the strangest and saddest crises in its long history.[7] In 1642 the Dominican Master General, Nicolo Ridolfi fell foul of the

*The Adventures of Philip*

Barberini family. The only cause of offence that has been adduced was that Ridolfi had done much to further the marriage of Paolo Borghese and Donna Olimpia Aldobrandini,* a young lady of very ample fortune that the Barberinis had designs upon. To fall foul of the Barberinis at this date was a serious business. The reigning pontiff, Urban VIII, belonged to that family and he had not been wanting in avuncular love. He had created two nephews cardinals; Francesco Barberini, Protector of England, whose name occurs so frequently in this book, and Antonio, who was among other things Protector of the Dominican order. The youngest nephew Taddeo had to be content with the lucrative position of Prefect of Rome. Urban built a sumptuous palace for them near his own palace of the Quirinal, conferred more than adequate benefices upon them, and the power of selling livings and privileges of all sorts. If they gathered handsomely they also spent handsomely. Francesco in particular was a man of cultivated tastes, who spent his wealth lavishly on works of art, on rare books and, let it be added, on numerous charities. He corresponded with most of the great virtuosi of Europe including Thomas, Earl of Arundel. By 1640 their wealth and influence were immense.

On 22 April 1642, on what proved to be a frivolous and trumped-up charge, the pope suddenly ordered Ridolfi to be removed from his convent of the Minerva and virtually imprisoned in the convent of S. Sisto. Next day a brief was issued ordering his trial, though nothing came of it for a time. Meanwhile a hunt was made for more substantial, or at least more credible charges against him, and they had not far to look. He had taken a firm line with many Italian Dominicans who had built up private incomes. The money (in some cases it was real estate) was put into the common fund and the erring brethren brought back to the letter of their vow of poverty. It required no great persuasion to enlist their co-operation in drafting charges of misappropriation, maladministration and the like. By a brief of 27 June Ridolfi was suspended from all his powers, and soon after moved to the appropriately named convent of St Peter-in-Chains, belonging to the canons regular of the Lateran. By the same brief Antonio Barberini as cardinal protector was granted all the jurisdiction of the Master General.

---

* She must not be confused with Olimpia Maidalchini, the notorious Donna Olimpia already mentioned.

He in turn nominated, for the day-to-day business of the order, a vicar general who was no friend of Ridolfi.

There was at this time in Rome an ambitious Dominican with powerful political connections. This was Michaele Mazarin, aged thirty-seven, brother of the cardinal who was soon to succeed Richelieu and was already an important figure in France. Michaele Mazarin made no secret of his desire and determination to be the next Master General. He used his own and his brother's influence to cause several vacant provincialates to be filled by nominees of the pope and therefore enemies of Ridolfi. He also persuaded the cardinal protector to appoint him president of the general Chapter that was to be held at Genoa in October 1642, seeing that Ridolfi would not be allowed to preside. Having further procured a brief inhibiting Ignazio Cianti, a faithful friend of Ridolfi, from voting at the Chapter or even leaving Rome, he set out for Genoa full of hope.

The Chapter was held in the convent of S. Domenico, and it was soon evident that is was packed with Mazarin's friends. Although there were only four French provincials the French delegation numbered eighty. The Polish and some Italian provincials had been put in by his machinations. The French influence was so overwhelming that it immediately aroused the hostility and suspicion of the others, most of them from provinces, in Europe or the New World, under the domination of Spain. After much heated protesting there was a schism. Led by Domenico de Marinis, the only Italian present who adhered to Ridolfi, the provincials of Hungary, Germany and Bohemia, and the diffinitors of Ireland, Bética (Andalusia) and Aragon and from five provinces in the New World, migrated to another convent in the suburbs of Genoa and there held a rival Chapter. Mazarin had no trouble in inducing his yes-men to declare Ridolfi deposed and himself elected. Meanwhile in the other convent, having paid tribute to the merits of Ridolfi and recorded an impassioned appeal to 'apostolic benignity' to restore him to favour, they proceeded to elect as Master General the diffinitor of Aragon, who was to act only till the restoration of their legitimate general. There were thus three generals at once; a situation that had never before arisen even during days of the anti-popes.

These proceedings did nothing to further the ends of Urban VIII, as they emphasized that there was a strong party, in the order as a whole, that sided with Ridolfi. He therefore suspended the acts of both Chapters and appointed a congregation of cardinals to go into the matter. In March 1643 he declared the acts of both Chapters to be null and void and in April ordered another Chapter to assemble in Rome in May 1644.

All this time Ridolfi remained a prisoner without being brought to trial. It would seem that Urban hoped that the unpleasant task of deposing him could be left to the coming Chapter. On 27 April, seventeen days before the Chapter was to begin, he annulled all processes against him and offered him a bishopric, which was refused. For two years the Barberinis had had full control of the appointments within the order and it was anticipated that the Chapter would do what was expected of them.

The Chapter met on 14 May. By order of the pope it was presided over by Cardinal Poli, who had taken no part against Ridolfi. This gave to the proceedings an air of freedom, which, however, was soon dispersed. Before any other business the cardinal rose and read four papal briefs. The first absolutely excluded Ridolfi from any participation in the Chapter: the others imposed a like exclusion on three eminent fathers, who had never wavered in their loyalty to Ridolfi, viz. Domenico de Marinis and his brother Giovanbattista and Ignazio Cianti. Without a word these four rose and left the room. Then followed a memorable scene. A large number of the capitular fathers escorted Ridolfi to the very door of the convent and begged him to tell them how they should vote. He inclined his head to one of his companions and whispered: 'Turco'. The cry was taken up: 'Turco, general'. The order had refound its unity. The fathers returned to the assembly and Tomaso Turco was unanimously elected at the first scrutiny. It was an unmistakable gesture of confidence in Ridolfi that was not lost on the Barberinis. It was inevitable that, as the nominee of Ridolfi, Turco would incur the enmity of Ridolfi's enemies. They were soon further angered by the favour he showed to his unfortunate predecessor. On 23 May, within a few days of the end of the Chapter, a correspondent writes:

> Cardinal Barberini is so incensed against Padre Turco that he has ordered him to turn P. Ridolfi out of the convent of S. Sabina and send him back to prison at St Peter-in-Chains. When the general gave this news to Ridolfi he replied that the case against him had been quashed, that he had been absolved and as an ex-Master General he had the right, according to the constitutions of the order, to choose his house of residence.[8]

How far the enmity of the Barberinis would have pursued the new general none will ever know, for on 29 July of this year Urban died and his nephews lost his powerful support. He was succeeded in September by Cardinal Pamphili (Innocent X), whose nephew was soon to marry that Donna Olimpia whose first marriage had been the cause of all the trouble. But the two Barberini cardinals remained; still immensely wealthy, still influential and not at all disposed to favour Turco or his friends.

The solution of this crisis in the order was scarcely a year old when Philip Howard received the habit in June 1645. That very month the new Master General set out on a visitation of France and Spain that was to keep him from Rome for nearly three years. He appointed Domenico de Marinis, vicar general, to take charge in his absence, the friend of Ridolfi and the enemy of the Barberinis. At the Roman court as agent of the English queen was John Digby, son of Sir Kenelm Digby. Kenelm was a friend of the Earl of Arundel and unlikely to imperil his friendship by any great activity on behalf of Philip. Thus in July 1645, when the earl began to move heaven and earth in order to reclaim his wayward grandson; there was nobody at Rome, apart from his brethren, who would champion Philip's cause.

III

The letters of 28 June notifying the earl of Philip's clothing must have been sent by special messenger for they reached him on the following day. He at once sent the doleful news to his wife at Antwerp. His letter took exactly a month to reach her, and in that time things had begun to move. The earl had also written to Cardinal Francesco Barberini and John Digby in Rome. They lost no time in carrying the matter to the cardinal secretary, Camillo Pamphili, son of the all-powerful Donna Olimpia. He referred it to the pope, and the upshot was a papal command that the novice should be removed from Cremona and lodged in the palace of Cardinal Cesare Monti, Archbishop of Milan, in order that his vocation might be thoroughly tested. Philip was accordingly conducted to Milan on 27 July.[9] Cardinal Antonio Barberini had written to the Master General on 18 July. His language is guarded. He asks the general to deal with this matter in the most dextrous and efficacious manner he can, that it may be settled with all possible promptness and without fuss or noise.[10] Francesco Barberini wrote on the same day to the earl asking him to forgive his grandson's imprudence, which was the result of his tender years and singular piety.[11] In a later letter that has not survived he evidently assured him of success, for on 7 August the earl comments:

> Although he writes that he still remains firm in his first determination, still I hope that with the continued favour of your Em[inence] he will be made to understand his duty towards a parent who deserves to receive from him a greater measure of obedience and love.[12]

For more than two months Philip remained the prisoner of Cardinal Monti, treated always with respect and kindness but rigorously cut off from any communication with his religious brethren. Only two days after his arrival his friend Fr Hacket drafted for him a petition to the pope. He tried to obtain the boy's signature. In this he was unsuccessful so the petition was never presented; but Hacket thought fit to send a copy of it to Henry Howard.[13] A copy eventually found its way to Rome via the internuncio at Brussels, with the comment: 'This petition was sent to His Holiness without the boy's knowledge'. It had not in fact been sent to the pope.

There are extant no fewer than sixteen letters from Cardinal Monti to Rome relating the efforts he had made and the arguments he had used to shake the constancy of his young prisoner.[14] He succeeded in excluding anybody who might have given the boy a word of encouragement or comfort, and he called in the services of several priests including the ex-general of the Oratorians. Henry Howard had a long walk with his brother in the garden on 9 August but could not shake his resolution. All this time the countess had been active in Antwerp, writing constantly through the internuncio. The greater distance from Rome meant a delay of nearly a month. Monti's instructions had been to keep Philip forty days and if he still stood firm to return him to the Dominicans. The countess's pleadings moved the cardinal secretary to order an extension of this period, but when his letter reached Milan on 6 September it was too late. Acting on his previous instructions Monti had restored the novice to his order; but because Henry Howard objected to his return to Cremona he had been consigned to the prior of the convent of S. Maria delle Grazie in Milan itself.

In order to satisfy the countess the boy's fate was now placed in the hands of the Cardinals of Propaganda. On 12 September at a congregation held at the Quirinal, presided over by Innocent X in person and attended by nine cardinals including the Barberini brothers, it was proposed that Philip should, according to the petition of his grandmother, be consigned to the custody of some lay person. The pope cut short all discussion by announcing that Philip had been summoned to Rome.[15]

The letter ordering this removal had been sent three days before on 9 September and reached Milan on the 20th. Monti waited to find a suitable escort and it was not till 3 October that Philip set out for Rome in the company of a certain Monsignor Terzago, who was returning to his duties there. They arrived about the middle of the month. It had been decided that Philip should be incarcerated in the sumptuous new palace of the Barberinis, but for reasons that will appear presently this arrangement was no longer convenient. Instead, he was placed with the Oratorians at the Chiesa Nuova. It was decided that Henry Howard should be sent back to Rome to press the claims of the family. He left Piacenza on 9 October and on 26 October he visited his brother at the Chiesa Nuova together with John Digby. They found him as constant as ever.[16] Then the family made one last desperate effort to obstruct Philip's vocation. A petition was prepared that goes far beyond anything previously asked for. Up till now the argument had been that he was very young and had been swept off his feet; that he had entered the order without due thought and under undue persuasion. They had asked that his vocation should be tested. Now that he had been subjected to an ordeal for more than three months and was still of the same mind his relatives showed their hand. They now petitioned that on no account should he be allowed to make profession in the Dominican order or any other and that any such profession if made should be declared null and void.[17]

How far the Barberinis, in their anxiety to please the earl and countess, would have supported this petition will never be known, for at this time fortune's wheel took a sudden turn. Almost at the moment when Philip received the habit in June of this year, inquiries were being instituted in the papal courts as to the means whereby the Barberinis had amassed their fabulous wealth during the pontificate of their uncle. There was nothing petty about the Barberinis, and this proved to be true of the discrepancies that were found in their accounts of expenditure of public money. Antonio Barberini, who was the chief offender, decided that the eternal city had lost its attractions, and on the night of 27 September, just a week before Philip set out for Rome, he slipped quietly away disguised as a sailor and got safely to France. There was a warm welcome awaiting him from Mazarin and the anti-papal court of Louis XIV. On 23 October Cardinal Capponi, prefect of Propaganda and one of the few remaining cardinals promoted prior to the election of Urban VIII, was named comprotector of the Dominican order with full powers of protector, to act during the absence without leave of Cardinal Antonio. The other Barberini brothers felt more secure as their financial dealings had been sanctioned by several briefs from their uncle. They stayed in Rome. On 15 October just about the time Philip arrived they ostentatiously displayed the arms of France and the French flag from the balcony of the palace that was to have been Philip's prison, as a gesture of defiance and a mark of family solidarity. However in the following January they thought it prudent to follow their brother to France, Taddeo adding his four sons to the party. They were pronounced contumacious and the vast Barberini property in the papal states was declared confiscated.

The petition drawn up by Henry Howard is undated. It is addressed to Cardinal Capponi. There is no record of its consideration by the cardinals of Propaganda, and there must remain a doubt whether it was ever presented at all. Henry writes to his grandfather on 7 November to say that 'we cannot possibly have any command from the pope to command my brother absolutely to be excluded from the order; for Cardinal Pamphili himself says it would be an extreme scandal to the world that by main force he should be hindered from it if it be a true vocation from God'.[18] This does not sound like a formal reply to the petition, but a hint that it had better be dropped.

Whatever the truth of the matter, when Philip's cause reached its critical stage the Barberini brothers were in no position to influence the papal court. By 22 January 1646 he had been restored to the Dominicans at S. Sisto and his ordeal was over. It is usually considered that Donna Olimpia was responsible for the disgrace of the Barberinis, and it was only when she herself was out of favour in 1648 that they were able to return to Rome and recover their property. So perhaps Philip and the Dominican order are indebted to this grasping woman. Philip nursed no resentment against the Barberinis. For the next thirty years we shall find him constantly invoking the protection of Francesco Barberini, whom he was destined to succeed as Cardinal Protector of England.

Philip (or Brother Thomas, as we must in future call him) passed the rest of his noviciate uneventfully. He was left in peace, if indeed any English boy could be said to enjoy peace when his country was torn by civil war, his king in the hands of the Scots rebels and soon to be executed, his family scattered, his grandfather dying at Padua, his eldest brother a helpless imbecile, his grandmother alone in Antwerp, his mother in exile in France. But at least there was no further attempt to do violence to his vocation. In the summer the novices were moved from S. Sisto to S. Clemente, and there on 19 October 1646 Br Thomas made his solemn profession in the hands of Domenico de Marinis, the vicar general. There were none of his English brethren present, but his profession was witnessed by two members of the Irish province, Thomas Bernadine alias O'Brien and Arthur D'Arcy, a professed novice. Five days before his profession his grandfather died at Padua. He was reconciled to the Church before his death,[19] so doubtless had forgiven his favourite grandson for becoming a beggarly friar.

## IV

Br Thomas was sent for his studies to the convent of S. Maria della Sanità at Naples, a house of strict observance directly subject to the Master General. Here the constitutions were observed to the letter, with matins at midnight, perpetual abstinence and the strictest poverty. Here also he came under the influence of a distinguished theologian, Ignazio Flume, who had been appointed regent of studies at an unusually early age. He was still in his twenties. In addition to his ordinary lectures Flume, by special precept of the Master General, gave Howard private tuition in the type of apologetics that was needed in England. His notes were later expanded into a substantial work in four folio volumes,[20] the third of which appeared in 1680, dedicated to his English disciple of thirty years before and with an appeal *ad Reges Angliae* to desist from heresy. In the following year Howard was able to repay his old master by procuring for him the See of Polignano.[21]

*The Adventures of Philip*

Howard always retained grateful memories of La Sanità, and in after years was responsible for sending there some of the most promising of his English brethren, including Thomas Worthington, several times provincial, and Dominic Williams, who became vicar apostolic in England. Indeed it is on record that he always spoke of it with tenderness, and said that were he not burdened with the upkeep of his own foundations, La Sanità would have had tangible testimony of his generous dispositions.[22]

Howard had missed the horrors of civil war in his own country but was soon to experience them at close quarters. In 1648 the citizens of Naples rebelled against Spanish rule and there was bloodshed and looting. He must have seen the Spanish armada in the bay. The revolt was easily suppressed and there followed the hangings and quarterings and the ghastly parade of traitors' heads on the city gates.[23]

One other incident of his years at Naples has come down to us. In 1649 he was visited by his uncle William Viscount Stafford, who was then in some sort of trouble, perhaps financial. Together they called on the nuncio, Emilio Altieri, who provided whatever help was required. Altieri was then a man of nearly sixty, the younger brother of a cardinal and without any expectations of being raised to that dignity himself. Not by the wildest flight of fancy could anyone have dreamed that these three men would be brought together again more than twenty-five years later, the nuncio seated in the chair of Peter, the young novice kneeling before him to receive the cardinal's hat, in the presence of that same uncle who, 250 years later still, would be raised, on that very spot, to the altars of the church as Blessed William Howard.

Meanwhile, with a sympathetic pope and the Barberinis far away, the Dominicans were able to breathe more freely. The Master General, Tomaso Turco, died in December 1649 and the pope appointed the recently disgraced Ridolfi president-general of the coming Chapter and ordered it to be convoked in Rome for the following Pentecost. It was an unmistakable sign of the pope's mind and there must have been many provincials, who, when they set out for Rome, had already decided to vote for Ridolfi. To their great grief he died on 25 May 1650, only a few days before the Chapter began. The fathers showed their sympathy and their loyalty by electing Giovanbattista de Marinis, one of Ridolfi's three faithful friends and fellow scapegoats. About this time Br Thomas's health was causing concern and it was decided to send him to France to finish his studies. Thus it happened that the arrived in Rome at the time of the Chapter in this Holy Year of 1650. Already the main ambition of his life was clear to him. He would establish the English Dominican province on a firm foundation after a century of most precarious struggle. He presented a petition to the Chapter pointing out that the number of Dominicans in England was very small and the number abroad still smaller. He asks that some priory may be set aside for their sole use, where they may train their own novices, or at least that provincials should be admonished to receive English, Irish and Scottish youths and prepare them as missionaries. This petition was considered by the Chapter and an ordination based on his proposals is recorded in the *acta*.[24] During these months in Rome Br Thomas appears to have made a deep impression on the new Master General; all the letters that he received in after years (we have none of Howard's own) breathe warmth and intimacy.

In November 1650 Br Thomas set out from Rome with a distinguished Irish Dominican, Dominic of the Rosary alias Daly, who was carrying letters form the Master General to the exiled English Queen, Henrietta Maria. They travelled together to Paris and thence Br Thomas made his way to Rennes in Brittany where he was to spend the next two or three years. Only one incident in his time there has been preserved but it is of some importance. Some time in the summer of 1651, though he was not yet ordained, he gave the habit of the order to two young men in the nearby convent of Morlaix. One was James Cunningham, a Scottish exile, and the other was Christopher Torre, who took the name of Vincent.[*] Like many of his nation who joined the order abroad Cunningham soon disappears from view. After his ordination he was given permission to go to Scotland for domestic reasons but was to return to his convent at Rennes.[25] There is no further reference to him. Torre, on the other hand, was destined to succeed Howard as superior, and later to become provincial of England.

---

[*] There is extant a draft of a letter from Vincent Torre to James II dated 22 September 1685. Speaking of Howard he casually refers to 'the 34 years experience I have had of him since he gave me unworthy the holy habit of our order' (Torre Papers). As he and Cunningham received permission (8 July 1652) to be professed together (Reg.91, f. 38) I have presumed that Cunningham was also clothed by Howard.

Howard was ordained priest in August 1652.[26] It was the intention of the Master General that he should return to Rome. There are minutes of letters to this effect dated 31 March 1653 and 30 May 1654,[27] but this journey was destined to be delayed for more than twenty years. In January 1654 he was in Antwerp and went thence to Amsterdam where his grandmother was living.[28] He was probably with her when she died on 3 June 1654. His father had died in April 1652 and it was probably business connected with the estates of both of them that suddenly called him to England. He writes to the Master General from London on 7 September to explain that the urgency of the summons had left him no time to seek permission.[29]

It was thirteen years since Howard had left England at the age of eleven. He had left a kingdom and returned to find a Puritan dictatorship. Cromwell had been declared Protector in the previous year. The House of Lords had been abolished and Howard's high birth was a hindrance rather than a help. Catholics were being crushed by fines and sequestrations. A month or two before his coming John Southworth had been martyred at Tyburn and none could foresee that there would not be another victim for a quarter of a century. In London Howard made his first contact with the handful of English Dominicans. There was the aged Thomas Middleton, who had ruled his little flock for thirty years, most of the time from the Clink prison. He had been tried for his life in 1651 while Howard was studying at Rennes. There was George Catchmay, who had been in England at least twenty-two years. At Stafford there was William Fowler and at Hexham the two brothers Armstrong, whose long-devoted ministry was still remembered eighty years later. There may have been one or two more, but these five are all that can be named with certainty. Three of them were in their sixties and the youngest was forty-seven. Middleton had been aware of the necessity of a house for training novices. In 1627 he had petitioned Propaganda for permission to receive them in private houses owing to the impossibility of having a formal convent in England. This petition had been rejected, as it was considered that they could be more effectively educated in a house of full observance in Flanders or France.[30] In 1636 he was licensed by the Master General to receive novices in England, provided they were housed together 'in some place where more secure quiet reigns' — a condition that could scarcely be observed in a country under the penal laws.[31] Hence nothing had been accomplished and (as far as is known) there had been no accession to the province during the twenty years prior to the clothing of Howard himself in 1645. This small band of veteran missionaries must have been heartened by his contacts with so many influential people at home and abroad. Through the internuncio at Brussels he had already established a way of sending letters safely to Rome. In the difficult undertaking of founding a convent they could not move a step without authority from the order and from Propaganda, and Howard's contacts in Antwerp and Brussels, and his friendship with the Master General and the Cardinal Protector of England were as essential as the wealth that had come to him from his father and grandmother.

On 1 October 1655 Howard wrote to the Master General proposing that Catchmay should be appointed vicar general in place of Middleton, who was worn out by age and toil. This was done. He also asked permission to open a noviciate in England, but this had to be refused because Urban VIII had made the conditions of a valid noviciate so much more stringent that they could not be observed in a country under persecution. Then Howard's letters cease for a time and Catchmay takes over command. Another general Chapter was meeting in Rome in May 1656 and Catchmay sent a moving appeal which 'called forth groans from many and tears from some'. The Master General replied with the heartening news that three English youths had offered themselves for the order and were being sent to France for their noviciate.[32] But the difficulties in the way of an all-English convent seemed insuperable. In November 1656, however, Catchmay received permission to try to establish a house in France or Belgium, and in June 1657 Howard once more crossed the Channel to see what he could find.[33]

Quite apart from the paucity of members there were other obstacles in his path. A few years earlier Peter Primrose, a Scotsman but a member of the Irish province, had been fired by a similar ambition to try to found a house for his compatriots. He had gone to Rome in 1650 and returned to France armed with warm recommendations from the Master General, asking the French provinces each to take two novices nominated by Primrose.[34] He had managed to place one at Toulouse, on his way to Paris, but in Paris he found the Dominicans uncooperative. He enlisted the kind offices of a number of Scotch exiles who were then in Paris, including Lord Grey, Sir James Hamilton, Baron Ridsal, a priest of the English queen's oratory, whose name is given as Thomas Bethaeus and a layman in the household of the Duchess of York named James Cunningham, who, as we have seen, entered the order in the following year. He was also helped by Ludovic d'Aubigny, a canon of Notre Dame, who was Howard's uncle. In spite of all this influential support nothing came of his schemes. One sentence in a letter to him from the Master General sums up the problems:

> We willingly grant you this permission provided you can first obtain the licence of the king, the *conseil*, the archbishop and our own convents.[35]

Perhaps it was the hopelessness of satisfying all these French officials that prompted Howard to look to the Spanish Netherlands.

## Notes

[1] B, 6816, f. 17.
[2] BL, Add. 5850, f. 95.
[3] H. Foley, *Records of the English Province S.J.*, 1877–83, VI, 627.
[4] Anstruther, *A Hundred Homeless Years*, 203.
[5] B, 7824, f. 75.
[6] Anstruther, *A Hundred Homeless Years*, 205.
[7] This section is based on A. Mortier, *Histoire des Maîtres Généraux de l'ordre des Frères Prêcheurs*, VI (1913), ch. VII.
[8] Ibid.
[9] Anstruther, *A Hundred Homeless Years*, 205–7.
[10] *Dominicana*, 5.
[11] *Ibid.*, 6.
[12] B, 7368, no. 3.
[13] B, 7824, f. 86; Anstruther, *A Hundred Homeless Years*, 209.
[14] B, 7824, ff. 67–89.
[15] Anstruther, *A Hundred Homeless Years*, 214.
[16] B, 8616, f. 98.
[17] *Dominicana*, 20.
[18] *Ibid.*, 22.
[19] Archivum Romanum Societatis Jesu, Epit. Gen. Anglia, 1642–98, f. 82.
[20] *Schola veritatis adversus mendacia Luteri, Calvini & Protestantium erecta*, Napoli, 1675–94. See Quétif-Echard, *Scriptores Ordinis Praedicatorum*, Paris, 1719–21, II, 736.
[21] P. T. Milante, *De viris inlustribus congregationis S. Mariae Sanitatis*, Napoli, 1745, 152; G. M. Cavalieri, *Galleria de' sommi pontefici, patriachi, archivescovi e vescovi dell' ordine de' predicatori*, Benevento, 1696, I, 662.

22. Fottaviano Bulgarini, *Vita del P. M. Domenico do S. Tomaso, OP, detto prima Sultan Osman Ottomano, figlio d'Ibraim Imperador de Turchi*, Napoli, 1689, 214.
23. Nunziatura di Napoli, 43, f. 80 (28 April 1648)
24. *Dominicana*, 23; *MOPH*, XII, 300.
25. Reg. 102, 233.
26. *Dominicana*, 23.
27. Reg. 102, 57, 112.
28. B, 6795, f. 24.
29. Reg. 101, 308.
30. AP, Acta Cong. Gen. 1626–7, f. 299 (9 Oct.).
31. Anstruther, *A Hundred Homeless Years*, 152.
32. *Ibid* 234.
33. Reg. 101, 467, 534.
34. Anstruther, *A Hundred Homeless Years*, 224.
35. Reg. 91, ff. 91–2.

2

## *Prior of Bornhem*

I

FROM THE EARLY YEARS OF ELIZABETH most of the exiled houses of English clergy, secular and regular, had been established in the dominions of the King of Spain. The money collected in England had never been sufficient for their maintenance, and many were in receipt of a Spanish pension. By the time Fr Thomas Howard sought to found a house for the English Dominicans the burden of these exiled religious had become more than the countries, particularly the Spanish Netherlands, could stand. Constant war with the Dutch Calvinists had exhausted the resources of a once flourishing country, and a law had been made forbidding any new foundations without licence from the Spanish king. Such licence was granted only when it could be shown that the proposed house had an adequate income and would not be a further burden on the local people. There were other stringent conditions that had never been imposed on the earlier foundations. The difficulties that thus confronted Fr Howard must have appeared as insuperable as those he had met in France.

One fact told in his favour. He was offered a convent that was already in being, so that his foundation implied no more than a change of ownership. This was the Convent of Bornhem, situated near the south bank of the Scheldt some twenty-five miles north-west of Brussels. The story of the foundation of Bornhem is the story of a relic. Peter Coloma, who had bought the property and the title of Baron of Bornhem, possessed a relic of the True Cross and in 1603, built a church and convent about a mile from his castle, as a worthy shrine for his treasure. The convent was entrusted to Flemish Franciscans but it never prospered. There was never more than a skeleton community, and for some years there was only a caretaker.[1] The baron's son, also named Peter, accordingly invited the Flemish Dominicans, and permission was given on 4 July 1637.[2] But there was strenuous opposition from the Franciscans and these were supported by the civil authorities. A royal decree of 16 July 1641 forbade the Dominicans to hold any assembly there and the baron was forbidden to build them a separate cloister, or to assist them in any way.[3] So things continued till 1653, by which time the Franciscans appear to have relinquished their claims. The baron offered the convent to the Flemish Dominicans through his confessor, Ambrosius Drewe, then prior of Brussels. On 8 November 1653 the Master General counselled the provincial to accept but made a condition that caused them to hesitate. He stipulated that the convent must be one of strict observance, with matins at midnight and perpetual abstinence.[4] Convents of this type had been established in many provinces in the hope of leavening less observant houses. They appear to have given a great deal of trouble and were never popular with the brethren generally. There was already one at Brussels that was constantly in the news, and perhaps the provincial thought that one was enough. At all events the baron's offer was not accepted. The convent was then entrusted to the Williamites, an order long since absorbed into the Cistercians, but these never obtained the royal permission to settle there.

Such was the position when Howard, arrived. He was not at first attracted to Bornhem. He tried to purchase a house in Termonde (where the English Dominican nuns had found a brief refuge a century before), and as late as September 1657 he was still negotiating for a house at Oudenarde.[5] Only when these overtures failed did he decide on Bornhem. On 15 December 1657 the Master General accepted the house and appointed Howard first prior.[6] Formal permission was received from the Spanish king on 9 March 1658, and the conditions imposed amply explain Howard's hesitations.

> 1. They must prove to our council that they have an annual income of 1000 florins.
> 2. They must enter it only as a refuge and may not increase their property.
> 3. There must never be more than thirteen religious and they are forbidden to beg.
> 4. If they depart, the order has no power to place other religious there.

5. They may not admit religious of other nationalities.
6. On Sundays and feast-days they must say Mass and Office behind locked doors lest the people be diverted from their parish church and miss the instruction.
7. They are forbidden to hear confessions, give communion or exercise other pastoral functions without permission from the local pastors.[7]

The formal gift of the convent was made by John Francis Coloma to John Baptist Verjuyse, the Belgian provincial, and Thomas Howard on 6 April 1658. The baron also had his conditions and they may account for the ill-success of the establishment during the past fifty years. No religious order would accept them unless very hard put to it.

1. There shall never be less than two priests and a lay-brother.
2. One of the priests shall say Mass at the castle whenever required by us and our successors.
3. The other shall say low Mass at 11 a.m. on all Sundays and feast-days: and on all Fridays, also at 11 a.m., for our intentions.
4. On our death and on every anniversary they are to say the nine-lesson office of the dead.
5. The relic of the Cross is to remain for ever in this convent in its silver reliquary, as it was received from the abbess of Coniuxdorp, except in time of war when it will be lodged with us till the danger is past.
6. They are given all the church furnishings enumerated in an inventory attached.[8]

Fr Howard took possession of the convent on 17 April 1658, which was the Wednesday in Holy Week. With him were Fr William Collins, a member of the Irish province, and George Daggitt, Howard's personal servant, who decided to become a lay-brother. On Holy Saturday they were joined by three others: Fr James Lovel, an Englishman born in Brussels and there professed, Br Martin Russell, who had been professed at Ghent, and Peter van den Berghe, a versatile Flemish lay-brother.[9] Thus Howard himself was the only fully fledged member of the English Domincans in the original community. Collins later transferred his affiliation to the English province, but Lovel remained a son of the convent at Brussels, and was one of the five members of that house who lost their lives ministering to the plague-stricken at Vilvorde where he died on 22 September 1668.[10]

## Philip Howard

Years of neglect had rendered the building almost uninhabitable. Windows were broken and stuffed with straw and there was a general air of decay and depression. The garden was less than half an acre, and they were surrounded by miles of swamp and fen. The castle stood as it still stands, hidden in trees a mile away, remote and melancholy. Roads were practically non-existent and the ordinary means of transport was the river, navigable for small craft as far as Brussels. Bornhem was in many ways a bad bargain, that only a desperate situation could have justified. Yet it remained our principal home for 150 years, and it still continues as a Cistercian abbey. The conventual buildings were entirely rebuilt in 1769, and since then the church has been burnt down and replaced, so that nothing now remains of the convent as it was known to Howard and his first companions.

With a small community and in a more rigorous climate Howard made no attempt to introduce the full observance that he had been accustomed to at Naples. There was no midnight office and they were allowed meat at four meals a week. They rose at 5 for matins and Mass, began schools at 7 and sang the community Mass at 10. Compline was sung before supper, which was at 6, and lights-out was at 8.45. The stipulation that the community should never number more than thirteen (including laybrothers) precluded any hope of establishing the observance customary in the great houses of study. Not that this restriction weighed heavily at first: it was to be some years before they even reached the maximum number. The regulation forbidding them to take members of other nations seems to have been evaded from the start. The presence of William Collins could no doubt be justified, as he was born of English parents, though in Ireland, but the same plea cannot be made for the Flemish laybrother who was in the original community, nor for another who joined within a year.

The conditions enumerated above were cramping enough but worse was to follow. On 23 December 1658 the vicars general sent him a document for his signature. It set out the conditions that he had already agreed to in the royal licence and asked for a solemn undertaking that they would be exactly observed *in perpetuum*. It subjoined a new condition, viz. that in any disputes that might arise over the meaning of these conditions, the Dominicans would bow to the decision of the bishop, or failing a bishop, of the vicars general, without right or appeal and notwithstanding any privileges, faculties, exemptions, indults or other graces granted or to be granted to the order by the Holy See or by kings and princes, that were contrary to the tenor of this agreement. This was too much for Howard. He sent a courteous reply on Christmas Day asking for time to consult his superiors.[11] Presumably he wrote to the Master General but no reply is extant. He also wrote to Francesco Barberini, enclosing a copy of the document, and this letter is the only one written by Howard during his residence at Bornhem that has come to light:

> I have not bothered your Em[inence] with my superfluous letters since the time I lived in France, for while I was a missionary of sorts in our stricken England nothing worthy of your notice came to my knowledge. Just a year ago it seemed to our general and to the few surviving English fathers of our order that it would greatly benefit the Catholic faith and the apostolic mission if we, like the other orders of our nation, could have a refuge in some neighbouring Catholic country for our fathers worn out with age and exhausted by the hardships of prison and persecution, and as a nursery where we could raise some tender shoots that in due season would bear fruit in the Lord's vineyard. I therefore girded myself and came to Belgium, and managed to obtain, though only just, and not without great hindrance and expense, a chapel dedicated to the Holy Cross with a house adjoining in a village in Flanders. At my own expense I have adapted this house into the form of a convent more or less suitable for our purpose. I obtained the necessary faculty from the king and council as well as all due permission from the vicars general of Ghent (our Diocese), *sede vacante*. My only motive was to ensure that the religious of our order and nation might live there without prejudice either spiritual or temporal.
>
> Nevertheless, though we have enjoyed quiet possession for about ten months, these vicars general are now threatening us with their authority and jurisdiction, and we are required to subscribe at once to the enclosed propositions. I leave it to Your Eminence's greater wisdom to decide whether it is right for religious and missionaries to give such an undertaking, and whether it is compatible with the true obedience which all Catholics, and our order in particular, owe to the Holy See.
>
> I am therefore constrained to seek the benefit of your protection as protector of our country, and beg you to be good enough to expose the state of our affairs to His Holiness. We humbly crave that we may be supported by his authority, to carry out our duties here in the same way as our order and other orders

are accustomed to do everywhere in this country, without any detriment to local rights. Indeed the bishops of other dioceses of their charity favour and protect the English religious of other orders. I dare confidently affirm that never have we given the slightest cause for complaint, except that we are unwilling to surrender the graces, favours and privileges granted or to be granted to us and our order by the Holy See.

I may add that it pleased Urban VIII of pious memory, by a brief of 19 November 1639, to honour this place with indulgences and to grant permission for Mass here. This has been the practice, with the consent of the ordinary at the time and without opposition until now, much to the comfort of the people of the neighbourhood who flock here out of devotion to the Holy Cross, which we possess, authenticated and approved by miracles, and in honour of which this chapel was built.

I could say much more but I must avoid prolixity; and I have said enough, I think, to enlist Your Eminence in defence of our cause, seeing it so greatly concerns the spread of the faith in our unhappy land. In doing this you will wonderfully add to your favours of the past. I hope in a few months to offer you my thanks in person; the main reason for the delay of my journey is that I want to settle this matter before I leave.

Bornhem, 3 January 1659.   Fr Thomas Howard of Arundel.[12]

For six years Howard had been expecting to return to Rome, though for what precise purpose is not known. We gather from this letter that he intended to set out in the spring of 1659 when Bornhem would have passed its first anniversary and could manage without him. Now political events turned his eyes to the west. Cromwell had died in September 1658 and there was much unrest in England. King Charles had moved his little court from Cologne to Bruges in March 1657 and spent much of his time in Brussels. Howard, like other loyal exiles, paid his respects and now the time had come when he could be of service. Early in 1659 the royalists planned a series of local risings in favour of the king and Howard was dispatched to England on this highly secret and perilous business. Indeed it was so secret that there is no mention of it outside the *Annals* of Bornhem. From this source we learn that he was to proceed to England in company with Robert Rookwood, an English Carthusian of Nieuport. Howard in vain warned the king that Rookwood was not to be trusted, and he took the precaution of deceiving Rookwood as to his movements. Instead of travelling via Nieuport as announced he travelled via Zeeland.

*Prior of Bornhem*

His only companion was a diminutive servant, John Jenkins, who later became a Dominican himself. In England Howard found that his worst fears were justified; Rookwood had betrayed the whole plan to the government. The risings were forestalled by the arrest of the leading Catholics, except for General Booth's rising in Chester, which was easily suppressed. Howard had to slip out of the country in the livery of the Polish ambassador, and beat a hurried retreat to Bornhem.[13] The king, who had waited at Calais ready to embark, now went south to attend the peace negotiations between France and Spain, returning to Brussels only in December.

The winter of 1659–60 was unusually severe. On 1 January General Monk crossed the border at Berwick with a small army and began his historic march to London. The roads were covered with snow and they never 'trod on plain earth from Edinburgh to London'. In Brussels the king's friends, unpaid and underfed, tried to keep warm before inadequate fires. Monk continued to march, so taciturn and inscrutable that it is still impossible to know when he first determined on the restoration of the king. He reached London on 3 February and placed his army at the disposition of the Rump parliament. The city fathers had refused to pay any taxes until a free parliament was convened. Monk was ordered to pull down the city gates. On Saturday the 11th he entered the heart of the city, met the mayor and aldermen and informed them that he had sent an ultimatum to parliament demanding an early dissolution and the summoning of a free parliament.

As it was growing dusk on the following day a man slipped unobtrusively into the king's lodgings at Brussels. He gave his name as Baily. He was excited and appeared to be rather drunk, but it transpired that he was really suffering from loss of sleep. He had an extraordinary story to tell. On the previous day he was at Lambeth House where a number of royalists were in custody. News came to them of Monk's ultimatum to parliament and soon the joyful pealing of all the church bells floated across the river. When darkness fell London was a blaze of bonfires. Baily had not waited for more. He posted to Dover and raced to Brussels with the news. The very speed of his journey made the king sceptical but Baily had a brief letter of credit from one whom the king could trust, as well as a copy of Monk's letter to parliament.[14]

If Howard at Bornhem knew of the bright hopes that were dawning he made no mention of them in his next letter to the Master

General written a fortnight later, on 6 March. He asked permission to complete his work by founding a convent of Dominican nuns, and the general, in granting permission, expressed his joyful surprise that English Catholics could find it in their hearts to attempt such a venture 'in the midst of their country's greatest calamity'.[15]

On 20 March the Master General penned yet another licence for Howard to come to Rome.[16] Long before it reached Bornhem the whole situation in England had changed. On 15 March a workman arrived at the Exchange just before closing-time carrying a ladder and a pot of paint. He climbed to the empty niche that had once held a statue of Charles I, and carefully blotted out the inscription that had replaced it—*Exit Tyrannus, Regum Ultimus*. ['The tyrant has gone, the last of kings']. Then he threw his hat in the air and shouted: 'God bless King Charles II'. The cry found an echo in every loyal English heart and not least in those of the hungry exiles in Belgium. Parliament was dissolved the next day.

On 30 March (which was 9 April in Belgium) Sir John Grenville delivered a message from Monk to the king, advising him to leave Spanish territory as England was still at war with Spain. Very early next morning, 10 April, Charles left secretly for Holland, only just in time to escape the attentions of a body-guard that was sent to detain him. This time Howard was abreast of the news. On that very day he wrote to Rome to ask if he could send a substitute owing to the changed state of affairs. How much more he said can only be gathered from the Master General's reply:

> By your letter of 10 April you deprive us of the joy with which we looked forward to your coming, and at the same time you substitute an even greater joy by telling us the most glorious cause of your stay: that the present state of your country and the anticipation of even more delectable news require your presence there. May the bloodshed by so many martyrs in England up to these very days now burgeon with new flowers and abundance of new fruit.[17]

From Breda on 14 April Charles issued his famous Declaration, and on 25 May (his thirtieth birthday) he received a jubilant welcome in London. The faith that had urged Howard to found a convent during the unpropitious days of the protectorate and in the face of such manifold difficulties seemed now to be fully justified.

## II

Howard soon followed the King of England (though the exact date is not known). In a dispatch of 31 July 1660 the internuncio at Brussels states that Fr Arundel went to England 'at the time of the return of the king',[18] so it is just possible that he was one of those who landed at Dover in the king's train.

It is necessary here to say something of the legal position of the English Catholics at the Restoration. Every enactment made against them since the days of Henry VIII was still on the statute-book, but only three of them need detain us. The earliest was the oath of supremacy of 1534. This denied the *spiritual* authority of the pope. Refusal to take it involved the penalties of high treason. Catholics had never doubted that to take it was tantamount to a denial of their faith, and it formed the pretext for executing the martyrs who suffered under Henry VIII. After 1570, however, this oath, though often presented to Catholics (especially during the civil war), was never made the grounds for a capital charge. After the Restoration it was dormant if not dead. The martyrs of 1585 and later were condemned under an Act of that year, which made it treason for a priest ordained beyond the seas to set foot in England, and misprision of treason (punishable by simple hanging) for anyone to shelter him. The third enactment was the oath of allegiance of 1606. This denied the deposing power of the pope, and its refusal involved the penalties of *praemunire*, i.e. forfeiture of goods and imprisonment for life. Most of the subsequent martyrs might have saved their lives by taking this oath but its refusal was not the legal cause of their deaths. They were still prosecuted under the Act of 1585. The oath of allegiance was condemned by two papal briefs but Catholics long remained divided as to the lawfulness of taking it, and it was the subject of much controversy and unhappiness. This oath was still very much alive in 1660.

Fierce laws led to plots, and plots to fiercer laws, till there was a veritable *codex tyrannicus*. The situation that called them into being had long passed away. No Catholic of the Restoration dreamed of redress by force of foreign arms. They tacitly acquiesced in the Elizabethan settlement. In all usurpations and conquests a time must come when undisputed possession confers a juridical right. None can define when that time has come, but come it must. History furnishes many instances of conquests, first condemned as aggressions, that in the course of time have been accepted as legitimate. Thus the popes recognized not only James II but his son James III as the lawful kings of England, but after the death of the latter forbade royal honours to be shown to Prince Charles, the young pretender. There are no exact rules to determine when a dispossessed dynasty cedes its rights to its usurper. There must be a space of life between, whose length none can predict, when the individual citizen is cruelly divided in his allegiance, and when he must follow his own conscience and if necessary suffer and die.

Catholics had suffered much for Charles I and Charles II, and their allegiance was unassailable. Yet the statutes that framed when their loyalty was suspect still remained and there was no hope that they would be repealed. For while the Stuart kings were favourably disposed towards Catholics, parliament was uncompromisingly Protestant and hostile, and it was parliament that made the laws. Under Charles I Catholics had often been shielded from the penalties of these laws by the royal prerogative, but this had helped to prepare for civil war and the death of the king. At best it was a precarious immunity. As long as the laws remained they could be invoked by bigots and in personal feuds, and impede the course of justice even in purely civil cases.

In his declaration from Breda Charles had promised

> a liberty to tender consciences, and that no man shall be disquieted or called in question for differences of opinion in matters of religion which do not disturb the peace of the kingdom, and ... to consent to such act of parliament as shall be offered to us for the full granting that indulgence.[19]

Three points should be noted. Charles promises freedom of religious opinions, not freedom of worship; that even this is qualified by the phrase 'that do not disturb the peace'; and that every concession is subject to the approval of parliament. This left the door open for parliament to declare that the opinions of Catholics disturbed the peace, thereby to deprive them of freedom even in the sanctuary of their innermost thoughts. This is substantially what happened. The indemnity bill, passed on 29 August 1660 after protracted discussion, gave freedom of worship to the established church and to Presbyterians, but Catholics were classed as 'intolerables' with anabaptized socinians and other fanatical extremists, and excluded from any advantage under the bill.

## Prior of Bornhem

Howard wrote the next day to some correspondent abroad:

> The Act of Indemnity is passed but we are excepted and only referred to a subsequent Act. God knows when that will pass. Yet I am made to believe that all will go well with us. It is also said that affairs will not continue long in this rigour. I do verily believe it, and that in a short time there will be something to do. The great ones of our country, as Ormond, Hyde and some others, are so full of business that there is no approaching of them but very seldom. Also their humours and inclinations are very much changed from what they were in times past. You cannot imagine how much prejudice we sustain by being excepted out of the pardon. Hardly a man of us can get any credit. I am for my own part reduced to extremity, and unless I am speedily supplied it will go very hard with me.[20]

By the same post he sent the following lines, so typical of his style, to his uncle, Ludovic d'Aubigny, at Paris:

> My Lord,
> Although I have not of late given you the trouble of my useless letters, yet I have taken the boldness to present you often with my humble service by the same hand as these, as I now take the liberty more particularly to assure Your Lordship of, and if my person might be as bold as my heart is free to speak, I should beg leave to say I hope you will soon grace your native country with your presence, it being conceived generally by those who have the honour of your relations that your own presence will be totally requisite here as well in order to your own concernments as the good of many more, and in particular those of our persuasion here. I shall not need further to trouble Your Lordship herein, being Count Marcin and others by this day's post give you such strong motives as I am confident you will hardly refuse.[21]

D'Aubigny answered the call and came to England the following month.[22] For the next four or five years he was to be the most prominent priest in England yet curiously little is known of him. Much of his work had to be carried out in the greatest secrecy for fear of arousing the anger of parliament, and it is only occasionally, principally in the correspondence of Patrick Conn with Francesco Barberini, that we get even a hint of his activities. His noble origin and kinship with Charles II made him *persona grata* at court, and his long residence in Paris surrounded him with a host of influential friends including Cardinal de Retz. But he was not a great letter-writer and such few letters as remain throw no light on his work in England.

Other royalists who had been for years in exile were now returning. In November came the queen mother, Henrietta Maria, accompanied by her grand almoner Walter Montagu, a priest who, like d'Aubigny, had spent many years in Paris and was better known there than at home. Her chapel at Somerset House had for twenty years been used by the Huguenots.[23] It was now redecorated and restored to her, and London Catholics once more had a public chapel where they could worship without molestation.

The most pressing question facing the Catholics was what their attitude should be to the oath of allegiance. The peers in particular were more concerned, for besides the penalties already mentioned the oath served to exclude them from the House of Lords. If parliament would not repeal or modify it, could they take it in the new circumstances? They swore allegiance not to parliament but to the king, and Charles was prepared to regard the oath, despite its wording, as nothing more than a protestation of civil allegiance. The leading Catholics therefore met in secret and sent a report to Propaganda.

> A meeting of Catholics took place at Arundel House on 14 November [1660] in order that they might agree amongst themselves whether the oaths of supremacy and allegiance, so often condemned by the Apostolic See, were lawful or unlawful, now that the king declares that he demands nothing in them but civil allegiance.

The only ecclesiastics present were d'Aubigny and Walter Montagu, neither of them representative of the English clergy. There were fourteen laymen: George Digby, Earl of Bristol, who had been secretary of state to Charles in exile and dismissed in 1657 for becoming a Catholic; Viscounts Montacute and Stafford; Lords Brudenell, Ward, Baltimore and Henry Howard; Lord Andover, eldest son of the Earl of Berkshire, and William Roper, brother of Lord Teynham. Of lesser degree though of greater weight were Colonel Samuel Tuke, Sir John Winter and Sir Kenelm Digby, who had all three suffered imprisonment in the royal cause and who were banished together in 1649. The others were John Thimelby and Charles Waldegrave. The Marquesses of Winchester and Worcester and Barons Teynham and Carrington were either not invited or did not accept. Most of these are familiar Catholic names, though it is surprising to find James Cecil, the future 3rd Earl of Salisbury, listed among the Catholics, as he was to prove himself their bitter enemy in parliament.

Sir John Winter, secretary to the queen mother, was in the chair. He had taken both oaths under Cromwell and was one of the few Catholics who defended the oath of supremacy. They appointed a committee consisting of Bristol, Brudenell, Ward, Howard, Thimelby and Digby, and deputed them to wait for a favourable opportunity to beg the king's mercy to his Catholic subjects.[24] It would appear that they came to no agreement on the main issue.

Parliament was dissolved on 29 December and no favourable opportunity offered itself till a new one met on 8 May 1661. It was probably then that Digby presented his appeal to the king, reminding him of his Declaration in favour of 'tender consciences' and plainly implying that it was these harsh laws that had led Catholics in the past to seek foreign aid, and that only toleration

> will free us from the imputation of having any foreign dependencies, when we shall no longer be in need of seeking redress from abroad in what rendereth us unhappy at home, and will be a means that Your Majesty may have the service of such your Catholic subjects as have talents to render you any, which by these laws is quite lost to Your Majesty and to the state, be the persons otherwise never so able and worthy.[25]

On 10 June the House of Lords appointed a committee to go into matter, and if they judged proper, to draft a bill for the relaxation of the penal laws. On 21 June Colonel Tuke was heard at the bar of the House but it was resolved that 'nothing had been offered to move their lordships to alter anything in the oaths of allegiance and supremacy'. The Catholic committee now approached the king. They professed that the doctrine of the pope's temporal authority was a problematical opinion, admitted by some individuals but no part of Catholic faith, and they offer to take an oath

> to oppose with their lives and fortunes the pontiff himself if he should ever attempt to execute that pretended power, and to obey their sovereign in opposition to all foreign and domestic power whatsoever, without restriction.

The findings of the committee of the lords came as a dramatic surprise. A bill was introduced to abolish all the penalties of treason, felony and *praemunire* imposed on Catholics by various statutes. There was no provision for the abolition of the fines for recusancy, but even so the bill exceeded the most sanguine expectations. Then came disillusionment. An opponent moved and carried a resolution that the Jesuits should be excepted from every benefit granted in the bill. Catholic solidarity was shot to pieces. Many were in favour of proceeding with the bill despite this outrageous clause; some perhaps willingly, others because they hoped that such an unjust and invidious exception would pass into oblivion.* But there was another party that would not incur the stigma of purchasing their freedom by sacrificing an order that had for so long laboured and suffered with them. They asked that the progress of the bill should be suspended and it was never heard of again. The entire body of penal laws remained for another century, often dormant but never extinct, needing only a Titus Oates to set them all in motion.

Fr Howard played no part in these negotiations, but he must have followed them with anxious attention. For the rest of his life these penal laws hung over the Catholics like a dark, threatening cloud, and much of this book will be incomprehensible unless this is borne in mind. The only policy left to them now was one of stealthy, slow consolidation, and a patience made just endurable by the flickering hope of better times to come.

III

The first event that promised to improve the lot of the Catholics was the return of the queen mother. She had been a source of solace during her husband's reign; she had interceded for the release of priests from prison and had saved some of them from death. Apart from the facilities provided by her chapel, her very presence was a comfort and a hope, as she had considerable influence over her sons.

---

\* In 1829 the Catholic peers voted in favour of an Act of Emancipation that expressly excluded from any benefit not only the Jesuits but all the religious orders; and since it was 'expedient to make provision for the gradual suppression and final prohibition of the same', a number of irritating and humiliating new restrictions were laid upon them. Yet no stigma attaches to these peers, because it was generally anticipated that these objectionable clauses would be still-born—and they were. The peers of 1661 could feel no such confidence in the good sense of their countrymen.

Soon after her arrival Catholics were further solaced by the prospect of another Catholic queen. Negotiations were in progress for a marriage between Charles and the Infanta of Portugal, Catherine of Braganza, and were brought to a successful conclusion by a treaty signed on 23 June 1661. Howard has been credited with a part in these negotiations, but there appear to be no grounds for this. In a very detailed account written by Francisco de Mello, the Portuguese envoy responsible for the treaty, the names of d'Aubigny and another English priest Richard Russell constantly recur but Howard is never mentioned.[26]

The marriage of Catherine with a Protestant required a papal dispensation but it is noteworthy that there was no attempt to obtain one. The protracted negotiations with Rome that were the prelude of other royal marriages—the abortive Spanish match, Henrietta Maria's, and Mary of Modena's—are entirely lacking for Catherine's. Articles very similar to those that safeguarded the religious freedom of Henrietta Maria were agreed to, but without any recourse to Rome. The first mention of a dispensation is not until six years after the marriage, when a new pope (Clement IX) had succeeded Alexander VII. There is extant the draft of a petition from Francesco Barberini to the pope, explaining that the queen had simply obeyed her mother and her governess and 'did not know and could not divine that a dispensation was necessary'. He asks the pope to condone her invincible ignorance of her obligations and to bless her marriage. With this draft are other rough notes from which it appears that the validity of her marriage had been 'bitterly disputed' in the time of Alexander VII, and the conclusion reached was that a marriage with a heretic without a dispensation was valid but illicit and could not continue without grave sin. It is stated that no petition had ever been received from the queen for a dispensation or for absolution from censures. All that Barberini could offer the pope was a letter from Catherine to himself, dated 1 March 1668, in which she asks him to convey to the pope her reverence for the Apostolic See and for His Holiness who so worthily occupies it, adding that she has always been and always would be a very faithful and obedient daughter of the church. She goes on to say that she has already expressed this in her letter of congratulation to the new pontiff but asks Barberini to reiterate it. The notes further suggest that such a testimony of her loyalty to the church was tantamount to a petition, and that the pope's brief should not mention a dispensation, but simply absolve her from any censures that might have been incurred.[27] This is certainly meeting prejudice more than half way.

Although the treaty was not signed until June, preparations for her arrival began months before. The royal chapel at St James's that had been looted and desecrated in the civil war was now put in order. Charles always had a tender spot for the English Benedictines. He never forgot that it was one of their number, John Huddleston, who had hid him after the battle of Worcester, and during his exile they had showed him a singular loyalty and devotion. Huddleston was excepted by name from every proclamation made against priests, and was to be called to the bedside of the dying monarch and to receive him into the church. It was Charles's wish that the Benedictines should have charge of the new queen's chapel, and as early as February 1661 two of them took up their residence at St James's. The very considerable sum of £1019 was disbursed for their maintenance during the next eighteen months.[28] By September their number had been increased to ten—six priests and four brothers—and they already had permission to wear their habits in their quarters, but at court only 'a soutane reaching to the knees'. In the London streets they were to appear only in secular dress.[29] We see already that fear of popular and parliamentary prejudice that was to govern the conduct of Catholics in every sphere of activity.

Patrick Conn, who visited London that spring, wrote to Barberini on 22 April, soon after his return to Paris. He said that the Benedictines were now a considerable body and very popular with the king because of their past services. He forecast (wrongly) that the new queen would have a Benedictine confessor.

The two other religious bodies, he continues, viz. the Franciscans and the Dominicans,

> are not numerous, and the only one who appears at court is Fr Philip Howard, Dominican, of the house of Arundel. He is admitted to the king's private apartments and he is on terms of familiarity with His Majesty. He is a young man of good parts, of average learning, of great goodness of life and is universally liked.[30]

This is the earliest appraisement of Howard's character and is in harmony with many later ones. Nobody credits him with any deep learning or discernment but all were impressed with his courtesy, his integrity and his goodness of life, and testified to his general popularity with high and low. Except at court he was not yet a very prominent figure but he appears to have been in the confidence of d'Aubigny and conversant with all the schemes afoot for the relief and well-being of the Catholics.

The most important problem was the provision of a bishop. As they dared not risk the hostility that the appointment of a bishop in England was sure to arouse they hit on an ingenious solution. Dunkirk had been captured from the French in 1658. Why not an English bishop of Dunkirk? His diocese would be English territory but would not trespass on any existing English see. Hence the bishop there could be a real diocesan and not a titular with a see *in partibus*, without, it was hoped, exasperating the Anglican hierarchy. Charles approved of the scheme and wanted d'Aubigny appointed, with jurisdiction over all the Catholics in England. The negotiations were kept very secret but became known in France. Charges of Jansenism against d'Aubigny caused a delay at Rome.[31] It was just as well, for in 1662 Dunkirk was sold back to the French.

Queen Catherine landed in Portsmouth in May 1662. There had been no marriage by proxy in Portugal and she had been assured that in England it would be performed only according to the rites of her church. On this point she resisted all Charles's persuasions and (again with an eye to popular displeasure) they were secretly married by d'Aubigny in her private chamber in the presence of a few Portuguese attendants and with Howard as the only English witness.[32] After the ceremony they were publicly declared man and wife by the Bishop of London.

D'Aubigny and Howard accompanied the king and queen to London. Howard writes from Portsmouth on 23 May to his brother Charles asking for hospitality for them both at his house (at Deepdene, near Dorking), which he had been told, somewhat loosely, was hard by Farnham where the court was to spend the night. With his usual flippancy he signs himself: 'Your magpie, Pippitt', evidently an allusion to the black and white habit of his order.[33]

It was not until August that the royal pair made their solemn entry into the capital. Soon the chapel at St James's was once more filled with regal pomp and splendour. D'Aubigny became the queen's grand almoner and Howard her chief chaplain. Four sub-almoners were appointed, and in addition she brought with her several Portuguese priests, including a Franciscan confessor and a Dominican preacher, Cristoval del Rosario, and also a community of eleven Capuchins. At the request of the king she built a convent, complete with cloisters and a separate chapel, for the English Benedictines.

There were now two stately chapels-royal as well as the chapels of various ambassadors and Catholics flocked to all of them quite openly and without causing much adverse comment. They were well attended even on weekdays. Thus the French ambassador reports on 19 April 1663 that he had six Masses daily in his chapel but these were not sufficient for the crowds that wished to assist.[34] There was, however, a limit. Patrick Conn complains on 27 January of this year that two Irish Carmelites in London, Plunkett and Carret, with their usual imprudence, had been holding a public school and catechizing and preaching in their habits. They had been arrested in their habits and taken to prison, though in a closed carriage. The watch had, however, waited till they had finished Mass, which they said with the door unlocked, 'against the style and usage of the country'.[35] This was an improvement on Tudor times but a warning against presumption.

English Catholics had long grown accustomed to the restrictions and humiliations of a proscribed body; avoiding the light of day, creeping furtively to Mass; cautious, suspicious and not a little cynical. The reestablishment of the two chapels-royal had done much to restore their self-respect, but it did not satisfy the queen.

Coming from a Catholic country she was not resigned to see Catholicism, then at the height of its external splendour classed with the extraordinary sects that were so busy in England. Presbyterians were ranting seditious sermons: a Quaker ran about stark naked save for an unnameable war-paint, proclaiming that the Lord would besmear their adversaries as he was besmeared; Fifth Monarchy Saints, shouting for King Jesus, were shedding blood and spreading terror everywhere. Catholics were officially classed with such as these and every new enactment to deal with this violent blasphemy applied equally to them. They had no bishop, no leader, no accredited spokesman, no representation at Rome, and something large and splendid was required to give them prestige.

In October 1662, only five months after her arrival, the queen dispatched her agent Richard Bellings to Rome. He carried a number of letters but none of them mentioned the real object of his mission. She asks the pope to give him credit and to hear from him the state of the church in the country to which she has come, and the matter of particular moment, viz. 'the petition he will make to you on behalf of Lord d'Aubigny my grand almoner'. To Cardinal Orsini she adopts the threatening tone used so often by Catholic monarchs towards the Holy See:

> I can assure you that I anticipate that many evils will result from the chagrin of the king my lord and spouse and of his ministers if the court of Rome persists in refusing him the favour which he asks for his relative, Lord d'Aubigny my grand almoner.

She enlisted also the good offices of Cardinal Barberini and the Prince and Princess of Tuscany.[36] Charles himself wrote to Cardinal Chigi, who replied on 9 April 1663 that he was doing all he could for Bellings in laying His Majesty's business before His Holiness, especially the matter concerning d'Aubigny.[37] If nobody spoke the word it was known to them all that Charles and his queen were pressing for d'Aubigny to be made a cardinal.

Howard and the other superiors of orders sent a joint petition to the same effect,[38] but there is no mention of the secular clergy or of the principal Catholic laymen. The request was received in Rome without enthusiasm but also without a blunt refusal. Negotiations continued for another year. On 23 April 1664 Cardinal Azzolini, secretary of briefs *ad principes*, wrote to Cardinal de Retz to say that he was doing all possible for d'Aubigny's promotion. The pope wished it to be known that delay was not to be taken as denial, but he required some assurance that parliament would in return grant freedom to Catholics and a salary sufficient to support the dignity. There was no point in sending a cardinal to England under present restrictions.[39]

This letter puts the difficulties in a nutshell. The whole business had been pursued with the utmost secrecy for fear of parliament. It is not easy to decide whether Charles would be more amused or terrified at the thought of asking parliament for £5000 a year for the maintenance of Cardinal d'Aubigny. Nor were the existing restrictions negligible. The main function of a cardinal at London would be to lend lustre to public assemblies and by his grandeur to inspire a certain awe and respect for the church of which he was a prince. This he could scarcely do if he had to attend court in a soutane down to his knees, or appear in London dressed like Pepys or perhaps a Puritan divine.

While these proceedings were pursuing their leisurely course Girolamo de Vecchii, internuncio at Brussels, arrived in London in September 1664. He came as Howard's guest and only Howard knew his identity. He thought he would be freer to investigate if he remained unknown. But in vain. Howard took him to Whitehall to watch the passing show and he was recognized by the king and the Duke of York, who had both known him in Brussels. He tried to withdraw to an antechamber but was summoned to the royal presence. Upon Howard explaining that he wished to remain incognito the king graciously concurred. He was allowed to see whatever interested him. He was shown the chapels of the two queens and the convent built by the queen mother for her Capuchins. He was told that Queen Catherine intended to do the same for her Portuguese friars. He discovered that the king thought highly of d'Aubigny and wished all priests in England to be subject to him.[40] Then he had an audience with the queen mother. She had known the English scene for close on forty years. She was there when the first vicar apostolic arrived in 1625 and had witnessed the quarrels that drove the second to France. She stressed very earnestly the crying need of a superior. De Vecchii then called on d'Aubigny and asked him if he would accept the office of vicar apostolic. Nothing was further from his wishes. He had no ambition to follow the last holder of that office through bitter controversies to ignominious exile. He was, however, persuaded by Howard and at last agreed to abide by the wishes of the Holy See. It was understood that the acceptance of this dignity was to be no prejudice to promotion to a higher one. Not that Howard thought it practical to have a cardinal in England. Far better for the church that he live in Rome leaving Howard as his grand vicar. The dignity of a prince of the church would, it was hoped, unite the dissident clergy in obedience to him and also make him a powerful ambassador at the papal court.[41]

By the end of 1664 these negotiations for a cardinal's hat had been in progress two years and there was still no sign of success. There we may leave them for a time, and turn to Howard's more personal affairs.

*Prior of Bornhem*

IV

Although Howard lived in London during these years he remained prior of his foundation at Bornhem. He contrived to spend a month or six weeks there each summer and for the rest of the time delegated his authority to a subprior.

His first visit to Flanders after the Restoration was in 1661. It was another milestone in the progress of the province. Although Bornhem was hardly established he was determined on completing his work by the foundation of the traditional counterpart of the friars, viz. a convent of nuns. He had received permission for this in April 1660 and had sent his cousin Antonia Howard to the Dominican nuns at Tempsche (now Temse), a mile or so from Bornhemm, to learn something of their rule and way of life. Now he took her from this convent, together with three Flemish nuns, to a house at Vilvorde, a few miles to the south. Next morning, 11 June 1661, he gave her the habit and the religious name of Catherine. One of the Flemish nuns, Louisa Hertogh, aged 32, was appointed superior.[42] These four, together with a few English girls too young to be received, at once began some degree of community life.

There were the same tedious preliminaries and restrictions that had delayed the start of Bornhem. Permission was required from the King of Spain before they could have the status of a convent. Howard sought permission from the Archbishop of Malines for them in the meantime to have Mass in their own house for themselves and the *domicellae*, i.e. the young ladies living with them. This would, he says, prevent the distractions consequent upon going to the public church and safeguard them from the danger of being recognized in the town by English heretics bent on causing trouble for their relatives in England. On 29 June they received permission to have one Mass a day, on a temporary altar, with locked doors and no bell-ringing, for themselves and the *domicellae* only. They were not allowed to reserve the Blessed Sacrament.[43] This abridged version of religious life continued for three years till Howard was able to satisfy the civil authorities that the nuns had a sufficient income to make them independent of local almsgiving. On 4 October 1663 the *conseil privé* permitted the foundation[44] and on 9 July 1664 the archbishop issued the formal faculty to erect a convent in honour of St Dominic at Vilvorde in la rue le Meer.[45] Thus after a lapse of eighty years the English nuns of the second order were once more established, though that first English novice was not destined to see the restoration of full conventual life. She died a holy death on 8 October 1661 after only four months of her novitiate, having been professed a few days before.[46] She was only sixteen, but in her brief religious life she links her English sisters of today with the first nuns of Prouille in seven centuries of unbroken tradition. *Beata animula*, wrote the Master General[47] to her grief-stricken cousin, *quae sic consummata in brevi explevit tempora multa* [Blessed little soul who, being perfected in a short time, she fulfilled long years (Wisdom 4:13)].

The next profession at Vilvorde was not until July 1664. In their own account the nuns complain of this long delay, 'the bishop and the country all that time persisting in rude denials to admit of an English convent'.[48] In fairness to the archbishop it should be added that he was powerless to grant the faculties until the civil authorities had given their approval.

Progress at Bornhem was slow but not unpromising. By the middle of 1661 there had been seven professions (including two laybrothers) and there were four simple novices, one of whom was already a priest. There was also a small school attached, with a number of prospective candidates for the order including two of Howard's own brothers. This was a satisfactory record for the first three years and Howard was already contemplating another foundation. He turned to the Mecca of the English Catholics, the little town of Douai. Douai with its university and, more important still, its English college had long before attracted the English Benedictines and Franciscans, and they had gathered vocations from the young men at the college or from the famous Jesuit school of St Omers that was some fifty miles to the west. For Howard the place had another attraction. There would be no need of long bargaining with the *conceil privé* or the King of Spain, for there was already a Dominican convent there belonging to the Flemish province. If only he could buy it for his own province! He had in April 1661 obtained sanction from the Master General, who promised to commend the project to the provincial of Flanders.[49] The Flemish fathers, however, were unwilling to part with it and on 20 June, just ten days after the opening of Vilvorde, Howard wrote to express his disappointment.[50] But he still hankered after it and in the following April the Master General asked the provincial to do all in his power at the coming provincial Chapter to get the fathers to agree to the transfer, pointing out how valuable Douai was for attracting English youths to the order.[51] The fathers remained adamant. Howard never relinquished his hopes. More than thirty years later when he made his will he left the residue of his estate 'to buy and found the college of St Thomas of Aquin of the Walloon Dominicans in Douai to make a college for the English Dominicans'. It was a dream destined never to come true.

Foreseeing that he would be in England most of the year he asked, in the summer of 1661, to resign his priorship. In his reply of 23 July the Master General not only declined to grant this release but instituted him vicar general in place of George Catchmay, who was growing old.[52] Thus at the age of thirty-two Howard became superior over all the English Dominicans at home and abroad.

By the beginning of 1664 the religious at Bornhem had increased to thirteen, the maximum allowed by their contract, and a new foundation was urgent. Howard tried to purchase a house in Dieppe but was again unsuccessful. In March 1665 he made one last effort to obtain a second house. He made his profession at San Clemente in Rome, and he knew that this convent was left virtually unoccupied for nine months of the year. He asked the Master General if he might have it. The reply was that the air at S. Sisto was so pernicious in the hot season that S. Clemente was essential as a summer house for the novices.[53] It never occurred to Howard to do what his Irish brethren were soon to do, namely to ask for S. Sisto as well!

The only expedient left was to use Bornhem for noviciate and house of philosophy and to send students for their theology to houses in other provinces. This became the practice for many years, and students were sent to Brussels, Louvain, France and Italy. This gave them a wider experience but deprived them of the special studies, especially in apologetics, that were deemed necessary for missionaries in England. But in spite of the disappointment over Douai the results of the first six years were gratifying and encouraging.

In England the situation was more difficult. Three veteran missionaries had died within a week, in May 1662, and they could not yet be replaced. There was little that Howard could do but wait till the new men were ready. Such few references as there are to him have nothing to do with his main work.

In August 1662 he dined with his grandfather's old friend John Evelyn, together with his brothers Henry, Charles, Edward and Bernard. Evelyn informs us that his son John 'had been much brought up amongst Mr [Henry] Howard's children at Arundel House, till for fear of their perverting him to the Catholic faith I was forced to take him home'.[54]

In a letter to his sister Henrietta Duchess of Orleans, dated 16 February 1663 the king recounts with much glee that the queen 'made my Lord Aubigny and two other of her chaplains dance country dances in her bedchamber'.[55] So perhaps this was another of Howard's duties.

Howard spent a few days in January 1664 with his brother Henry at Norwich in the sumptuous palace of the Dukes of Norfolk, where Christmas had just been kept with great splendour and extravagance. Henry does not appear to have been much impoverished by recusancy fines.

> They had dancing every night and gave entertainments to all that would come. He built up a room on purpose to dance in, very large and hung with the bravest hangings I ever saw. His candlesticks, snuffers, tongs, fireshovels and andirons were silver. A banquet was given every night after dancing, and three coaches were employed to fetch ladies every afternoon, the greatest of which would hold fourteen persons and cost £500 without the harness, which cost six score more. I have seen his pictures, which are admirable: he hath prints and drafts done by most of the great masters' own hands; stones and jewels, as onyxes, sardonyxes, jacints, jaspers, amethysts, and more and better than any prince in Europe; rings and seals, all manner of stones and limnings beyond compare. These things were most of them collected by the old Earl of Arundel, who employed his agents in most places to buy him up rarities, but especially in Greece and Italy, where he might probably meet with things of the greatest antiquity and curiosity.[56]

In February 1664 Henry and his brother Edward set out on a special embassy to Constantinople, attended by his servant John Burbury, the very same who had escorted young Philip Howard on his momentous visit to Fr Hacket.

In June 1665 came the plague. The roads were filled with carts and coaches as rich and poor fled from the capital, some of them carrying the dread infection with them. The queen went to Hampton Court and thence to Salisbury. The plague followed her and she moved to Bristol. The queen mother retired to France. Normally when she went to France her Capuchins remained to administer to the London Catholics. It is not known whether her chapel or that of the queen at St James's remained open during the three months of horror. Howard was presumably with the queen but there is no evidence. On 13 July d'Aubigny sailed from Dover taking four horses as though for a long stay or a long journey.[57] Few besides his nephew knew his plans. He was on his way to Rome to place before His Holiness the situation in England, to accept the office of vicar apostolic and to petition for the more eminent dignity of the red hat. With these honours he intended, for the greater profit of the English Catholics, to reside abroad, delegating his authority to Howard.[58] This uncle-nephew relationship was well understood in Rome, where for two centuries the pope had invariably made a nephew his cardinal secretary. D'Aubigny got no further than Paris. He was only forty-five but in poor health and he died there on 10 November. There is an oft-related story that he had been nominated cardinal and that a messenger arrived with the news just after his death. He was certainly never named in a consistory. The nuncio at Paris refers to him several times, records his death 'after a long illness',[59] but makes no mention whatever of any messenger from Rome bringing such important news. Another scheme for the betterment of Catholics had gone awry. On 3 January 1666, by letters patent of the queen, Howard was appointed grand almoner in his place.[60]

## Notes

[1] C. R. Palmer, *Life of Philip Thomas Howard*, London, 1867, 98–100.
[2] Reg. 70, f. 144.
[3] AB, Conseil Privé Espan. no. 1120.
[4] Reg. 101, 174.
[5] *Ibid.* 551.
[6] *Ibid.* 115 (pt. I), 13; *Dominicana*, 26.
[7] B. van Doninck, *Het Voormalig Engelsch Klooster te Bornhem*, Leuven, 1904, 413–15.
[8] *Ibid.* 415.
[9] Palmer, *Life*, 105.
[10] Dominican Archives, Ghent, MS 22, 529.
[11] *Dominicana*, 27.
[12] B, 2170, f. 127; the enclosure is B, 2693, f. 126.

13. AFOP, XXVIII (1958), 317.
14. E. Clarendon, *History of the Rebellion*, Oxford, 1839, 942.
15. Reg. 115, 133.
16. *Ibid.* 130.
17. *Ibid.* 139.
18. NF, 44, f. 287.
19. The original document will be found as Parliamentary Archive, HL/PO/JO/10/1/283, Main Papers, 4–14 April 1660—The King's declaration from Breda. Lords Journals, XI. 7. In extenso.
20. BL, Add. 34713, f. 18.
21. *Ibid.* f. 16.
22. B, 8669, f. 50.
23. SP, 29/16, no. 83.
24. AP, Lettere Riferite nelle Cong. Gen., Angliae (etc.) 1653–63 (t.12), f. 57.
25. Peterson, R., *Sir Kenelm Digby*, London, 1956, 291.
26. BL, Add. 15202; cf. *Quadro Elentar das relaçones politicas e diplomticas de Portugal*, tt.XVII and XVIII.
27. B, 8616, ff. 163–8.
28. Bod, Clarendon MSS, 78 ff. 79–80.
29. NF, 45, f. 474.
30. B, 8669, f. 71.
31. C. Cochin, *Dunkerque éveché Anglais*, in *Bulletin du Comité flamand de France*, Blois, 1908, 331–52.
32. AAW, A33, no. 137, 326.
33. *Dominicana*, 93.
34. J. J. Jusserand, *Recueil des instructions données aux ambassadeurs*, XXIV, Paris, 1929, I, 332.
35. B, 8669, f. 127.
36. BL, Add. 22548, ff. 32–41.
37. Bod., Clarendon MS 79, f. 135.
38. *Dominicana*, 32.
39. Bod., Clarendon MS 84, f. 124.
40. NF, 49, f. 221.
41. *Dominicana*, 32–4.
42. AB, 16542–57, 1–10.
43. AB, 14512, f. 117.
44. AB, Conseil privé Espan., no. 1159.
45. AB, 14512, ff. 118–20.
46. *Dominicana*, 177–8.
47. Reg. 115, 230.
48. *Dominicana*, 179.
49. Reg. 115, 194.
50. *Ibid.* 212.
51. *Ibid.* 194.

52 *Ibid.* 212.
53 *Ibid.* 376.
54 *Diary of John Evelyn*, ed. W. Bray and H. B. Wheatley, London, 1906, II, 147–8.
55 A. Bryant, *King Charles II*, London, 1955, 124.
56 *Sir Thomas Browne's Works*, ed. S. Wilkin, London, 1836, I, 44.
57 Cal.SP Charles II, IV, 53, 474.
58 *Dominicana*, 33–4.
59 Nunz.Fr., 130, f. 954.
60 Stuart, I, 2.

# 3

## *Grand Almoner*

### I

WHILE CATHOLICS THROUGHOUT THE REST OF ENGLAND were worshipping in secrecy, attending Mass in garrets and country houses, the Catholics of London were enjoying facilities that compare very favourably with those of today. Within a semicircle of scarcely a mile radius they had a choice of four chapels attached to foreign embassies, as well as the chapels royal. They could attend High Mass and Solemn Vespers celebrated with lavish appointments, and without need of secrecy or fear of arrest. These amenities attracted to London a multitude of clergy out of all proportion to the needs of the faithful there, and only at the price of leaving whole counties deplorably understaffed. While in some parts of the country a priest had to ride many miles to minister to his scattered flock, in London there was diplomatic protection and often a small but regular stipend paid by a foreign government. Most of the surviving documents emanate from London and give a picture of clerical life that is far from being typical of the clergy as a whole.

Of the public chapels in London the greatest prestige naturally belonged to those of the queen-regnant and the queen mother. Queen Catharine had a small chapel in the palace at Whitehall as well as the more spacious one attached to St James's palace. It was of these two chapels and their attendant clergy that Howard found himself the superior at the beginning of 1666. The earliest list of these clergy is that given in Edward Chamberlayne's *Angliae Notitia*,[1] a year-book that began to appear in 1669. The names remain substantially the same till the close of the chapels in 1688, and it may be assumed that most of these priests had been there from the beginning. The list does not always give the full name, but with the help of other sources it may be completed as follows:

*Philip Howard*

| | |
|---|---|
| Grand Almoner | Philip Howard, OP |
| Confessor | Antonio Fernandez, OFM |
| Almoners | Richard Russel, Bishop-Elect of Portalegre |
| | Patrick Ginn, an Irish Franciscan |
| | Manoel Pereira, Trinitarian |
| | Paulo de Almeida, OP |
| Preacher | Cristoval del Rosario, OP |
| Treasurer | Dr Thomas Godden, *vere* Tilden a secular priest. |

There were also six English Benedictine monks and eleven Portuguese Capuchins, but their names are never given in these lists.

Many distinguished visitors have left their impressions of the chapel in St James's, and at the risk of some repetition it will be better to let them speak for themselves. One of the most detailed descriptions is that written by the secretary of Cosimo Prince of Tuscany, who in 1670 succeeded his father as Grand Duke Cosimo III. He travelled extensively and in the spring of 1669 visited Ireland and then England:

> 19 April 1669. Good Friday.[*] His Highness was conducted to the royal chapel of St James for the ceremonies, which were performed with music. The queen was present. His Highness was given a private place at a glass partition in the quarters of my Lord Philip Howard, grand almoner to Her Majesty.
>
> 20th. The functions and blessings proper to Holy Saturday having been performed in his house, His Highness went to St James's (occupying the same place as yesterday) to watch those that were performed by the religious in charge of the queen's chapel. This is a small church within the precincts of the royal palace of St James, not very far from the other palace of Whitehall with which it is connected by a large park enclosed by walls on every side. The park contains a long, straight and spacious walk, used for the game of pall-mall, and flanked by great elms, whose shade enhances the pleasure of walking there in the summer. Close to this walk and running nearly the whole length is an artificial canal made in Cromwell's time, the home of several species of waterfowl that have grown quite tame. The rest of the park is allowed to run wild and forms

---

[*] Cosimo follows the New Style. In 1669 Easter according to both styles synchronized, though the *date* in England was ten days earlier. The instrumental music on Good Friday is merely a sign of the times. Had Cosimo come in the following year he would have discovered that on his Good Friday the queen was celebrating the feast of the Annunciation.

> woodlands for deer and other game. The queen's chapel is on the left of the main entrance of the palace, in a remote corner and without any external semblance to a chapel. The way to it is across the main courtyard and down a passage that opens into a smaller courtyard connecting the chapel with the grand almoner's apartments.
>
> As you enter the little church there are two side-chapels. The one on the right is dedicated to our Lady, and the queen herself says the rosary in it on all big feasts, when she comes to assist at the divine office. In the middle of an inner wall, that rises from floor to ceiling, and just above the door, is a glass partition, and here Her Majesty is accommodated whenever she comes from Whitehall palace (her ordinary residence) to assist at Mass and Vespers in this chapel. In the church itself there is only one altar, lavishly carved, with a tabernacle, covered with a veil of the appropriate liturgical colour, in which the Blessed Sacrament is reserved. On top of it is the crucifix. There are no other statues or pictures ... A great number of Masses are celebrated every day for the convenience of the faithful, who flock there.*

He goes on to name the almoners, and tells of the little convent of the Portuguese friars and of the six English Benedictines.

> All these, together with the musicians and others are under the control of the grand almoner, who because of this office is favoured by the king with the title Milord. He is the only one who is allowed to walk in the streets of London in clerical dress. Although a Dominican he wears by dispensation the garb of a secular priest. The rest remove their habits and go in the city in lay clothes. All are bound to assist when the queen is there, sitting chorally on benches. The grand almoner has his seat on the gospel side, raised above the rest, and there he assists, always wearing amice, surplice and stole.

Cosimo saw a great deal of Howard, went with him to Somerset House to see the world's largest telescope, to cock-fighting, to Hampton Court, and for a trip on the Thames. On 11 June they went together to Islington to see a man who could walk on water,†2

---

\* By a papal brief of 3 October 1664 the high altar of the queen's chapel became a privileged altar, it having been represented that more than fourteen Masses were celebrated there every day (SB, 1365, ff. 453, 456).

† 'Thursday 3 June 1669. One captain Stoupe, a man pretending knowing in the mechanics, having found out an art of walking upon the surface of the water, on Tuesday morning he showed the experiment to the Prince of Tuscany at the pond at Islington, in his way to Harwich, with which His Highness was

finishing with dinner with William Lord Petre at Thornton. He was not impressed with English cooking. The pastry was coarse, with too much spice, and badly cooked. There were no forks and they all washed their fingers in the same basin; some dipped the end of their napkins into the water and so cleaned their teeth. He much preferred the gentility of the Italians.

Cosimo also visited Windsor and there made friends with a little boy, John Green, who seems to have had the run of the castle where his father was master of the music of the Chapel Royal. Cosimo does not mention the incident, but the boy who as Raymund Green was destined to become provincial of the English Dominicans recalled the fact sixty-four years later, and was sure that the grand duke would still remember the little boy who had sat at his feet in Windsor castle.

Cosimo made many lasting friendships during his visit. For years afterwards he shipped from Leghorn large consignments of choicest wines, sometimes as many as two hundred cases, to those who had been kind to him, and the Howard family figures largely in his gifts. He also employed his minister and his friends to procure all that was best in the England of that time; portraits by Lely, Rubens and Van Dyke, miniatures by Samuel Cooper, the Historical Collections of Rushworth and the English works of John Milton; clocks, furniture and the latest inventions, including an apparatus for sweetening sea-water. Bernard Howard was busy buying horses, and Milord Philip, as he is always called, undertook the shipment of six fawns, a gift from the king to the grand duke to stock his deer parks. There is much correspondence over these delicate creatures, and even more when they eventually arrived and proved to be all stags. There were rich damasks and satins, wines from the Canaries, and deerhounds from Ireland, all testifying to the wide culture of the Medicis which had made Florence the Athens of Italy. In one letter Cosimo thanks Philip for his political news-letters from London, and there is evidence

> much pleased with the rarity of it and gave the person twenty guineas for his pains. He presses much to have the king see it and to have a patent for fourteen years... Wednesday 25 August 1669. This evening the same person that formerly walked upon the water before the Prince of Tuscany showed the experiment before His Majesty and Royal Highness, etc., upon the Thames in Chelsea Reach, where he walked very orderly for about half an hour, to the great satisfaction of His Majesty' (Bulstrode Papers 1897, 104, 113).

in plenty that a friendship had been forged that was to endure till Howard's death. The time was to come when Cosimo would repay, with all the lavish grandeur of a Medici, the hospitality extended to him by the grand almoner.

On 23 January 1667 Samuel Pepys records in his diary one of several visits he paid to the chapel:

> To St James's to see the organ Mrs Turner told me of the other night, of my late Lord Aubigny's; and I took my Lord Brouncker with me, he being acquainted with my present lord almoner, Mr Howard, brother of the Duke of Norfolk. So he and I did see the organ but I do not like it, it being but a bauble with a virginal joining to it, so I shall not meddle with it. The almoner seems a good-natured gentleman. Here I observed the desk which he hath [made] to remove, and is fastened to one of the arms of his chair. I do also observe the counterfeit windows there was, in the form of doors with looking-glasses instead of windows, which makes the room seem both bigger and lighter, I think; and I have some thoughts to have the like in one of my rooms. He discoursed much of the goodness of the music in Rome but could not tell me how long music had been of any perfection in that church, which I would be glad to know. He speaks much of the great buildings that the pope (whom in mirth to us he calls antichrist) hath done in his time. Away, and my lord and I walking into the park I did not observe the new buildings: and my lord, seeing I had a desire to see them, they being the place for the priests and friars, he took me back to my lord almoner, and he took us quite through the whole house and chapel and the new monastery. So away with the almoner in his coach, talking merrily about the difference in our religions, to Whitehall, and there we left him.[3]

Pepys came again for midnight Mass the following Christmas but found it rather too much for him:

> With a great deal of patience stayed from nine at night to two in the morning, in a very great crowd, and there expected but found nothing extraordinary, there being nothing but a High Mass. The queen was there and some ladies. But Lord: what an odd thing it was for me to be found in a crowd of people, here a postman there a beggar, here a fine lady there a zealous poor papist, and here a Protestant, two of three together, come to see the show. I was afraid of my pocket being picked very much. But all things very rich and beautiful; and I see the papists have the wit, most of them, to bring cushions to kneel on ... And there I left people receiving the sacrament.[4]

## Philip Howard

Another celebrated visitor in 1669 was Saint Oliver Plunkett. His partiality for the Dominicans is well known. He had been appointed Archbishop of Armagh on 9 July 1669, and on 24 August received letters commendatory from the Master General[5] to lodge at Dominican houses on his journey to Ghent, where he was consecrated on 30 November. He writes to Barberini from London on 30 December:

> I presented the letters of Your Eminence to the queen, who gave me a most gratifying audience ... I also delivered your letter to Father Howard, grand almoner, a truly worthy man. He secretly lodged me for ten days in his own apartments in the royal palace. With great kindness he often conducted me in his carriage to see the principal curiosities of the city. He is truly hospitable and munificent, and the refuge of all foreign Catholics; he enjoys great favour with the king and queen, and is loved by all, even the Protestants, for his great gentleness and courtesy. I request you to thank him in your next letter for the kindness which he showed me out of esteem for Your Eminence. Fr Fernandez also, in consequence of your letters, made many professions of readiness to serve me, and showed great courtesy. In my opinion he is not very influential and has little weight with the queen; *est bonus vir*, a good simple man.[6]

Finally we may give Howard's own account of his life at this time. It is a very long Italian document that is a summary of several of his letters, of various dates, and is headed:

> What Fr Howard writes concerning the articles of marriage in England 30 September 1667.
>
> In case it is desired to know what life is like in the queen's household, and in case Your Lordship should be asked about it, I send the following account, which will help you frame your reply and also inform the Apostolic See.
>
> The queen's majesty by virtue of the articles and treaty of marriage has a great-almoner, who has his quarters in the court in the royal palace of Whitehall, where there is also a chapel, quite small but open to the public. Here the queen and all who wish may come daily to hear Mass. A third part of the rosary, with litanies and other prayers is recited aloud about four in the afternoon. It is also customary to have a sermon in this chapel, especially when the queen is indisposed, and for the sake of the servants who must remain with Her Majesty and cannot go to the other chapel in the palace of St James, where most of the preaching is done, and from a pulpit.

## Grand Almoner

The grand almoner has another apartment in the royal palace of St James half a mile from Whitehall through the park. Here is the principal chapel of the queen, with a high altar and two other altars, all sumptuously and correctly built. Every first Sunday of the month and on all the feasts of the rosary Her Majesty, candle in hand, walks in procession, in company with her ladies, gentlemen and servants and with the clergy all in their habits or clerical garb, as is done in a Catholic country, led by a cross-bearer etc. She goes to a cloister built near the apartment of the grand almoner.

In this chapel Her Majesty assists at High Mass and Vespers on all Sundays and feast-days, and in Lent at least three times a week, and very often at the sermons. There is an Italian choir which sings a good deal of the Mass and Vespers, and the Portuguese friars sing the rest. These latter say their office in choir every day and therefore Her Majesty has built them a proper cloister at the side of the chapel, where they always wear their capuchin habit. In the middle of the cloister appertaining to the grand almoner is a cemetery for the interment of the dead and in particular of the queen's servants, and a house for the Dominicans, one of whom, a master of theology and a Portuguese, is Her Majesty's preacher. In another part is a house for the English Benedictines, also Her Majesty's chaplains. As for the rest of the officials and servants of the chapel—the treasurer, the sixteen sub-almoners, who serve four at a time in rotation,* and others—they live out and have a lodging and maintenance allowance.

The grand almoner has two personal chaplains who live with him, besides his own brethren. He goes about in a caped soutane of black silk down to his feet, and in this dress he appears in public on all occasions; but in church he wears a surplice with stole and the square biretta, and he solemnly sings the Mass and presides at the office on all the greater feasts. He publicly says grace at the royal table, morning and evening and makes the sign of the cross openly, but only after the Protestant bishop has said his *Benedicite* for the king. The same almoner always has his place in the queen's first carriage, if for any reason he does not wish to go in his own coach with his chaplains.

During a progress, i.e. when Her Majesty goes on a journey, he has assigned to his use one (or two if he wishes) of the great carts belonging to Her Majesty called 'wagons' to carry his luggage and his servants. They are like the army vehicles, long

---

* This is a misunderstanding. There were four sub-almoners serving one at a time.

and covered and four-wheeled. He has lodging always in the queen's house. He has another carriage reserved for the chaplains who accompany him on the journey. He has pack-horses and another wagon or cart to carry the furnishings of the chapel and the luggage of the chaplains.

It is worth mentioning that one of the four chaplains or almoners who are under the grand almoner, is a bishop-elect in Portugal and is publicly known here by the title of Bishop Russell, Bishop of Portalegre, and he is an Englishman. It can be seen from this that the name of bishop is tolerated here and does not cause jealously in anyone. Hence one may infer that any similar appointment will have the like effect.

Furthermore an Irish Dominican named Darcy, Bishop of Dromore in Ireland, remained here some time on his way to Ireland, and officiated publicly in the queen's chapel in full pontificals, and went to many other parts of this kingdom, administering Confirmation and conferring Holy Orders in public. And it is most important to note that those who receive Holy Orders within the realm of England are not subject like the others to the penalties layed down by law against priests etc., for these laws taken literally refer only to Jesuits and priests coming from the seminaries, and all these laws speak of priests ordained beyond the seas, and not of others.

To be brief, all the processions and ceremonies of the church are carried out with as much solemnity and care in this chapel as in any cathedral church, the only difference being a biretta in place of a mitre.

The grand almoner uses the very pastoral staff that belonged to St Thomas of Canterbury, made from the horn of a unicorn, with a cross at the top, whereas other pastoral staffs have a crook. But the saint had his in this form.* Nor would anyone

---

* This venerable relic is doubtless the *baculus pastoralis* of St Thomas, made of pear-wood with a top of black horn, which is mentioned in an inventory of relics preserved at Canterbury in 1321 (J. Dart, *The History and Antiquities of the Cathedral Church of Canterbury*, London, 1726, appendix, XII). It was shown to Erasmus on the eve of the Reformation, when it was kept in the sacristy. By then it had been encased in silver. Erasmus tells us that it was without any decoration or cross, and that it came up to his waist. (*Colloquia. Peregrinatio Religionis Ergo*). When the shrine was looted it passed to the crown, and perhaps the lack of any religious symbol saved it from further desecration. In an inventory of the 'jewels remaining in an iron chest in the secret jewelhouse within the Tower of London', signed by James I, is the item: 'One long piece esteemed for an unicorn's horn' (J. Bayley, *The History and Antiquities of the Tower of London*, I, London, 1821, p. 192). Panzani was shown round the Tower in 1635, and saw among other things 'the archiepiscopal cross of St

here take scandal at seeing an ordinary crosier any more than they do at the sight of this precious staff of so great a saint; nor would a mitre annoy them any more than a square biretta does. And in any case it would be no more than a nine days' wonder, as happened the first time the queen appeared.

But nobody can believe what good effect these ceremonies of ours have on the minds of a very large section of the populace. Many came and still come out of curiosity and partly to laugh and poke fun at our goings-on; but it often happens to them what happened to the Jews. Manhu? What is this? They asked and they found; they knocked and it was opened unto them. Wonderful is God in all his works.[7]

In addition to the presence of three Dominicans in the queen's household, Dominican influence in her chapel is evident in many small points. We have already referred to the daily recitation of the rosary either in the domestic chapel in Whitehall palace or on greater feasts in the side-chapel at St James. This chapel was dedicated to the Immaculate Conception, two hundred years before the doctrine was defined, and here in 1663 the rosary confraternity had been established.[8] Fr Howard was probably the author of a little book entitled, 'A method of saying the rosary of our blessed Lady, as it was ordered by Pope Pius V of the holy order of preachers, and as it is said in Her Majesty's chapel of St James. Printed in the year 1669.' The only known copy of the first edition is preserved at

---

Thomas of Canterbury, kept with the silver because of its value, being the bone of a unicorn' (NI, VI, f..141). An inventory made in 1650 of the effects of Charles I gives 'An unicorn horn' (Pegge, *Curalia*, London, 1806, IV, 122). Such horns were believed at one time to belong to the legendary unicorn and were credited with preternatural powers. They are often mentioned in old wills and were greatly treasured. They are in reality the horn of the *rhinoceros unicornis*, the common rhinoceros that had never been seen in England. Evelyn records in his Diary on 28 October 1684: 'I went to see the Rhinoceros or Unicorn, being the first that I suppose was ever brought into England'. Queen Catherine had evidently been permitted to use this staff in her chapel three years before this letter of Howard's. She took the liberty of altering it out of all recognition by turning it into a processional cross of conventional design. When she eventually returned to Portugal she took it with her. It was discovered there in the Coach Museum (once the royal palace) in April 1956. It bears the following inscription: 'Crux Pastoralis Sancti Archiepiscopi Thomae Cantuariensis, a Regina Catharina in Ampliorem Formam Reducta Anno 1664'. It is about 6ft 9in. In the back is a small door covering a circular hole through which may be seen the wood of the original staff. What was the fate of the horn? I suspect it became the figure of a very beautiful crucifix long treasured by Howard's brethren in London, but no longer forthcoming.

Downside, though there are copies of later editions in the British Library and at Edinburgh.

By papal brief of February 1669 written from the Dominican priory of Santa Sabina the queen was given permission to keep the feast of Bl. Rose of Lima, who had been beatified the previous year.[9] Another brief of 1672 allowed her to keep the feast of Bl. Gonsalvo, a Portuguese Dominican, and, rather surprisingly when we think of the times, of Bl. Pius V, the Dominican pope who had excommunicated one of her predecessors.[10]

II

These accounts of the queen's chapel portray a small Catholic community living a normal, carefree life under a religious-minded Catholic queen and an indulgent king. They are not only far from representative of Catholicism in England as a whole: they are a misleading commentary on the state of Catholicism even in the metropolis. The glamour of baroque chapels and Italian music hid a situation full of anxiety and scandal. All the penal laws remained on the statute book and many were still in force and it required only a common informer to set in motion the wheels of violent persecution. While Cosimo was watching the ceremonies of Holy Week at St James's, Titus Oates was preparing for Holy Orders at Cambridge. There had already been incidents that showed how thin was the veneer of security that shielded Catholics from the fury of parliament. In the very year that Howard became grand almoner there had occurred the great fire of London, in September 1666. This had been maliciously attributed to the papists, and on 10 November an edict was published barring them from London. No exception was made for English Catholics in the service of the queens. Such was their confidence in the royal prerogative that the London Catholics took no notice of this edict, and a couple of months later, while the city of London was still a blackened ruin, Howard, full of merriment, was showing Pepys round the two cloisters at St James's that had sprung up in the heart of Protestant London. Thoughtful Catholics, however, were not lulled into a false sense of security by the apparent impotence of parliament. They knew that the fires of hatred smouldered and needed only an ill-wind to fan them into a flame.

Far more disquieting than the fear of persecution was a canker at the heart of the clergy that was destroying their zeal, poisoning their minds, warping their judgment and driving the laity to despair. This canker itself was the result of persecution and the destruction a century before of the church's normal means of government. It might be expected that persecution would unite Catholics into a close comradeship of fellow-sufferers. This was true only for a few years. Then the lack of authority and leadership made itself felt; all the old rivalries and the new ones as well had by now had half a century of unrestrained dominion over the hearts of men who had given up so much to become ministers of Christ. There was the ancient jealousy between seculars and regulars, heightened by the fact that the regulars were forced by circumstances to lead the lives and to do the work of secular priests. There was the rivalry between the various religious orders that was by no means restricted to the realms of theology. There was the scramble for chaplaincies in the houses of the dwindling number of Catholics who could afford to support a priest. There were the obvious dangers that flowed from their utter dependence on a lay patron.

The unity of the clergy was also rent by divergences of views on the extent of papal jurisdiction. There had always been some to defend the oath of allegiance and to blame the Roman court for the disabilities under which they groaned. They believed they could come to terms with a persecuting government by repudiating what they considered the extravagant claims of the church to meddle in temporal affairs. There were some who had imbibed the views of a section of the French clergy who practically advocated a national church under the jurisdiction of the most Christian king. These Gallican views were expressed with much force by an able secular priest, Thomas White *alias* Blacklow, who had a considerable following, though it is impossible to determine to what extent his writings reflect the views of the clergy as a body. The same applies to the charges of Jansenism that were recklessly hurled at any opponent. We know the opinions only of the minority that recorded them in writing, and it is all too easy to attribute them to the inarticulate majority.

The effect of all these divisions on the life of the church would be tragic in any age, but was much more so for a generation living under the strain of the penal laws, with frayed nerves, short tempers and the type of controversial writing that attacks an opponent's morals rather than his tenets.

The root of all this evil, as many saw it, was the lack of a properly constituted superior over the clergy. Rome was also painfully aware of this crying need, but all attempts to supply it, by arch-priests and then vicars apostolic, had had the effect of accentuating the divisions and intensifying the discord. Considering the magnitude of the task it is not surprising that none of these superiors was an unqualified success. The two vicars apostolic in particular had done much to turn a difficult situation into an impossible one. Bishop William Bishop, appointed in 1623, left a legacy that was to trouble the church for sixty years. Relying on the wording of his brief of institution which gave him all the powers of an ordinary, and regardless of the fact that he was ordinary of Chalcedon, not of England, he erected a Chapter with dean, archdeacons and vicars general, and only afterwards applied to Rome for approval. Rome neither approved his action nor condemned it. His successor, Richard Smith, again without previous recourse to Rome, confirmed this Chapter, and the story of the church for the next half-century is largely dominated by the efforts of the Chapter to obtain papal recognition. Smith also stirred up a hornet's nest by calling in question the validity of the faculties enjoyed by the regulars, unless renewed by himself. This led to the brief *Britannia* (9 May 1631), which upheld the privileges of the regulars and censured the bishop for want of tact. Smith retired to a convent in Paris, though he claimed he had never resigned. Thus since 1632 there had been no effective superior, and since his death in 1655 not even a nominal superior over the secular clergy. The Chapter now claimed all the powers belonging to a canonical Chapter *sede vacante*, though it was only too conscious that it had no legal standing in the eyes of Rome. It exacted an oath of obedience from all secular priests coming to England[11] and this, despite its illegality, does not appear to have been resented. In default of any proper authority it performed a useful function in ensuring some degree of order, particularly in the distribution of priests, but it could not exercise any effective disciplinary powers. Priests coming to England received their faculties from Propaganda through the rectors of the colleges abroad, and the Chapter could not suspend them even in extreme cases. Over the religious the Chapter dared not attempt any control whatever, though there were some religious working as free-lances without any superior in England, and in cases of grave scandal they could be suspended or recalled only after protracted negotiations with their superiors abroad.

At first sight Rome's attitude to the Chapter appears hesitant and timorous, but even when the problem is seen in perspective and with the experience of three centuries, it is not easy to decide what the cardinals of Propaganda should have done. They could hardly ratify the Chapter as it stood. It had been erected without reference to them: it included men suspected of unsound doctrine. It was anti-religious and bitterly anti-Jesuit and nobody wanted a repetition of the stormy days of Richard Smith. Also it was not representative of the secular clergy as a whole. It was almost entirely the preserve of priests educated at Douai. In a 'roll of the Chaptermen as it stood at the beginning of this assembly' (10 September 1661),[12] Valladolid is represented only by Anthony Whitehair, and Lisbon by Humphrey Ellis (part-educated at Douai) and Thomas Godden. There were three from the English College at Rome, if we count John Falkner, who had been expelled from it. The other twenty-eight, including all five vicars general, were from Douai. On the other hand there were grave arguments against a forthright declaration that the Chapter was null and void. It would leave the church in England without any semblance of organization or discipline. It would cast doubts on the validity of all its past acts, including the marriage of the king and queen, for which d'Aubigny had asked faculties from the Chapter. It might even lead to schism. Perhaps it was wiser to allow it to function in this uncanonical fashion till the political situation in England was more stable. At times an oblique reference to the Chapter crept into letters from Rome and was eagerly pounced upon as an acknowledgement of the validity of their body. By such small crumbs, inadvertently scattered, the hopes of the Chaptermen were just kept alive.

What the Mass of the lay Catholics thought about the appointment of a bishop we shall never know, for they were inarticulate. The alacrity with which they flocked to receive Confirmation when the chance occurred is indicative of a general desire to have a pastor in episcopal orders. The views that were recorded and have come down to us are the views of the Catholic gentry with property to lose. Recent memories of sequestrated estates made them timorous of any move that might provoke persecution. They preferred to let sleeping dogs lie and to wait for better times. Howard's elder brother Henry is probably representative of his class. He expressed his fears in letters to William Leslie, who acted as Rome agent for many purposes.

> Now at so mad a cross season all we papists desire is to tire out the severity with patience and steady honesty; no tricks and at long run I believe we shall appear the best subjects to monarchy. We talk much of the French, their landing in Ireland or some of our dominions, but much is not to be feared from a company of squibjacks whose doublets and breeches meet not by two handfuls in this frosty weather, and believe me, let us grumble what we will at one another at home, yet if a foreigner appear, both the Protestant sectary, papist, presbyter, quaker, Jew and all are instantly one, and all to club them out. And we laugh at invasion, for whoever enters our Peel-basket shall never break it or out of it more.[13]

When at this time George Leyburn, President of Douai, began another agitation for the appointment of a bishop, Henry Howard expressed his standpoint in a letter of 30 August 1667:

> As to Mr Leyburn's pretensions and business I do assure you I am not sorry you say you almost despair of it, for I believe when the truth is known he has consulted more his own hot-headed fancy than the dictates of the papists in England, for I have been lately spoke to by divers here of the very prime and best quality of them, and neither they nor I do so much as know what 'tis he aims at, and therefore I do most reasonably believe 'tis what we should little approve of. And I could wish when he or any from him are to have an answer to their requests that they were told they believe the papists of England scarce know or desire what he does, and vouch for a reason mine and many others saying so. Nay farther, that I in particular (who should know something) and many, nay most besides, do not desire at this time any alteration or innovation or new rules or authorities to be procured.[14]

On 15 November he writes:

> I desire you would see and read from your patron [Barberini] my brother's long letter, well stating the case of our affairs here, in which I think he says he hopes that nothing Mr Leyburn or any other from abroad shall say to be the desire of the Catholics here, ought to pass for such unless it be seconded and repeated hence, where we (whose estates and concerns are liable to censure for the folly or precipitation of others) ought to be asked ere anything is done. And I assure you as yet as matters go we

desire nothing at all of new to be done from your part towards our relief, lest instead of a courtesy you offer us an injury.[15]

The letter of his brother here referred to is a Latin one dated 18 November. He writes to Francesco Barberini:

> It is the unanimous feeling of the community, both of ecclesiastics and of the principal laity, that it would be very inopportune at this time to determine anything of this nature until it is seen how things are going to turn out here.[16]

He goes on to say that he has been asked by the greater part both of the clergy and of the leading laity to represent this to His Eminence and to ask that nothing be done without consulting those who were living in England and would have to bear the brunt of persecution. It is certainly an exaggeration to say that the clergy were unanimous on this topic or any other. Howard dismisses them as a negligible minority.

### III

As distinct from this question of a bishop to rule over the clergy was the question of a bishop to rule over the queen's chaplains, and of this matter Howard took a very different view.

The treaty of marriage had stipulated that Queen Catherine should have the same number of chaplains, and of the same quality, as had been permitted to her predecessor, now the queen mother. All the world knew that the chaplains of Henrietta Maria had been under the control of a bishop, and as soon as Fr Howard became grand almoner he began to plague Propaganda to implement this part of the agreement, though the Holy See was not a party to the marriage treaty. The question was not as simple as it sounds. Henrietta's bishop was a Frenchman, and as a foreigner was not subject to the penal laws. There never was any difficulty about a foreign bishop residing in London, but parliament was always extremely hostile to any suggestion of an English Catholic being made a bishop in England. They cited not only the penal laws, but the old laws of Catholic times, which forbade the appointment of bishops without the sanction of the king.

The obvious person to be made bishop over the queen's chaplains was the grand almoner, and Howard was convinced that such an appointment would not meet with serious remonstrances from parliament. He consequently pressed to be given episcopal rank, full jurisdiction over the queen's household, and complete immunity from the jurisdiction of any bishop or vicar apostolic; privileges enjoyed by all royal chaplains in Catholic countries. Yet the situation in England was so different that the comparison with Catholic countries has little value. In Paris or Madrid such chaplains were concerned exclusively with the royal household and had no jurisdiction beyond it. In London, where there were no public churches, large numbers of the faithful came to worship in the chapels of the queens and received the sacraments from the royal chaplains. It was essential that they should have for this purpose the ordinary faculties granted to the missionary priests. By no arguments from precedents abroad could it be pretended that the grand almoner was the normal or rightful fount of missionary faculties.

It was reasonable that the grand almoner should have full and effective control over the chaplains, as chaplains. They were a heterogeneous body of seculars and regulars, English, Irish and Portuguese, and it was his duty to ensure order and uniformity within the small world of the queen's own court. Uniformity was not then such a simple matter as it is today. On top of all his other difficulties Howard had to cope with a problem that happily no longer exists but was then a source of much confusion and must be explained.

In 1582 Gregory XIII had reformed the calendar, which in the course of centuries had got ten days ahead of the sun. He ordered that in that year the day after 4 October should be the 15 October. He also restored the old pagan 1 January, which had persisted through all the Christian centuries, and made it the first day of the Christian year. Most Catholic countries accepted the papal reform. Queen Elizabeth herself wanted England to follow suit and a proclamation to that effect was actually printed.[17] Then the Archbishop of Canterbury persuaded her that such a move would show subservience to the pope, and so the proclamation was never published.[18] Thus the English calendar remained ten days behind most of Europe, and 25 March remained the legal new year till 1752. For historians this discrepancy is a well-known pitfall. Letters that passed between people living in England followed the old style, though even in these, there was a tendency to adopt 1 January as the new year. For letters sent to and from abroad there was no uniformity of practice. The foreign ambassadors writing to their courts from London invariably used the new style. English ambassadors abroad used the old, or sometimes gave both. Ordinary people pleased themselves. Fr Howard used the new style, but thought in terms of the old. In a letter dated 2 October 1671 he speaks of events happening on the fifth of this month.[19]

This may seem merely academic, but for the London Catholics of the seventeenth century it was a practical problem. In the queen's chapel they followed the English calendar, but in the chapels of the Catholic ambassadors (except the Venetian) they followed the new. When the queen was celebrating Christmas the Spanish ambassador had reached 4 January and was preparing for the Epiphany. Although the difference was but ten days, there were occasions (e.g. in 1663 and 1671) when there was nearly a month between the two Easters. A man might have gone to Mass at St James in 1664 and found the chapel draped in purple for Palm Sunday while his wife was listening to the organ pealing forth the joys of Easter in the chapel of the French ambassador. No wonder Fr Howard wanted full powers to prevent this sort of thing happening in the queen's own chapel. Without such control there was nothing to prevent the Portuguese Capuchins from following the new style while the English Benedictines followed the old. Indeed there was nothing to prevent the people, on their second Sunday of Lent 1663, being wished a happy Easter by a Portuguese preacher. All sorts of practical problems were affected by this choice of styles. The time allowed for making one's Easter duties, the days of fasting and abstinence, holydays of obligation, the period when solemn marriages were prohibited, and many kindred regulations were rendered chaotic.

It was not long after he assumed the office of grand almoner in 1666 that Howard began to make his opinions heard in Rome. Sometimes he writes direct to Propaganda or to Cardinal Barberini, but more often to William Leslie, the Scots priest who seems to have been almost everybody's agent in Rome. His letters to Propaganda are couched in formal and restrained language, but to Leslie he wrote with the greatest freedom. It is a pity that these furious letters survive only in Italian versions adapted by Leslie to the ceremonious traditions of the papal courts. In one letter Howard says:

> Please note that what I write to you is not to be translated verbatim and exactly as I colloquially express myself. You must put it into proper form *quia non omnia omnibus* [because I am not all things to all men]. I write to you fully and frankly as to a friend, and you must use this information in the way that the negotiations require.[20]

How much pruning these letters in fact received before they reached the august ears of the cardinals it is impossible to say. Even in their Italian dress they are not outstandingly reverential, and Leslie did not think it necessary to omit, for instance, the passage just quoted.

It cannot be pretended that Howard is consistent in his demands. At times he claims to have all the jurisdiction he requires and asks only for the rank and 'mere title' of bishop as a mark of honour due to the queen: at other times he asks for a considerable increase in real authority. At times he is concerned only with the queen's chapel: at other times he deals with the problems facing Catholics generally. But he had best speak for himself.

> All that I believe could be done and all that I write to the cardinal protector would cost nobody anything and would commit nobody to anything. It is merely a title due to me by article eight of the treaty of marriage between the king and queen. If the supreme pontiff grants this favour nobody will be able to complain that it will affect the *status quo* in England. It cannot give me more prestige than I now enjoy (without anyone complaining) and on the other hand will be a great consolation to the poor Catholics, who have been deprived for so many years of the sacrament of Confirmation. It will make no difference to my control over these chaplains of all sorts and over the numerous servants of the queen my patron: they are already under my jurisdiction, so that I should get no more than a mere title, as I've said.[21]

How can this be reconciled with the following?

> In order that the grand almoner may perform his office fully as regards both the clergy of the royal chapel (who are partly seculars and partly regulars of various orders and nationalities) and the large number of layfolk of various qualities and nationalities, it is not enough, living as we do in an heretical country, that he should have the ordinary power and jurisdiction such as bishops have in their own dioceses. He needs also certain extraordinary powers at least over the clergy of the royal chapel and over the whole royal household; powers similar to those

enjoyed for a brief space by the archpriests in England. That is to say, he should grant missionary faculties at pleasure to such chaplains as he should deem fit, and none of them would enjoy faculties or privileges except such as they receive from him or from his vicar in his absence, since he is the pastor and ordinary of the court. All other priests in England, both secular and regular, obtain their faculties for the mission from their respective superiors. Therefore similar power should be given to the grand almoner (who is the superior of the chapel and of the chaplains) to grant or withhold faculties according to his judgment. Indeed royal chapels in every part of the world are exempt from the jurisdiction of the ordinary and from all other jurisdiction than that of the grand almoner.[22]

By 1669 Howard had very considerably modified his views. He is insistent that the queen's almoner should be a bishop; he is still very sensitive to supposed affronts offered to the majesty of his patron. But these questions take a secondary place. He is growing more and more concerned with the chaos and scandal, not in his chapels but at large among the Catholics, and due to the lack of a superior. These problems were not his responsibility but he felt that if he did not speak, the very stones would cry out. In this year there had been some confusion in England because according to the old style the vigil of St Matthias (23 February) fell on Shrove Tuesday. The vigil was a day of fasting and abstinence and the rules were much stricter than most. It was impossible to combine the austerity of the vigil with the hilarity of the carnival. Rome had naturally made no provision for the contingency that arose only in the countries that had refused the reformed calendar. Howard arranged a meeting with superiors of other bodies to ensure uniformity. It was not his job, but nor was it anyone else's and it was a matter of public concern that could brook no delay. He reported the incident to Leslie two days later:

> I would like you to know, that I published on the doors of Her Majesty's chapels the resolution passed among ourselves concerning the vigil of St Matthias, seeing no reply had come from Rome. I did the same when it was a question of publishing the indulgences and the jubilee. I had them printed in English and affixed to the doors of the royal chapels, and copies were sent to all the countries of the realm. But in the two last jubilees there was a certain amount of confusion because before I could get them printed and published, the provincials of the various orders

had caused them to be made public to their penitents, saying that they had received their own copies. However Her Majesty decided that she could not and ought not to take cognizance of it until it had been notified by public authority and by myself, as being the only and proper pastor of the court and of all the household and servants of Her Majesty, as also of the servants of the Duke and Duchess of York and in general of the entire personnel of the court. I was not favoured with due notification of this latest jubilee, which should have been communicated by lawful and public authority. I sent to the nuncio at Paris (there being then no internuncio in Flanders)[*] and he ordered me to publish it as I have done. The previous jubilee was sent to my predecessor from Brussels by the internuncio of that time. Would you therefore be good enough to signify to those it concerns that Her Majesty considers that her chapel and her grand almoner should have at the very least as much authority, jurisdiction and exemption in these countries as is enjoyed by other royal chapels and their royal almoners. And in the first place they should be exempt from all episcopal jurisdiction in whatever district they may sojourn with Her Majesty. Also please ask all these gentlemen on my behalf that all orders which are sent may be addressed to me, because otherwise I shall be unable to take cognizance of them.

And apropos of this I hear it said that those who call themselves here Chaptermen have written to their agent in Rome to procure the deliberation of that tribunal, and they

---

[*] Howard here implies that the nuncio at Paris functioned only in the absence of the internuncio at Brussels. The situation was not as simple as that. The Paris nuncio had been made 'ordinary' of England in 1615 and so remained at this time. When Propaganda was founded in 1622 the cardinals thereof made their own arrangements. They divided their vast territory into thirteen groups and entrusted each group to a nuncio or his equivalent. Group five, comprising Flanders, England, Ireland, Norway and Denmark, was entrusted to the internuncio at Brussels. By a geographical misconception that was soon rectified, Scotland was grouped with Greece, Asia Minor, Bulgaria, Russia etc., and entrusted to the vicar of the Patriarch of Constantinople (AP, Acta Cong. Gen. 1622–5, f. 3). As most English affairs were the concern of Propaganda, the Brussels internuncio became far more important than the 'ordinary' at Paris, and five months after this letter from Howard, by decree of 14 July 1669, the office of ordinary was transferred to Brussels (AP, Audienza I, 1666–79, f. 71). A similar confusion arises over the correct cardinal for appeals. Propaganda put each of the above groups under the care of one of its own body. Group five came under Cardinal Odoardo Farnese. It was a coincidence that he was Cardinal Protector of England. He was not the protector of the other nations, but henceforth we find petitions from them addressed to him rather than to their own protectors.

say that His Holiness has received their agent as agent of the Chapter, thereby recognizing them as a legitimate Chapter, which other popes have never been prepared to do. Would you please inform me accurately of the truth of this. If it really is true and is followed by the appointment of a bishop, he can have no authority whatever over the chapel, household or servants of Her Majesty, nor perform any function in the royal chapel, any more than the Archbishop of Paris or the ordinary of Madrid has any authority in the royal chapels of their Majesties. Please advise these gentlemen in good time and make due representations to them and to His Holiness, to prevent the trouble that might ensue.

Here there is a great division concerning the feastdays because some observe the old feasts and some the new, and neither side will move into the views of the other. There is just as much to be said for one side as for the other, but nothing to be said to defend the scandals that follow on the wake of these discords. The whole evil is due to the lack of any legitimate authority.

Likewise we are not in agreement about the fasting on all Fridays of the year, not knowing whether some ought to observe it or none. We are not in agreement about eating meat in Lent. Many do it publicly at table in the presence of heretics, while others maintain that it is not lawful. This causes not only merriment among heretics but scandal as well, when they see our divisions in these and in other matters which I've pointed out again and again till I'm sick and tired of doing so. I see no attempt made to find an effective remedy, as though we were more contemptible than Holland and lots of other countries that have far fewer Catholics and of less standing, and no such favourable king or pious queen. Yet we are now the most miserable of all, we who in the days of the very pagans were *non Angli sed Angeli* [not Angles but angels].* Now we're left without any authority at all and with no one to administer the sacrament of Confirmation.

As for the reason you adduce that our divisions are the cause of this evil, I reply that there is no nation that hasn't its factions and discords just as bad as ours, if not worse, especially if they are left, like us, without a shepherd. There always will be factions and discords where there is no firm authority to deal with them, and if shepherds are sent who won't or can't defend

---

* This is the remark of Pope St Gregory the Great on seeing young English slaves being sold in Rome. The story is recounted by the Venerable Bede in his *Ecclesiastical History of the English People*, II.i.

the flock with vigour and pastoral devotedness, the very sheep become so many wolves.

Will you please beg and implore these Signori not to heed the flood of reports supplied by scamps and trouble-makers; not because I doubt for one moment the prudence of these Signori, but because I fear that the lies and false reports that are spread with such industry may possibly make some slight impressions on them that will prejudice them against the truth when they hear it from responsible sources.

You should not apropos of the Fridays that the representatives of France, Spain, Italy etc. allow themselves to be persuaded that here the said Fridays of the year are no longer days of fasting by precept and obligation, and their households dine lavishly in public with great scandal while English Catholics who take part in the very same meals keep the fast. And so the heretics who come to these meals are filled with derision and are scandalized to see such diversity of opinion in matters of mortal sin, due to no remedy being provided by superiors laying down the law to be observed. Please represent all this strongly.

I omit very many other things that also need immediate remedy because it seems to me superfluous to make representations as long as there is no legitimate authority to enforce their due observance by the faithful.[23]

In another letter to Leslie of 30 April 1669 he says he has written to Cardinal Barberini and told him again of the 'chaos which arises, continues and spreads through lack of legitimate authority to deal with it'. The sense and promptitude with which bishops were appointed in Ireland, while nothing was done for England, and in particular the appointment of Talbot on the recommendation of the Spanish ambassador made Howard very angry.

After this letter I won't write again until I know more exactly the will of His Eminence and of the Holy See, but I can't hide my feelings from you that I find it a bit strange to see so much done for other Catholic subjects of His Majesty while we, like lost and wandering sheep, are not given a thought. But what strikes me as even more surprising is that this remedy is applied on the recommendation of foreigners and that their information, though they are ignorant of our affairs, prevails with the sacred congregation. It is quite certain that these foreigners judge according to their own passions, factions and interests, but when all this leads to trouble we are the ones to suffer the ill-effects. I don't say all this for your benefit because I believe that you will faithfully and promptly pass on all the requisite information that

I've already sent you, but you will allow me to let myself go, because I'm on the spot and see things going from bad to worse, and I cannot remain dumb. Two years ago when I was received by Cardinal Rospigliosi at Brussels, His Eminence commanded me to write to him and keep him informed of everything. You know that I wrote twice but seeing no effect and getting no answer, I thought it better not to bother him further till I saw what was being done about the matters already put to him. I tell you quite frankly that I have no intention of employing the mediation of foreigners in our affairs and I've always refused it because I supposed that my demands were just and necessary and did not need to be bolstered up with other motives. But for the life of me I can't understand what is holding up the decision of the Holy See. My only comfort is that I've unburdened my conscience before God and men.

When I showed the internuncio the letters about the vigil of St Matthias he was astonished, and he told me he had never heard of or seen any ruling about it. Therefore, to put an end as far as possible to any disagreement I called a meeting of the heads of the clergy, secular and regular, to try to come to some unanimous decision. To have delayed any decision would have led to some scandal and confusion. I foresee the necessity of doing this sort of thing in all other matters until some legitimate and undoubted authority is established. But I see that this does nothing but stir up unpleasantness between us and Rome. It is heart-breaking.[24]

On 1 June the internuncio said the same but more respectfully to Propaganda, recommending an early settlement of Fr Howard's oft-repeated demands, as the suspended animation of English affairs was causing great trouble and disorder.[25]

Howard continues the attack in another letter to Leslie of 18 June. He strongly dissents from the view that the name of bishop is so odious to parliament that it would cause great commotion, and bemoans the facility which the cardinals believe any false information which tends to the destruction and not the betterment of the church in England. He then produces a new argument in favour of his need for episcopal powers:

> Not having the authority of the keys from Rome I was compelled a few days ago to have recourse to the authority of the sword of my patron in order to expel from here a man who had gone crazy, and I shall probably have to get rid of some others as well, who are reacting unworthily here. I am extremely reluctant to use such means, but urgent necessity and the lack of other means

leaves me no alternative. For the love of Jesus Christ beg these signori to issue some regulations for our affairs, and to put the authority into the hands of anyone they like, and so put a stop to evils which follow one upon another and are on the increase.[26]

By October 1669 Howard had received some sort of control over the faculties exercised by his subordinates but it did not extend to the Portuguese members of the household. After further representations this matter was rectified, and the secretary of Propaganda was able to write to Brussels.

Praise be to God that Fr Howard this time will be satisfied with the new faculty sent to him, in which the Portuguese are also comprised. It is most important to keep this man contented.[27]

It was, however, over-optimistic to say that Howard was contented. His principal request had not been granted. There was still no sign of a mitre to give greater honour and dignity to the queen's grand almoner. The cardinals of Propaganda can hardly be blamed for this. Even in Howard's own letters the two quite distinct questions, of a mitre for the royal chapel, and a superior to govern the church, had become inextricably entangled. To add to the complications, at the very time when Howard began to agitate for adequate jurisdiction over the chapel, the Chapter began to consider him as the most likely candidate for the wider and more onerous position of head of the English Catholics.

## Notes

1. E. Chamberlayne, *Angliae Notitia*, London, 1669.
2. *Relazione del viaggio d'Irlanda et Inghilterra*. Biblioteca Nazionale Centrale di Firenze, II, III, 429. Eng. Trans.: *Travels of Cosmo III Grand Duke of Tuscanny through England*, London, 1821.
3. *Diary of Samuel Pepys*, ed. H. B. Wheatley, London, 1904, VI, 142.
4. Ibid. VII, 247.
5. Reg. 115, 9.
6. P. Horan, P., *Memoirs of the Most Rev. Oliver Plunkett*, Dublin, 1861, I, 43.
7. AV, Misc. Arm. I, t.17, ff. 290–4; also AP, Sc. Rif. Anglia, I, f. 238.
8. Reg. 112 (ter), f. 534.
9. SB, 1439, f. 418.
10. SB, 1583, f. 135.
11. Ushaw MSS, XVIII, F.6, 'The general assembly of the Chapter of the Catholick English Church held in May 1667'. The text of the oath is given under the third session on 8 May.

12 AAW, A32, no. 63.
13 M. V. Hay, *The Jesuits and the Popish Plot*, London, 1934, 102.
14 *Ibid.* 106.
15 *Ibid.* 108.
16 *Dominicana*, 34.
17 SP. 12/160, no. 28.
18 BL, Add. 32092, ff. 26, 29.
19 NF, 60, f. 537.
20 *Dominicana*, 40.
21 AV, misc. Arm.I, t.17, f. 294.
22 AAW, A32, no. 68; cf. *Dominicana*, 36–42.
23 AP.Sc.Rif.Anglia I, f. 310.
24 *Ibid.* f. 316.
25 *Ibid.* f. 338.
26 *Ibid.* f. 299.
27 AP, t.54, 41.

# 4

# *Bishop-Elect*

## I

THE CHAPTER OF THE SECULAR CLERGY, that sometimes called itself the London Chapter and sometimes the Chapter of the English church, had been formed in 1623 and had spent the next forty years in seeking approval from Rome. If it lacked all validity it made up for it by the zeal of its members. Few cathedral Chapters can have worked so hard. The dean and his consultors met in London every month for 'consults' and there was an annual meeting that was usually well-attended. Funds were collected for the support of an agent in Rome and for charitable purposes. The secular clergy appear to have accepted its authority without question. On the other hand it had incurred suspicion and odium by the advanced Gallican views of some of its members, notably Thomas White alias Blacklow, and its enemies never lost an opportunity of using this as an argument against its recognition by the pope. It was militantly anti-Jesuit and generally anti-religious.

Howard refers on more than one occasion with open contempt to the 'so-called Chapter' and nowhere has he left a word in writing that can be interpreted as agreement with their claims. Yet he managed to give them the impression that he was on their side and would, if he could, work for their recognition. Like so many who write violent letters Howard was a mild man to meet. There are many references to his courtesy and amiable manner towards everyone, and the Chaptermen may have mistaken this for approval of all their deeds and pretentions. The dean of the Chapter in 1668 was John Leyburn, Howard's lifelong friend, and another prominent member, Thomas Godden, was treasurer of the queen's chapel and to that extent under Howard's authority. There were, then, friendly relations that might well give rise to exaggerated hopes.

It seems a fair deduction from the correspondence soon to be given that the sole aim of the Chapter was their own preservation and formal ratification. They want a bishop, but he must be an Ordinary and not a petty vicar apostolic. Why? Because a vicar apostolic, with a see *in partibus*, has no power to form or confirm a Chapter. This is the burden of all the letters that passed between the dean and his agent in Rome. Never do they mention the grave scandals and confusion that weigh so heavily on Howard. Never will they compromise even for a time, even for the good of the Catholics.

The Roman authorities were fully alive to the need of a pastor in England with valid and effective jurisdiction. But England had been placed under Propaganda. For administrative purposes it was just as much a mission-field as China or darkest Africa. The long Catholic past, of which English Catholics were so conscious, had no weight in their deliberations. Howard may remind them of the privileges of grand almoners in medieval England; Benedictines may claim the wide privileges they once enjoyed at Westminster and Canterbury: all this meant nothing to Propaganda. England was a *provincia desolata* and subject to the rules that applied to all foreign missions. It must walk before it can run. It must begin with a vicar apostolic with a titular see somewhere in Asia minor. He will have ordinary jurisdiction there and may if he wishes form a Chapter there, though his brief of appointment always dispensed him from the obligation of visiting his see 'so long as it remains under the dominion of the infidel'. But in England he will have only such authority as Propaganda chooses to delegate to him. When this desolate region is sufficiently developed will be the time to consider the establishment of a hierarchy. Such has always been, such is still, the procedure in missionary countries.

But could not an exception be made for England with its glorious past, its Catholic queen and its surviving Catholic aristocracy? Must it be classed with the Gold Coast or the West Indies that had never known such glories? Such sentimental arguments made no appeal to Propaganda. They had their rigid laws and they kept control firmly in their own hands. They were reluctant to depart from precedent. They would not, for instance, delegate to priests the power to administer Confirmation, though England had been without a bishop for nearly forty years. They were reluctant to delegate the power to grant even the simplest dispensations. Judged

## Bishop-Elect

by modern standards this over-centralization seems incredibly unrealistic. At a time when it was not only extremely difficult and expensive, but also a matter of high treason to correspond with the Roman courts, English Catholics had no easier means of obtaining urgent and highly reasonable dispensations. Roman archives furnish many examples of their pathetic petitions. In 1627 a Dominican in England writes to the Holy Office for permission to go about in secular dress, when it was suicide to appear as a priest.[1] In 1650, when priests were being shipped as slaves to Jamaica, an Irish Dominican in London asks for a dispensation to eat meat sometimes during Lent when dining with heretics, so as not to give himself away.[2] It was not until the time of Innocent XI (1676–89) that the students at the English, Irish and Scots colleges in Rome were dispensed from the obligation of having their banns of ordination read publicly in the Lateran and in their parish church, for every spy to hear and transmit to England ahead of them.[3] If Rome was not prepared to modify procedure in small ways when it was a matter of life and death, what chance was there of her relaxing the strict regulations that governed the appointment of bishops in the vast mission-fields?

There was another consideration that doubtless influenced the Italian cardinals. They were familiar with Italian sees that were usually no more than a single city and its surrounding villages. Within his domain the bishop ruled, it is true, with ordinary jurisdiction subject immediately to the pope; but his authority was very limited in extent. How could anyone conceive of a single bishop having ordinary jurisdiction over an area the size of England?

In asking for an Ordinary the Chapter were crying for the moon, but in their anxiety they continued to cry. It was for them a matter of self-preservation. Though so often rebuffed they continued to send to their agent the names of three of their own body that they considered worth of a mitre. By 1668 they were beginning to despair. It was probably the dean John Leyburn who first suggested Howard. If they could not have one of themselves, what did they think of asking for him? He was brother of the Duke of Norfolk, queen's almoner, a friend of the king, full of energy, well-disposed, still under forty, and one who knew how to talk to those cardinals. It is true he was a religious, but if they had to have a religious it was far better to have a Dominican than a Benedictine or a Jesuit; for the Dominicans were so few that there was no danger, even with a bishop, of dominating the country. On 2 December Leyburn deliberated with his advisors.

> The dean and nine consultors being present it was put to the vote whether or no our agent should have order to move His Holiness the second time for a bishop, and it was carried in the affirmative by eight votes. A second question was hereupon proposed, viz. whether in case the persons nominated by the last general assembly should be waived and the lord almoner offered for a bishop, His Lordship should be accepted or no. This question being put to the vote was also carried in the affirmative by nine voices. And accordingly order was sent to our agent to proceed accordingly. But in regard the matter of the capitular brethren in the country, this was ordered to be done by a circular letter to the purpose.[4]

The replies of seven of the capitular brethren are extant. Not one of them shows any enthusiasm for the proposal, though there is never a word against Howard personally. Only one, Francis F., gives an explicit 'no':

> I received your letter wherein you desire my vote. I here declare that my vote shall be the same I gave in our general assembly; only for one of these nominated there. I desire to be excused that I vote not for Mr Howard, lord almoner, nor for any other regular whatsoever. It will not be convenient here to name the reasons that move me.[5]

Extracts from other letters will show the temper of the Chapter:

> Methinks we should not refuse it although they confer it not upon any of the persons by us nominated, because they accomplish the substance of our request, albeit not in the manner we desire it. Indeed, considering the opposition of regulars touching the manner of our request, how could they better please them (who must not be displeased) and us (who deserve some compassion) than by giving them one who is as they are, and us him who having so inconsiderable a body of his own is apt to favour and hold more intimate correspondence with ours than any other body of the regulars ... I am not ignorant how opposite this vote is to the sentiments of our predecessors, and I doubt will prove now to some of our more ancient brethren. Nevertheless considering the long vacancy and our almost despair of obtaining our own wish, I judge it better to accept of such a person as this we now suppose, by whose authority we may hope for redress of many disorders, than by refusing, to render ourselves obnoxious

to the obloquy of them that call us Independents, and say we would have no bishop. (unsigned)

What can the judgement of one so far off, so little acquainted with great persons and courts and as little versed in the study required to the resolution of this point, add to the completing of it? I know not the person proposed, his ability, nor how he stands affected, nor what hopes of his espousing our concerns as a father. I know he is of a noble descent and of an order that best suited me in all countries. But who can tell, if we calmly digest a prior now, under that denomination, but that the next may be a rector [i.e. a Jesuit]. But, sir, the main ignorance is, I know not whether our acceptance or non-acceptance, our will or nill, signifies anything there where we begged confirmation and were repulsed, so as when we were boys or young men we had no power or *ius* to propose or nominate who should be our master in figures or grammar and our rectors and ministers of our college, we must be so still ... Whoever that one in ten was I must love and honour for a resolute stout clergyman, but too desperate for me ... Why cannot we hope, nay expect from one who accepts that dignity and charge, the just procedure and patronage which it requires? I am sure God will exact it. I give my vote to you. If that will not serve I give it myself hobb nobb for the affirmative, that this noble person Fr Philip H. is to be accepted if he be proposed for bishop ... And now I think of it, many of this gentleman's coat were decried for Jansenists. Why may not he then be zealous for those who have been and are still trampled on under the same stones? (Thomas Forbes).

I fear I shall not acquit myself prudently in the case, for first I am altogether a stranger to the gentleman, ignorant of what temper and inclination to our body. Again I am in my private judgement for the negative, especially he should be imposed upon us without our consent. My reason is, they that reject so many worthy persons of our own body, so often propounded, can mean us no great good in imposing a regular upon us; one perhaps that will be easily guided by their counsels. Nevertheless, swayed by the leading authority of our venerable brethren, who thoroughly understand the case, I freely give my vote for the affirmative. (George Hodgson).

I must confess I have some difficulty to give a positive resolution. For on the one side, considering the obligation incumbent on us to choose one whom we shall judge, all things considered, the most fit and worthiest, truly I can hardly approve of the person proposed. Not that I have any reason to think him unworthy of

> that dignity, but that I am persuaded there are others that may claim it by a more just title. But on the other side ... there may be reasons unknown to me that may induce others to recede from this general maxim. Wherefore, in confidence of your being better able to judge of the present circumstances than myself, I freely make over my powers of voting unto you, and shall own for mine whatsoever you shall determine in my name in this point. (Francis Gage, from Paris).
>
> My vote is for the affirmative, relying herein more on nine of ten counsellors than any reason of my own, who I presume have weighed all inconveniences may ensue better than I possibly can who am totally ignorant of things of this nature, though I conceive it would be very hard measure none should be thought worthy we have proposed. (Francis Williams).
>
> I am glad that we are not past hopes: it shall be my prayer to quicken them and bring them into possession. What you intimate concerning my lord almoner, God direct you for the best. I give my vote to you: bestow it as you please, and I beseech God direct you in this and all other important affairs. (George Middleton)[6]

Armed with this almost unanimous, if somewhat tepid support from the Chapter, John Leyburn began to make their views known in Rome.

## II

The Rome agent of the Chapter in 1669 was Alexander Holt, who wrote under the name of Silverio and addressed his letters to William Fulton, who had just succeeded Leyburn as dean. His task was not an easy one. As the Chapter had no legal existence, so its agent had no standing in the papal courts. He was never received in audience. He had no legitimate access to information. He pestered Baldeschi, the secretary of Propaganda but got little out of him. He had to pick up what he could by pumping and by bribing minor officials. The information thus acquired was of very varied value, and even the more successful scoops left room for doubt as to their accuracy and completeness.

The Chapter had met again on 31 December 1668, considered the overwhelming vote in favour of Howard and instructed Holt to present another petition to the pope.[7] It was always just as well to ask for more than you expected, but on the other hand it was wise to avoid adding requests that had no chance of success and could lead only to the rejection of the whole petition. But Holt could not bring himself simply to petition for a bishop. He prays the pope to grant them Philip Howard as Ordinary in England with the title of archbishop, and at the same time to confirm the Chapter with apostolic authority.[8] But perhaps it made no difference what he put in his petitions. This one now exists only in draft. The original never reached Propaganda. Indeed it is significant that there is not a single petition from any agent of the Chapter in the archives of Propaganda nor any reference to one. It would seem that they got no further than the papal wastepaper basket. Still Holt continued to hope, and to pump, and on 27 July 1669, some six months later, wrote with something like jubilation:

> Mine of late gave you to understand that the decisive Congregation had met, but that the communication of their results by any direct means was flatly denied me who treat the business, which though a strange kind of policy yet usual and much affected here. My next endeavours therefore have been employed in lying perdue and pumping for private intelligence, and I doubt not that I have made a total discovery, which I herein communicate unto you, *sed sub sigillo* lest we injure the intelligencer. Not that I desire you to conceal any point of it from our venerable brethren, who I know bestir themselves towards the perfecting of that which hath cost so much pains and moneys to advance to this posture. My request therefore in point of secrecy is only this, that you keep it amongst yourselves; and where necessity requires that lay friends or patrons know, by reason of imploring them to assist you, that you own not the news from me. Thus much premised my discovery is this.
>
> First, that the Congregation, *annuente Sanctissimo*, hath condescended to my main request, i.e. resolved to give us an *absolute ordinary* to govern our church.
>
> Secondly, after he is consecrated and installed in his employment, to confirm also our venerable Chapter, if he prove so honest as to be willing of it. This latter is a point never mentioned by me but judged convenient by these politicians whereby to oblige us, because they see that we have so much brains in our heads as to stand upon our legs without their helping hand.
>
> Thirdly, by reason they will believe none but their own ministers, they have appointed Signor Agretti to come over to

you with speed, to observe whether my words be true, and to take information of the fittest person for the foresaid employment.

Fourthly, his instructions are that he address himself immediately to the Venice ambassador and make use of him in all occasions.

Fifthly, that here are arrived two letters, one from my Lord Almoner, Mr P. H. and another from the Lord Archbishop Talbot, both speaking very honourably of our venerable dean and Chapter, but the latter earnestly recommending the other as the fittest person to be our ordinary, which is not so willingly hearkened to here for divers reasons, i. because regulars in this nick of time are not judged the fittest to govern missions, ii. because they conceive he may be satisfied with the dignity of bishop alone, and may be a means to bring in another of our body to govern, who may be more active than his employments would permit, to the end no side complain, etc.

Sixthly, 'tis also resolved that Agretti stay amongst you after the bishop is made, and continue with this title of *ministro apostolico*.

Seventhly, the Congregation also resolved upon Mr Plunkett for the primacy of Ireland, i.e. Armagh. He was a school-fellow of mine and professeth much affection to us and our cause. This last is blabbed abroad all the town over, but all that concerns us, most secret.

This is all of substance which I have to say at present, from whence I hope you will conclude with me that, all circumstances considered, viz. my small capacity, my want of recommendation, the difficulties of treating with this court, the manner how we were looked upon there through the many obloquies and aspersions cast upon us, together with the power and watchfulness of our adversaries—these and the like reflections, I say, being made by you, I doubt not but so favourable conclusion or construction may be made that my part upon this stage may be allowed to have been acted, if not according to your wishes, yet at least as thoroughly as my power extended to.

He goes on to counsel Pulton to anticipate the enemy and gain the ear of the Venetian ambassador.[9]

Part of this information was irreproachable. Plunkett had been appointed to Armagh on 9 July, but that information was public property. Agretti had been instructed to proceed to England on the affairs of the Chapter. Talbot had written recommending Howard as the most suitable person to rule over the clergy and had deprecated the use of the title of bishop. But he wanted to see

## Bishop-Elect

the Chapter dissolved.[10] Howard had also written, but hardly in commendation of what he refers to as the 'so-called Chapter'. He had, however, strongly dissented from the opinion of Talbot that the title of bishop was odious to parliament and should not be used.[11] Thus far Holt was reasonably well informed, but the rest of the story was really not worth the fee that produced it. A great deal of information had been submitted to Propaganda of which he had no inkling. There was, for instance, a long dispatch sent on 22 June by the internuncio Airoldi reporting an interview he had given to the provincial of the Jesuits:

> He discoursed at great length on Catholic affairs in England, but the principal question I asked was concerning the creation of a bishop as head of the English clergy. He replied that such a step could not be taken without causing commotion and risking an outbreak of persecution against the Catholics, because the title of bishop is so odious to the whole Presbyterian sect (of which parliament is almost entirely composed) that even the Protestant bishops are being slowly reduced to a state of almost total impotence. I opposed two considerations to his arguments. First that the seventh article of the marriage treaty promised the creation of a bishop, and secondly that before I left Rome there had already arrived an agent from the said clergy to press for a bishop. He replied that these marriage treaties envisaged that the grand almoner should be a bishop, but honorary and without jurisdiction, simply out of regard to the Majesty and the queen. Secondly, it was quite true that the clergy had sent an agent to Rome to ask for a bishop as head of the clergy, but, nonetheless, their intentions had been that he should be chosen from their body; a body which, infected with opinions that had been condemned, would thereby have kept the whole contagion of their corruption. Also when His Holiness would have created a bishop independent of them and of sound doctrine they would not have him at any price. He made a further point which seems to me worthy of consideration. It is this. Parliament is due to meet in October and it is customary in their assemblies to pass new laws prejudicial to Catholics. They might well seize upon the creation of a bishop as a further excuse to vomit up laws sanctioning even more violent anti-Catholic persecution.[12]

Nor was it only the Jesuits who complained of the corrupt opinions of the Chaptermen. Airoldi had reported on 19 January:

> George Leyburn president of the college of Douai has been here and has represented to me the necessity of bringing back to

their duty the priests in London, who, without any foundation, usurp the title of Chapter of the English church. They cause a great deal of harm because the greater part is infected with the pernicious opinions of the Sorbonne, of Jansenius and of Blacklow alias White.

Leyburn suggested that the only remedy was a vicar apostolic with episcopal character and he thought Fr Howard the best choice.[13]

Howard's own fervid letters had certainly stressed the urgent need for a bishop, but they served also to warn Propaganda of the appalling difficulties that he would have to face. With all this information before them the cardinals had a special congregation on 12 July and on the 14th were received in audience. They first suggested that the office of Ordinary of England should be transferred from Paris to Brussels. This was approved. They next dealt with Howard's complaint that the grand almoner had never been given episcopal rank. The pope agreed that he should be informed by some third party that 'the delay in consoling him with this rank was due to the fact that the queen had never communicated to them her desire that the choice should fall on him'. Then they came to the heartbreaking question of a pastor for the English flock.

> The cardinals are only too aware that this country needs a pastor, but they are at a loss to find a subject capable of bearing such a burden, as long as the candidates proposed by the clergy are for the most part suspected of unsound doctrine and the seculars so hostile to the religious. It seemed best that the Congregation should propose that Fr Howard be raised to episcopal rank and then granted little by little a certain amount of authority in order, in this way and without any danger, to make trial of his fitness and to accustom the clergy by imperceptible degrees to give him obedience. But before coming to any decision they judge it necessary to hear the opinion of Agretti.
>
> His Holiness approved.[14]

Thus the grandiose story that Holt had picked up boils down to this: that the cardinals had decided nothing at all and would not do so till they received Agretti's report.

Holt was soon aware of the inadequacy of his informer and of the undue optimism he had inspired. He writes again on 3 August:

> Since my last I have made trial of other private ways whereby to gain intelligence of what passed in the thrice-mentioned congregation, and I am told that though some part of what was

in my last be true, yet that these people have an intention first to try if they can make Mr P. H. bishop, and next, if will relish, to give only authority of vicar apostolic: that no recommendation is yet come from his mistress for to promote him to the dignity, but that they hope it will. The relation, you see, is less favourable than my other, which at that time truly I had no reason to doubt of. Now you have both, as clear as I, and though I always suspect the worst, yet tis remitted to your discerning judgement to conclude what's best to be done in the circumstances. This I have to add, which is most certainly true, that the Venice ambassador with you is the man relied upon both for advice and intelligence in all transactions there, and that there is newly arrived a letter from the internuncio enclosing another from the said ambassador which counsels thus: that if no positive resolution be already taken here concerning the business of Mr P. H., that twere good to defer it till the sitting of the two ensuing parliaments, ours already known and the Scotch now newly summoned to meet at the same time.[15]

The information concerning the Venetian ambassador was not without foundation, but it does not appear that he played a leading part. He wrote to urge the appointment of a bishop, but as he says himself: 'I wished to lend a hand quietly to an affair in which I do not wish to cut a figure'.[16]

By the end of July Agretti had reached London, with a letter of credence to Howard, by whom he was introduced to the king and queen. He stayed in London till October when parliament met, and, as his identity and mission were by then widely known he was asked by the king to retire from the capital. He returned to Brussels in the autumn and his detailed report is dated 14 December 1669.[17] As a fairly full summary of this report has already been published[18] it will be enough here to give his estimate of Fr Howard and the arguments for and against the appointment of a bishop.

> That the king is quite willing that a bishop should be appointed, or at least a superior for the Catholics appears from His Majesty's discourse which I sent to the Archbishop of Cesares [the internuncio] on the 8 of last month. Fr Howard told me in confidence that His Majesty positively wished that a bishop should be appointed, but that bearing in mind the parliament the king asked, just before my arrival in London, that as nothing had yet been done such a promotion should for the love of God be deferred till after parliament so as not to give a handle to the extremists.

## Philip Howard

The problem remains to find a candidate competent for this burden. I had not the opportunity of getting to know many priests, and in the present discord among the clergy I know not where to lay my hand on a person free from bias and endowed with the high qualities that are required.

I gave the king an opportunity to say whether he had any special predilection for Fr Howard. His Majesty made no reply. I don't know if this means that His Majesty is merely indifferent, or whether he was unwilling to discuss the matter, with parliament so near.

Fr Howard has quite considerable ability for the post, and if the organization of the church was already on its feet and running smoothly I consider he could be proposed without any scruple. But here the vicar apostolic will enter a church that has been deprived of pastors for so many years that he will in all probability have to contend with the members of the Chapter, and with the regulars, and on top of this he may have some opposition from the heretics.

I had a lot to do with Fr Howard in the greatest secrecy, in order to form an opinion of his ability. He has none of that profound learning, shrewdness and maturity which are requisite for bearing such a heavy burden. From what I heard, this was also the opinion of the king and queen and of certain other people of intelligence that I sounded on some other pretext.

On the other hand, Fr Howard

1. Is of an exalted family known to Your Eminence.
2. Of great zeal and goodness, of holy intentions and of exemplary life.
3. Of sound doctrine and submissive to the wishes of the Holy See.
4. Is neither a secular nor a Jesuit, which seem nowadays to be the two extremes in the church. I found him impartial between seculars and regulars, and if anything, tending to side with the secular clergy.
5. Is of an order which up till now has not been prominent in England. Therefore his promotion will not arouse the jealousy of the religious nor of the capitulars as would that of a member of a more prominent order.
6. Does not belong to the French or to the Spanish faction and does not meddle in politics.
7. Is *persona grata* with the king, and highly thought of by the queen (though they regard him as stated above), and his being grand almoner will be an additional advantage.
8. He will not be resented by the capitulars though they would prefer one of their own nominees. During my last few days

in London I noticed that the capitulars showed increasing confidence in him.

9. From what I could learn he will be welcomed with approval by the faithful both high and low.

Some of the best informed among the religious to whom I put these points made no objection to Fr Howard personally and it appears that the Jesuit fathers would prefer him as vicar apostolic to anyone else, and intimated that they gathered this was the inclination of the king. But they were at pains to acquaint me with his above-mentioned defects.

In case His Holiness should deem it expedient to lay on Fr Howard the government of the church in England it will perhaps be as well, over and above the instructions and the specification of his faculties, to enjoin him not to ally himself with the Chapter nor with the regulars, particularly the Jesuits and Benedictines, except in so far as it should be ordained by the papal court, and to be governed by those principles with the counsel and supervision of the internuncio, in order to avoid the disturbances caused by Bishop Smith of Chalcedon.

It is worth considering whether it would not be better to make Fr Howard bishop of the queen's chapel first of all, and then little by little charge him with the affairs of the mission, in order to make trial of his sufficiency. He, however, is unwilling to be a bishop in that form, declaring that when, either by the death of the queen or by some outbreak of persecution he should lose his post of grand almoner, he would find the title of bishop an embarrassment. Nevertheless I think that if he is wanted to undertake the office of vicar apostolic, he will not refuse to take the episcopal character.

From what little I was able to learn it would appear to be much better to make Fr Howard vicar apostolic, in spite of his shortcomings already enumerated than to leave things any longer in their present state. I judge, however, that Your Eminence should defer this business until after the session of parliament, both because that is what the king wishes and also to see the outcome of the great projects which (so it is said) have been made in parliament in matters of religion.

As for the capitulars, perhaps the kindest way to regularize them would be this. That the vicar apostolic in the name of His Holiness should ratify all that they have done up till now so as not to trouble consciences, tell them that His Holiness will soon form a permanent Chapter, examine the attitude of each member and of other priests and pick out the best of them. His Holiness might then create a true and perpetual Chapter from those so chosen, making it clearly understood that he reserves to himself forever the right of appointing to vacancies ...

I come now to the faculties that Fr Howard would wish for. I asked him about them when I first saw him, but every time I broached the matter he changed the subject. Later on he told me that in the faculties so kindly granted him by Your Eminence he would have liked a clause enabling him to communicate them to the priests secular and regular who are the queen's chaplains, because the patents sent were those of a simple missioner. Towards the end of my stay in London he began to make it clear little by little that he would wish for jurisdiction over all the priests, secular and regular of the queen's chapel in some form as enjoyed by the principal chaplains of Catholic crowns. He considered that those of the queen of England ought not to be in a lower category, and he conjectured that the principal chaplains of the Catholic kings of England must have had the same prerogatives. Over and above this, because it was an heretical country, he would like the power to depute as missionaries such of his chaplains as he thought suitable and to revoke their faculties at will; in other words, that Your Eminence should not grant faculties directly to any of them, but send them through him. With such jurisdiction and authority he would have means to enforce proper discipline and to punish those who were remiss in the work of the mission. I was not greatly impressed by this proposition, finding it too sweeping, and I answered vaguely. I said that for such powers he ought to be a bishop, because it was not the way with popes to confer jurisdiction on persons especially regulars who were not dignitaries. I threw out this remark to see if he would be willing to be made bishop for the chapel, for if such were the case I would have asked him again to move the queen to solicit this grace for him. But he stood firm on this point, he did not wish to be made bishop for the chapel.

I added that he should take steps to consult the ancient registers of the palace to see whether there was any proof of what he had said, that before the schism the grand almoners were exempt from the jurisdiction of the ordinary, because such a document would help forward his claims. And that is as far as the business has gone. I took my leave of the queen without her saying a word about all this, though I talked with her for a considerable time, but that night Fr Howard came to look for me with Fr Patrick Ginn and these two together proposed the above request in the name and (so they said) by command of the queen. I excused myself by saying in so many words that Fr Howard had delayed too long in explaining himself on this matter, and that I had no time to ponder a matter of such gravity,

and therefore thought it necessary to defer it till I returned to
England or till Fr Howard crossed to Flanders (as he does from
time to time). This would enable me to put the matter to the
internuncio and see what could be done (without committing
Your Eminence) to serve Her Majesty and satisfy Fr Howard.
He replied that if necessary the queen would write to Your
Eminence. In order not to involve Your Eminence I answered,
citing similar cases, that it was quite certain that such a grace
would not be granted without Her Majesty's petition, but that
I thought it better to consult the internuncio first and to ask for
light from a friendly party in Rome, because a letter from Her
Majesty would cause much embarrassment to Your Eminence
if it should perchance prove impossible to gratify her.

As an appraisement of Howard's capabilities and shortcomings this report is valuable and shows considerable discernment, but in general it is a far too roseate view of the state of the church in England. The wounds were too deep to be probed by a foreign visitor and were not to be healed by any ingenious formula, however well-intentioned.

This report might, however, have led to the immediate appointment of Howard as vicar apostolic, had it not so happened that Clement IX had died five days before it was written. There was soon a change of policy and a new internuncio at Brussels, and the whole dreary business had virtually to begin all over again.

III

After a discordant conclave of more than four months the cardinals resorted to compromise and on 29 April 1670 elected Emilio Altieri, who took the name of Clement X. He had been a cardinal less than a year and was only three months short of his eightieth birthday. Fr Howard wrote to congratulate him, asked his blessing and immediately launched an appeal on behalf of the English Catholics. He reminds the pope of how they had met twenty-five years before:

> For my part I have known the tenderness of your heart towards
> the Catholics of this nation, ever since (when at Naples in
> the convent S. Mariae Sanitatis) I payed my respects to Your
> Holiness; and later on when with my uncle Viscount Stafford (in
> 1649 before I left Naples) and with letters of our special patron
> Cardinal Altieri of pious memory, Your Holiness's brother (who

> had bound us to him for ever) we attended on Your Holiness, and you were pleased at once to help us in our pressing and immediate necessity.[19]

It was good to have a pope that he had actually met, though so long ago, and there was another meeting in far-off days that now assumed an unexpected importance in the destiny of Fr Howard. The new pontiff gave the office of cardinal nephew, or cardinal secretary, to Paluzzi-Altieri, an uncle by marriage of Laura Altieri the last surviving member of the pope's own family. The cardinal nephew was always a very influential person but never more so than under an octogenarian pope. Caustic Romans declared that the pope reserved to himself only the pontifical functions of *benedicere* and *sanctificare*, while Cardinal Altieri busied himself with *regere* and *gubernare*. Certainly there is evidence in plenty that the cardinal secretary exercised enormous power, and of supreme interest to Fr Howard was the fact that his confessor was none other than John Baptist Hacket, the Irish Dominican who had first fired young Howard with a love of the order and had conducted him to his novitiate at Cremona. Hacket became the principal target of the attack on the order launched by the Howard family, and he was forbidden by the Master General to have anything to do with his protégé. Such a prohibition, however, could not destroy a friendship so deep as it was sudden. Hacket never relinquished his early hopes of seeing Philip Howard a cardinal, and though there is no evidence of any converse between them during the next twenty years they had not forgotten each other. With the election of Clement X, Hacket's name begins to appear in letters from Rome as the confidant and agent of Fr Howard, and it would be strange if the old Dominican never mentioned the subject of red hats to his all-powerful patron.

Howard wrote to congratulate the new cardinal nephew though they had never met,[20] and it was perhaps the good offices of Hacket that drew them together in mutual esteem. Howard now added Cardinal Altieri to his list of correspondents, and twice in 1670 wrote to him direct on the crying needs of the English church. He continued to make his clamour heard through the 'normal channels'—Francesco Barberini, Cardinal Protector of England, and Baldeschi the secretary of Propaganda—but affairs had reached such a pass that he did not hesitate to write direct to the pope and to the cardinal secretary.

*Bishop-Elect*

There is, however, a noticeable change of emphasis in his letters. He no longer hammers away at the rights and privileges of the queen's chapel, or the claims of the grand almoner to episcopal rank. He protested strongly because the queen was not officially notified of the election of the new pope, and he was not mollified when it was explained that the etiquette of the papal court did not extend this honour to queen-consorts, but only to queens reigning in their own right. The special case of a Catholic queen married to a heretic does not appear to have been envisaged. Howard must have enjoyed pointing out that the queen had received a brief announcing the accession of Clement IX.[21] Apart, however, from this alleged breach of etiquette, the affairs of the queen's chapel no longer find a place in Howard's letters and the question of a mitre for the grand almoner is quietly dropped.

An event in 1668 must have opened his eyes to certain inconveniences that he had not foreseen. Some of the French Capuchins attached to the chapel of the queen mother were causing grave scandal, and Howard wrote to Propaganda via Leslie suggesting that they should be deprived of their missionary faculties. On 25 August Propaganda concurred. They wrote to the missionaries, to their provincial in Paris and even to their general. They sent the first of these letters to be delivered by Howard. Soon there were protests from Walter Montagu the grand almoner and complaints from the queen mother that this high-handed action had been taken without any reference to them. In vain Propaganda pointed out that these priests had been deprived only of their *missionary* faculties which were not controlled by the grand almoner. An affront had been offered to a queen and Howard was blamed for his interference and officiousness.[22] A year before he had been clamouring for power to grant or withhold these very faculties in respect to all the priests subject to his authority: now he was denying the same power to his fellow grand almoner.

Worse was to follow. In June 1669 the queen mother, nearing her death, retired to France. She took her grand almoner with her but left the Capuchins to administer the chapel for the benefit of the faithful. Soon three or four of them publicly apostatized but still exercised their faculties as priests.* A year before, Howard had

---

\* 'Yesterday [3 April 1671] at the French church in the Savoy two young Capuchin friars did publicly, in the face of the whole congregation, renounce

## Philip Howard

so loudly insisted that the clergy of the queen's chapel should be exempt from the jurisdiction of the ordinary even for missionary faculties. But what happened when the queen died and the chapel was closed? Who was to prevent them going on using their faculties and forming an independent 'diocese' of their own? What was to prevent a similar insubordination when Catherine of Braganza died and the grand almoner automatically ceased to exist? The danger of vesting large and exclusive authority in a nominee of the crown must have become painfully clear. Howard writes to Barberini on 22 April 1670:

> I am compelled to reiterate to you my request for the household of Her Majesty in particular and for the common good of Catholics, for both are suffering extremely from this lack of properly established authority to deal with the grave disorders that daily multiply, especially by the coming and continual increase of so many foreign priests. Many here by virtue of faculties obtained independently of local superiors horribly abuse the sacraments. Their scandalous lives are an obstacle to numerous conversions and gravely offend the Catholics. Many of them are already apostates and heretical ministers, belching forth horrible and disgraceful lies about us to palliate and defend their licensiousness and vicious living with their concubines and bastards. The greater part of these are French Capuchins and Portuguese Recollects, though there are also Italians, Spanish, Belgians and Irish, and one Englishman. All these at first claimed to be apostolic missionaries, and now some of them are ministers and preachers in the churches of Italian, French and Flemish heretics, and the rest are not much better.

He goes on to say that if only something had been settled for England he would set out for Rome to communicate orally these and many other similar matters.[23] In May he reports to the internuncio that four French Capuchins had apostatized and he queries the faculties exercised in London by their Irish brethren.[24] In June there is a report from the nuncio in Paris that Charles II had asked for the appointment of a bishop because of the recent apostacy of three Capuchins formerly of the chapel of the queen mother.[25]

>> and abjure the Roman Catholic religion and embrace the Protestant, in which they were unanimously received to the great joy of all those present' (Bulstrode Papers, 180).

## Bishop-Elect

One thing appears to have been virtually settled by the middle of 1670. The acts of the various congregations held by Propaganda and all the correspondence that flowed from them speak of Howard as the person chosen to rule over the English church. He had been recommended by all sorts of people including Oliver Plunkett and the Grand Duke of Tuscany, and there is no other name ever mentioned. The nominees of the Chapter were taken seriously only by the Chapter. Nor was there, outside the Chapter, any serious doubt that he was to have the title of vicar apostolic and not ordinary. Two questions remained to be settled; the opportune moment for publishing his appointment, and the extent of his jurisdiction. On 9 September 1670 these questions were discussed by a particular congregation of Propaganda, and next day their decisions were submitted to the pope.

> Audience with His Holiness, 10 September 1670.
> A particular congregation was held concerning the special affairs of England, and consideration was given to the necessity of appointing a superior and to the needs of the Catholics. In order that there may be a superior for the clergy and also a person who will inform the Apostolic See sincerely and distinctly of everything concerning religion in that kingdom. The cardinals advise the appointment with the title of vicar apostolic and with episcopal rank, of Fr Philip Howard, Dominican, grand almoner of the queen, of a most noble family, of good life, integrity of manners, sufficiency of learning, esteemed by the king and wished for by the queen and the court, as appears from the relations of the internuncio of Flanders and of Claudio Agretti, who were sent to investigate. It remains for His Holiness to approve of this resolution, so that the matter may proceed.
>
> Rescript
> His Holiness approved and ordered the matter to proceed. But no resolution was taken as to the faculties and jurisdiction which he should exercise. Great caution is to be used to prevent a reoccurrence of the disturbances of previous vicars apostolic, and in determining what powers shall be given him over the regulars. There is in London a Chapter of secular priests instituted by the first vicar apostolic, the Bishop of Chalcedon, but never approved by the Holy See. It is *de facto* exercising ecclesiastical jurisdiction, and it must be decided whether to confirm it or annul it. As this is a question of grave importance its solution is deferred to another congregation.[26]

The choice of a superior was thus at last agreed upon, but the principal problems remained unsolved. A superior with ill-defined and disputable faculties was worse than no superior at all. We must now see what the unfortunate Chapter was doing; how much they knew and what they thought of the decisions that so vitally affected them as a body, but in which they were not consulted. Indeed the tragedy was that they *could* not be consulted, for the cardinals could not very well treat with a body without acknowledging its existence.

## IV

Alexander Holt's last extant letter from Rome is dated 29 March 1670. He had just had an interview with Baldeschi, who, though he comes in for so much abuse, was one of the few who treated the agent with civility:

> We fell to discourse of our other affairs, wherein I told him that though at present we had no P[relate] yet I conceived it not wise to signify unto him that you did nominate Mr H. for to be our bishop. He replied that the time was always convenient, that he was continually labouring to serve us beforetime, that he could not forestall the resolutions of the congregation but that he believed we should have all satisfaction in that point, that he was very glad Mr H. was so grateful to the clergy, because he really judged him the person appointed by providence as an instrument of great good for our country in this present age, that he had heard such good of him etc. I added divers reasons and commendations of him, and moreover the caution viz. that though his lordship was so eminently qualified for that office yet we should hereafter not let it pass for an example of regulars coming into that charge, and that so much I was obliged to declare at present unto him.[27]

In June Holt was replaced by Thomas Forbes. There was no change of policy. Forbes's style is as familiar and rather more disrespectful, and his capacity for pumping and bribing was at least equal to that of his predecessor. His first letter is dated 3 July:

> Since Mr Holt departed hence, which was three weeks ago, there hath been nothing done here. The secretary Baldeschi promises much, but I who know him too well believe nothing. He says

that within a few days the congregation concerning England will be holden and in it three things principally will be treated, to wit the granting of a bishop, the confirming or annulling or tolerating of the Chapter and the retaining or dismissing of those Dr Leyburn put out of Douai College.

Concerning the first point I told him that the clergy hath very often caused represent to this court the great desire that the whole body and every particular member of it hath ever had to see the hierarchy, which is composed of bishops and priests, established there, and this I amplified so much the more, largely because I was told by a person that knew it well that lately Agretti hath written here that the clergy really desires no bishop. I did show him that if you had not really desired a bishop you could never have proposed Fr Howard, a person that hath so many qualities fit to facilitate the effect of what you propose. I told him that the desire generally of all is that he be honoured with the title of archbishop, and that he be ordinary, and I see that they would only give a vicar apostolic like him that is in Holland, and so much the more that Agretti hath written here lately, as I am told in confidence by one that knows well, that the clergy desire no more. This seems very strange to me and much contrary to what Mr Holt and I have ever judged. So sir, I pray you write me your mind in this point, and whether I shall continue to ask an ordinary or at the least a delegate power with the whole jurisdiction of an ordinary, and whether in any case I shall admit the name of vicario-apostolico, to which only here they seem to incline.[28]

A fortnight later on 29 July he writes again:

> There being shortly a congregation to be holden I went to inform the cardinals and the secretary Baldeschi concerning the two points, to wit, the granting of a bishop and the confirming of the Chapter. I did find in them all a great desire to grant a bishop and a great propension to Fr Howard's person, and no great reluctancy to the title of archbishop *in partibus*, but as for the title of ordinary of England, here we did stick for I pressed hard that an ordinary should be granted and they urged a vicario-apostolico with the power of an ordinary. I seeing the repugnancy to the name of ordinary, proposed that at the least they would innovate nothing and so grant a bishop with that same name, title and power the last two bishops had, to which they seemed not to repugn much, so we must find out a copy of the brief or bull of the said last bishops ... But above all things agree first there with Fr Howard in the title and power

> foresaid, lest I press one thing and he or his agent here another. For I am told that there is an old religious of his order, who is an old friend of the cardinal patron and lodgeth with him in the palace. He is an Irishman; his name is Borgo. This father as I am told agents for him here. I shall go and see him and if I find it be so, I shall offer my service to him, expecting your particular orders hereabouts.[29]

By 26 July he had discovered the true identity of Borgo:

> I have discovered since, the father Dominican I named in my last is not called Borgo. His name is Hacket. The Reverend Fr Howard hath written here to the secretary Baldeschi that he purposes to come here to this court. I believe it is the said Fr Hacket that hath put him in this design, for he says that both the pope and cardinal nephew, with whom he stays, have great designs both for England and for Fr Howard's person.
> 
> This Fr Hacket is a good simple old friar who takes smooth words for real effects. Besides I hear he is about a founding a convent of Irish friars here, and purchasing a rent to maintain them. Perchance he fancies that Fr Howard being here would help him much in compassing this his design, which he esteems of a very great consequence for the good of the Catholic religion in all His Majesty's dominions. The Jesuits here have given up a memorial to the cardinals of the congregation. I have not as yet discovered any other particularity of the said memorial but that they propose Dr Leyburn for bishop. I know that this hath been laughed at. The congregation will be shortly holden, yet I believe that you will have time enough to write me what you desire I should represent here in your name.[30]

The convent for the Irish friars was that of S. Clemente. Howard also had designs upon it for the English province. It had been refused on the grounds that it was needed as a summer house for the novitiate at S. Sisto. John Baptist de Marinis, the Master General who had been so friendly with Howard and died in 1669, and the Chapter of 1670 elected John Thomas de Rocaberti. Howard at once sent his congratulations. He asks to resign his office of vicar general and permission to come to Rome; he renews his petition to have S. Clemente for the English province. The new Master General replied on 6 September. He would not allow Howard to resign his office or come to Rome, saying he hoped soon to be travelling beyond the Alps and could meet him there.

## Bishop-Elect

> As for the two convents of S. Sisto and S. Clemente [he continues,] We have already disposed of them. Her Serene Highness the queen of Great Britain graciously deigned to petition our recent general Chapter to grant these two convents to our Irish missionaries. His Excellency the ambassador of Portugal came personally to our Chapter and commended this matter to us and to the fathers. Therefore when we have consulted with His Holiness we shall at once put our Irish brethren in possession.[31]

Whether Forbes was right in making Fr Hacket a prime mover in this matter is impossible to say, but he was certainly wrong in surmising that it was the purpose of Howard's projected visit to Rome. On 15 September Forbes writes to Holt:

> I received a letter of two lines from you yesterday with an enclosure from Tho Howard for Fr Hacket, which I have delivered this morning, but the good old man did put the letter on his table, so I know not as yet what it contains ...
>
> This week the congregation hath been holden. What hath been resolved none knows as yet for they have imposed a rigorous silence, so that none as yet knows but by conjectures what hath been done. By the next post I hope to write you what I shall discover, if it be possible. Fr Hacket says, although but only by conjectures that it is resolved to make archbishop my lord almoner. So I believe also, but only by conjectures. This I know certainly that a great packet of letters hath been sent out this morning by the secretary Baldeschi to the internuncio of Flanders concerning what hath been resolved in the congregation, and I believe in this packet was likewise one for my lord almoner.[32]

A week later Forbes had made himself familiar with the contents of Howard's letter to Hacket:

> That letter of Fr Thomas Howard you sent me for Fr Hacket, he read it to me the other day I went back to see him. This letter shortly carries that he takes very ill that these here offer to make him only a vicar apostolic, and that they will not confirm the Chapter, and desires the said Fr Hacket to write himself with Mr Leslie and make to obtain the one and hinder the other. But after some discourse I discovered that this father will never trouble himself much for the Chapter, which he called an imaginary thing. This did not surprise me, for I never could imagine that an Irish friar would promote much your interest. My lord almoner had done much better to signify to the secretary Baldeschi this his favourable desire for the confirming of the Chapter ...

> The congregation was holden near a fortnight ago, but so closely that none as yet hath been able to discover certainly anything they have resolved. Fr Hacket told me that Cardinal Altieri, although very earnestly asked by him, would tell him nothing. Mr Baldeschi gives fair words, but I know certainly that he hath done and said all he could to hinder the confirming of the Chapter, Yes, I know he said that Fr Howard was of his mind in this point, which I believe to be a calumny, the said person being too honest and noble to promise you there one thing and write the contrary here.[33]

In another letter of 20 September Forbes informs us that Dr Leyburn says:

> That the Jesuits have told him that my lord almoner shall only have the title of bishop as was agreed in the article of His Majesty's marriage but no jurisdiction, and that there will be another bishop, although not so soon, made for the government of the church. Fr Hacket, who is, although a very old man, a young courtier, doth hope shortly to see my lord almoner not only archbishop but cardinal.[34]

It was twenty-five years before, when he had first made friends with the youthful Philip Howard, since Hacket had first said that 'he hoped to see him a cardinal'. Even now the idea appeared fantastic, but the old man was not such a young courtier as Forbes supposed.

On 4 October Forbes was still in the dark:

> All things here since the congregation have been so closely kept that I have not, with all possible diligence used, been able to discover what hath been the precise resolution of the said congregation. Yet having seen some papers wherein are contained many things that were proposed by some in the same congregation, I suspect that the resolution hath been either this or something like this, to wit: to make the said father bishop without giving him for the present any settled jurisdiction till they try him little by little in some little affairs they intend to commit to him, and if they give now, or when they shall give him the said settled power, to rule or limit it so, that he undertake nothing against the religious, especially the Jesuits, but what shall be enjoined him from this court; that he govern and do everything, at least in the beginning, with the counsel and superintendence, as they call it, of the internuncio; but especially and above all that his hands be tied so that he cannot confirm the Chapter, and this they say is a point must be done with much dexterity and cunning that neither he himself not the clergy perceive it,

for the clergy's agent published here that if the power of the bishops of Chalcedon be diminished in the least it shall not be received there. This is the advice and opinion of the foresaid three persons. Whether it hath or in what it hath been followed I have not been able as yet to discover, for I never, since I have been here, see any business kept so closely, which makes me suspect the worse. They give me fair words, and promise that you shall all be contented, and I must not seem to believe otherwise lest I betray these friends to their great prejudice, who have given me the former notice, and so deprive myself in time to come of the means to know anything more ...

Assure yourselves that this court cannot nor dare not do anything to your prejudice if you will be well united among yourselves and with your bishop, although here they think the best way to undo the Chapter is by the making of a bishop. Continue therefore more than ever the exercise of your jurisdiction till the bishop be made and his power established, and then do all Chapters can canonically do, *sede plena*, especially making the bishop ask your consent *prout de jure*. You see your adversaries' designs, and so prepare yourselves to prevent them, which you can do no ways better than taking heed, as you say very well in your last letter, of *falsi fratres*. You understand me. And trust none but those who are as earnest in your interest as you are and have been in theirs.[35]

The next letter is undated. The document which he enclosed would seem to be the copy, still preserved,[36] not of what Baldeschi had just said to the pope, but of the actual minutes of the congregation held on 9 September, in which (as we have seen) the choice of Howard was approved. This letter was received in London on 28 October so probably was sent soon after the one just given of 4 October.

Not without great pain and importuning my friends here I have got at the last a copy of what Baldeschi, in his audience two days ago only, said to the pope concerning what has been resolved a month ago in the congregation. I send it you here enclosed, but I request you, make use wisely and discretely of it, lest it being discovered here, my friend should suffer for it. Above all beware Fr Howard know it, for he hath correspondence of letters with the said Baldeschi.

Notwithstanding all we have done and said you see they here will call bishops, whatsoever power they have delegate them from this court, vicars apostolic, and this in the acts that passeth here or elsewhere among themselves. We cannot hinder: but in those papers, as bulls, faculties and such like we receive from them, we must not suffer such a title. Neither do I believe they will put it in, more than they did in the other two bishops of Chalcedon's faculties, whom likewise you see they call vicars apostolic. It seemeth that here they have assurance from I do not know whom there, that an arbitrary power and altogether dependent from them and their ministers will be more easily received there that I here strive to make them understand.

Fr Hacket told me that the Cardinal Patron Altieri said to him that first the bishop must be made, and afterwards for his titles and faculties the queen's writing here will obtain what she desires. You will do well to write both to the cardinals of the congregation freely your mind concerning this their proceeding, and yet more boldly to Baldeschi; and make Fr Howard write also, for this court's maxim and principle is to grant nothing but what maketh for its own advantage, unless fear make them do otherwise.[37]

The cardinals of Propaganda had kept Howard's appointment a dead secret for several reasons. The nature of his jurisdiction had yet to be decided, a premature revelation would raise a storm, and it was the king's wish that no such move should be made till after the session of parliament, which was due to meet in October. Now Forbes had bribed his way into the secret and sent an accurate copy of their confidential Acts to his venerable brethren in England.

In October 1670 the internuncio Airoldi paid a visit to London. His subject was not to investigate the sufficiency of Fr Howard, which had been done by Agretti, but to sound the clergy on the far more vexatious question of the jurisdiction to be given to the new vicar apostolic. He lodged with the Venetian ambassador and was introduced by Arlington to the king and queen and Duke of York, Howard being also present. He had interviews with three leading Chaptermen. He was advised to leave before parliament assembled on 24 October.[38] His report, dated 29 November, occupies forty-two pages. Much of it is taken up with descriptions of the queen's chapel and kindred matters and it does not do much more than state the divergent views that should by now be familiar to the reader. He says that Howard is recommended by clergy and laymen and by the ambassadors of Spain, Venice and Portugal, but there was general agreement that nothing should be done till the end of the parliamentary session.[39] Certain points were discussed that do not, however, appear in the report. This we learn from a letter to Forbes from Alexander Holt dated 28 October:

## Bishop-Elect

You must know that Signor Abate Airoldi hath been here and for ought we could perceive did not communicate with any of our adversaries. My lord almoner was in Flanders. When he began his journey hither and so recommended him to one of our brethren, but unknown, until my lord's return. It pleased God that I also came up two nights before the abbot's departure; wherefore four of us did visit him and spoke our minds boldly and freely in our own behalf, as also in defence of ourselves and you. His accusation against you was this, that you made three propositions in our name, viz:

First that we should be content the election of the bishop should be made by His Holiness.

Secondly the nomination of divers of our chiefest Chapter-officers in like manner.

And thirdly that we were content to have a formula or formulary imposed upon us in point of doctrine, particularly for the renunciation of Mr Blacklow's opinions.

This news he said was sent unto him from Baldeschi. We replied that we could not yield nor consent to any of these three propositions for divers reasons which we gave him there by word of mouth and are now writing more at large to send to him. And as soon as I have time to copy them you shall have them, perhaps by the next post. As for your part he said that Baldeschi conceived that you had exceeded your commission, because after that you had proposed those three things, twas a long time ere you came to him again. We replied that we were well assured that you never made any such proposition, but that such propositions were invented by our adversaries and partly proposed to you (that is the two first) by Baldeschi. And to prove that you made them not I produced your letter, which says that you will not advance anything of your own nor without our advice. So much for those things. I assure you I spared not the gentleman at all, and my lord almoner spoke well and home to the purpose.[40]

This is the first hint in all this correspondence that the Chapter were not prepared to accept a bishop nominated by the pope. They had long ago agreed to accept Fr Howard if their own nominees were rejected and if he were offered. On the other hand it is also the first mention of any formulary of orthodoxy. If the Chapter were to be confirmed as it stood, some such formulary might be justifiable, but as the intention was to form a new Chapter by selecting individuals of approved doctrine, any such formulary seems superfluous as well as aggravating. When

Airoldi returned to Flanders the two parties were further apart than ever.

On 21 November 1670 the Chapter resolved:

> That my lord almoner be acquainted with what we were informed of the Roman court's intentions, which were to give him the title of vicar apostolic with some small, limited jurisdiction altogether delegate, and which could arbitrarily be revoked; that they intend also to tie his hands so that it shall not be in his power to confirm the Chapter; and lastly that they joined his name with our adversaries as an adviser to annul it, desiring him not to be ordained until he first saw and gave us leave to consult upon the faculties or jurisdiction offered by them at Rome, to the end no occasion of differences might arise afterwards.[41]

Airoldi had been amazed to discover that the highly confidential deliberations of Propaganda were accurately known to the Chapter, and he wrote to warn Baldeschi that there was a leakage. It was a great blow to Forbes. He writes on 3 January 1671:

> I have only to tell you that the internuncio hath written here that you had known that most particularly all that had been done or said. The secretary Baldeschi answered him that he had put away the under-secretary Giovanni Battista, who, as he imagined, was the person that had revealed all. You must know that some days before the internuncio his letter came here Baldeschi had turned out the said Giovanni Battista imputing him to have given secret notice of a certain business resolved in the congregation, to the court of Vienna. This was a particular providence for us, for if the said internonce his letter had come sooner, undoubtedly the said Giovanni Battista had been put away upon the other cause, which had been an unspeakable grief to me. The internonce hath sent here lately a relation of twelve sheets of paper of what he has seen and done there ... One that did not see it but heard of another who had seen it, tells me that he praiseth much my lord almoner, but yet not so much as was expected here, and that you did speak very rudely to him.[42]

Without this disreputable but valuable link Forbes was much handicapped in his quest for information, and it was long before he had a like success. Not that there was much to discover at the moment. Parliament had reassembled in the previous October and it was wise to wait and see what sort of a rod they had in pickle for the papists. Charles had in May 1670 made a secret treaty with Louis

## Bishop-Elect

XIV whereby he undertook to declare himself a Catholic in return for a large sum of money and a promise of French arms, if necessary, to keep him on the throne. Until the right moment arrived he had to humour an anti-Catholic parliament and allow them to vent their hatred in further acts against popery. In the meantime Forbes's letters are devoid of news, but not without interest.

> I am infinitely glad to see you so united with my lord almoner and so resolute in not letting yourselves be supplanted by this court who mindeth nothing else, as you may have fully seen in these papers I have already sent you. I know Baldeschi is much troubled in seeing you and my lord so unanimous, for it was by him he thought to supplant you. Assure both yourselves and my lord that this is the only way to get any tolerable condition from this court. The vicar apostolic of Holland here, for so they call him here and never bishop, is so tossed betwixt the fathers his adversaries [the Jesuits] and the congregation of Propaganda that I am sure that such a title and delegate-power will never be accepted of by any that sees and hears how the prelate has been, both in his own country and here, persecuted by his adversaries and ill-protected by those who would make the world believe that they are the upholders of episcopacy. (31 January)[43]

A fortnight later there was still nothing to report:

> There is no great appearance that the congregation will hold so soon, although Baldeschi said to me yesterday that once in this Lent he will call it. He gives me fair words and great promises but I know of a person of honour that Baldeschi said to him that the business of the Chapter and bishop vexed him and kept him so perplexed that on his salvation he did not know what to do. This is the effect of your great union among yourselves and with my lord almoner, for their aim here was to supplant you by giving him a power so restricted that he should have done all they commanded him and nothing more. (14 February)[44]

The Chapter had no doubts that Howard would not accept the title of vicar apostolic, but that was not the impression he gave to others. He had written to Cardinal Altieri on 5 December 1670, begging his help. He was 'thrice-happy' that the new pope should remember their meeting in Naples and that His Eminence is pleased to extend to him the patronage he formerly showed to his uncle Aubigny. No country had suffered more for the faith than England, and never since the schism began had they been blessed with more kind and indulgent sovereigns than the present king and queen. All their ills, be it said to their shame and his great sorrow, were of their own making. *Inimici nostri sunt nostri domestici* [Our enemies are of our household; cf. Matthew 10:36]: disorderly lives, scandals of false brethren, laxity, and factions that had torn that to tatters, as though Christ were divided. And all was due to the lack of solid authority.[45] He had said all this before but now he had a new and very powerful advocate. Altieri instructed his secretary, Signor Cataloni, to find out what the position was at Propaganda, and the following Informations dated 22 March 1671 were drawn up for his benefit:

> In the congregations that have been held concerning the affairs of England it has always been unanimously resolved that it was not expedient to defer any longer the appointment of a legitimate superior for the ecclesiastics of England; that he should be honoured with the episcopal character and be made vicar apostolic and not yet ordinary in that country.
>
> There was considerable uncertainty whether the person agreed upon for this dignity, namely Fr Howard, would be prepared to accept it and therefore first Claudio Agretti, who was acting as apostolic minister in Flanders in the absence of Cardinal Rospigliosi, and then the present internuncio ought to discover his mind. Both of them wrote that he would have accepted with the utmost satisfaction.
>
> These are the reports that appear in the archives of this Congregation.[46]

The truth would seem to be that Howard was not very concerned about the title he was to be given. What he so constantly stresses is the need for a superior who could deal with the wayward religious. That was the crux of the question. It was not until 1748 that it was finally settled that religious on the English mission must have faculties from the vicar apostolic to administer the sacraments. They had always before received their missionary faculties from their own superiors and therefore claimed that only their own superiors could revoke them. It was on this rock that Bishop Smith had made shipwreck. These privileges, however, were not absolute. The moral procedure was for religious superiors to present their subjects individually to Propaganda for approval, and Propaganda then referred them to the Holy Office for faculties. Thus their faculties, although they came *through* their own superiors, were in fact granted by the Holy Office on the advice of Propaganda, and surely they could be revoked by these congregations without reference to the religious superiors. It was on this assumption that Howard asked for the revocation of the faculties of the French Capuchins. Propaganda could delegate this power of revocation. But after a century of uncertainty the situation was extremely delicate. They considered it wiser to appoint a vicar apostolic with very limited faculties and when he was established and recognized, then to increase his powers so that he could deal with urgent cases without recourse to Rome. It would seem that Howard was not content with such limitations, but it was for reasons quite different from those adduced by the Chapter.

Even assuming that Howard could be persuaded to accept the solution offered by Propaganda there still remained the question of the opportune moment to announce his appointment. It was the merest common sense to do nothing that would call down upon their heads the further anger and revenge of an already vindictive parliament.

## Notes

[1] AGOP, II, 734.
[2] AP, Sc. Rif. Cong. Gen., Anglia e Scotia (t.297), f. 150.
[3] R. Honorante, *Praxis secretariae tribunalis ... urbis vicarii*, Roma, 1762, 172.
[4] OB, Orders of the Consult in London 1667–93, 71.
[5] Agen. no. 62.
[6] *Ibid*. nos. 59, 60, 63, 77, 27, 65.
[7] OB, Orders (see note 4), 72.
[8] OB, MSS 1649–94, no. 102.
[9] Agen. no. 110.
[10] P. Moran, *Spicilegium Ossoriense*, Dubin, 1874, I, 477.
[11] AP, Anglia I, 614.
[12] AP, Sc. Rif., Anglia I, f. 342.
[13] B, 6828, f. 27
[14] AP, Audienza I, 1666–79, f. 71.
[15] Agen. no. 111.
[16] Cal.SP Venice, XXXVI, 127.
[17] AP, Sc. Rif., Anglia I, f. 126; Agen. No. 137.
[18] W. M. Brady, *Episcopal Succession*, Rome, 1877, III, 107.
[19] NI, 10, f. 2 (1 July 1670).
[20] *Ibid*. f. 3; *Dominicana*, 53.

[21] AP, Sc. Rif., Anglia I, f. 515; *Dominicana*, 53.
[22] AP, Lettere circa il Settentrione 1665–8, ff. 12–16; cf. *Dominicana*, 40.
[23] AP, Sc. Rif., Anglia I, f. 498.
[24] *Ibid*. f. 510.
[25] *Ibid*. f. 526.
[26] AP, Audienza 1666–79, f. 88.
[27] OB, MSS. 1649–94, no. 117.
[28] Agen. no. 176.
[29] *Ibid*. no. 178.
[30] *Ibid*. no. 180.
[31] Reg. 140, 7.
[32] Agen. no. 188.
[33] *Ibid*. no. 189.
[34] *Ibid*. no. 190.
[35] *Ibid*. no. 192.
[36] *Ibid*. no. 186
[37] *Ibid*. no. 194.
[38] Cal.SP Venice, XXXVI, 294.
[39] AP, Sc. Rif., Anglia I, ff. 625–67.
[40] Agen. no. 197.
[41] OB, Orders of Consults 1667–93, 118.
[42] Agen. no. 198.
[43] *Ibid*. no. 215.
[44] *Ibid*. no. 217.
[45] AV, Particolari 49, f. 606.
[46] AP, t.54, 287.

# 5

## *The Gathering Storm*

### I

THERE IS A LITTLE NEWSLETTER printed in far-off Bologna on 1 April 1671 giving news from London of 6 March; news that does not appear anywhere else:

> The queen's confessor having publicly displayed a bull of jubilee sent from the pope, the lower house resolved to petition the king that he will put a break on the excessive liberty of Catholics and that they may be made to take the oath of allegiance according to the rite of the Anglican church. Also that Sig. Plunkett, who has the title of Primate of Ireland and Sig. Peter Talbot, who has been publicly announced as Archbishop of Dublin, have been arrested and conducted to London; also that they have sent to the upper house to approve of these petitions.[1]

There was no truth whatever in the rumours concerning the Irish archbishops, but there may have been some grounds for this garbled story of a papal bull. Howard more than once affixed one of these to the door of the queen's chapel, though on the inside. Perhaps this was the spark. On Monday 13 March

> This morning His Majesty was pleased to be present in the Banqueting House attended by both houses, who made their humble address to him to take some speedy course for the preventing of the growth of popery, which His Majesty graciously received and returned his answer to this effect, that he would take care of all their requests and would issue out his proclamation for the banishing of all papist priests and Jesuits and cause the judges and all other officers to see that the law against papists be put in execution and all other things that may induce to the prevention of its growth, but supposed no man would wonder if he made a difference between those who have newly changed

their religion and those who were bred up in the name and had served his father and himself faithfully in the late war.[2]

On Thursday 24 March it is reported that 'His Majesty in council was yesterday pleased to allow of three proclamations'. The third was for the banishing of all papist priests and Jesuits. It was already in print and appeared on Thursday morning.[3] It made no distinction between recent converts and the rest but royal chaplains were exempted. That same day Holt sent the news to Forbes in Rome:

> For news, this very day was published a strict proclamation against popish priests, who are either to be gone before the first of May or else suffer according to the rigorous laws, as also against all popish recusants, who are to suffer likewise. What the execution will be God knows, but this same day also is a bill to the same purpose referred to a committee of the house of lords. Doubtless this news is represented to your grandees all ways and so will stifle all our affairs at present, if not for ever hereafter.[4]

Howard was less perturbed. He had written to the internuncio the day before that 'the Catholics had good friends and that when the decree against them comes to be published there will be the routine storm but it will quickly die down'.[5] In a later letter he said that the proclamation would have no effect because the very heretics recognized the impractability of such rigorous laws and the king would do all in his power to negate it.[6] No notice whatever seems to have been taken of this proclamation. Parliament was again prorogued in April, and in May public attention was diverted by Colonel Blood's desperate attempt to steal the crown jewels. Howard paid his regular visit to Flanders in June, and on 26 September accompanied the queen to Norwich. Once again they were lavishly entertained by Henry Howard.[7]

There is extant a letter of Howard's to his brother Henry concerning this visit, and although it is of no importance, it is one of the few of his purely domestic letters that survive, and it reveals the same boyish humour that was noted and recorded on a former occasion by no less a critic than Samuel Pepys.

> Dear Brother,
> Before I received yours (yesterday) of the 18 current, my Lord Arlington sent me from the council-board a copy of yours enclosed in Sir Robert Paston's letter to him; wherefore I went immediately unto Her Majesty, who I found very willing to do

Sir Robert all the honour she could, but how to compass the affair he desireth, of having both their Majesties to dine at his house on Saturday, had many difficulties, His Majesty having appointed to be at the Lord Townsend about that time, and Her Majesty at my Lord Arlington's the same day. However after counsel Her Majesty was graciously pleased to give me leave to argue and urge the business hard, as I did, although my Lord Arlington could not well (as he told me) appear further in it, being it would deprive him of the honour of having Her Majesty that day at his house. However after much ado (which were too long to write) my importunity prevailed and His Majesty is contented to expect the queen to dine with him on Saturday morning, but it must be an early dinner at ten of the clock without fail, at which time Her Majesty will be there from Norwich where Your Lordship's palace must have the burthen of us, and bestow your Friday's collation on us papists, and what else you will please to grace the true Protestants withal.

Whether or no we shall dine with you on Sunday cannot be resolved certainly until we see first how you treat us beforehand. Wherefore until then, as always I remain
Your most affectionate brother
and humble servant
P. Howard

21 Sept. 1671.
Your Lordship will no more be troubled with a parliament until next October come twelvemonth.[8]

There are passages in the correspondence of the internuncio that will correct any false idea that Howard's influence in court circles was used only for arranging dinner-parties. He had a large circle of friends in public office and was constantly corresponding with the internuncio on a variety of subjects over and above his regular requests for ever-wider faculties. Thus he was called upon to avert a diplomatic crisis in relations between London and the Vatican when a certain Captain Jennings tried to sail his ship into Civita Vecchia without firing the customary salute of guns. A great deal of ink was spilt over this, including letters of complaint from the cardinal secretary, and of apology from Arlington and even from the queen. But Howard's name constantly appears as the mediator.[9] In October 1671 he recommended to the internuncio Sir Robert Southwell, who was being sent to Brussels as ambassador-extraordinary. The English consul at Tangiers had been murdered and a punitive expedition despatched. Howard says:

If they call at Civita Vecchia they will behave themselves better than heretics usually do with Catholics. I have many personal friends Catholics, who are going on this expedition, and the Admiral Spragg is my particular friend* and a Catholic at least at heart. Some years ago I treated with the king and Arlington to have an English consul at Civita Vecchia and I found a person who was a Catholic. But the English merchants did not want it as being an extraordinary expense and not justified by the small traffic and contact the heretic has with the papal states. It would be a very useful thing to have a good contact with England, albeit heretical, because from this reciprocal exchange of views much fruit and advantage might accrue to the Church.[10]

When John Lord Berkeley, the new Viceroy of Ireland, was about to set out in September 1671, it is reported that

> Howard has had a long and friendly talk with him concerning the affairs of that realm, and that at his insistence and that of the said Berkeley the king has granted an annual pension of £200 to the Archbishop of Armagh [Oliver Plunkett], and the viceroy undertook to see that the taxes paid to the king by the Irish were stabilized. The Archbishop of Dublin [Talbot] will not miss the opportunity to complain of that prelate, although the internuncio hopes to keep him quiet and calm him down because in the past he received a pension himself from the king. He has written a nice letter exhorting him to live amicably with Armagh.[11]

The Chapter correspondence of this year shows them complaining bitterly of the delays at Propaganda and at the same time doing all they could to impede it by their intransigence:

> I received none from you since your seventh, wherein you gave little news of a congregation, but my lord almoner had news at that time that it would be held speedily and great matters done for us. Dr Leyburn also writ to his nephew the president that the congregation was to be held a month ago and the lord almoner to be installed, but I believe as you say that such correspondents are old men but young courtiers. For news, our queen is removing to Somerset House. Our Lord Chamberlain Montagu E[arl] of Manchester is dead and the

---

\* 'Saturday 12 December 1668. This evening Sir Edward Spragg is gone down the water to embark for Ostend, being accompanied with the lord almoner Howard, who goes upon his private affairs into those parts for some time' (Bulstrode Papers, 1897, 78).

E[arl] of St Albans is in his place. Also five rogues attempted to steal the king's crown out of the Tower of London, but were by chance discovered and three of them taken with the crown. (Holt to Forbes, 19 May)[12]

Somerset House was closed soon after the death of Henrietta Maria in 1669. At first it was proposed to rent it to the Portuguese ambassador but Catherine decided to move there herself, and her chapel at St James's was taken over by the Portuguese embassy. Thus for the rest of his time in England Howard officiated in the more ornate chapel built by Henrietta Maria in 1632. The register at St James's bearing the royal arms was continued by the chaplain of the Portuguese ambassador and is still preserved at the embassy.[13]

> Old Dr Leyburn is in town as the report goes, but appears not as yet. He says you offered him many great preferments, but his zeal to his mission made him come to lay his bones in holy London, and truly as Ben Jonson used to say, I take him for a very hopeful old man ... My lord almoner is gone to Flanders and we here all in good order. If the old Dr [Leyburn] endeavours to disturb any his *dimittimus* will not be long in drawing. (Holt to Forbes, 20 June)[14]

> To Mr Forbes.
> 1. He is desired by the English Chapter and clergy to solicit for the confirmation of the said Chapter, *prout de jure.*
> 2. To move for the making Mr Philip Howard an archbishop with a title *in partibus*, but that he have ordinary jurisdiction in England, i.e. over all that kingdom; and that by no means he accept any such title as vicar apostolic.
> 3. He is required to put a stop to all strangers invading the English Mission and endeavour the expulsion of those already in it, because they do much hurt both by the scandals they commit and also cause disturbance; neither have they faculties. (Undated; about end of June)[15]

> Believe not what is written by any from this place concerning my lord almoner's business, unless it come from me; for I may say without vanity that I discern better than any of those that write to his lordship, when we may believe or not believe the fair words and promises of this court. For the present there is nothing but great desires, as they say, to advance the foresaid business. (Forbes to Holt, 10 July)[16]

> I am ashamed that you there are at so great changes and I have [been] so unprofitable. Yet I persuade myself that you see that

> I am not the cause of this slowness. Baldeschi promises even with great oaths great matters, but I believe it all will turn to nothing. Card. Barberini by reason of his brother Cardinal Antonio's death is altogether taken up with the interests of his heritage and the visits of *condoglienza*, so that till these be passed no congregation will be holden. I am of opinion that this month of September will give us one as it did the last year. I am glad you see and know there the little trust that the great assurances of old young courtiers deserveth. (Same, 15 August)[17]

On 18 September Patrick Conn joined in the chorus. He wrote to Barberini expressing his amazement at the long delay and suggested that in addition to Howard, Walter Montagu, who was now out of a job and who had private means should be made a bishop in England.[18] Although he does not say so this solution would have settled the Chapter controversy, for they acknowledged that they would automatically cease to exist on the appointment of a plurality of bishops.

September came and went and still there was no congregation for English affairs. Howard continued to write regularly to the internuncio but his letters scarcely refer to the subject that he had so much at heart. Now that the choice had fallen on him it would have been unbecoming to have shown his impatience.

Forbes's last letter of the year is less bleak:

> The secretary told me yesterday that he would call the congregation the next week and that he hoped that it should be resolved the same jurisdiction for my lord almoner which the two former bishops had, except only that this jurisdiction would be somewhat restricted towards the regulars to avoid those contestations which the Bishop of Chalcedon had with the said regulars. I told him that I believed that my lord almoner would not accept this restriction, since all bishops everywhere have an illimited power over regulars *in iis quae pertinent ad curam animarum saecularium et administrationem sacramentorum* [in all things pertaining to the care of the secular souls and the administration of the sacraments]. Besides, that excepting the regulars in this manner from the bishop's power would be cause and occasion of greater disorders. I spoke to him concerning the title of archbishop and confirming of the Chapter. He said that after the settling of the bishop's power these other things should be likewise ruled. (6 November)[19]

There was, however, no congregation in November or in Decem-

## The Gathering Storm

ber. In a whole year the business had made no progress whatever. The long delay had had only one effect. The secret of Howard's nomination was by now a very open secret. Far away in Bremen the Italian Vicar Apostolic Valerio Maccioni had heard of it. He wrote to Altieri on 15 December offering to cross to England incognito and consecrate Howard with the assistance (in default of bishops) of two mitred abbots.[20] Altieri replied on 27 February 1672 that he was very edified by his zeal and would bear him in mind when the time came, but at the moment his services were not required.[21]

II

By the beginning of 1672 Forbes seems to have lost heart, and it would have been wiser to have sent a new agent. His letters grow more and more petulant and distrustful, and he was hardly in the right mood for long and delicate negotiations. He writes on 2 January:

> I wrote to you in my last that the secretary Baldeschi assured me that shortly the congregation would be holden and that the business would be totally resolved. And yet a year and four months are passed since the last congregation and nothing has been done as yet, nor is like to be done. He puts the blame upon the cardinals and particularly Chigi, who, as he says, hath kept by him the papers that were sent *per manus* to the said cardinals, without either perusing them or sending them back. To be short and free with you, sir, I see very little hopes or appearances that these here will do anything for you. The secretary says that the high pretensions of the Chapter do so trouble and keep perplexed this court that they do not know what to do. Some weeks ago the news book here called the *Folietto Secreto* said that a congregation had been held at the Propaganda and had resolved to make bishop my lord almoner of England. This made secretary Baldeschi go mad, for he thought that this was a jest put upon him.
>
> I do not write you often because really I have nothing to write you. In the meantime the jurisdiction of your Chapter takes deeper root, so that I hope that if ever here they would harm you they shall not be able, and you may assure all those that desire to see your authority confirmed from this court that all possible means hath been used, but that the negligence in

affairs altogether spiritual is so great here that hardly once in a year do they so much as think on you.²²

This topic of the Roman courts' neglect of their primary work becomes a regular theme of his letters and almost an obsession. Yet the archives of Propaganda make it abundantly clear that amid all the lavish banqueting and magnificent displays, the day-to-day work, painstaking and ponderous and patient beyond belief, continued even through the summer heat. In particular the hard-working Baldeschi comes in for scathing criticism. The next letter is dated 6 February 1672:

> I desire nothing more than to serve you, but you know what sort of people these be here and how little they mind any business that hath not joined with it their profit. Baldeschi has been altogether taken up these days passed in negotiating a marriage betwixt a son of the Prince Corboniana his kinsman and a niece or brother's daughter of Cardinal Altieri, who now owes two cardinal's hats and will give them at the first promotion, one to Mons.Colonna, son of the said Prince Corboniana, and one other to a Dominican friar, brother to the Duke of Gravina of the house of Ursini, who married almost a year ago another niece of the said Cardinal Altieri. They talk here that Baldeschi, in consideration of the pains he has taken in this *parentado* will get some employment, yea the report goes that he is to be nonce in France. I would be glad they give him any employment providing they take from him that which he has, for we can expect no good from such a person.²³
>
> Here all this court is now and has been taken up this long time with the marriage of Cardinal Altieri his niece, and especially Baldeschi, who has been a chief mediator in this affair as I write you in my last. I pray God they give him some employment for his recompense more suitable to his quality than that which he has.* You must have patience, for so long as we have to do with him we will obtain nothing; and besides many other proofs of this you must know that he is now become a great friend of your adversaries the padri [Jesuits]. They have, as I am informed, lately gained him with presents and *regali*. He obtained not long

---

* Shortly afterwards (22 March 1673) Baldeschi became Assessor of the Holy Office. He soon got his reward for promoting the marriage of the pope's grand-niece with Egidio Colonna. As there was not a suitable person in the Colonna family upon whom to bestow a red hat, and as Baldeschi was a relative of sorts, he changed his name to Federico Colonna and was made a cardinal on 23 June. He spent the rest of his life in curia and died in 1691.

ago from the congregation of Propaganda for a padre of theirs that is sent by the general of their order to visit their missions on the Indies, a thousand and five hundred crowns, and I believe that the fathers left him his share. My lord almoner, if he had sent him some *regali* [gifts] it may be he had got his business done sooner, but this betwixt you and me. Here we have no news. All this court is now taken up with the marriage of the papelins and carnival-sport. (20 February)[24]

On 5 March he reports that the Dominican friar Gravina will not accept the cardinal's hat 'but the pope hath sent his general to him with a brief commanding him to accept this dignity'.[*25] On 25 March he bemoans that 'this is a pontificate so languishing that nothing can be expected in it but delays and nothing else'.[26]

Of Charles's five chief ministers, the cabal of Clifford, Arlington, Buckingham, Ashley and Lauderdale, the two first were suspected of being crypto-Catholics, but whether from conviction or expediency it is not easy to say. They were both signatories of the secret treaty of Dover already mentioned. With these councillors Charles decided on renewing war with the Dutch. The main objects were to plunder the richly laden ships returning from the Levant and to break the Dutch seapower that menaced English trade. The piracy began even before the declaration of war. In order to ensure that there would be no trouble from the various religious malcontents at home it was decided to grant them some measure of toleration.

On 16 March 1672 was published a declaration of indulgence for tender consciences. In it the king claimed that as supreme head of the church he had the right, recognized by several statutes, to suspend laws concerning religion. He declared his determination to maintain the church of England but he willed that 'all manner of penal laws in matters ecclesiastical, against whatsoever sort of non-conformist or recusant should be from that day suspended'. A sufficient number of places of worship would be licenced for dissenters but this benefit of public worship should not be extended to papists, who must confine their religious assemblies to private houses. For the nonconformists this was toleration indeed. It enabled, for instance, John Bunyan to leave his prison at Bedford carrying his precious manuscript of *Grace Abounding*. Towards

---

* This was Vincenzo Maria Orsini, then aged 23. In 1724 he became Benedict XIII, the last Dominican pope.

## Philip Howard

Catholics the Declaration was not so generous, but it gave as much as parliament could be expected to swallow. Howard was said to have had a hand in it. The internuncio wrote to Altieri on 2 April:

> They say that Fr Howard has a great part and great merit in this move and that this would seem to be the moment that His Holiness should be pleased to seize to comfort those Catholics and to appoint someone to take care of them and govern them.[27]

In Rome the news was received with satisfaction and the cardinals of Propaganda decided that the moment had come to act. A particular congregation was held on 26 April. It was decreed that Howard should be appointed a bishop *in partibus* and, with the title of vicar apostolic, should be given jurisdiction over the whole of England. The vexed question of whether to confirm or annul the Chapter was discussed but, as a 'matter of grave importance' was deferred to a subsequent congregation.[28] At an audience next day they suggested to the pope that the new bishop should have the same jurisdiction as had been granted by Gregory XV in 1623 and by Urban VIII in 1625 to the two bishops of Chalcedon. They further urged the necessity for secrecy and asked that the matter might be passed on at once to the secretary of briefs. His Holiness approved and ordered the expedition of the briefs.[29]

Forbes was more than usually successful in making this highly confidential information his own, though more by inspired guesswork than by bribing. Only three days later, on 30 April, he reports:

> The news you write me in your 24th we had them the last week. Immediately the congregation was holden, but for greater secret it was intimated *pro rebus Hiberniae* [for matters of Ireland]. What has been resolved in it I have not, nor any other, been able to discover; the silence has been hitherto so great. Yet I believe certainly that by this post they send order to the internonce to call to Flanders my lord almoner and there cause consecrate him bishop. I believe they will give him the same jurisdiction the others before had, but desire him that he beware that in his faculties he suffer not the word of *vicario apostolico*. For I know that the same morning Baldeschi was very busy seeking out in the Propaganda a copy of the faculties they used to give to apostolic vicars. If my lord stand it out they will grant him this and much more, for they are afraid here that now there being so good correspondence betwixt your court and the French, if they should continue in doing nothing as hitherto they have done, you have recourse to the French clergy, and this fear made

them, presently that they did see the king's declaration, hold
the congregation to prevent any resolution the French clergy
might possibly take in your affairs at your request, which is
the thing in the world they fear most here, and although this
fear is foolish, yet it is good they have it, and we ought daily to
augment it in them, for no motive we can bring them, sets them
so on work as this. Yea they are in a great rage against the French
ambassador here, because a business of so great consequence as
liberty of conscience in England being a-treating, not without
his king's participation as they imagine, he never has given the
least notice of it . . . I pray you be vigilant there in this affair and
let not my lord almoner go over to Flanders alone without some
of you to counsel him in an affair that concerns you both. No
resolution has been taken about your Chapter, nor will be till
the bishop's faculties be settled.[30]

Forbes repeats much of this in his letter of 7 May, and stresses even more strongly the power of the French pistol.

> They desire the internonce to proceed in all this affair so warily
> and circumspectly that I believe there shall be as little effected
> now as before. Nothing was spoke concerning the Chapter.
> They are still here afraid of your intelligence with the French
> and if you there with the internonce make any show of it, it
> will so affray him that it will procure you no little advantage.
> Therefore if my lord go over to Flanders you will do well to
> send one of your body along with him, to hinder that name of
> *vicario apostolico* and any other thing in his faculties that may
> prejudice you. This week Pio Quinto the pope was beatified
> here, yet there was great opposition made by some cardinal who
> does not approve so frequent beatifications and canonizations.[31]

The letter of 30 April conveying the rumour of Howard's coming consecration reached London on 24 May. Holt's answer shows that Forbes was not alone in using the French clergy as a threat:

> Mr Dr [Pulton] and I went immediately to my lord almoner, who
> as we hope will beware not to accept of a disgraceful jurisdiction,
> especially at such a juncture. If your court imagine that we shall
> play our cards by the assistance of the French clergy rather than
> be too much abused *hanno ragione* [they are right]. For upon
> our request of their opinion concerning the bull of His present
> Holiness, which calls Mr Russell, now bishop, *canonicum capituli
> Catholici in civitate Londini*,[*] etc., and in the latter end also decrees

---

[*] This was one of those slips that the Chapter pounced upon. At the congregation

his canonry to be vacant by the promotion of him to Portalegre, the Sorbonne say that 'tis a clear acknowledgement and strong confirmation of our Chapter. But your people are strange in all proceedings, for they need not scruple the authority of our Chapter, because upon the coming in of two or more bishops 'tis void of itself.[32]

A few quotations from Forbes's letters during the rest of the year will be enough to show the hostility and suspicion that were not the best attributes in an agent. It should, however, be borne in mind that they were private letters to a friend and that his official attitude was doubtless more circumspect.

> This court being much Spanishly affected, gusts nothing although never so good that comes either from France or allied with France, so that the total conversion of your nation in this conjuncture would breed more displeasure than pleasure here.[33]
>
> I desire nothing more than to be useful here to you, but this generation of vipers mind nothing less than religion.[34]
>
> Even when they would execute their decrees I believe neither my lord almoner nor you would accept them, for they tend to nothing else but to make him a petty apostolic-vicar ... If once you admit this slavery you will never be able to get out of it, for this court aims at nothing else but to make you altogether dependent, even in trifles, from the congregation of the propaganda: that is to say from Baldeschi.[35]

The brief appointing Howard Bishop of Helenopolis is dated 16 May 1672. It dispenses him from the necessity of visiting his see 'so long as it remains in the hands of the infidels' and allows him to be consecrated, if need be, by one bishop only, assisted by two priests.[36] On the following day was issued a brief conferring on him all the faculties granted to the archpriests by Clement VIII and Paul V and also those which ordinaries enjoy in their cities and diocese. The term 'vicar apostolic' is not used, but so closely have the Chalcedon briefs been followed that Howard is instructed to have recourse in matters of special gravity to the nuncio at the court of the King of France, notwithstanding that the office of ordinary of England had been transferred to the internuncio at Brussels.[37]

<blockquote>held on 26 April it had been ordered that the copy of the brief in the register should be amended by expunging the words 'canon of the Catholic church in London' (Brady, III, 129).</blockquote>

*The Gathering Storm*

According to Baldeschi the briefs were sent at once to the internuncio, but it would seem that this was true only of the brief appointing Howard bishop. As late as 16 January 1673 the brief conferring his jurisdiction was still in the secretariat of briefs, for on that day Propaganda wrote thither asking that the clause instructing Howard to have recourse to the nuncio at Paris should be corrected and the internuncio at Brussels substituted. The pope gave his approval on 21 January and the brief was duly amended.[38]

All that concerned the appointment of Howard was to be treated with the utmost secrecy lest a premature disclosure should provoke some new anti-Catholic law. Howard himself was not informed and pleaded ignorance of the briefs as late as December 1673.* In Elizabeth's time the government had its paid spies in the heart of Rome. These were no longer necessary as the agent of the Chapter was doing their work.

In a month or so Charles had got to hear that Howard's briefs were in the hands of the internuncio. The reaction to the Declaration of Indulgence had been much more violent than expected and the appointment of a bishop at this juncture would only have added fuel to the flames. Arlington, Buckingham and Halifax were setting out in May as plenipotentiaries to conclude a peace with the Dutch. Charles gave Arlington secret instructions to ask the internuncio not to publish the briefs.

All this matter has been shrouded in secrecy. Baldeschi's successor, Urbano Cerri, in a report to Innocent XI in 1677, states that all affairs relating to England for some years past had been removed from Propaganda to the Holy Office for greater security.[39] It would seem that Baldeschi, who was promoted Assessor at the latter in 1673, took these papers with him. None of the original correspondence is now to be found in Propaganda. But Baldeschi must have overlooked one important book. It contains copies of all the deliberations concerning England from 1637 to 1672 and summaries of the letters that were laid before the cardinals. The

---

* 'Try whether you can privily get a copy of a certain brief which (as we are informed) was made above a year ago in a congregation. It was made for my lord almoner and in it some authority granted him as a vicar or bishop, but what the limits of it were is unknown to him and us. A copy of it would be very acceptable to both. And that such a thing was done is certain, as divers have asserted both of the court and others, though your grandees deny any such thing now to have been done' (Holt to Forbes, 12 December 1673).

following account is compiled from a very long report that Baldeschi prepared for a congregation held on 16 September.[40]

He refers first to the decision of 26 April to appoint Howard bishop and to give him the faculties given to the bishops of Chalcedon; also the decision to send the briefs to the internuncio and to leave the rest to his discretion. There were two points arising from this. 1. The best means to prevent the elect not only confirming the Chapter but recognizing it in any way; and 2. The best way to proceed was to declare the Chapter null and void.

With regard to the first it was decided to instruct the internuncio to procure a letter from Howard explicitly promising not to approve or recognize as a Chapter 'the collection of priests who arrogate that title to themselves'. With regard to the second point it was resolved to wait for the internuncio and Howard to suggest when the right moment had come, how it should be promulgated and what subjects should be chosen to form a new body.

In due course the internuncio replied that he would do his best, but that it was doubtful if Howard's election could remain secret for long and it might be made public inopportunely; that if Howard discovered that the briefs were in his hands he might complain of any delay. But as long as the business was secret he would see that all went well. That the Benedictine who had recently delivered the letter from Arlington recommended that, things being as they were, there should be no innovation because it would wreck all the king's plans, plans that were for the advantage of religion; that it was necessary to wait till the end of the present campaign and also till parliament, due to meet in October, was over; parliament was the most dangerous obstacle to the whole business and therefore he should wait till a person of judgment and trust arrives from London, with whom he may consult about the best course of action.

In another letter the internuncio acknowledges the receipt of the briefs and says that before forwarding them to Howard he will obtain the promise not to recognize the so-called Chapter or to erect another without approbation from the Holy See; that Robert Pugh[*] has written to say that the Chapter is arguing that the title of *Canonicus Ecclesiae Londinensis* in his faculties is equivalent to

---

[*] Pugh was an ex-Jesuit. He died in prison during the Oates plot (H. Foley, *Records of the English Province of the Society of Jesus*, 8 vols., London, 1877–83, V, 34).

papal recognition of the Chapter and that they need to be enlightened; and that only one or two of the Catholic nobility adhere to the Chapter and many were amazed that it had not been annulled.

Clifford had written to the internuncio saying that the King of England had received notice that the bulls creating Howard a bishop were in his hands and had ordered Clifford to ensure that they were not sent to England because their publication at that present juncture could only be injurious to the purpose for which they were issued.

This letter was enclosed in one from the internuncio saying that it had arrived only just in time; he had been merely waiting for a convenient opportunity to forward the briefs to Howard; that it could be gathered from Clifford's letter that the election was already known in London and that the times were not propitious to proceed with it. After receiving this letter business had taken him to Antwerp, and two days later the two plenipotentiaries arrived there.* At a banquet given in their honour he was seated next to Arlington and thus had an opportunity of a long discussion concerning Clifford's letter.

Arlington said that he too had been ordered by the king to write to him for the suspension of the briefs of the bishop-elect but he had not had time. The internuncio stressed the need of a superior for the English Catholics in order to put a stop to the troubles that arise in a land of liberty; that the articles of the queen's marriage allowed the character of bishop for her almoner and it could not justly be refused. Arlington agreed that a superior was necessary but said it was not opportune to appoint one at the moment; that it would be better to delay it because the king and he himself would let him know when the right moment had come. He also agreed that the articles of marriage allowed for the almoner to be a bishop but he said that Howard was not capable of this office: he was a good subject and well thought of at court, but it seemed he lacked the qualities and the adroitness required for governing. Hence it was necessary to consider that either Rome or the king would have to give him a capable assistant, one adept at the task of ruling. It could, said Arlington, be inferred from this that the king

---

* Airoldi went to Antwerp on 9 July (NF, 61, f. 482). Arlington may also have visited Bornhem for there is mention of a donation from him of 20 florins on 25 July (*Dominicana*, 140).

would make no difficulty about a bishop in London but he simply reiterated that the moment was not opportune. The internuncio added that he would have liked a longer discussion but had to beware of arousing the suspicions of Buckingham and the others.

In another letter he confirms all that he had said in the preceding and adds that from Arlington's conversation he gathered that he was well disposed to the Catholics and thought it was quite likely that he was secretly a Catholic. The same was true of Halifax.

The cardinals having heard this long report praised the internuncio for retaining the briefs and judged that no further instructions need be sent him since it was clear by his letters that he would not publish them until he was assured that the English king would not take the publication amiss.

As for the question of an assistant they thought it would be a good thing if the internuncio appeared ready to agree to one deputed by the pope, in order by this prompt agreement to remove any desire on the part of the king to nominate his own candidate, seeing that such a nomination might create some difficulty on the part of the Holy See.

They also approved of the replies to Arlington as given in the letter of 23 July. Although they did not wish to add anything, still, out of curiosity the internuncio should try to discover the reason why Fr Howard, who had been considered by the king and by all his ministers as worthy to exercise the functions of a bishop, should not be judged so now.[41]

By devious means that we can only guess copies of Baldeschi's *scrittura* and of the minutes of the meeting found their way to the Chapter in London. They are mentioned in a list of documents in their archives,[42] though they appear to be no longer extant. They probably came some considerable time after as there is nothing in the Chapter correspondence to suggest that they had even a clue of what had transpired. And surely we should have expected some vitriolic comments on the decision to annul the Chapter.

Howard's correspondence is also strangely silent about the matter. He still keeps the internuncio informed of English affairs but there is never a note of impatience, and he no longer recounts the scandals and divisions that were crying out for reform. Perhaps he had at last realized the futility of it all. Only Patrick Conn continues to pester Barberini with complaints about the lack of a bishop and with warm commendations of Howard.[43] After all these years of

## The Gathering Storm

constant clamour and patient discussion nothing whatever had been achieved. The acceptable time (if there ever was one) had come and gone. The see of Helenopolis was given in December 1673 to a German Benedictine, and from that moment presumably (for there is no official cancellation of his briefs) Howard ceased to be bishop-elect.

Catholics had to look elsewhere for some amelioration of their lot.

### III

By 1673 it was evident that Queen Catherine was unlikely to bear a son and heir. The next in succession was James Duke of York, the king's brother. He had long been a Catholic at heart though he had never openly professed the fact. It was his custom to attend Protestant services with the king, but after 1671 he had refused to take communion. In March 1673 parliament forced the king to cancel the Declaration of Indulgence and to sanction the Test Act, which imposed on all who held office under the crown an oath that explicitly denied the doctrine of transubstantiation. James refused it and resigned all his offices, though still he did not declare himself a Catholic. His first wife Anne Hyde had died in 1671, and the question of a second marriage now assumed a new importance. As heir presumptive it was imperative that he should find a bride in one of the royal houses of Europe.

After negotiations with the royal house of Austria had failed, it was decided to approach the d'Este family, whose head was Duke of Modena. There were two possible candidates; Eleanora, sister of the late Duke Alfonso IV, and Maria Beatrice his daughter. Eleanora was thirty and her niece Maria Beatrice was only fourteen. Both had set their heart on taking the veil, and neither was willing to forgo a religious vocation in order to become Duchess of York and probably Queen of England. Louis XIV as well as the family chaplain, P. Garimberti, SJ, were in favour of Eleanora, as being of a more suitable age for the duke, who was nearly forty. The duchess Laura, widow of Alfonso IV, wished the honour to go to her daughter Maria Beatrice, though she seems at first to have had some scruples about sending so young a princess into a distant, heretic country.

## Philip Howard

In August 1673 Henry Mordant Earl of Peterborough was despatched to Modena on this important business. His instructions were to sue for the hand of Maria Beatrice, and if that failed then to transfer his addresses to her aunt Eleanora. He was to be careful not to let Maria Beatrice discover that he had a second string to his bow. The important thing was to ensure that the duke was well and truly married to somebody before parliament met in October. It would be best to face them with a *fait accompli*. He carried a written pledge that King Charles would honour whatever promises were made by him. He was to remain incognito till there was some certainty of success. This meant the farce of using the backstairs of the palace instead of the front, for everyone knew him and his mission.

By the time he arrived in Modena in mid-September Eleanora had been ruled out as a possible candidate. Her resolution to become a nun (as she did soon afterwards) proved unshakable. All exertions were now concentrated on overcoming the opposition of Maria Beatrice. The French King had sent a special ambassador, M.d'Avaux, and Francesco Barberini, both as Cardinal Protector of England and as a relative of Laura, and was interested enough to send one of his secretaries, Giovan Battista Hussoni.

It was the story of Philip Howard's struggles over again. The young girl remained unshaken in her vocation. Her mother tried every argument she could think of. She told her that princesses were not born to be stay-at-homes, but must follow fortune wherever it leads. She pointed out that the Duke of York was next in succession, and dangled before her the glittering prize of a royal throne. It was all in vain. 'She's as hard as this' declared Laura to Hussoni, banging the table on which she was leaning. At last the poor girl was prevailed upon to submit the matter to the pope and to hear his paternal sentiments. A special messenger was despatched to Rome, and a hortatory brief, dated 19 September 1673, reached Modena on the 21st. Clement X spoke of the great harvest of joy that God was preparing for the Catholics in England as a result of this alliance, and the anxiety caused him by her repugnance to marriage. He exhorted her to reflect on the great advantages to the faith that this marriage would bring, and to open to herself a field of meritorious work wider than that of the virginal cloister. She was not to be held back by the fear of living amongst heretics, for he would insist on adequate safeguards for the practice of her religion.

## The Gathering Storm

Before the counsel of the Vicar of Christ, Maria Beatrice could only bow in agonized submission. Next day the Earl of Peterborough on behalf of the king and his brother solemnly swore before witnesses that the Duchess of York would enjoy the free exercise of her religion, with the same rights and privileges as were enjoyed by the Queen of England. He would not, however, put this solemn pledge in writing for fear of repercussions in the coming parliament. Another special messenger hastened to Rome to obtain a dispensation from the impediment of 'disparity of cults'. For although generally considered a Catholic, and although three months before he had resigned all his offices rather than subscribe to an anti-Catholic oath, the Duke of York still attended Protestant churches and had never formally declared himself a Catholic.

It was Friday 22 September, and the solemn nuptials were fixed for Sunday 1 October. There is ample time for the dispensation to arrive but obviously preparations must begin at once. The guests are invited, the cathedral sumptuously decorated and the whole population of Modena prepares to celebrate with all its traditional, elaborate pageantry. On Wednesday the 27th there is no news from Rome, and Hussoni writes urgently to Barberini pointing out the inconvenience and the anxiety that this delay is causing in Modena. On Friday the 29th there is still no letter of any sort from Rome and the situation is desperate. A council of theologians is hastily convened. There were five of them 'of various orders'. As the Dominican priory adjoined the palace perhaps the Dominicans were represented. What was to be done? The Earl of Peterborough made it clear that if there was any question of a postponement of the marriage he would at once return to England. Was a dispensation really necessary, the duke being so generally considered a Catholic was not the pope's hortatory brief tantamount to a dispensation? The Bishop of Modena refused to have anything to do with a marriage without the dispensation, and Fr Garimberti took the same line. At last it was decided that the granting of the dispensation could be presumed, but out of deference to the pope the solemn nuptial Mass in the cathedral was cancelled. The marriage ceremony was performed privately in the chapel of the palace the following morning (Saturday), and on Sunday there was a Te Deum in the cathedral to assuage the disappointment of the populace. Thus Mary Duchess of York (as we must now call her), having with such agony of soul obeyed the vicar of Christ, was married without his blessing.

And what, it will be asked, was happening in Rome? There the situation did not appear in quite the same light. The bitter disappointment of the whole population of Modena was as nothing compared with the pope's disappointment at the turn of events in England. It was all very well to guarantee the new duchess the same rights and privileges as were enjoyed by the English queen, but at this very time those rights and privileges, solemnly sworn to in the marriage treaty between England and Portugal, were being flagrantly dishonoured by parliament. The following report sent via Brussels on 24 March 1673 shows that Altieri, the Cardinal Secretary, was fully informed:

> The proclamation made here against the priests states in express terms, which I have seen and read in print, that the queen may have in her chapel only foreign priests, and that those who are natural subjects of the king are to withdraw, on pain of incurring the same penalties as the others. It has been strongly represented that by the articles of the queen's marriage she is permitted to have so many who are natives of the country. In reply it is said that the articles of this marriage cannot derogate from the fundamental laws of the realm. You will see how their fury goes to the lengths of attacking a queen who thinks only of living for God, and of being in the world as though she were not of it. What Catholic princess could have the temerity to come into a nation which has so little regard for those to whom it owes infinite respect? The trouble is that the king has signed an agreement not to impede parliament in the execution of any law they please to make.    (SB March, 1673)

In his hortatory brief the pope had promised Mary Beatrice adequate safeguards for the practice of her religion, and the news from England made it painfully clear that not even the word of a king was a sufficient guarantee when he was at the mercy of a hostile parliament. What value, then, had the verbal promises made by Peterborough on behalf of the Duke of York? The matter was submitted to a congregation of eight cardinals, and they agreed that the dispensation could not be granted until some better assurances were found. The Bishop of Modena was secretly instructed to return the hortatory brief,* but no open declaration of the pope's

---

\* The copy of this brief in the papal register has the marginal note: *Non fuit*

mind was sent to Modena. Had he immediately signified his decision there was certainly one person in Modena who would have been overjoyed to obey, and there could be no marriage without a bride. It was not, however, till 30 September (the very day of the marriage) that he signed the brief ordering the delay. Cardinal Altieri sent this brief to the cardinal legate at Bologna, asking him to send it on to Garimberti, *'without, however, any extra-ordinary diligence'*. It would seem as though Altieri hoped it would arrive too late to interfere with the arrangements at Modena. If the marriage proved a success it could be rectified later; if the causes concerning religious freedom were broken, then no responsibility rested on the Roman court.

When this brief eventually found its way to Modena the Duchess of York had already left for England. The journey across France was a succession of leisurely festivities and it was not until November, when England is not at its best, that the unhappy victim reached London. She confided years afterwards to the nuns at Chaillot that her first sentiments on meeting her husband could be expressed only by tears. Had she had the heart to look out of her window on that first dismal night she would have seen a glow in the southern sky. Beyond the Thames a huge effigy of the pope was being burnt by way of welcome. 'I find', writes a correspondent, 'making of popes a great trade here and burning of them as great a diversion. The night the duchess arrived, a pope of £50 was burnt in Southwark.'

When the news reached Rome that the marriage had been celebrated without waiting for the pope's answer Cardinal Altieri wrote a stern letter to Laura on 7 October, denying that the hortatory brief gave any grounds to suppose that the pope would grant the dispensation without more ado, and expressing his grief that they should have acted with such haste and presumption. There the matter rested for a time. On 8 January 1674 the Duchess of York wrote herself to the pope begging him to bless her marriage, but there was no reply. In April Louis XIV took up her cause, offering his own guarantee for the observance of the stipulations concerning religion. In October Cardinal Barberini presented a petition explaining all the extenuating circumstances. This produced a brief that is not very cordial in tone. It does not grant the dispensation

*missum* [it was not sent].

or even allude to the necessity for one. It accepts the fact that the marriage has taken place with solemn assurances of religious freedom, absolves the duchess from all censures, and, for the quiet of her conscience and the good of religion, sanctions the parties' living together, provided that all the promises made by the king and his brother and backed by the King of France, are faithfully honoured, and that the children of the marriage are under the care of the duchess and her assigns until the age of puberty. There is no explicit blessing on the marriage, but a few months later, on 16 March 1675 Clement wrote more tenderly, commending her readiness to offer herself as a victim for the good of the English Catholics, and imparting his fatherly benediction. By the time it reached London a new proclamation had been published, banishing all priests, even those 'pretending privilege to attend the queen or foreign ministers'. Before she was eighteen her name was to be disgracefully dragged into the Oates plot, her secretary done to death at Tyburn, and she herself forced with her husband to flee the country. There were grounds enough for the papal apprehensions that had delayed the dispensation.

In all these marriage negotiations, so fully documented, there is no mention whatever of Fr Howard. Yet he claims to have played a decisive part in securing for the Duke of York the hand of Mary Beatrice, rather than that of her aunt Eleanor. Why he should have had any special interest in this choice still remains a mystery. Both were good Catholics, and Eleanor was of a more suitable age for the duke. One would have expected him to have had sympathy for a young girl whose plight was so similar to what his own had been. As a novice of fifteen he had to face almost alone the hostility of his family to his religious vocation, and the powerful intervention of several cardinals. But at least he had had one friend and eventually the pope had taken his part and allowed him to be professed. She had just as strong a longing for the religious life and was meeting with much the same sort of opposition. She was only a girl and a year younger than he had been, and nobody seems to have shown her the slightest sympathy. She must sacrifice her vocation, stifle her repugnance to marriage, be wafted to a sunless country she had never before heard of, to live among heretics, the wife of a widower of nearly three times her age, whom she had never seen, and whose standards of conjugal fidelity was to be demanded of her for the good of the English Catholics.

## The Gathering Storm

Howard's part in these negotiations is known only from a letter written by him in 1676 after he had become a cardinal and two and a half years after the events. This letter has survived only because it was one of many that were seized by the English government during the scare caused by the Titus Oates plot. They were all addressed to Edward Coleman, secretary to the Duchess of York, whose foreign correspondence, especially with France, was deemed treasonable and who was executed for his alleged part in the plot. A selection of his foreign correspondence was published by order of parliament in 1680 to justify his execution. The selection includes several letters from Howard, as proof that the Duke and Duchess of York were secretly corresponding with the pope. In the panic of the Oates plot even the most innocent exchange of courtesies with the pope appeared as a sinister menace to the lives of all good Protestants.

The only letter that concerns us here is a very long one dated 14 March 1676 from Rome. It is so long that Howard complains: 'My time is quite spent and eyes almost out, writing so much'. As printed it is an extraordinary production, with clumsy, tortuous phrases that are almost unintelligible. The explanation is that the original letter, like all important letters that had to cross half a continent and were liable to be intercepted, was written in cipher. This particular cipher, however, was woefully inadequate. It consisted simply of a list of numbers representing prominent people whose identity it was safer to veil. From a deciphered copy of another of his letters to Coleman, we gather, for example, that 155 stood for the Duke of York, 150 for the pope, 330 for Cardinal Altieri, 55 for Rome and 990 for Cardinal Norfolk, as Howard was always called. Where Howard would normally have written 'I think', he writes '990 thinks'; This is always decoded as 'Cardinal Norfolk', and this gives his letters a quite unfair pomposity. Howard complains in this very letter that the cipher 'is not large enough, and besides hath not the alphabetical letters necessary to make words'. Thus when he wanted to encode an ordinary word he had to resort to a circumlocution. For 'Dominican' he could only say 'the confederates of 990': similarly for 'Jesuits' he had to use a phrase which when decoded becomes 'the confederates of the French king's confessor'. Such subterfuges are not conducive to chaste and limpid prose.

We gather from this letter that Fr Vincent Torre, Howard's successor as vicar general in England, had found a place in the duchess's household, and apparently other Dominicans as well. The Benedictines and Jesuits were now trying to oust them, and Howard was annoyed. The duke should show more gratitude to Howard, who had rendered such good service in securing for him the hand of Mary Beatrice. Such is the theme of this section of the letter, which is all that need be given here:

> But now I must tell you that I cannot but be sorry to understand (by witness which I can produce) that some of the chief of Mr Sheldon's confederates [the Benedictines] have informed that the duke's affection is so much and only for those and the confederates of the French king's confessor [the Jesuits] that he absolutely declared it, and said he would be served by them only; which if so, Vincent de Torre and Cardinal Howard's confederates [the Dominicans] may shut up their shop and traffic elsewhere; and I should be glad to know it to provide accordingly. For although it is most clear and true what I said often in England, that if Cardinal Norfolk had not sent Fr White in post haste from Rome [to] where the duchess was then [Modena], and that he and other of his confederates had not stoutly resisted and conclusively argued against the potent confrater of the French King's confessor [Fr Garimberti, SJ], that the duchess [Eleanor] and none else (as the other would have, to put off the concluding with this duchess) [Mary Beatrice] was fitting and to be had for the duke, the whole business (which was then broken off) would have been spoiled and broken off for ever. But Cardinal Norfolk having notice from Paris at first of the breaking off of the other treaty, a particular friend of his there thought first of that duchess which (God be praised) is [Maria Beatrice] and spoke to Lord Peterborough of it, etc. (of all which the said Lord Peterborough can tell you). And at the same time Cardinal Norfolk wrote to several at Rome about it, and posted the above-named Fr White with full instructions to employ all his little wits and those of his confederates (whose house joineth to that of the duchess) to act all possible, as they did to right purpose, and (*nolens volens* the juggling of others) argued so hotly and well, that it was concluded quite contrary to the intention and expectation of the jugglers. My Lord Peterborough can tell you something of it and I much more; but since the business is done it's no matter. I did it not to pick thanks or for recompense to me or mine, but to serve the duke and Catholic religion in England.[44]

Howard's correspondent in Paris was Patrick Conn. There are several letters from him to Barberini concerning the marriage and he was much involved in the preliminary stages before Peterborough left Paris. Fr White on the other hand now makes his first appearance. As he has a tiny niche among the immortals something must be said of his career.

Among those who fled from England on the outbreak of the civil war was Richard White of Hutton, Essex, brother of Thomas White alias Blacklow, whose Gallican views had given the Chapter such a bad name. He settled first at Pisa with his wife, Catherine Weston daughter of the Earl of Portland, and a family of three sons and five daughters. In 1642 they moved to Rome. Tragedy followed on tragedy. His wife died after much suffering and was buried in the chapel of the English College on 27 October 1645. He was left with this large family, the eldest only seventeen, and no means of obtaining money from England. The eldest boy George entered the English College in January 1646. The other boys were Charles and Jerome. In 1648 the father petitioned Cardinal Barberini to find a place for Charles, aged twelve, in the College of Propaganda.[45] This was not granted. There was a strict law forbidding them to receive students of any country that had a national college in Rome, and also Charles was well below the minimum age. In 1654 Charles joined the Roman province of the Dominicans, changing his name to Thomas. Henceforth he was known as Tommaso Bianchi. Under such a thorough disguise he might have lived and died without anyone, then or now, suspecting that he was English. He had left England at the age of seven or eight and was bi-lingual. One wonders how many Englishmen at this time, when the English mission had no attractions, joined orders abroad, buried their identity under some foreign form of their names and carried their secret to the grave. Not so Tommaso Bianchi. There was another member of the province with the same names, and the Englishman is often distinguished by the addition of 'alias Albus' or 'alias White'. After studies at Naples he was ordained at the Lateran on 13 March 1660. Being seven months short of the canonical age (24) he needed a dispensation. In his petition he speaks of his desire to return to England to preach the faith, but fate decreed otherwise. He settled down in the Roman province and to the normal routine. In 1664 and 1665 he was appointed to preach the Lent and his life at this time, as procurator at Viterbo and subprior at Civita Vecchia was not in any way unusual. Then in February 1671 he was given permission to go to London and elsewhere to settle his private affairs and it was doubtless then that he first met Howard. When he returned to Rome in October 1672 it was to act as Howard's agent. Soon his name begins to appear in the letters of Thomas Forbes, who first mentions him in a letter of 6 February 1673:

> Padre Thomaso has not had any letter from my lord almoner since he came here, nor long before. This court here says my lord's affair and its effectuation depends totally now upon yours, and this is the answer they give to all that speak to them of this business, so that the said padre is now about another affair, to wit, to procure the church and convent of Ss Giovanni and Paulo for the English Dominican friars. But besides the difficulties he will find in getting the said church or convent (it belongs to an abbatia of Cardinal Rospigliosi) I do not see how he can maintain his friars there without a sum of money.[46]

This is the earliest mention of overtures to acquire Ss John and Paul's for the English Dominicans. Forbes's pessimism was not justified, for two years later this ancient basilica was entrusted to Howard, and soon became a fully constituted convent. Forbes's next piece of information is as false as it is mischievous:

> Padre Bianchi has received from my lord almoner, as I am informed, a case or box by way of Leghorn full of rich stuffs, I believe to make a present of to Baldeschi, secretary of Propaganda. This is not an ill way to advance business in this court, if it were taken at a more fit time.[47]

How unfair was this charge of bribery may be seen from Howard's own letter, which makes it clear that this rich stuff was a present of scarlet cloth from King Charles to Cardinal Barberini.

It must have been in August or early September 1673 that White received instructions from Howard to proceed to Modena. At that time there was a danger of a complete breakdown in the marriage talks, and his object was to allay the scruples of the Duchess Laura and persuade her to consent to the marriage of her daughter even at the tender age of fourteen, and to oppose the candidature of Eleanora, which was supported by Louis XIV and Fr Garimberti. There is no account anywhere of these transactions. They must have ended before the middle of September when Hussoni arrived, for then there is no longer any question of Eleanora. Perhaps Thomas White was one of the theologians later called in for the hurried consultation that sealed the fate of the young bride.

## The Gathering Storm

There are two very different accounts of what happened in the private chapel of the palace on that fateful Saturday morning. A long narrative of the festivities and of the journey to England was compiled by a court secretary. This is his account of the marriage ceremony:

> All the princes and princesses betook themselves to an apartment of gold and stucco on an upper floor, together with the English ambassador and the French envoy. At the altar of a chapel there D. Andrea Roncagli, the parish-priest of the court, asked and received the reciprocal consent of the contracting parties and celebrated the marriage privately, except that, besides the aforesaid princes of the serene house, there were present the three *maestri de camera*. [Here follow their names and the names of other privileged guests, who filled three rooms]. Everything was done according to the rite of Holy Mother Church and the form laid down by the Council of Trent, but because England and her ambassador were of the Protestant religion, it was not done *inter missarum solemnia*, as is customary among Catholic spouses.

This is ambiguous. *Inter missarum solemnia* may mean 'during the principal Mass'. He does not say explicitly that there was no Mass, though it might be implied from the reason he gives, *viz.*, because Peterborough was a Protestant. Peterborough has also left an account. He recalls the trouble over the dispensation and says:

> The Bishop of Modena was then applied to for the performance, but he refusing, a poor English Jacobite was found, brother to Jerome White, who after served the duchess,* who having nothing to lose, and on whom the terror of excommunication did not so much prevail, did undertake it, and so he performed the ceremony.[48]

What was the ceremony performed by Thomas White? Peterborough is not very clear, but his words seem to imply that there *was* a Mass. What other ceremony could have been obnoxious to his Protestant sensibilities? He says he was

---

* Jerome did not serve the duchess for long. On 31 October 1674 he was very ill and dictated his will to his brother George. He does not mention his Dominican brother but he leaves his sister Frances 'my jewel of diamonds given me by Prince Rinaldo'. The will was proved 10 November 1674 (The Prerogative Court of Canterbury, PROB.11/346, f. 134).

conducted to a chamber near the chapel, where he reposed himself till so much of the service was done as seemed abnoxious to the religion he did profess; after which he was led to the chapel where the princess expected him, and there between them was performed the ceremony designed for a perpetual marriage between this admirable princess and the Duke of York his master.[49]

Which of these accounts are we to believe? The court secretary is writing a version for the family and must avoid any suggestion that there was a cloud over the proceedings. It is a masterpiece of understatement. He does not hint at the perturbation caused by the non-arrival of the dispensation. He does not explain why the marriage was performed by the *parocco* and not by the bishop or the family chaplain. He leaves the reader to suppose that out of deference to Peterborough there was no Mass, but that otherwise all went smoothly and happily. It is possible that Peterborough on the other hand is not quite accurate. When he says that White 'performed the ceremony' he may mean that he said the Mass, a function that a Protestant might well consider the marriage proper. Whatever the truth of the matter it does not seem reasonable to dismiss his account as false merely because it does not agree with the court version.* There is no conceivable reason why he should have invented the part played by Fr White: there is every reason why the court secretary should wish to suppress it.

Fr Howard does not mention White's part in the ceremony but only in the preliminary negotiations. It is reasonable to suppose that White would have stayed on at Modena till the marriage was concluded, and Howard's letter, taken in conjunction with Peterborough's account, makes it scarcely disputable that he played

---

\* In his *Derniers Stuarts* (I, 97) Campana, having given the account of the court secretary, comments: 'This passage of the chronicler is a complete rebuttal of the statement of certain English historians that the fear of displeasing the pope having deterred every ecclesiastical dignitary from performing the marriage, they had to have recourse to a poor Irish priest who was passing through Modena. The intervention of the parish priest of the chapel is moreover certified by another eye-witness, Muratori, in his *Antichità Estensi*.' Muratori may have been an eye-witness though he was only eleven months old at the time of the marriage. When he came to write his *Antichità Estensi* he was librarian and archivist of the Duke of Modena, and doubtless relied on the very document that Campana says he corroborates.

## The Gathering Storm

a part in the actual marriage. Perhaps it never became generally known. White was not sent to the papal galleys. He returned to Rome and in the following December received a brief confirming his reaffiliation to the Minerva. A year or so later he became prior of Civita Vecchia.

Whether in the years of tribulation that were to follow, Howard felt quite the same satisfaction with the part he had played is a question to which he never vouchsafed an answer. The time was to come when the name d'Este sounded less sweetly to his ear.

### IV

The Declaration of Indulgence so incensed parliament that it had to be revoked. There followed the passing of the first Test Act that required every employee of the crown to take the oath of allegiance and supremacy, to deny transubstantiation and to receive the Protestant communion.

In March 1673 a new proclamation was issued, and this time it touched the chaplains of the queen and of the ambassadors. In previous proclamations they had always been exempted, but now it was ordered that the queen was to be served only by foreign priests, and that all priests who were subjects of the king were to depart the realm within thirty days. The queen protested against this flagrant breach of the articles of marriage, but all in vain.

In the summer the Duke of York, on the eve of his wedding resigned his office of lord high admiral and his other commissions. In December Catholics were denied access to St James's Park and the chapel there.

In February 1674 the internuncio asked for a papal brief commending Howard's brother Henry Duke of Norfolk for his steadfastness in the face of persecution.[50] This was duly issued, dated 17 March, and dispatched to Brussels.[51] On 28 April, however, the internuncio reports that letters from England cast grave doubts on the duke's constancy; that, following the example of the Duke of York and others, he had taken the oath with the qualifying clause allowed by the king, *viz.* that his oath implied nothing contrary to the primacy of the pope. The internuncio therefore judged it better to suspend the delivery of the brief.[52]

Accounts of the persecution reaching Rome seem to have been exaggerated, for the Master General writes to Howard on 2 June asking for details of the Irish Dominicans who were reported to have been executed in Dublin.[53]

The *Annals* of Bornhem, on which all later accounts are founded, states that Howard's final departure from England was in this year, 1674. This is a mistake. He paid his annual visit to Bornhem in September but was back in London before the end of the year. It does not appear that any of the royal chaplains had obeyed the proclamation. Perhaps they hoped to ride out the storm as they had so often done before.

On 3 February 1675 a proclamation was issued by the king in council ordering all romish priests pretending privilege to attend the queen or foreign ministers to leave within fourteen days. This was followed on the 5th by another proclamation ordering all Jesuits and priests (except Mr John Huddleston) to depart the realm before 25 March and never to return.[54] On 10 February the Mass was forbidden throughout England, 'the chapels of our dearest consort and the chapels of foreign ministers only excepted', and none but the queen's servants were to attend Mass in her chapel.[55]

According to *Annals* the parliamentary attack was directed in a special manner against the grand almoner. The charges against him are carefully tabulated by the annalist.

1. He was reputed the author of the Declaration of Indulgence.
2. He had converted to the Catholic faith and sent to his convent at Bornhem to become religious, a certain Dr John Davis, a minor-canon of Windsor and chaplain of Magdalen College, Oxford, together with John Green, who had been sent to study at Magdalen by the dean and Chapter of Windsor. This was the little boy, already mentioned, who had made friends with Cosimo in Windsor Castle.
3. That he had ordered to be printed in English pontifical bulls of indulgence for saying the rosary.[56]

The annalist might have added that Howard had caused to be printed and distributed in England certain papal bulls, and had actually affixed them to the door of the queen's chapel. Such defiance of the law had not been heard of since John Felton had nailed Pius V's bull of excommunication on the door of the Bishop of London's palace, and paid for it with his life.

A report of Propaganda of 19 July 1677 states that the heretics had got to hear of Howard's appointment as bishop, and for this reason it was judged prudent for him to leave England.[57] This report is worthy of credence, for by this time Howard was himself a member of Propaganda and must surely have consented. In a letter written only a month before this report he had blamed the Benedictines for broadcasting prematurely the news of his appointment as bishop; though he does not make it the reason for his departure:

> The Benedictines and others played the fools to stop the execution of it [the appointment] in England, when it was not intended to be made use of but in due time, which others (at least as good as the Benedictines and the Caballers) ought to judge.[58]

He does not, however, attribute his departure to this untimely disclosure.

Apart from the account in the *Annals* there is no evidence that any special attack was made on Howard personally. The proclamation applied to him and to his sub-almoners, but the story of a pending arraignment on the charges listed by the annalist seems to be, to say the least, an exaggeration. Cosimo's minister in London wrote to his master on 12 February (old style):

> Your Highness will find enclosed ... the recent proclamation against the priests. In compliance with this, milord grand almoner of the queen is preparing for his departure, with the intention of crossing to Flanders, then to France, and so to Rome, calling on the way to kiss your Highness's hand. There are other Catholics also who intend to avoid the rigour of the law by departing the realm. Others have decided to stay and see what happens in the coming parliament.[59]

Thus it would appear that it suited Howard's plans to obey the proclamation. He had already made up his mind to go to Rome in any case. With letters of commendation to Cardinals Barberini and Altieri from the king[60], and with a liberal present of religious objects from the queen's chapel, he left London, arriving at Dover on 20 March. The navy yacht had been put at his disposal and arrived in the early hours of the 23rd, two days before the time allowed in the proclamation expired. He went aboard at 8 a.m. and set sail with a fair nor'westerly wind.[61] Little did he realize that for him it was the last sight of England.

Meanwhile parliament were consolidating their victory. On 5 May it was proposed

> That no Romish priest attend the queen but such as are foreigners, and such now attending her as are otherwise, may be removed, and that after the death or removal of such other servants as at present attend her, none be admitted in their rooms but such as are Protestants or foreigners.[62]

The barefaced repudiation of the marriage agreement shows how little parliament could be trusted when it came to matters affecting Catholics. It makes one wonder whether Howard had been right in maintaining that the appointment of a bishop would have caused no more than a passing fit of hysterics. In 1671 it might have been done without peril, opportunity had been missed and was not to come again for many years.

V

When Howard became grand almoner at the beginning of 1666 the number of English Dominicans had risen to 25 — 12 priests, 7 students, 2 novices and 4 laybrothers. Nine of these, including Howard and his inseparable laybrother Henry Peck, were working in England. Then came the lean years. Between 1666 and his return to Bornhem in 1675 only eight new subjects had joined, and as four had died there had been an increase of only four in nine years. There were now 29 — 17 priests, 5 students, 3 novices and still only 4 laybrothers. Eleven were in England. The little school had been reopened about 1670 but it was not till 1679 that it provided another vocation to the order.

The progress of the nuns had been equally slow though rather more uniform. In 1669 Howard had removed them from Vilvorde to Brussels, as being a safer refuge in times of war and unrest. At that time, after eight years, nine had been professed, one of whom had died. In March 1675, after fourteen years, thirteen had been professed, of whom three had died, so there was a community of ten.

Besides the problems raised by inadequate and almost static numbers there was a serious financial problem. Earlier foundations had received annual grants from the kings of Spain and the Holy See. Bornhem received neither and was dependent on the interest from Howard's endowment and such help as could be sent from England. Howard was able to save something out of his salary as almoner. There is a record of his sending £200 in 1669 and doubtless this was not his only gift.⁶³ But the general picture presented by the account books, such as they are, is one of stark poverty.

Such was the position in the spring of this jubilee year, 1675. Howard wrote to Cardinal Altieri on 13 April informing him of his arrival and of his intention to stay a considerable time in order to attend to the quiet of his own soul. He expressed his determination to travel to Rome before the end of the Holy Year.⁶⁴ He was full of hope that the storm in England would blow over like others before it. He explained to the internuncio that the reason why the king had himself issued this harsh proclamation was because otherwise the deed would have been done by parliament by an irrevocable law that would have been far worse for the Catholics. It was much easier for the king to connive at breaches of his own orders than breaches of statutory law.⁶⁵ Howard added that all this trouble had profoundly upset the queen; that she had refused to participate in any of the festivities of the court even when urged by the king.⁶⁶

He had been at Bornhem just two months when an event occurred that was to tear him away for ever. A special courier was crossing Europe as fast as horses could carry him, publishing wherever he passed that Philip Thomas Howard had been made a cardinal.

## Notes

1. Avvisi 40, f. 127.
2. *Bulstrode Papers*, London, 1897, 176.
3. Ibid. 178.
4. Agen. No.223.
5. AP, Sc.Rif.Anglia I, f. 720.
6. NF, 60, f. 236.
7. *Narrative of the visit of King Charles II to Norwich, 1671*, ed. Dawson Turner, Yarmouth, 1846, 18.
8. Arundel Castle, Autogr. Letters 1632–1723, no. 409.
9. NF, 60, ff. 539, 542, 592 etc.
10. Ibid. 536.
11. AP, Acta Cong. Gen. (t.41), f. 396.
12. Agen. No.228.
13. CRS, 38.
14. Agen. No.231.
15. Ibid. no. 209.

16 *Ibid.* no. 234.
17 *Ibid.* no. 236.
18 B, 8669, f. 199.
19 Agen. no. 231.
20 Brady, *Episcopal Succession*, III, 127.
21 AP, Lettere delle S. Cong. 1662, f. 10.
22 AAW, A34, no. 1.
23 *Ibid.* no. 4.
24 *Ibid.* no. 6.
25 *Ibid.* no. 8.
26 *Ibid.* no. 12.
27 NF, 61, f. 253.
28 AP, Anglia Misc. IV, 275.
29 *Ibid.* 277.
30 AAW, A34, no. 16.
31 *Ibid.* no. 19.
32 *Ibid.* no. 22.
33 *Ibid.* no. 23 (10 June).
34 *Ibid.* no. 25 (2 July).
35 *Ibid.* no. 27 (20 August).
36 SB, 1491, f. 13.
37 *Ibid.* f. 21.
38 *Ibid.* f. 22.
39 Accad. dei Lincei (Rome), Corsini 283, f. 12; Eng. trans. by R. Steele, London, 1715; Brady, *Episcopal Succession*, III, 130.
40 AP, Anglia, Misc. t.I, 285–93.
41 *Ibid.* 294.
42 AAW, A34, no. 37.
43 B, 8669, ff. 227, 231, 241.
44 Letter of Cardinal Howard, 16 March 1676 in *A collection of Letters ... relating to the horrid Popish plot, printed from the originals in the hands of G. Treby, Esq.,*, London, 1681.
45 B, 8624, no. 45.
46 AAW, A34.
47 *Ibid.*.
48 D. Jones, *The Life of James II, late King of England ... with A Supplement*, London, 1705, Supplement, 37–8.
49 *Ibid.*, 38.
50 NF, 63, f. 86.
51 AV, Epist. ad Prin. 71, f. 127.
52 NF, 63, f. 167.
53 Reg. 140, 129.
54 *Catalogue of Proclamations*, London, 1928, 69.
55 TNA, PC. 2/64, 372.

## *The Gathering Storm*

56 Arch of Eng. Province (London), *Annales*, 146.
57 AP, Cong. Part. 1677 (t.21), f. 218.
58 Treby, *Letters*, 90.
59 Med. 4241, 306.
60 B, 8661, f. 27; AV, Principi 102, f. 126.
61 SP.29/369, nos.41, 57.
62 Cal.SP Dom. 1675–6, 100, 109.
63 *Dominicana*, 138.
64 AV, Partic. 54, f. 90.
65 NF, 59, f. 410.
66 NF, 64, f. 139.

# 6

## *The Red Hat*

### I

THERE SEEMS TO BE NOWHERE IN ENGLISH a detailed account of the ceremonies that accompanied the making of a cardinal at the time when the splendour and external magnificence of the church was at its apogee. The ceremonial has not changed substantially in the course of centuries but, with the loss of the Papal States, the disappearance of so many Catholic kings, easier communications and less expansive and expensive fashions, it has been shorn of much of its former pageantry. It may therefore be of interest to follow in detail all the elaborate pomp and circumstances that lie behind the simple statement that Philip Howard was made a cardinal. Most of it would apply to any cardinal made at that time, but there was a situation affecting Howard in particular, that must first be explained.

France under Louis XIV was strongly Gallican. He claimed powers over the French church and clergy that, if allowed, would have made him practically the pope of France. No papal bull could be published in his domains until it had been scrutinized by his ministers and declared to be harmless to the liberties of the French church. The king nominated the bishops and was particularly solicitous to ensure that France got what he considered was its fair share of cardinal's hats. With so few great countries still faithful to the church, the pope had to be more than usually circumspect in such appointments and to avoid giving offence to France by nominating a Spaniard, and *vice versa*. This was one reason why so many Italians were chosen, for Italy was a congeries of small independent states, none of which could rival France or Spain or the Empire, and their cardinals did not upset the balance of power. At Rome Louis was represented by two brothers d'Estrées, one his ambassador and the other a cardinal. Their instructions were to impede the creation of any cardinal who might act independently of the French faction and interest. The quarrel between pope and king was to grow very much more intense, but already in 1675 it was a grave anxiety to the aged Clement X, and it was to cast a shadow over Howard's promotion. The unpleasantness began with a most objectionable breach of curial etiquette.

On 27 May the pope held a secret consistory (at which only cardinals were present) in the Quirinal and announced the names of the new members of the college. There were six in all.
1. Alessandro Crescenzi, a Roman and the pope's *maestro di camera*, aged 68
2. Galeazzo Marescotti, a Roman, nuncio in Madrid, aged 47
3. Bernardino Rocci, a Roman, the pope's majordomo, aged 48
4. Mario Alberizzi, a Neopolitan, nuncio in Vienna, aged 65
5. Fabrizio Spada, a Roman, nuncio in Paris, aged 32
6. Philip Howard, aged 45.

Thus the pope had avoided arousing the jealousy of the rival great powers by ignoring all three and creating five Italians and an Englishman. The announcement of the new creations was made in the following form.

> Venerable brethren,
> For the greater glory of God we have resolved to create cardinals of the Holy Roman Church. [Here the names were read out finishing with that of Philip Thomas Howard.] the virtues of all of whom are well known.

The pope here added a special word of commendation for Howard, praising his meritorious work for the church in England. Then came the question: '*Quid vobis videtur?* What is your opinion?'[1]

It had been the custom for well over a century for one or more of the cardinals at this point to rise and deliver a few well-chosen words on the felicity of the pope's choice and the merits of their new brethren. On this occasion, however, instead of the usual compliments, Cardinal Grimaldi, who was Vice-Protector of France and a partisan of the French, delivered a strong protest. No consideration, he said, had been given to the repeated requests of Louis XIV for a hat for the Bishop of Marseilles. He concluded by saying that it would be far better if cardinals were chosen by the votes of the college as was the custom in antiquity, and he then stormed out of the room.² Thereupon Cardinal D'Estrées arose to express his agreement with Grimaldi and made a thinly veiled attack on Cardinal Altieri:

> I agree absolutely with the most wise words of Cardinal Grimaldi, words so in keeping with the spirit of the church. I may add that it cannot possibly be unknown to Your Holiness that my king and master has been convinced for the past six months that through his ambassador Your Holiness had promised that this time the cardinals were to be created according to the wishes of kings. Indeed there are many letters to corroborate this. Hence Your Holiness might not and by right cannot proceed further without first deliberating with the most Christian king. To do otherwise would be a grave injury to this most puissant king, the eldest son of the church, who above all should be favoured by the Apostolic See both for his own merits and good deeds and those of his predecessors. Out of my duty to the church I cannot dissimulate before Your Holiness what great ills I foresee will follow. Your Holiness's kindness and sincerity, which are known to all the Christian world, render it impossible to suspect Your Holiness of such counsels as these, and compel us to attribute them solely to those who serve you, and serve you so ill. I go so far as to say that they serve you merely for their own ends and private ambitions, and in this matter too, whatever happens it must have evil consequences.³

The pope made no answer but brought the consistory to a speedy end by pronouncing the regular formula:

> By the authority of almighty God, the Holy apostles Peter and Paul and our own we create cardinals of the Holy Roman Church (N. N. etc.). *In nomine patris*, etc. Amen.

Only two of the new cardinals, Cresenzi and Rocci, were in Rome at this time. They were summoned by Cardinal Altieri, sumptuously banqueted with the élite of Rome, and then admitted to kiss the pope's foot. The pope himself invested them with the red biretta. That night and the following, the windows of the whole court and of all the relatives of the new cardinals blazed with myriads of candles and flares. Three great buildings, however, remained as black as night. They were the palaces of cardinals Grimaldi and d'Estrées, and that of the French ambassador.

On the same day as the consistory (27 May) a courier named Filipponi set out for Brussels with Cardinal Altieri's letter to Howard. He reached Paris in a mere matter of ten days. He delivered the news to the nuncio Spada, who was himself one of the new cardinals. It happened that there was in a convent there a young lady of fifteen, a niece of Howard, and she was the first of the family to hear the great news.[4] Filipponi proceeded to Brussels. The internuncio, Falconieri, had been recalled and his successor had not yet arrived. Claudio Agretti was in charge, with the title of minister-apostolic. The cardinal secretary instructed him to accompany the courier to Bornhem, but in a post-script left this decision to his own judgment.[5] He decided against it and Filipponi made his way to Bornhem alone. It was Trinity Sunday, 9 June. Filipponi looked at the shabby building and wondered if he had lost his way. Could this wretched-looking convent really be the end of his long journey? Enquiries confirmed that indeed it was. He asked for the prior and presented his credentials. The little community was summoned. Was this at long last the appointment of a vicar apostolic? When Altieri's letter was read to them they remained stunned and silent, and in the midst of a silence when seconds seemed like minutes Cardinal Howard burst into tears.[6]

Next morning Howard, uncertain whether to accept, went to Antwerp to consult the bishop, who was a Dominican and an old friend.[*] He was accompanied by a Flemish laybrother, Hyacinth Coomans, who wrote the first *annals* of Bornhem and is the authority for these details. They called first at the Dominican convent and Coomans could not contain himself. Soon the porter and the community knew as much as he. Then they visited the bishop. Asked by Howard whether he should accept, he led him without a word to his private chapel where both remained some time in prayer. Then the bishop arose and intoned the *Te Deum* and the fateful decision was made. Next day, 11 June, the news was known in London.[7] It was not, however, till 15 June that Howard wrote to the pope and to Cardinals Altieri and Barberini to express his

---

[*] Marius Ambrosius Capello. He is of some interest to the English-speaking world as his episcopal lineage can be traced to Louis Floride Berlaymont, Archbishop of Cambrai (1570–96) who ordained many of the early priests of Douai. (*Gallia Christiana, qua series omnia archiepiscoporum, episcoporum et abbatum Franciae vicinarumque ditionum ab origine ecclesiarum ad nostra tempora per quattor tomos deducitur, et probatur ex antiquae fidei manuscriptis Vaticani, regnum, principum tabulariis omnium Galliae cathedralium et abbatarium*, rev. Denys de Sainte-Marthe, 1725, III, cols, 55 and 242; V, 311, 12, 164, 135, 20).

## The Red Hat

homage and thanks.[8] By this time another special messenger had left Rome for Brussels. He was carrying the red biretta and a papal brief addressed to Our Beloved Son Philip Howard, Cardinal of Norfolk, and dated 2 June.[9] He began his journey on the 4th furnished with many letters of commendation.[10] At the same time others set out for Paris, Vienna and Madrid on similar missions.

These messengers were papal chamberlains. The one sent to Howard was Peter Dominic Joseph de Gereuse de Cabanes, a young man, a native of Avignon, who was seeing the world for the first time and thoroughly enjoying the experience. From almost every stopping-place he sent to Altieri a full account of his adventures. (He never mentioned any companions but presumably he was escorted by servants, for the roads were infested with bandits. It would not do to be robbed of that biretta!) He was able to arrange his journey so as to call on his relatives at Avignon. He reached Paris without mishap, and as Belgium was notoriously unsafe for travellers, from bands of unpaid Spanish troops, he entrusted his precious burden to the nuncio there for safer dispatch to Brussels. It was just as well. Between Paris and Brussels he was held up by these soldiers and had to purchase his freedom with a substantial bribe. Filipponi had done the journey in twelve days; Cabanes took forty-two, arriving on 16 July. The new internuncio, Tanara, who had arrived some days before, allowed him to repose himself for a couple of nights in his house and to do some sight-seeing, and on 18 July they went together to meet the new cardinal.[11]

The past month had been a busy time for Howard. He stayed with the bishop at Antwerp and sometimes at his villa at Lierre, though with frequent visits to Brussels and Bornhem. He had to make provision for his brethren and his nuns. There was also the financial problem of how to sustain his new dignity. Princes of the church were expected to keep up a certain standard of external splendour and in Howard's time the standard was extravagantly high. Most cardinals received a substantial salary from their own country, and the great powers were only too anxious to buy the adherence of other cardinals for their political ends. If red hats usually went to rich men it was because of this fear that poor men would be almost compelled to accept pensions which tied them to particular countries. From the start Howard set his face against accepting any such financial help. Altieri had sent him a bill of exchange for a thousand scudi (some £250), which he gratefully accepted, but a similar gift from Cosimo III he felt it his duty to return.[12] His own brother Henry came to his aid, offering the loan of £1000 (to be repaid on the cardinal's death) and such family silver as was still at Padua. He also agreed to pay all the expenses of his son Tom, who was to be one of the train for the journey to Rome.[13]

There was also a vast number of letters to be answered — letters of congratulation from cardinals, ambassadors and friends — and all in the high-flown prolix style of the times. Some of these had to be repeated, including one to the Master General, for the courier was robbed on the way and reached Rome empty-handed.[14]

A letter from the Chapter, written towards the end of June will serve as an example of the prevalent epistolary style:

> May it please your Eminence,
> Though the proceedings of our parts of the world concerning dissenters in religion (particularly the Roman Catholics, who are always aimed at above others) continue in the like threatening strain as formerly, so that we can promise ourselves no security at home, yet we cannot but infinitely rejoice at Your Eminence's happy promotion abroad, and humbly cast at your feet our Chapter's and clergy's hearty congratulations for the truly looking upon it as the greatest step towards the future good both of our clergy and nation that ever was gained since the days of Queen Mary, and hoping that the same providence which hath beyond our expectation bestowed upon us so eminent a patron will likewise give a blessing to those pious endeavours which we are well assured Your Eminence will use in order to the rectifying the decayed walls of Jerusalem. And as we have always experienced your gracious favours towards our Body, so shall Your Eminence, God willing, ever find us devoted to your service and obedient to your commands to the utmost of our power. The news of the severe bill against Catholics, which was twice read in the house of commons, as also of their differences with the lords concerning privileges, and their prorogation thereupon till the 13 of October next, we conceive will ere this be transmitted by other hands. Since which, here is nothing of novelty, neither can the wiser sort frame any conjecture what measures will be taken for the future. Therefore, supposing Your Eminence to be called upon by more weighty affairs, we will forbear to be tedious, and wishing Your Eminence many and happy years, beg leave to subscribe ourselves
> Your Eminence's most humble and most obedient servants.[15]

Howard replied asking how he could help them in Rome. They had — need it be said — only two requests:

> Whereas the Cardinal of Norfolk desired our instructions as to what we wished him to do for us at the great court, 'twas first resolved (in confirmation of what was formerly agreed to when Mr Holt was agent at Rome, and in testimony of our continued affection towards His Eminence) that we should first desire that His Eminence be made absolute ordinary of England, secondly that His Eminence would please to endeavour to get our Chapter confirmed; and these two requests were all that were judged convenient to be moved in the present circumstances: and unto these resolves that our brethren's votes in the country should be desired. (7 July 1675)[16]

They also sent a letter of gratitude to Clement X. It was subscribed: *Onuphrius Eliceus Decanus capituli ecclesiae Anglicanae sede vacante.*[17] Altieri nearly fell into the trap. The first draft of his reply is addressed 'to the canons and Chapter of the English church in London'.[18] But when the letter reached the Chapter it was carefully directed to 'Onuphry Ellis and the other priests of the English church'.[19]

The news of the promotion got a mixed reception in England. Queen Catherine was informed by a letter of Altieri of 27 May and later by a papal brief of 4 June and sent a gracious reply to both.[20] Henry Howard wrote his thanks via his brother to cardinals Altieri and Barberini.[21] Fearful of the consequences of corresponding with Rome he asked his brother to open any replies from these cardinals and send only the gist to his chaplain Fr Kemys.[22] Many waited anxiously for the repercussions of parliament. Would they use it as an excuse for further anti-Catholic legislation? The Venetian ambassador at Rome had written on 1 June:

> Many have misgivings that the promotion is ill-timed; indeed that it may produce evil effects against the Catholics of that country under present circumstances when parliament is in session and may conceive the suspicion that the royal house is cherishing intelligence with the court of Rome and is corresponding with it.

The Senate passed this information to their ambassador at London, expressing their satisfaction at the promotion and asking him to make their sentiments public.

In the meantime it will be worthwhile to observe what effect the news of this promotion will produce at that court, and we shall look to your diligence to supply us with the information about this.

This information was supplied in a reply of 15 July:

> While the Catholics have been consoled by this event, which they attribute to a pure miracle of almighty God, the heretics have been correspondingly cast down, although outwardly they affect not to esteem that dignity. When one of the leading peers of the realm, finding himself in company with other religionaries, asked who was responsible for Howard's promotion, the Duke of York replied: It was the rest of you by your persecutions. My lord retorted that he only regretted that the Roman Church could now boast of having one cardinal who was a true Catholic. I may add that while this most worthy individual was considered here as a good servant of God and esteemed for his high rank and the adherents of his house, he has not been credited with any ability, so there is not the smallest apprehension among the bishops or other religionaries of receiving any molestation from him. When the earl-marshal, brother of His Eminence, asked whether His Majesty would be graciously pleased to receive a letter from the cardinal, the king said that he would not only be pleased to see his letters but would answer them. Some Catholic lords want me to believe that the king would be willing for this individual or some other honest man to be appointed Bishop of England with full authority over the priests, friars and Jesuits.[23]

He goes on to complain of the need of such a superior. There are 600 priests living too freely and careless of their obligations. There are frequent scandals. They go about dressed in the height of fashion, wearing swords and periwigs, and are lavishly entertained. The king would like to see them brought to order or driven out.

On 17 June John Leyburn wrote in very much the same sense:

> This very day I have had letters from England signifying that the recent promotion of Fr Howard to the cardinalate has aroused a great deal of clamour. The avowed enemies of the church openly exclaim against it; others judge it according to their predispositions; some still doubt whether it be true because neither the king nor the queen have been notified of it. Meanwhile with the more dutiful of the church's sons I give a thousand thanks to God for inspiring His Holiness with this wisdom and for granting such a consolation to the afflicted church in England.[24]

Relatives and friends were now arriving in Belgium for the formal ceremony of giving the new cardinal the red biretta. Viscount Stafford came with his son John; Henry Howard's son Thomas with Fr Joseph Kemys, OP, who had been chaplain to Howard's mother till her death in the previous year and was now chaplain to her son Henry; and John Leyburn from Douai. The imposition of the biretta could be performed either by the head of the state of by the principal prelate of the country. Both the governor (the Duke of Villanova) and the Archbishop of Malines sought the honour, and Howard, unable to choose one without offending the other, gave it to his friend the Bishop of Antwerp.[25] The ceremony took place in the cathedral there on Sunday 21 July after the High Mass and closed with a solemn *Te Deum*. For the occasion Antwerp produced the first and the worst of the many engravings that are supposed to be his likeness.[26]

On 5 July Leyburn had written to Barberini for permission to resign his post as president of Douai so that he could accompany Howard to Rome and stay there as his auditor.[27] Without waiting for an answer he wrote at the same time to the Chapter desiring them to suggest a successor. At a consult on 7 July they chose three names,[28] and it is significant that the first on their list, Francis Gage, was duly appointed by the cardinal protector. The Chapter was worth listening to, even if it did not exist. Gage proved an excellent choice.

Howard had intended to be in Rome by the middle of November, but the possibility of carrying out a delicate diplomatic mission caused a delay. Cardinal Altieri suggested that on his way to Rome Howard should seek an interview with Louis XIV and try to lessen the tension between that king and the Holy See—tension that had been increased by the pope's action in ignoring the king's demand for more French cardinals. Howard wrote a letter to Louis and sent it to Patrick Conn. Conn's instructions were to sound the French ministers on the likelihood of the king agreeing to receive a letter from the cardinal. If there was danger of a definite refusal the letter was not to be presented. It was soon made clear that the king would refuse to receive either the letter or Howard himself.[29] Howard then enlisted the support of Charles II, Queen Catherine and the Duke and Duchess of York. These represented to the French ambassador in London that it would be a disgrace for the most Christian king to refuse to receive a prince of the church, especially one who had been shown all due honour by the heretic King of England; that it would be an affront to England to repulse a member of the first family in the land, and one who came with the recommendation of the English King.[30] But Louis was determined to have nothing whatever to do with any of the newly created cardinals. He had refused to show any mark of honour to Cardinal Spada, the nuncio at his own court, and he resisted the pressure of the English royal family to grant an audience to Howard. He said that if Howard would accept a pension from France he would then receive him. Otherwise he would grant him a passport to cross his territory and that was all.[31] Howard had no intention of accepting a pension that would tie him to France, and thus the negotiations came to naught. The only effect was to delay his departure for Rome.

Throughout the summer Howard was fully occupied with the affairs of his two foundations and the preparations for his journey. He still stayed mostly with the Bishop of Antwerp, but was often in Brussels incognito, when he invariably stayed with the nuns. He entrusted to them some of his silver, which they have zealously guarded to this day. He had moved them from Vilvorde to Brussels for their greater security in time of war, and now he made a similar provision for his brethren at Bornhem. On 3 August he purchased two contiguous houses in Antwerp 'sur la plaine vulgairement nomee d'Ysere Waegh' one called 'la Poielle d'Or' and the other 'le St Beaques'. It was not, however, till 1682 that he petitioned the King of Spain for amortization. In his petition[32] he explains that the religious had often been compelled by the upheavals of war to vacate Bornhem and seek safety in Antwerp, the nearest fortified city. There appears to be no other reference to these houses or to any temporary flight from Bornhem.

On 24 August he went to Bornhem to make a Retreat, returning to Brussels on 7 September. Owing to the delays already mentioned it was not until 12 October that he finally left Brussels. A hurried visit was made to Bornhem, which he was destined never to see again, and then he set out for Rome.

II

There were several recognized routes to Rome, but none of them was easy. The route through Germany was longer and not without its danger in those days of constant unrest. The direct route was inevitably through France, which Howard, after the rebuff from Louis XIV, would have preferred to avoid. There was then no easy route across the Alps, and Howard decided to try to avoid them. On 17 August he wrote to Cardinal Altieri asking if it would be possible for two papal galleys to wait on him at Marseilles and conduct him to Leghorn or Civita Vecchia.[33] On the same day he also wrote to his old friend Cosimo III, Grand Duke of Tuscany for the like favour.[34] Altieri replied, regretting that the only available galleys were already bespoke to carry the new nuncio to Spain and to return with Marescotti, one of the six new cardinals. He suggested that Howard might be able to arrange to join these galleys at Marseilles.[35] Marescotti was quite agreeable, but when Howard realized that he would be delayed by his negotiations with Louis XIV he advised Marescotti to proceed without him direct to Civita Vecchia.[36] Cosimo also regretted that he could not lend his galleys to the cardinal without offending other important people whose requests he had already refused.[37] There was thus no option but to prepare to do the whole journey by land.

From Brussels the party travelled to Lille, arriving on 16 October. The new cardinal was welcomed with a salvo of guns.[38] After a stay of three of four days they moved on to Douai. Here they were honourably entertained by the English Benedictines at St Gregory's. A student recited a very long *Carmen Panegyricum* written by a recent convert minister, Richard Reeve, who had just joined them. It was afterwards printed.[39] The visit was also commemorated by the production of another engraving purporting to be his likeness. He also visited the English College at Douai but no account survives.

The next stop of which there is any mention was Paris. Owing to the attitude of the king, Howard remained incognito. He stayed nearly three weeks in a small Dominican priory at Gonesse, some ten miles to the north, paying several visits to the nunciature.[40] The nuncio, the new Cardinal Spada, had already left for Rome. It was not until 14 November that the party, now increased to thirty, set out again,[41] reaching Lyons on the following evening.[42] On 19 November, when they were on the point of continuing their journey, Howard wrote to Cosimo to say that the republic of Genoa had kindly offered him a galley as far as Leghorn, where he would await the grand duke's commands.[43] Thence they travelled, presumably through the Mt Cenis pass, to Turin, arriving on the

23rd. In order to avoid the delay that would be caused by a public reception, the party stayed quietly at the Carthusian monastery of S. Giovanni Moriano outside the city.[44] On 27 November Howard informed Cosimo that he had been dissuaded from attempting the sea-passage owing to its uncertainty at that season of the year, and instead was travelling via Ferrara. He regretted that this change of plan would deprive him of all chance of visiting Florence and paying his respects to its sovereign.[45] Soon they were again on the move, but now they left their carriages and embarked for Piacenza on the wide waters of the river Po.[46]

Travel in those days involved so many difficulties and hazards that it was not possible to predict the day of arrival at any particular place, or even the precise route to be taken. Although Howard wrote to Altieri from every stopping-place, there still remained some doubt as to where he would turn up next. The cardinal secretary wrote repeatedly to the cardinal legates at Bologna and Ferrara, the nuncio at Florence and even to officials as far east as Ravenna and Urbino, warning them of the possible arrival of the new cardinal, and ordering them in the name of His Holiness to receive him with all the marks of honour due to his rank. These officials sent their couriers scouring the countryside for news of the present whereabouts of Howard and his train, and there were frequent interchanges of letters with each other and with Rome, all concerned with their anxiety to carry out the pope's commands. Sometimes rumour sped ahead of the news. Five English horsemen arrived at Bologna on 4 December, and one of them, who said he was a Benedictine, asked to say Mass at the shrine of St Dominic. The cardinal legate was very suspicious and thought this might be Howard himself, travelling incognito, but the prior of S. Domenico assured him that he knew Howard quite well, and that this was not he.[47]

At Piacenza there were fresh carriages and horses awaiting the cardinal, sent by the Duke of Parma, and he continued their journey through Parma to the borders of the papal states at Bologna, arriving there on 6 December. The legate of Bologna reported that Howard had six gentlemen at his table, four at a second table and five or six postillions.[48] Evidently some of the original servants had returned to France with the carriages. At Bologna and probably at every great city Howard received a civic welcome. The cardinal legate and the cardinal archbishop with all the nobility of Bologna awaited him beyond the city walls and conducted him in state, with a long cortege of carriages-and-six, to the legatine palace where he was magnificently lodged and banqueted. Presumably he visited the Dominicans but the fact is not recorded. It was expected that he would continue along the easier road through Imola, Faenza and Forli, and elaborate preparations were made for his reception. Cosimo, however, would not lightly release him from his long-standing promise. He sent to Bologna a special litter for his use, and on Saturday 7 December the party, accompanied some of the way by the two cardinals of Bologna and a great concourse of grandees, took the route over the Apennines and out of the papal states into Tuscany.[49]

It was very late on Monday night when they reached Florence, but even so the grand duke and a great gathering of the nobility were waiting outside the city walls to escort them, with a brave display of torches to the ducal palace.[50] The Palazzo Medici had been abandoned by the family some years before and Cosimo was now living in the Palazzo Pitti, with its celebrated terraced garden of Boboli, situated beyond the Ponte Vecchio. It was here that Howard and his train were sumptuously entertained for four days. Writing to his minister in London on 10 December Cosimo reports the cardinal's arrival and says he is in excellent health, but gives no other particulars.[51] From another source we know that he was entertained by the Dominicans with a disputation held in his honour, but whether at S. Maria Novella or S. Marco is not stated.[52] He was shown all the sights of Florence and himself gave a banquet to fourteen Florentines who he had known in Flanders and England. Very early on the morning of 13 December they set out for Siena, with a parting gift of six beautiful horses, and in carriages also provided by Cosimo.[53]

Meanwhile the other new cardinals, with similar ceremonies and entertainment were slowly converging on the eternal city. Cardinal Spada, the nuncio from Paris, was the first to arrive, reaching the outskirts of Rome on 30 October.[54] Here he remained incognito, outside the city walls, awaiting the arrival of his confreres. Cardinal Alberizzi, the nuncio from Vienna reached Bologna one day ahead of Howard. But of Cardinal Marescotti, the nuncio from Madrid who was coming by sea, there was no sign and no news. The papal galleys had in fact been chased by pirates and driven miles off their course.[55] It was just as well that Howard had decided not to travel that way, for Marescotti did not reach Rome till after the end of the Holy Year.

Howard reached the outskirts of Rome on 16 December and that day assembled with the other three new cardinals and their followers without the Flaminian Gate—the northern gateway into Rome, perhaps better known as the Porta del Popolo. Cardinal Altieri sent his own coach-and-six for the use of the cardinals, who led a cavalcade of eighty coaches through the cheering crowds to the Quirinal. Here they changed their travelling garb, put on the rich cardinals' robes, and were introduced to kiss the pope's foot and hand. Then they rose to receive the kiss of peace, and to render their thanks to His Holiness. Next they paid the customary ceremonial visits to the pope's relatives.

On Thursday morning, 19 December, the pope held a public consistory at the Quirinal when the three new cardinals were admitted to the embrace, and after retiring to the chapel to take the usual oath, returned to the pope's presence and received the red hat. There was a splendid banquet provided by Cardinal Altieri and attended by the two other new cardinals who had already received the hat, as well as by the nobility of Rome. In the afternoon they crossed Rome with a great cortège to visit St Peter's. That night Rome was gay with illuminations at all the windows of its innumerable palaces, and once again the palaces of the French ambassador and the two protesting cardinals remained in utter darkness.

On Christmas Eve came the ceremony of the closing of the Holy Door and on 16 January 1676 Cardinal Marescotti, having escaped the pirates, reached Rome. He received his red hat on 6 February and was banqueted by the other five cardinals of the same creation.[56]

On 31 July Tommaso Bianchi had been granted permission to go to London for his domestic affairs.[57] He probably carried a papal brief of 30 July to Queen Catherine acknowledging her letter of thanks for Howard's promotion.[58] It was expected that Bianchi and Howard would meet somewhere on their routes,[59] but whether they did so it is not recorded. Another English Dominican, Lewis Thursby, who was studying at Naples, was granted permission on 21 December to go to Rome in order to pay his respects to the Cardinal of Norfolk.[60]

Cardinal Howard had been invited to make his home in the great Dominican convent of the Minerva. Patrick Conn was not at all enthusiastic. He wrote to Cardinal Barberini on 7 September:

## The Red Hat

The Master General of St Dominic has invited him to lodge in the Minerva. I cannot help thinking that this lodging would be decorated after the fashion of religious, that is to say, white walls and no furniture. Your Eminence could remedy this by inviting him to avail himself of more fitting apartments in your most sumptuous palace at Quatro Fontane.[61]

This was the palace that had been chosen as his prison thirty years before, when as a sorely tried novice he had first been summoned to Rome. Eventually there was a compromise. Howard took up his abode at the Minerva, and Barberini provided rich tapestries to hide the whitewashed walls that offended Conn.[62] Thus he was able to combine the simplicity of the friar with the magnificence of a prince of the Church.

## Notes

1. AV, Consist. Acta Misc. 74, f. 355.
2. BV, Vat. Lat. 12339, f. 213.
3. C. Gérin, *Louis XIV et la Saint-Siège*, Paris, 1894, II, 597.
4. Nunz.Fr., 153, f. 325.
5. NF, XX, 145, f. 364.
6. *Life*, 155.
7. HMC, Laing MSS, I, 402.
8. AV, Cardinali, ff. 178–82.
9. SB, 1568, f. 97.
10. AV, Epist. ad Prin. 71, ff. 261–5.
11. AV, Particolari 54, ff. 178, 193, 209, 224.
12. Palmer, *Life*, 157.
13. M. A. Tierney, *History and Antiquities of the Castle and Town of Arundel*, London, 1834, II, 530.
14. Reg. 140, 166.
15. AAW, A34, no. 94 (undated draft).
16. OB, Orders of Consults 1667–93, 144.
17. AAW, A34, no. 92 (undated draft).
18. AP, Lettere delle S. Cong. 1675 (t.64), f. 79.
19. AAW, A34, no. 93.
20. AV, Epist. ad Princ. 71, ff. 261, 291; AV, Princ. 101, ff. 204–5, 327–8; *Dominicana*, 68.
21. AV, Princ. 101, f. 401.
22. Tierney, *History and Antiquities*, II, 530.
23. Cal.SP Venice, XXXVIII, 411, 429.
24. B 8623, f. 144.

25. AV, Particolari 54, f. 235.
26. BL, King's 179, ff. 256 et seq.
27. B, 8623, f. 146.
28. OB, Orders of Consults 1667–93, 144.
29. Nunz. Diverse 98, f. 179; NF, 59, f. 426; Cal SP Venice, XXXVIII, 457.
30. AV, Cardinali, 39, ff. 273, 429.
31. NF, 59, f. 431; Cal SP Venice, XXXVIII, 462.
32. Sim. Secretarías Provinciales, log.2497.
33. AV, Cardinali 39, f. 254.
34. Med. 3827 (17 Aug.).
35. NF, 45, f. 388.
36. AV, Cardinali 39, f. 291.
37. Med. 3827 (17 Aug.).
38. NF, 64, f. 479.
39. A. Wood, *Athenae Oxoniensis*, 3rd edn (1820), IV, col.387.
40. AV, Cardinali 39, f. 354.
41. AV, Legazione di Bologna, 53, f. 377.
42. AV, Cardinali 39, f. 378.
43. Med. 3827 (19 Nov.).
44. AV, Leg. di Bologna, 53, f. 375.
45. Med. 3827 (27 Nov.)
46. AV, Cardinali 39, f. 385.
47. AV, Leg. di Bologna, 53, f. 375.
48. *Ibid.* f. 382.
49. *Ibid.*
50. Nunz. Firenze, 62, ff. 553–5.
51. Med. 4241, f. 383.
52. Nunz. Firenze, 62, f. 555.
53. *Ibid.* f. 578.
54. AV, Leg. di Bologna, 53, f. 336.
55. Avvisi 118, f. 362.
56. *Ibid.* ff. 368, 384, 409.
57. Reg. 139, f. 51.
58. AV, Epist. ad Princ. 71, f. 291.
59. Reg. 139, f. 87.
60. Reg. 148, f. 377.
61. B, 8669, f. 245.
62. SP. 101/85 (21 Dec.).

1. Engraving of Cardinal Howard

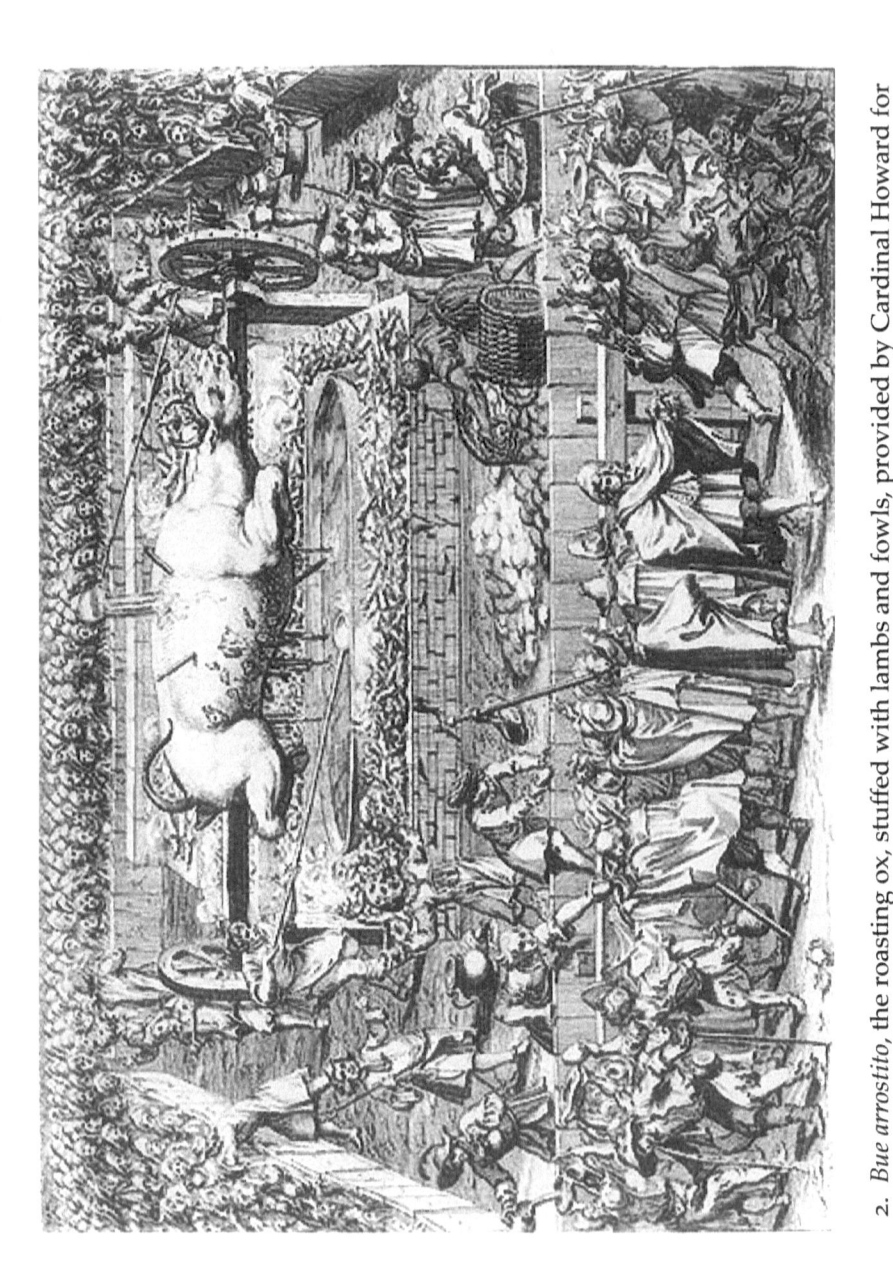

2. *Bue arrostito*, the roasting ox, stuffed with lambs and fowls, provided by Cardinal Howard for the people of Rome to celebrate the birth of a son to James II and Mary of Modena in 1688

3. The Church and Convent of Santa Sabina, Rome

4. Martyrs' Chapel, Venerable English College, Rome, constructed during the tenure of Cardinal Howard as the College's Cardinal Protector.

# 7

## Cardinal in Curia

### I

AFTER RECEIVING THE RED HAT, two more ceremonies remained before the new cardinal was fully fledged. On Monday 24 February, in a secret consistory held in the Quirinal the four newly arrived cardinals attended the brief function of the ceremonial closing of their mouths. The pope pronounced the traditional formula:

> We close your mouths so that you are unable to utter your opinion in consistories, congregations or other cardinalitial functions.

A month later, on 23 March, a similar ceremony took place when the pope opened their mouths and thereby gave them full powers to speak and to vote. On this occasion they received their titular churches, Howard's being that of St Cecilia. Marescotti was at the same time appointed legate at Ferrara. They then kissed the pope's foot and hand and were received to the formal kiss of peace.[1]

Two days later Howard fulfilled what may be considered his first public engagement in Rome. For more than two centuries the Minerva had been the scene of an annual event that always drew a crowd. In 1460 the Dominican Cardinal Torquemada (uncle of the inquisitor) had established there a sodality known as the *Annunziata*, and built the beautiful chapel that still bears that name. The object of the sodality, composed of two hundred Roman citizens, was to provide dowries for girls who were too poor to marry or to enter a convent. Pope Pius V raised it to the status of an archconfraternity, generously endowed it, and established what was known as a papal *capella*, or an occasion when the whole college of cardinals was invited to participate. The pope himself came in cavalcade with most of the cardinals. There was High Mass followed by the bestowing of the very generous dowries on some four hundred girls, who came in procession in bridal dresses. The archconfraternity and its work still continues, but since the destruction of the papal states the *capella* and the presence of the pope have ceased. The feast-day of the Annunziata is the 25 March, which in 1676 was the Wednesday in Passion week. There was an industrious master of ceremonies, who kept a diary in which he delighted to record any breach of rubrics. The aged pontiff was beyond riding and was drawn in a litter from the Quirinal to the Minerva, at the door of which all the cardinals were waiting, wearing red copes over their scarlet robes. Cardinal Cybo, the senior cardinal present, received the pope with incense and holy water and they proceeded to the altar of St Dominic where the Blessed Sacrament was exposed. Thence to the sacristy where the pope vested, and wearing a white cope and tiara he was carried on the *sedia gestatoria* to the high altar. The Mass was usually sung by the cardinal who had the Minerva as his titular church, but this year the honour was given to Cardinal Howard. After Mass the dowries were distributed by Cardinal Barberini, who was protector of the archconfraternity, and the ceremony finished by the pope receiving the various officials. Then the pope returned to the Quirinal followed by a stream of cardinals of his own creation.[2]

It was not long before Howard was given his share in the responsibilities that went with the honour of the cardinalate. He was appointed a member of the congregation of Propaganda and attended his first meeting on 22 April.[3] He was also put on the congregation of Rites, and attended his first meeting on 9 May, when fifteen cardinals were present. Their principal business was to consider the canonization of St John of God.[4]

His elder brother Henry, Earl of Norwich had advised Philip to

> make haste to be near his great patron, for if he do not establish him in his lifetime, the next officer [pope] which succeeds in his place certainly will never take half, nor no part of the proportion, of that care of him as this will do: and now or never, in his lifetime, must he fish, after which all that interest dies.[5]

Apart from placing him on the two congregations Clement X does not appear to have done anything to promote Howard's interests or to alleviate his poverty. Cardinals belonging to Catholic countries were largely financed by their sovereigns, and Howard felt

## Cardinal in Curia

strongly that, albeit England was not a Catholic county, Charles II should do something to support an English cardinal.

> Is it not a shame for them all to thrust me totally on the pope and Rome, who have already *motu proprio* done so much, beyond all imaginable expectation? Nay, is it not worse that the king or others should endeavour to thrust me on France, Spain or the Emperor, by most of which I have several years since had great offers, but would never bite at, and since made cardinal, more powerful offers. But if the king and the rest judge me not worthy of my own master's livery, I will rather appear so naked as yet to cover the shame of my father (or fatherland) with my own simple coat, rather than embroider it with another's livery, to appear like a bastard to my ungrateful country.

He goes on to suggest that the king should 'grant a barony unto such a one whom I may name ... for which I may lawfully get a pretty sum of money.'[6] It does not appear that he ever received any financial help from England, either by the common practice of selling honours or in any other way. He retained the office of grand almoner with its salary of £500 a year, but, as we shall see, there was the greatest difficulty in obtaining any payment even of this sum. He received generous gifts from Cardinals Altieri and Barberini, but little in the form of a permanent income. What was to happen when Clement X died and Altieri, who was so unpopular with the strong French faction, lost his dominating position of pope's nephew?

There was no doubt about the power and the hostility of Cardinal d'Estrées and his followers. They still kept up their opposition to the pope and to all his works and were waiting impatiently for his death. The cardinals of his last creation were sent to Coventry. This made life unpleasant enough. There were great social and religious functions that all the cardinals felt it their duty to attend, and the rival parties would not even exchange ordinary civilities. They eyed each other like two school teams forced to use the same changing room. As early as February 1676 Howard writes:

> Although the French ambassador nor his brother the cardinal do neither receive or give any visit or converse with any of the cardinals of the last promotion, yet the said cardinal hath sent many excuses and compliments to me how sorry he is that he cannot at present visit and confer with me, as he doth mightily desire. And I have as often sent the like compliments to him.

> And finally the other night at a great assembly at the Queen of Sweden (who often in public speaks mighty well of England and our nation) Her Majesty spoke to me *ex abrupto* in French (although she used always before in Italian) and presently called on the Cardinal d'Estrées (who was there with fifteen cardinals more) to hear how well I spoke French (as she said) better than herself. And he approaching to Her Majesty and me, who were alone talking, could not well but speak to us both, which when he did to me I answered accordingly. And presently the queen left us alone, so that I then began to talk to him of the business you know, of which he said much, and I answered as much, hoping that after the fury will be past, these preliminaries may conduce to a good effect.[7]

Howard was not destined to enjoy for much longer the patronage of Clement X. In spite of his eighty-six years the pope worked almost to the last. It was only in June 1676 that his doctors felt any anxiety, and he continued to give audiences up to the middle of July. Then on the 22 July the cardinals were summoned to his bedside, and he died the same afternoon. He bequeathed to every cardinal a book from his library. Howard received *L'Ateismo schernito, coll' esempio d'Arrigo Ottavo* (Atheism scorned, with the example of Henry VIII), a book I have not been able to identify.[8]

For nine days the cardinals performed the obsequies of Clement X, and on the tenth day, as the law then demanded, they entered into the conclave to elect the successor.

The elaborate procedure for the election of a pope has not changed substantially in the last thousand years, though it had received modifications by Howard's time, and it has been further modified since. The essential feature, however, has always remained. The cardinals were solemnly led in procession into the Vatican, the doors were locked, and they remained cut off from the outside world till one of their number received the two-thirds majority required for an election. The medieval regulation whereby they had to live and sleep in common had long been abolished and each cardinal had a separate cell. Another medieval regulation concerning meals had also been relaxed. In order to expedite their business it had formerly been the rule that after five days their refreshment was reduced to one course, and after a further five days, to bread and water. Now they were allowed two meals a day, each of two courses, which were brought from their own palaces by the *dapiferi* in gaily decorated carriages—a custom that continued till the secularization of Rome in 1870. However long the conclave lasted they were not allowed to receive or send letters, or to see visitors in private. If they left the conclave (except for illness, with the doctor's certificate) they could not return. Every precaution was taken, at least in theory, to prevent political pressure from without. Each cardinal was allowed to take a secretary with him into the conclave, and it would appear that Howard took John Leyburn. At all events Leyburn's letters to Edward Coleman cease during this period, and in their place are letters signed 'W. L.', which are evidently the initials of William Leslie, the Scots priest who had served so long as Howard's agent in Rome.

In practice, the isolation of the cardinals was by no means complete. They seem to have both received and written letters. Thus Leslie writes on 5 September, when the conclave was more than a month old:

> Cardinal Norfolk hath received letters from the king and the duke enjoining his adherence with France, which he answereth by this post; that to the duke, the secretary of the duchess will see. I refer to other particulars to what I have writ unto my Lord Arundel, and Cardinal Norfolk to Mr Hays. Cardinal Norfolk will not accept the offer from France of Albi, dreading the dependence which would follow. A like offer from Spain hath been refused. Many are of opinion the conclave will last long, especially if the French persist in their animosity against Altieri, who will be able in spite of them to hinder the election of any whom they would endeavour to have chosen without his concurrence. It would be a great service to the Church if this quarrel (which seems to have no deep bottom) were taken up. The present conjuncture seems most proper for it, and Cardinal Norfolk might be a proper instrument. I hear he hath his health well in the conclave, and gains much in the opinion of his brethren.[9]

Howard's reply to King Charles (who would not support him) ordering him to vote with the French cardinals (who would not speak to him) is unfortunately not extant.

The sacred college at the death of Clement X numbered sixty-seven: three French, three German, two Spanish, one English and no less than fifty-eight Italians. Forty-four were in Rome when the conclave began on 1 August. Voting began on 3 August. There were two scrutinies a day, morning and evening, but after each there was what was known as the *accessus*. Without a second scrutiny any cardinal could add his vote for a cardinal who had been voted for in the last scrutiny. This was really equivalent to four scrutinies a day, as is now the rule. The early voting, while they awaited the arrival of the rest of the cardinals, was of an exploratory character. In the very first scrutiny, Howard got three votes, with one *accessus*; but it was not very serious. Howard was associated with a body of cardinals who were determined to vote for the best candidate regardless of political affiliations, and who earned the name of *zelanti*. It was an open secret that their candidate was Benedetto Odescalchi, who had a reputation for holiness of life and great personal austerity. There were two obstacles to his election. First, he himself was most reluctant, and it was feared that he would refuse. Secondly there was the powerful opposition of Louis XIV. Custom, for more than a century, had accorded the great Catholic powers a right of veto, or exclusion of a candidate obnoxious to them, and it was feared that Louis would exercise this power against any nominee of Cardinal Altieri. So for the time being; they refrained from voting for Odescalchi and gave their votes to almost anybody else.

The French cardinals entered the conclave on 30 August and the struggle began. Next morning they let it be known that they would not visit the six new cardinals nor receive visits from them, and that this was the command of their king. The most objectionable of them was Cardinal de Bouillon, whose 'disedifying' life shocked even the court of Louis XIV. The sequel is best told in a report sent to the King of Spain by Cardinal Portocarrero on 5 September.

> The six cardinals of the last promotion sought to visit the French cardinals who had recently entered the conclave, but under various pretexts they were not admitted.
>
> The day before yesterday the English Cardinal Norfolk, either piqued by this rebuff and the lack of good manners in the French, or else egged on by Cardinal Altieri and his party, sent a message to Cardinal Bouillon that, as one of the new cardinals, he would like to call on him, adding that he had already met him in Paris. He would be glad to be informed whether or no Bouillon would receive him. Bouillon sent a reply couched in vague and ambiguous terms declining the visit. Shortly afterwards the two of them met near Howard's cell and Howard asked Bouillon very forcibly why he refused to receive him; he wanted to know if he had been ordered to do so by the king, or was it for particular motives of his own? If the latter, they

could hardly be so weighty that they could or should prevent a meeting. If the former, then he would write to the King and Queen of England and the Duke of York complaining of this order of the King of France, convinced as he was that his king would defend the honour and reputation of his own subjects; that he was not a subject of the King of France nor in any way dependent on him; that Louis having granted him a passport recognizing him as a cardinal when he passed through France to Rome, it was very strange that he would not recognize him as a cardinal in Rome; that the French cardinals visited the Spanish cardinals and received them in return in spite of the fact that the two countries were at war, while the kings of France and England were at peace and on the best of terms. He concluded with the remark that his king was just as great a prince as the French King. Then they both fell to furious abuse, Bouillon calling the English 'Heretics', and Norfolk calling the French Huguenots.

A little later the two met in the chapel of the scrutinies and started again, till Bouillon pretended he was indisposed, stormed out of the room and went to his cell to confer with his companions. This fracas has truly set tongues wagging through the whole conclave causing no small anxiety to the sacred college.[10]

There is a more detailed account of this first interview, this time from the standpoint of a Frenchman. It would appear that the meeting took place as they emerged from the morning scrutiny and that it was witnessed by most of the cardinals. Howard opened the attack, speaking in Latin.

> Bouillon (abstractedly): Plait-il?
> Howard continued in Latin.
> B. (in French): Monseigneur cardinal, I understand little enough Latin when it *is* Latin; but when it's disguised as English—*mufui*, I just don't recognize it at all.
> Howard hereupon changed to French, which he spoke fluently though with an English accent:
> H. Monseigneur, this is not the way to behave to colleagues and equals; men who have travelled so far to settle a matter so serious.
> B. Serious, did you say? Don't I know it.
> H. And therefore it seems to me that it's most unbecoming that you hold yourselves aloof and show so little esteem for the rest.
> B. That's a matter of opinion.
> H. I lived in the midst of heretics. What are they going to say?
> B. You can write and let us know, if that will amuse you.
> H. (exasperated by the other's levity, and speaking heatedly):

What the heretics will say is that the Holy Ghost can't have any place in the election of a pope when there's all this rowing and hatred.

B. Oh well, Monseigneur, if that's all the English say, you must agree they're very naïve or very good children.

H. But your king, Monseigneur, your king must surely feel concerned for the dignity of our solemn action in the service of God and the whole church.

B. Hum, I very much fear, Monseigneur, that His Majesty Louis XIV is far more concerned with his wars and his amours with de Montespan than with the conclave. However, if it beguiles you to think that he cares, where do we go from there?

H. Monseigneur, I don't speak for myself in this matter. I belong to a House where the insults you offer your colleagues just don't penetrate. But I'm convinced that His Majesty Louis XIV never ordered you to treat the College like this.

B. You really think so, Monseigneur?

H. I'm convinced of it by the worthy treatment I myself received from His Majesty on my way through Paris. And I beg Your Eminence to ponder well on the scandal you're causing by going on in this unseemly way.

B. (who up till now had been casual and half-amused, suddenly becoming fierce): I'd like you to know first of all Monseigneur, that you can keep your sermonizing to yourself. I don't need advice from you or anyone else on how to behave, I know what I'm doing, and what I'm doing is my duty. Secondly I'm surprised, Monseigneur, that you know the orders of my king better than I do. I can't find words to express my astonishment that you should imagine you are better informed of the secrets of the King of France than I and my colleagues who heard them from his own lips; and that you have the cheek to tell us how to carry them out. So keep your impudent suggestions to yourself. They're not of the slightest interest to us.[11]

Then, nose in air and with a rustle of scarlet, the ruffled eminence of France sailed past. There was a murmur of protest and disgust from the other cardinals but none spoke a word. It was a bad augury for a speedy and peaceful election.

The French candidate was Cardinal Grimaldi, who entered the conclave on 7 September bringing the number to sixty-two. He received a total of seven votes in the second scrutiny that afternoon, and again seven the following morning. It was soon clear that he could never get a two-thirds majority. Cardinal d'Estrées had written on 22 August for Louis's consent to the election of

Odescalchi. His letter alone might have been ineffective, but with it went letters from Cardinals Chigi and Rospigliosi informing the king that Altieri's sponsoring of Odescalchi was a mere pretence in order to hide his intention of springing his real candidate on the college at the psychologically opportune moment. This was enough. Louis gave his consent to the election of Odescalchi. Never was king more successfully hoodwinked. Not only was Odescalchi the true candidate of Altieri, but he was to prove an energetic and redoubtable antagonist to Louis's Gallicanism. The king's letter of approval was laid before the cardinals on 20 September. By now there were sixty-three. That evening there was a memorable scene. After supper Odescalchi retired to the private chapel; soon all the cardinals followed and kissed his hands. It was virtually an election by acclamation and he could no longer hold out. In the scrutiny held the following morning he received twenty votes and immediately after there were forty-two *accessi*. Thus Odescalchi became Innocent XI by the unanimous vote of the brethren. The conclave had lasted fifty days. The pope's coronation took place on Sunday 4 October. Cardinal Howard had a small part to play. It was the privilege of the three most recent cardinal priests to wait upon His Holiness in the Sistine chapel, where he vested, and after the kiss of peace to escort him to St Peter's where the solemn coronation was performed by the cardinal deacon.[12]

One event took place during the conclave that Howard would not willingly have missed. His earliest Dominican friend, John Baptist Hacket, to whom he owed so much, died on 23 August and was buried in the common vault of the brethren before the altar of St Dominic in the Minerva.[13] Thus these two men who had met so strangely at Milan were destined to be buried in the same church in Rome, the older having lived to see his dream come true after a lapse of thirty years.

Although Howard had been given his titular church of St Cecilia in March 1676 it was not until the feast day of that saint (22 November), which this year fell on a Sunday, that he took possession. There is a long account by the master of ceremonies, almost entirely concerned with the niceties of the rubrics, when the celebrant happens to be a bishop. It was a very wet day and only seven of the many prelates invited graced the occasion. Howard presided at the High Mass celebrated by an archbishop, and afterwards he was told by the master of ceremonies that if on a future occasion he wished to exercise his jurisdiction, bless the incense and give the blessing at the end of Mass, he should take care that the celebrant was not in episcopal orders.[14]

The new pope was by nature austere and economical, and as he found an exhausted treasury it was just as well. What money he could find was wanted for the war against the Turks, who were threatening to overrun eastern Europe. It was not to be expected that he would provide adequate pensions for the poorer cardinals, and Howard, who was perhaps the poorest, was forced to look elsewhere for an income. Soon after the pope's coronation he asked to be considered for the post of Cardinal Protector of Portugal, which carried with it a pension from the Portuguese government. The other candidate, however, was the most pugnacious of all the French party, Cardinal d'Estrées, and he was duly appointed in January 1677.[15] Howard's name was on a shortlist for the office of vice protector, but it was judged that an Italian cardinal would be more 'active', and it is unlikely that he had the support of d'Estrées.[16] In April 1677 Howard received a small pension of 1600 crowns for six years upon benefices in Portugal. 'This help' wrote Leyburn, 'is thought, by those who know his condition, to have but small proportion to his necessities, but in this interested country and thrifty pontificate, any little provision of this kind is thought considerable.'[17] In June 1677, after only eighteen months in curia, Howard petitioned the pope to allow him to become Bishop of Nepi, in central Italy, so that he could retire from Rome and devote himself to pastoral work. This was not granted.[18]

An event of great importance for the development of the English Dominican province took place at his time. This was the acquisition of the ancient basilica of SS John and Paul on the Coelian Hill, with its adjacent buildings and gardens. It was accepted by the general Chapter that met in Rome in June 1677. The buildings were dilapidated and needed a great deal spent on them, which may account for Howard's success in obtaining them. His drastic restoration of the basilica has been deplored by all subsequent generations but doubtless in his own day and in the prevailing fashion it was considered a fine achievement. Conventual life began at once with Thomas Cooper as the first prior.

This foundation was important for another reason. It brought the English Dominicans one step nearer Howard's dream of re-establishing the full status of a province. The constitutions required that a province must possess three formal convents, but in exceptional circumstances a dispensation may be given to enjoy all the rights and privileges with only two. Perhaps it was the unhappy state of affairs in England that caused Howard to delay obtaining such a dispensation. Eight more years were to pass before he saw the realization of all his hopes.

In May 1678 he moved from his white-washed rooms in the Minerva to quarters that Patrick Conn would have considered more worthy of his rank. Cardinal Gastaldi had been appointed legate at Bologna, and allowed Howard to use his palace near the Ponte Sisto, complete with all its furnishings, during his three years absence.[19] Innocent XI was equally generous. It is said that he never once walked in the gardens of the Vatican or the Quirinal and would have considered a visit of the papal summer-house at Castel Gandolfo as a most unseemly luxury. In October 1678 Howard was indisposed and he writes from Castel Gandolfo on the 21st to the cardinal secretary:

> By your gracious letter I see very clearly how exceedingly great is the kindness of His Holiness in my regard. If he had done no more than to allow me to enjoy the sweetest fruits of his fatherly love in this palace of his (which to me is an earthly paradise) it would be enough to make me utterly happy. But not content with this His Holiness further honours me with most choice wines and other comestibles in abundance, the effects of his supreme generosity.[20]

While Howard was enjoying the quiet and the wines in the pope's own country palace, pursuivants in London broke into the house of Edward Coleman and seized three bundles of letters, so to London we must return.

II

Mention has already been made, in the account of the marriage of the Duchess of York, of the letters that passed between her secretary Edward Coleman, and a number of ecclesiastics resident abroad, including Cardinal Howard. Written in an elementary and far from adequate cipher they are, in their published form, intolerably tedious and involved. The constant repetition of proper names where we should expect pronouns, and the cumbersome circumlocutions that were necessary to disguise names that had not been given a number, render these letters unique for laborious awkwardness.

They were published during the scare that followed the revelations of Titus Oates. They were meant to demonstrate that the Duke of York was holding secret and treasonable converse with the pope. Nobody can seriously contend that the correspondence with Rome has any political, much less treasonable, intent. Coleman was wise to surrender the key to his code, though he would have been wiser, in the excited state of public opinion, to have destroyed his correspondence altogether. Here, however we are concerned only with Cardinal Howard. Ten of his letters to Coleman were printed. There are others from John Leyburn and two from William Leslie, both of whom were writing on behalf of the cardinal. There is no reason to doubt the authenticity of any of them. Coleman himself acknowledged them,[21] and many are still extant, together with a few that were evidently not considered sufficiently incriminating to warrant publication.[22] Seven of Howard's letters belong to the first half of 1676, soon after his arrival in Rome, and three belong to the summer of 1677. The longest of them—that of 14 March 1676—has been extensively quoted earlier in the account of the marriage at Modena. There are echoes, in some of these letters, of the quarrels and jealousies that were only too evident in the church both in England and Ireland. Some of these quarrels are still so obscure that no detailed account is possible, and all that can be done here is to quote the comments of Cardinal Howard, in his typically outspoken letters to the duchess's secretary.

Soon after Howard left England the Portuguese members of the queen's household began to intrigue for the well-paid post of grand almoner that Howard still retained. He writes on 8 February 1676:

> I have written pretty full to Mr Hayes (at my brother's as you know) to confer with you, what my time is too short to repeat, about the old business, in which the Portuguese would get the queen to give my place to a Portuguese, under several specious pretexts, as some of your friends give out here will speedily be done; and if the king had not at first hindered, would have been done by the queen. Now therefore you are desired to deal with the duke, that he speak privately and efficaciously with the king, to hinder it on all scores, both at present or at any time hereafter etc., as Mr Hayes can tell you.[23]

## Cardinal in Curia

By 18 April 1676 this matter seems to have been settled to his satisfaction, and he retained his office and income till the king's death:

> I am much obliged to the duke and duchess for endeavours, if need be, that the Queen of England should think of removing me. But by what I hear from the Portuguese and others I think there is no such interest, it having been only the invention and malicious reports of some. However, my obligation unto the duke, duchess and secretary is the same.[24]

In March 1676 Howard dispatched Patrick Conn to England with a number of commissions. The principal was to expedite the marriage of Elizabeth, the second daughter of the cardinal's brother Henry, who was soon to become 6th Duke of Norfolk. She married George, 4th Marquess of Huntly.

> The second part of my commission [writes Conn to Barberini on 10 December from Paris] was to convey his dutiful homage to their Majesties and to procure the subsidy necessary for his maintenance. This proved to be far more difficult than I had anticipated. The laws made in that kingdom by Henry and Elizabeth are so rigorous and precise against those who give aid, directly or indirectly, to persons in Holy Orders, that the queen herself is able only with the greatest difficulty, and under another name to pay the stipend that goes with his office. Also Her Majesty's secretary told me that the treasurer of her household being a heretic refused many times to pay the amounts due to the cardinal for fear of being denounced to parliament. His promotion has been praised and welcomed by many but everyone is afraid of having the slightest dealings with him. The dangers are so great that even the Catholics cannot give him the least assistance without evident peril of losing all that they possess.[25]

Another topic, and one that evokes Howard's bitterest comments, was the feud between Oliver Plunkett, Archbishop of Armagh, and Peter Talbot, Archbishop of Dublin. Talbot was an ex-Jesuit and had exercised considerable sway in English court circles, especially with the Duke of York. Howard had not been enthusiastic when he was appointed to Dublin, though, on the other hand, Talbot had warmly recommended Howard for vicar apostolic in England. Talbot also appears to have been suspect as a favourer of the Franciscan Peter Walsh and his followers, who had lax views on the deposing power of the pope. Plunkett was a personal friend of the cardinal and made no secret of his love for the Dominicans. Talbot was supported in England by a Benedictine named Edward Sheldon, who was a member of the household of the Duchess of York, and Howard's *bête noire*. Indeed there are hints that Howard's relations with the English Benedictines generally were far from cordial. Fr William Hitchcock, prior of the Benedictines at Douai, where Howard had been so warmly welcomed only a few months before, writes to the procurator of his order at Rome on 20 February 1676:

> Fr President has writ to our cardinal that you may have an apartment in his lodging, that you may seem to have his countenance, and also be in better circumstances to observe the motions of him and such as are about him. If His Eminence should not prove moderate in order to us religious, then you know how to join forces with the rest of the regulars of our nation. I think it would not be amiss to acquaint some there how he is much of his uncle Aubigny's spirit, a sufficient Jansenist, and in his practice a sworn enemy of all regulars. Mr Leyburn, although he always seemed smooth, yet certainly is a great adversary. Hinder his removing from Douai if you can, for he had much better be here than there ... I beseech you burn this when perused.[26]

Howard's bitterness towards Talbot and Sheldon is much in evidence. He resented their influence with the Duke of York, who seems to have preferred them to his Dominican adviser, Vincent Torre. Howard writes of 14 March 1676:

> What you write of the Archbishop of Dublin, his apparent victory at Rome against his adversary [Plunkett], is quite the contrary, for the Archbishop of Dublin is not in esteem here, for that nor his practices there, which are very ill relished. Neither did I ever write or trouble the duke with those affairs which were more out of faction than otherwise, and I took order long since, that no proceeding should be in it before his arrival, that all might be well examined, and those unto whom it was committed do much approve of the archbishop's adversaries' books. I wonder Mr Sheldon maketh so much noise in that affair also, having had so much commission to trouble himself or other in it, and if (as you say) he came thither chiefly about that business, he might more quickly return as wise and to as much purpose as he came ... And let the duke be assured, I will serve him and all the Catholics whether they will or no, although the Achbishop

of Dublin and his friends are enough to enflame all, if their malice were not well known at Rome, and by Cardinal Altieri, Francesco Barberini and many others. But I dare answer I am of no faction, but against the factions, who are in great number but cannot prevail *in iniquitatibus suis* [through their iniquity, cf. Psalm 106:43] ... The Archbishop of Dublin wrote hither to Cardinal Altieri a very foolish, ridiculous, malicious letter against Cardinal Fra. Barberini, as he hath often other suchlike and worse ones to others, of manifest falsities, which I myself have seen and have, actually written by his own hand; besides his forging false letters is a constant old custom of his. I will say no more at present lest I should say too much, but this I dare say, that if the duke make use of him or shew him his favour he will much disgrace himself and his cause, and put both English and Irish Catholics in great division, which will be the easiest way for the Protestants to destroy them. And everyone wonders how Mr Sheldon should be of late so great a protector and friend of the Archbishop of Dublin, when to my knowledge (and many others) he was quite the contrary (as he told me) not long before, the archbishop pretending to Mr Sheldon's place about the duchess. But it appeareth that Mr Sheldon and his confederates, by their late violent bending for the archbishop and his ways against the order, is more out of faction than zeal ... I must again take leave to tell you that it may do the duke no small prejudice, if the Catholics of England, or the pope and Cardinal Altieri with his confederates of Rome, should be persuaded of the duke's partiality to any whatsoever. He may be a good friend to any in general or particular, but partial to none, so far as to the exclusion of others.[27]

He writes again on 16 May 1676:

If the duke or duchess employ the Archbishop of Dublin or his adherents in Rome it will but confound their and the Catholics' affairs with chimerical visions. Neither will Rome esteem a Benedictine coming on such things as belong not properly to his trade, but [I] suppose his business is to get a little money for himself, which is not so easily parted withal ... And as to the Archbishop of Dublin prevailing with the duke in his late resolution [not to attend Protestant churches], a few or none will believe it here, he being used to write falsehoods and forgeries that his saying it maketh it not believed. But if it were so, *de bono opera, non lapidamus te* [it is not for a good work that we stone you, John 10:33]. He did his duty, for which God recompense him. And as to what Fr Sheldon pretends to say in the other point, betwixt the Archbishop of Dublin and his adversary, Rome needeth not such learned wits to teach those who know better. Others have already as foolishly been fiddling, but neither fiddler or fiddlestick is regarded. They may teach fools to dance if they can, for the tune soundeth not right where a better is used. The best employment Mr Sheldon can [do] for the duke and duchess is to become a Benedictine and pray for them quietly.[28]

Another topic that finds a prominent place in these letters is the ambiguous conduct of the Duke of York. Though generally considered a Catholic he allowed himself a latitude that caused Rome to eye him with suspicion. He went openly to Protestant churches, a practice so clearly forbidden by papal decrees. Howard more than once implies that he was acting on the advice of Talbot and Sheldon and that they were in this matter scandalously lax. Howard contended that the duke was not bound to declare himself a Catholic but must avoid acts contrary to Catholic practice and discipline. Yet it is difficult to see what Howard expected him to do. Refusal to go to Protestant churches had been for a century the one great external mark of a good Catholic and was accepted universally as a full profession of Catholic faith. The oath of allegiance should have been the acid test, but there were many Catholics, priests and layfolk, who held that it could be lawfully taken. Refusal to take it was not, in practice, the act that distinguished Catholics from Protestants. Refusal to attend Protestant churches was, on the other hand, universally upheld by Catholics. It was this refusal that gave them their distinctive name of recusants. For the duke to refuse to go to church would have been universally interpreted as an explicit profession of Catholicism. Howard writes on 18 April 1676, concerning the pope's refusal to grant the marriage dispensation for the Duke of York:

> That which then gave him doubt of the duke's being a Catholic, and which yet doth not at all satisfy the pope or at Rome, is the duke's doing (as they esteem it) the contrary, by going (as you know) with the Protestants, which you know was long since condemned by former popes, that the Catholics could not etc., and in this point I confess I was put to my trumps in Rome when it was objected to me, although I must as duly confess it was never yet my opinion in England that any Catholic could do it, and so I did clearly declare myself when and wherever I thought I ought, or that it was asked me. But I was informed

## Cardinal in Curia

> not long before I left England that other wise people proposed something confusedly (not to term it otherwise) to some whom they thought convenient to pick out ... I cannot perceive the right way hath been taken by the duke and Rome to understand thoroughly one another, nor the Catholics and the pope neither, but by confused, undigested and too often factious notions, which will never do rightly the Catholics of England's affairs. The pope doth not at all desire the duke to do anything indiscreetly or precipitantly, that all England may openly say the duke is a Catholic, leaving that unto his own discretion for a due time. But to do anything to the contrary, as Rome thinketh, the pope cannot approve of. I have, however (I am sure), done my best with Rome for the duke, who is not so much to be blamed on his side, if others who should know more do not condemn but rather approve, or at least connive therein.[29]

When the duke's daughters received Protestant confirmation, Howard comments:

> I was glad to hear (although I virtually believed it) of the duke's endeavours to hinder what the Protestants did to his daughters of late. You understand me. And if I had letters [for a code] I could write more clearly of somewhat else in which the pope was not so well satisfied as I wished, but I have cleared the best I could, although I declared always my opinion against it. But others more wise and politic went the contrary way, and knowing my opinion would not ask it me, as they did others whom they thought to draw to theirs.[30]

On 9 November 1677, the duke wrote himself to Innocent XI:

> The news will surely have reached Rome of the marriage between my eldest daughter Mary and the Prince of Orange, and I cannot doubt that this sudden resolution will have caused some thoughts in the mind of Your Holiness. I must protest that although she is my daughter I could not prevent this absolute and free act of the king, my brother and master. I again assure Your Holiness that I will never be lacking in diligence and care in the preservation and furtherance of the Catholic religion in these realms.[31]

If the pope was disappointed that a daughter of James should be married to a Protestant, James himself was to rue it in after years when Mary returned to England to supplant him.

It is necessary to dwell at some length on these quarrels that are so evident in Howard's correspondence. They prepare us for the debacle that is to follow. Here is a picture of priests and religious jockeying for positions in what they anticipated would one day be the royal court. Here is evidence of the entire lack of sympathy and understanding between the English cardinal and the clergy at home, who were destined to become the advisers of a Catholic king. It is noteworthy that nowhere in Howard's letters is there any mention of the English Jesuit, Edward Petre, who was soon to exercise such influence over James and the affairs of the church in England.

Soon these domestic squabbles, disedifying as they are, were put into the shade when the fantastic revelations of Titus Oates suddenly burst upon an eager and overcredulous Protestant populace. How far Oates was the tool of anti-Catholic politicians has never been established, but it seems beyond belief that an obscure apostate church-student could have carried all before him without powerful support from above. Certainly the atmosphere was suited to his purpose. The hostility provoked by James's Catholic marriage and virtual profession of Catholicism, the Test Act and the proclamation that was the occasion of Howard's leaving England, had all helped to stir up the latent animosity of the people, especially in London. There had been steadily increasing pressure upon the papists, and the king was powerless to stem the tide. Marriage agreements meant nothing. On 3 October 1676 was issued an order in council whereby His Majesty 'straitly commands that no others presume to resort to Her Majesty's chapel but such as are Her Majesty's domestic servants'. Officers were appointed to watch there and at the homes of ambassadors 'without stopping or questioning any as they go thither, but at their coming from thence they are to apprehend and bring the said persons to the Board'.[32] As early as February 1676, soon after Howard reached Rome, the English Chapter wrote to him, thanking him for the appointment of Francis Gage to succeed Leyburn as president of Douai college, and reminding him of the need for a bishop:

> 'Tis true at home the clouds seem still to gather more and more, and we have great reason to apprehend that the storm will fall severely at last, being so many persons are already convicted and so many seizures of estate already made, though now all non-conformists are threatened likewise. However it prove, having Your Eminence's patronage we hope at least not be to traduced as formerly at the See Apostolic, whiles we suffer for it in our own country.[33]

Patrick Conn was less pessimistic. He writes to Cardinal Barberini on 17 April 1676 from his safe refuge in Paris:

> Great commotion has been caused in that city [London] by the resolve of the Duke of York not to accompany the king to his chapel on Easter day, as was his wont. This news has stirred up everybody, especially our pseudo-bishops, who called a meeting immediately afterwards in the house of the Archbishop of Canterbury in order to excite new persecutions against the Catholics. As, however, there are numerous other sects in this kingdom not subject to their episcopal authority, and comprising many powerful interests, they cannot launch their censures against the one without involving them all. This famous assembly had no such intention. They send their satellites all over the country with orders to prosecute the Catholics according to the old laws, and recently they caught a Jesuit father. He was hauled before a justice, who showed him such favour that after a cursory examination he was released on bond to appear at the next session.[34]

The forebodings of the Chapter proved to be right, though perhaps there is something to be learned from the letter of Patrick Conn. A comprehensive attack on all non-conformists was too dangerous. What was required was a good popish plot on traditional lines that would bring persecution only on the Catholics. This is precisely what Titus Oates provided. It was on the familiar lines of all the plots that had been invented for the extermination of Catholicism, but the net was spread wider. It was not a Babington plot or a gunpowder plot, but the popish plot *par excellence*. The Protestants were to be eliminated, the king shot and poisoned, and England restored to the faith by force of arms. Oates had ready the names of the new bishops and of the principal ministers of state, and this gave him scope to inculpate all the leading Catholics, from the Duke and Duchess of York downwards. Attempts were even made to involve the queen. By now the English Dominicans were more numerous than they had been for a century, and for the first time are prominent in a persecution. How well-equipped and thorough Oates was is shown by the fact that he cited nine out of the eleven English Dominicans known to be in England at the time, and added for good measure Cardinal Howard and Vincent Cooper, who were far away in Rome. In his imaginary popish hierarchy Howard was to be Archbishop of Canterbury 'with an augmentation of 40,000 crowns per annum for the maintenance of his legantine authority'. Other Dominicans are nominated to the sees of Ely, Peterborough, Bristol and Bangor.

Apart from his appearance as the head of Oates's popish hierarchy, the evidence against Howard may be quoted as a fair example of the slender foundations upon which the whole chimerical plot was based, and of the connivance given in the Lords to barefaced perjury:

> 5 April 1679. This day the Lords did very little; only one Sedway found them discourse, who told a story that being some three or four years since at Rome, Cardinal Howard with others expressing great hopes of the speedy establishing their religion in England, he argued its impossibility from the zeal of the bishops. They answered that several of them were favourers of it, naming the Bishop of Ely, the Bishop of Gloucester and the Bishop of Bath and Wells; and that he came over, having often waited on the Bishop of Ely. At last he acquainted him with his resolution of exchanging popery for Protestantism, and that the bishop should seem to discourage him, saying that his [Sedway's] own was a better religion than was generally believed to be.
>
> 8 April 1679. Sedway was brought to the bar, who had aspersed three reverend bishops with the scandal of popery, but he was so far from making anything like truth appear against them, that whereas he pretended he derived his knowledge of it from Cardinal Barberini and Cardinal Norfolk some three or four years since at Rome, yet gave contrary accounts of both the cardinals and a very mistaken one of every part of Rome itself. Yet because he was called the king's evidence and was ushered in by an eloquent earl, it was carried but by five votes for his commitment.[35]

Of the nine Dominicans in England who were cited Thomas Fidden died in the midst of the plot and Vincent Torre, the superior, escaped to Flanders. Edward Bing and Maurice Gifford were never captured. The other five were imprisoned. William Collins, an Irish Dominican who had been affiliated to the English province, was begged by the Spanish ambassador and was allowed to cross to Bornhem. Joseph Kemys, who is described as a 'very old man' was judged too ill to stand his trial, and died in Newgate prison on 27 January 1680. The other four were tried, and as we would expect, not a word was whispered about the plot. They were tried under the sanguinary laws made by Elizabeth and accused simply of being popish seminary priests. Alexander Lumsden of Aberdeen successfully pleaded that these laws did not apply to Scotsmen. Dominic Maguire, an Irishman born in Spain, was similarly outside the law. Lionel Anderson and Peter Atwood were condemned to death, but later together with Dominic Maguire of the Irish province were reprieved, Atwood at the eleventh hour when he was actually awaiting the hurdle to drag him to Tyburn. Thus the Dominicans provided no martyr. Of the twenty-one executed, eight were Jesuits, two Franciscans, one a Benedictine laybrother, six secular priests and four laymen. Among those put to death were several of Howard's friends. The first victim was his correspondent, Edward Coleman, and the last his old friend Oliver Plunkett. Even more closely affecting him was the martyrdom, on 29 December 1680, of his uncle William Viscount Stafford, who five years before had accompanied him to Rome.

There are no letters of Howard extant in which he expresses his anguish at the return of Elizabethan ferocity after so many years, free at least from bloodshed. It would appear that he sent his sympathy to the London Chapter, for there is a draft of a reply, dated 28 March 1679:

> If it be a comfort to the miserable to have companions in their affliction, it is a double one to us to have Your Eminence not only a fellow sufferer with us, but also at the same time a patron also and reliever of our sufferings, for we are most sensible of the great share Your Eminence beareth in the calamities of our distressed country, so we cannot but acknowledge with all gratitude your compassionate affection of our part thereof, which hath moved Your Eminence to suggest both to His Holiness and our protector the difficult straits which we are reduced unto, so that whatsoever help or redress we shall receive from that court we shall ever look upon it as an effect of Your Eminence's goodness and bounty towards us, and we beseech God to reward your charity towards us with all prosperity in this life and an eternal crown of glory in the next.[36]

This letter was written when the Oates plot was only a few month's old and when only six executions had taken place. Nobody could foresee the extent of the persecution, and in the midst of the frenzied and panic-stricken populace even the Chapter did not consider the moment opportune to press for a bishop.

It was at this tragic moment that the Chapter was to receive a blow from which it never recovered. For nearly twenty years its secretary had been a priest named John Sergeant, a prolific writer and an able controversialist, though unstable, violent and obsessed with a hatred of Jesuits that amounted to a mania. Howard claims to have been the means whereby in 1668 he was relieved of this office in favour of the more moderate John Leyburn.[37] Sergeant was suspected of holding the condemned views of Blacklow and of supporting the Irish firebrand Peter Walsh. He thought it prudent to obey the proclamation of 1673 and retired to Paris, highly commended by Humphrey Ellis, the dean of the Chapter and by Peter Talbot, Archbishop of Dublin. Talbot later changed his opinion of him and publicly stigmatized as heretical a new work of Sergeant's that appeared in 1676. Sergeant corresponded with Cardinal Barberini, and in a letter of 17 October 1675 bitterly complains that Fr John Warner, SJ, has stolen his penitent, the Countess of Shrewsbury[38] — a significant complaint when we consider the sequel.

In 1679, in the midst of the Oates plot Sergeant returned to England, his expenses paid by the government. For the next two years his name appears with those of Oates, Bedloe, Dangerfield and other perjured witnesses as the recipient of an allowance of £5 per week: money that he earned by services scarcely less disreputable than Oates's, and, in a priest, infinitely more reprehensible.[39]

It does not appear that any other member of the Chapter associated with him or approved, or even knew of his vile treachery, but he remained a prominent member of the Chapter and as such brought suspicion on them all. How could Rome feel any confidence in the probity of a body that harboured men like Blacklow and Sergeant? Had there ever been any solid hopes that the Chapter would be confirmed, this sorry exhibition of Sergeant's must have finally destroyed them.

## Notes

1. AV, Act. Consist. 22, ff. 194, 197.
2. BV, Vat. Lat. 12340, f. 8.
3. AP, Audienza 1666–79, f. 233.
4. BV, Vat. Lat. 12340, f. 12.
5. Tierney, *History and Antiquities*, II, 535.
6. Treby, *Letters*, 83.
7. *Ibid.* 80.
8. SP. 85/11, f. 176.
9. Treby, *Letters*, 92.
10. Sim. Leg. 3124.
11. Petruccelli della F. Gattina, *Histoire diplomatique des conclaves*, Paris, 1864–5, III, 290; Med. 3396 (4 Sept. 1676).
12. BV, Vat. Lat. 12340, f. 34.
13. T. de Burgo, *Hibernia Dominicana*, 1762, 544.
14. BV, Vat. Lat. 12341, f. 60.
15. F. de Bojani, *Innocent X, sa correspondence avec ses nonces 1676–9*, Rome, 1910, I, 149.
16. *Corpo diplomatico portuguez*, ed. J. C. de Freitas Moniz, t.XIV, Lisboa, 1910, 390.
17. Treby, *Letters*, 94.
18. SP. 101/85 (5 June 1677).
19. *Ibid.* 14 May 1678.
20. AV, Cardinali 42, f. 320.
21. HMC, Ormonde, IV, 482.
22. HMC, 13th Report, app. VI, 100. Fitzherbert MSS.
23. Treby, *Letters*, 79.
24. *Ibid.* 87.
25. B, 8669, f. 249.
26. C. Dodd, *The Church History of England*, London, 1737, III, 392.
27. Treby, *Letters*, 81.
28. *Ibid.* 89.
29. *Ibid.* 85.
30. *Ibid.*
31. AV, Princ. 164, f. 340.
32. TNA, PC. 2/65, 349.
33. AAW, A34, no. 103.
34. B, 8669, f. 247.
35. HMC, Ormonde, V, 33, 35.
36. AAW, A34, no. 130.
37. *Dominicana*, 41.
38. B, 2170, f. 214..
39. *Secret Services of Charles II and James II*, Camden Soc., London, 1851, 8, 10 etc.

# 8

## *Protector of England*

I

IN MARCH 1680, when persecution in England was still raging, Howard received an appointment that identified him still more closely with English affairs. In succession to Cardinal Francesco Barberini, who had held the office since 1626 and who had recently died, Howard became Cardinal Protector of England. The brief was dated 7 March and another brief of 8 March constituted him Protector of Scotland as well. Howard returned the briefs, asking that the two appointments might be united in a single brief,[1] thus for ever linking the two countries.* The news must have leaked out before the brief for on 17 February there is a note in the account book of the English College of the expenditure of more than two scudi 'for the arms and portrait of Cardinal Howard'.[2] The college was expected to display a portrait of their cardinal protector.

Among those who wrote to congratulate him was Fr John Warner, the Jesuit provincial, then at St Omer. His letter, which has not survived, was answered on 6 April:

> Amongst the many congratulations addressed to me upon account of the protectorship which it hath pleased His Holiness to entrust me with since the decease of Cardinal Barberini, not any gave me greater satisfaction than that which I received this week from you by the hands of Fr Anderton. These therefore are to render you my thanks and to assure you of my readiness to employ this new power in the manner that shall appear to me most conformable to the good intentions of His Holiness who gives it, and more advantageous to those on whose behalf it is

---

\* It would appear that this request was not granted for there is in the Scots College at Rome (I, 4/4) a copy of a brief appointing Howard Protector of Scotland *only*.

given. I cannot but foresee many difficulties to be encountered considering the circumstances which our country at present is in, for surmounting whereof both the prayers and counsel of my friends will be necessary. And as I have a confidence that neither of these helps will be wanting from you and those of the Society who are under your government, so likewise I desire you to remain firmly persuaded that the light which I may receive from such assistance and the capacity it may put me in will accordingly be made use of for the good of Catholics in general and with due regard to the just satisfaction which may be challenged from you and yours in particular.

If we were all united in hearts and minds as we are involved in the same persecution, what we suffer from the malice of our adversaries would be recompensed by the comfort received from one another, but the scandals particularly by promotors of the oath, do unfortunately deprive us of this advantage. I find these scandals mentioned not only in your letter but also in several others which of late are come to my hands. You will easily believe that I am heartily sensible of the prejudice caused thereby, and that I shall not leave unattempted anything within my power for removal of it. The disorder is such as doubtless doth require application of some remedy, but the difficulty consists in choosing a remedy that may be efficacious and adequate to the evil. My endeavours are employed for discovery of such an one. In order hereunto I consult those persons here whose prudence, piety or authority may be relied upon. I shall be glad to know what you can suggest in order to the same, or any other concern which you judge fit to be recommended unto, very Rev. Father,

Your most affectionate friend
Cardinal Norfolk.[3]

Four days later, on 10 April, Howard wrote in a similar strain to Alexander Holt, then in Paris. He praises the work of the seculars, 'the principal part of the spiritual militia', and exhorts him and his colleagues to follow in the footsteps of the martyrs, and to refuse not only the oath of supremacy, which they all do, but also the oath of allegiance, about which they are divided:

> There are not wanting persons who (as you may easily imagine) do urge this point to the disparagement and disadvantage of your body. Nor will it be in my power, without your concurrence, to hinder the ill impression that may be caused by it in the minds of His Holiness and those on whom you must necessarily depend for obtaining what you judge most important for a right

government amongst yourselves and the flock committed to you. I hope you will receive this intimation as an argument of the desire to serve you which I have ever made profession of. I am now in a capacity of giving more effectual proofs than formerly of the sincerity from which this profession does proceed. But it will belong to you to remove such obstructions as have been hinted by me, and which otherwise, by stopping up the way I am to take, may frustrate my best intentions and render my endeavours unsuccessful. A disappointment of this kind will be very unwelcome to, your most affectionate friend,

Cardinal of Norfolk.[4]

John Warner promptly accepted Howard's invitation to suggest remedies for the divisions in England. There is a draft of a very long letter endorsed: 'Letter designed for the Cardinal of Norfolk, but only an extract of it was sent, 1 May 1680'.

My most humble thanks for the honour of Your Eminence's letter of the 6 of April. It is a singular comfort to us all, myself in particular, amidst the difficulties which have dispersed and almost oppressed the small remnant of English Catholics, that the divine providence hath placed that power designed for the relief of our nation in your person, of whose inbred goodness we have all had so long an experience, and whose readiness to benefit all is by new arguments every day confirmed. And seeing at that distance things passing amongst us here cannot be known but by letters, and Your Eminence is pleased to demand what I can suggest in order to remedy what is amiss, I shall do so in the best manner I can.

In the first place I most humbly beseech Your Eminence to receive this, not as a judge but as a father; not as a judicial information in order to a legal indictment of the persons concerned, but as a secret relation of the state of things; not as designed to get any punished for what is past, but to prevent what mischief may be hereafter feared, by such mild means as the times will bear and the persons are capable of, which Your Eminence's prudence and experience shall suggest. I shall speak nothing but what I think true: if I am deceived I shall be as glad to correct the mistake as, if myself were spoken of, I should desire others to do it.

Had all Catholics been of one mind and concurred unanimously to the quenching this fire it could have done no great hurt and had been soon extinguished. But some were persuaded, though their neighbour's house was on fire their own was in no danger, as not being built with such combustible matter, and hoping that the burning down of the other would give their own a fairer prospect and leave them at liberty to enlarge upon its ruins. They threw oil into the fire and endeavoured to hinder its quenching.

Oates gave the first overture for this discrimination of Catholics in the 25th article of his narrative, where he exempts the secular clergy from the number of plotters.[*] This put some of them in hopes that the regulars were aimed at and might be ruined, and they tolerated. And they were so possessed with this opinion that the imprisonment of several and the execution of some of their own could not correct it.

The means they used to attain that end, the expulsion of regulars, Jesuits particularly, and their own toleration, were that they are harmless and we dangerous to the State by reason of our obedience to an extern superior and our dependence on a foreign prince, viz. the pope: which are not only the sense but the very words of Oates in the dedicatory epistle of his narrative to the king. But chiefly by promoting the oath of allegiance, which they pretend we refuse out of a treasonable design against the government. All this is contained in their letters, which, as I am informed, are sent to Rome.

To get lay Catholics to join in taking that oath great art was used. To Rome they writ that no head of any of the bodies of churchmen abetted them nor others, but only some few private and inconsiderable men. In France they boasted that all, even Jesuits themselves, in England allowed them. In England they charged the Jesuits as the only opposers of them, and very lately have informed the king that Jesuits at Rome solicited His Holiness to excommunicate all oathists: an odious thing which I think was never mentioned. At least I am sure I never heard nor thought of any such thing, and which I think would in this conjuncture give a greater wound to Catholic religion then the persecution itself. They had their designs in spreading these contradictory rumours. That at Rome was to lull that court asleep with representing the thing as inconsiderable: that in

---

[*] Oates wrote: 'Item XXV ... The Jesuits there [St Omers] advised the fathers in one [letter] of March 1st that the secular clergy should be treated withal about the business, but they finding them then at that time to be men inclined to live in peace and obedience to their prince, the Fathers, viz. Thomas White etc. answered them in one of March 10th that the clergy were a sort of rascally fellows that had neither wit nor courage to manage such a great design; and did pray them of Ghent and them of St Omers to be of good cheer, for their designs went on well both in Scotland and Ireland, and the fatal blow should be given to the black boy at Whitehall with all speed that might be' (*A True Narrative of the Horrid Plot*, London, 1679, 16).

France, to increase their interest with the numerous Catholics who flocked thither: that in England, to make themselves grateful to the State, and the Jesuits odious. I need not mention to Your Eminence how much these *est et non*, these contrary reports, are contrary to the spirit of truth, as we find in 2 Cor. 1 *a versu* 17.

That Dr Holden framed a design to exclude all regulars who would not renounce all dependence on any foreign superior, the pope particularly, is evident, I hear, out of his own writings. That this same design died not with him, we have great reason to believe. It showed itself sufficiently when Mr Sergeant was permitted in London, for then his friends in Paris openly talked of it, as being unavoidable. They reflected not on their own condition, and that they whetted a knife which could cut their own throats. For what danger to the State from the Jesuits' fourth vow to go on missions wherever the pope commands, which is not the ordinary vows of our seminaries to return to England when commanded? Yet that is one of the reasons alleged for our exclusion.

The success of all these endeavours have not answered their expectation, though in the promotion of the oath they have been too successful. But that being not the end but only a mean used to obtain it, when they see by experience it is insufficient they will easier be induced to lay it aside. At the beginning a small matter would have put a stop to their acting. Now the number of oathists is increased so much that to use severity towards all would endanger a schism. Yet such enterprises, directly contrary to lawful authority, ought not to pass uncorrected. Probably it were good that one or two ring-leaders were suspended *a divinis*. The pain would involve a few but the fear reach all, and the visible disappointment of their main intent would dispose them to a compliance with their duty.

Thus in obedience to Your Eminence's commands I most humbly represent to your consideration what occurs to me in this present conjuncture. We shall hope for a fit remedy in due time, and the meanwhile comfort ourselves with expectation of it, seeing Your Eminence is convinced there is need of it, and that the news of these disorders was not grounded on any ill will to the persons but on their real actions. Never any dispute in religion more unseasonable started, first because of the danger for the persecution, and secondly for the probability of settling religion greater than at any time since its fall in England. God forgive the authors, but it is certain that nothing could in all probability more ruin our hopes than this ill-timed dispute.[5]

This letter is an eloquent testimony to the havoc wrought in the ranks of the English Catholics by the oath of allegiance. Warner's strictures on Sergeant were fully justified, but he does not provide any evidence that other secular clergy were pleased at the outbreak of persecution or poured oil on the flames. Oates was able to make capital out of the dispute and to represent the 'oathist' as more loyal than their opponents, but this was a mere side-line, and does not appear to have influenced the judges. Thus Lionel Anderson, OP, at his trial defended himself on the charge of saying Mass by informing the court that he had been excommunicated for ten years 'for scribbling and writing against the temporal power of the church of Rome'.[6] This admission did not save him from being condemned to death. The priests who were martyred were tried and condemned under the old Elizabethan laws that made priesthood treason. It does not appear that any enquiries were made concerning their attitude to the oath.

The question that poses itself is the question that haunts us all through these tragic years. What should be done? What could Howard or Propaganda or the pope himself do to heal the wounds in the English church? Even being wise after the event, and three centuries after, it is still far easier to criticize Rome for inactivity than to suggest a policy that had a chance of success. Warner's suggestion that some of the principal clergy should be suspended is not very helpful. It would have been unjust to suspend them without a judicial enquiry, and such an enquiry, in the heat of the persecution, was out of the question. Nor are censures of much avail unless they can be effectively imposed. Without a bishop on the spot church discipline was no more than a name, and it was those who most strenuously opposed the appointment of a bishop who were loudest in their complaints at the disunity and indiscipline that ensued.

The office of Cardinal Protector of England in those troubled times was certainly no sinecure. One has only to examine the papers of Francesco Barberini, who held the office so long, to see how much he was involved in the affairs of the English Catholics. The protector had very wide powers and control over all the English colleges on the continent and was consulted at every turn by the various congregations on points touching the realms under his protection. Now that the protector was himself an Englishman and a member of Propaganda his influence was unusually strong.

All the powers he had clamoured for while in England had now fallen into his lap, and with them a new caution and perhaps a sense of hopelessness that rendered them largely ineffective. Unfortunately he spent the last six months of his life destroying his personal papers, so that there remains nothing comparable to the vast Barberini collection. But enough remains, scattered over Europe and preserved often by the merest chance, to show the extent of his correspondence and the variety of the problems and complaints that he was expected to deal with. Those that follow belong to a later period of his life, but they are given here simply as samples from what must have been a very bulky postbag. How should he deal, for instance, with the following complaint against the Spanish Jesuits who ran the English College at Seville?

> They give no clothes to the students but let them go naked with rags like beggars. I have worn a shirt nine months together and a pair of sheets a twelvemonth without changing. They give us nothing but few olives, granades and oranges with water for our diet, but they themselves eat flesh even upon Fridays and fastdays, besides the provision of jocalate and sweetmeats in their chambers.[7]

Then there was the Scots missioner who wrote thirty-five pages, 'not by way of accusation against anyone but by way of question'. He manages to excogitate no less than forty-seven questions, of which the three following will perhaps prove more than enough:

> 8. Why do the Jesuits in Scotland make use of faculties which they have not? As is clear in the marriage of my lord chancellor, dispensing with him and his lady in 2°gradu, which they cannot do. Whether they are obliged to show to my lord protector all the faculties that they have, that he say what they can exercise, what not? Why do they boast and vaunt in Scotland before laics that they have greater faculties than the clergy priests? Without any necessity, but only to magnify themselves as the only beloved and esteemed by the Apostolic See, and to vilipend and depress the clergy as if the Apostolic See had little esteem for it, granted it but common powers and faculties, had little or no confidence in it, and that the whole esteem, love and confidence was and is in the Jesuits? If such discourse be capable to edify the laics, or rather to raise up factions and pernicious emulations and at last scandals. Why do they not rather observe the precepts of Jesus Christ, Luc. 22 v.24 et seq. when *facta est contentio inter eos*

*quis eorum videbatur esse maior?* [a dispute arose among them, which of them was to be regarded as the greatest, cf. Luke 22:24]
33. Whether missioners satisfy their duty and obligation, not going to visit Catholics but in fair days and good seasons, when meat, drink and other conveniences are to be easily and in abundance had for man and horse?
35. Whether it be lawful to say that Rome with its decrees does more harm than good; that it is not practique of the mission of Scotland and that for this reason it should not be informed of what passes therein. Whether it is lawful to keep hidden from Rome all that passeth there, and that all cases, though never so doubtsome may and ought to be resolved within Scotland itself, and no recourse to Rome thereanent.[8]

The office of cardinal protector gave Howard authority over the English College in Rome, and no student could be admitted without his approval. Probably he delegated this power to the rector, though the cardinal's name is always mentioned as the authority for each student's admission. Only once does he appear to have made a new regulation. The college still preserves a decree dated 13 December 1680 ordering all scholastics to assemble in the great hall at the customary signal and there on their knees to make their morning meditation in common. 'Moreover we declare that the Fr Minister, or one of the other fathers in his absence at the discretion of the rector, shall be present in the said hall to see that this order is carried out.'[9] Perhaps the college was in such good order that during his fourteen years as protector no other ordination was necessary. Perhaps it is merely a freak of fortune that this one, so typical of the age, is the only one to survive.

For other details of Howard's rule over the English College there is a volume of petitions made by some of the students to Francesco Barberini (the younger) in 1704.[10] It is not easy to appraise their historical value or to say how representative they are of the views of the students as a whole. There are three matters that concern their late cardinal protector. These students complain that, in building his palace, Howard destroyed a property that had been left to the college by Bernadino Pipi, the rents from which were to provide a free burse. There is no suggestion that Howard misappropriated this fund, but it is complained that the rent he paid to the college for his palace went into the general accounts, and that the free place for a poor student had lapsed. Howard had always been concerned about the poor quality of the English spoken by priests whose studies were done abroad.

> They came over young and retained all the English that they brought over with them, which was only the language of boys. But their education being among strangers they had formed themselves so upon that model that really they preached as Frenchmen or Italians in English words; of which he was every day warning them for he knew this could have no good effect in England.[11]

He therefore abolished the custom in the college of speaking Latin (except at recreation) 'because these youths were beginning to forget their mother tongue'. In 1704 the students themselves petitioned for Latin to be restored.

The most drastic of Howard's innovations was the banning, in 1684, of the *convictors*, who had been a feature of the college since its inception. The convictors were from families that could afford to pay fees, and most of them came for their general education without any thought or obligation of taking priestly orders. They had been of considerable financial assistance to the college and they were reinstated immediately after Howard's death. In this matter the students were on Howard's side. They complain of the arrogance and the snobbery of this privileged class and of their exemption from the common duties of the college. They record one recent case of a convictor striking a divine, without retaliation, and of another who said he would rather be a blacksmith than a secular priest. However the *alumni* were far more numerous and not inferior in physical strength. The convictors normally contented themselves with putting up rude notices in indifferent Latin. If we may judge by the only example quoted* these were incomparably less witty and abusive than the pasquinades against cardinals and popes that appear to have delighted the victims as much as the general public.

The cardinal protector could hardly remain indifferent to the need of Catholic books for the English laity, and within a few months of his appointment Howard brought out a catechism of Christian doctrine. As there has been some confusion over this

---

* *Procul O procul esto maligni / Et odi profanum vulgus et arceo* [Keep away, O keep far away, you malignant ones / And I hate the unholy rabble and keep them away (a notice based on poems of Vergil and Horace)].

book, some details must be given here. The first to associate Howard with this work is an Italian Dominican, Domaneschio, whose book was published in 1767.

> For the spread of the faith, in the time of Innocent XI and with his approval he compiled a book in English in which the principal dogmas of the Catholic church, and especially those impugned by heretics, were set out and explained so solidly and clearly that nothing more useful for its purpose could have been desired. Although he printed this book in Rome he published it as though from Basle and under a false name, lest the heretics (as was vehemently suspected) would intercept it on its entry to England, Scotland and Ireland. Six thousand copies of this work were shipped to those provinces and everywhere caused such a stir that every copy that fell into the hands of the heretics was publicly burnt.

He adds a footnote to say that a copy is preserved in the Dominican convent of Our Lady of Grace at Gibello near Venice, with a manuscript note by Fr Patrick O'Flynn, an Irish Dominican, that gives the above particulars.[12]

With all due respects to Father O'Flynn, Howard has no claim to the authorship of this book. What he did was to print a new edition of a very famous catechism: *AN ABRIDGEMENT of Christian Doctrine WITH Proofs of SCRIPTURE for Points controverted Catechistically explained, by way of Question and Answer.*

The address of the reader is subscribed 'H. T.', which stands for Henry Turbeville, a priest and professor of Douai college. There are many editions, all very rare. The earliest I have traced is the third edition of 1649 or 1650, of which there is a copy in the British Library. There are editions of 1661, 1676, 1684 and 1687 all with the imprint of Douai. Here we are concerned only with copies that bear the imprint BASILEAE Anno MDCLXXX (Basle 1680). It had long been a common practice for Catholic books, printed secretly in England or smuggled in from the continent, to bear false imprints or none at all. Nobody appears to have thought before of the far more effective ruse of choosing a centre of Calvinism as the supposed place of origin. Overworked customs officials who would raise their eyebrows at 'Douai' might well pass a catechism from Geneva or Basle, especially when the work 'Catholic' had been carefully excluded from the title page. But what makes the Basle edition of special interest is that there are two quite distinct editions both with the imprint Basle 1680. They are so similar that only when they are brought together and closely compared are the differences on the title page apparent. Once these differences have been noticed, a study of the book reveals different ornaments and slight variations in lay-out, but it is obvious that every effort has been made in one of them to produce a facsimile of the other. The most noticeable difference is an unfortunate printer's error. One has a TABLE of contents, the other a THABLE. It is not possible to say which is the earlier. Judging by the ornaments the edition with a TABLE was printed on the newly established press of Propaganda, which has now developed into the Vatican Polyglot Press. There are two copies in the Barberini Library (now part of the Vatican library) (Stampa Barb. V. XIV, 106, 107), and one in the English College, Rome. The other edition, with THABLE, is in the Barberini Library (ib. 105), and the British Library. The latter edition was perhaps published at Douai, though there are indications that suggest an English origin.

It is probable that Howard procured a copy of the 'Douai' edition and imitated it as closely as the limitations of the Propaganda press would allow. There is no explanation of why he should have gone to this trouble in days before copyright, when pirated editions troubled nobody's conscience. So much for the authorship of what became known as 'Howard's Catechism'. A Franciscan missionary setting out from Rome for Ireland asked to be supplied with copies of F. Molloy's *Grammatica* (1677) and *Lucerna Fidei* (1676) (both in Irish) and *Doctrina Christiana Em. Cardinalis Howard*.[13] All three were printed by the Propaganda press, and were still offered for sale in their catalogue of 1793.[14]

Another of Howard's literary activities during these years needs some preliminary explanation. There lived in the Black Forest in the middle of the seventeenth century, a secular priest of great holiness of life, named Bartholomäus Holzhauser. He had a burning desire to work for the conversion of souls and particularly of England. He was a mystic with the gift of prophecy. He is said to have foretold the execution of Charles I, and to have had visions that convinced him that England would be converted when the priests there were of one mind and heart and lived in a manner more becoming their calling.[15] When Charles II was in exile he was the guest, in 1655, of the Archbishop of Mainz at his residence at Ringrave on the Rhine. The archbishop spoke to him of the fame of this priest who at the moment was at Bingen on the other side of the river. Charles expressed the desire to meet him, and in the dead of night, when the Rhine was lashed by storms the priest was rowed across at considerable risk to kiss the hand of the exiled king. They passed the night in earnest discussion and Holzhauser warmly commended to the king the Catholic faith and the priests who were labouring in England in its defence. Charles promised that he would be mindful of these fervent supplications if ever he came into his kingdom.[16] Doubtless his life-long tenderness towards Catholics and his death-bed reconciliation to the church owed something to this romantic meeting on the banks of the Rhine, on that wild night five years before his restoration.

In order to foster a more worthy mode of life for the secular clergy, Holzhauser founded what was known as the 'Institute of Clerics living in common'. Priests who joined this Institute were pledged to a quasi-monastic way of life. They lived together, with only male servants, pooled their resources and followed a timetable as exacting as that of a house of religious. Whatever his prowess at prophesying, Holzhauser's Institute is very much a product of his times. One would have thought that for priests living together the obvious common prayer would be the divine office. Priests were bound to say it in any case and might have derived more profit from saying it together. In the constitutions of the Institute the divine office is never mentioned. The common prayer, which is much insisted upon, consists of the rosary, litanies, popular prayers and at least an hour of communal meditation, which was then much in vogue.[17]

The Institute was embraced by a small number of priests in most countries of Europe and was highly commended by Innocent XI. Howard considered it the most appropriate means of sanctification for the clergy in England, and promoted it with enthusiasm. There is evidence that he contemplated imposing it on the English College in Rome, but nothing came of it.[18] On 7 April 1684 he issued his only encyclical letter to the clergy of England. The original manuscript with his signature is still extant, and there are printed copies at Westminster Diocesan Archives, Stonyhurst and in the Vatican.[19] He first expresses his concern at the way of life led by the clergy working in England. There were three principal dangers. First, that of idelness; secondly the 'promiscua cum mulieribus cohabitatio' (which must not be translated literally); and thirdly the uncontrolled administration of property, and of ecclesiastical property in particular. He therefore commends the Institute to the English clergy as the most suitable remedy. His encyclical was carried to England in June 1684 by his secretary Thomas Codrington. It cannot be pretended that it met with any conspicuous success. A Jesuit considered it an 'inept speculation that could in no way be reduced to practice'.[20] In an edition of the constitutions of the Institute published in Rome in 1688 only four priests in England are claimed as members.[21] Codrington did his best to propagate it but was strongly opposed by the Chapter. John Ward, its secretary wrote:

> It may be wondered what should move or rather transport some few of our brethren to invent a particular body or society of clergymen, called *in communi viventium*, in imitation, though but in very few things, of the German Institute, wholly impracticable here and unsuitable to our circumstances, having in Bishop Smith's golden treatise, *Monita utilia pro missionariis in Anglia* and the appendix all that is proper for our state and condition in England.

The venture received its death blow in 1698 when it was strongly attacked by John Sergeant in *A letter to our worthy Brethren of the New Institute*.[22] The English clergy, so long accustomed to complete freedom, did not view it benignly, and as far as England is concerned the Institute must be written off as a dismal failure.

The subjects that gave Howard the greatest anxiety during these closing years of Charles II, were the status of the English Chapter and the problem of a bishop for England. During the Oates plot both subjects were in abeyance, but when more peaceful times returned the Chapter renewed their demands. Perhaps enough has been said on these topics in previous chapters, though Howard has never explained his position. It was assumed by the Chapter that he wholeheartedly supported their claims, and it now came as a bitter blow to find that his view was that consistently taken by Propaganda and by the Roman court generally. Long as it is, the correspondence should be printed in full, for it was the last time that they ever appealed to him. One more bond of confidence between Howard and the English Catholics was severed.

On 16 November 1684 two letters were addressed to Howard, one a common letter from the whole Chapter, the other from John Perrot, the dean. The following is taken from the original drafts that are now the only copies extant. In their general assembly held in June 1684 it had been unanimously resolved to send six names, in the forlorn hope that Rome might accept one of them for bishop.[23] Later it was intimated to them that Howard himself would not be unwilling to be their bishop,[24] and this correspondence is the result.

> May it please Your Eminence
>
> Although it may seem a great presumption in respect of the purple Your Eminence gives splendour to and receives reciprocal lustre from, to beseech you too stoop so low as to be our pastor and bishop, yet the many years experience of Your Eminence's extreme goodness and kindness to our body and the signal veneration we also have for Your Eminence will, we hope, render this our address pardonable, especially the great service of God and Catholic religion that from the condescendency to our most humble supplication must needs result, will, we confide, prevail upon Your Eminence to give us herein a favourable and consolatory despatch.
>
> My Lord, Your Eminence knows the temper of our nation: knows it forbids, even by our Catholic laws made under Catholic kings and yet in force, to receive here in the clergy from His Holiness any other authority than ordinary, and we humbly conceive no other can here be received as hath been formerly made out both by reasons and laudable examples, without great prejudices if not the ruin of the clergy. We therefore jointly supplicate both that Your Eminence will not accept of any other, and would vouchsafe also to instruct us how we may effectually compass as secure the desired blessing of Your Eminence's pastoral superiority over us, in case there be anything further requisite on our side after Your Eminence's representation of this our most humble request to His Holiness, whom we hope God will inspire to hear us and grant what will be to all so advantageous.
>
> Now in this pleasing supposition that Your Eminence thus far vouchsafe to contribute to our general good, there will lack only this farther addition to make us as happy as present times will permit, viz; that since we cannot expect the consolation of Your Eminence's presence, that, of the six named to be presented to His Holiness in our last general assembly one, whom Your Eminence shall consider most proper, be made bishop and your coadjutor to reside with us. The six that were named by private scrutiny came forth in this order:
>
> D. John Godden.
> D. John Perrot.
> D. John Bethan.

*Protector of England*

D. B. Giffard.
M. John Leyburn.
D. James Smith.*

And here we should break off, knowing how precious Your Eminence's movements are to the whole church, but that the good of this afflicted country, which notwithstanding hath the honour in history to be styled *primogenitum Ecclesiae* [firstborn of the Church] presses us to beseech Your Eminence that nothing be done inconsistent with the *esse* and *bene esse* [being and well-being] of our Chapter, which under our late most reverend bishops and *sede vacante* since their decease hath flourished above 60 years, and however obscured by intervals with great calumnies is yet illustrious with signal suffering in many of its members, both for the faith it professeth to God and respective fidelity to His Holiness, whose blessing as most obedient sons of the church we most humbly beg by Your Eminence's interposition, as also the continuance of Your Eminence's favour upon
My Lord
Your Eminence's most obedient
and most faithful servants.
Nov.16, 1684.

(My formal letter)
May it please Your Eminence the common letter which this bears company had long since most humbly kissed Your Eminence's hand but that there have been some necessary retardments, which notwithstanding I have just reason to hope will conduce much to the better success of our desires both there with Your Eminence and here also. It may indeed seem a gross omission that at our general assembly which was partly made in order to a nomination of such persons that His Holiness might out of many worthy choose one whom he judged most proper and make him an ordinary, Your Eminence was not prenamed, and others only in case of Your Eminence's non-acceptance, but with all candour and sincerity I must beg Your Eminence to believe that considering the most eminent station you are in, it did not so much as enter into our thoughts that we might hope so great a happiness, as from Mr Goderington's relation of Your Eminence's extreme goodness and tenderness for us, we have took confidence to supplicate for now, though it was our misfortune to know how particularly Your Eminence intended to favour us, so lately. Mr Goderington being no longer over, yet

---

* It is worthy of note that the last three named in this list were eventually chosen by Rome as vicars apostolic.

extremely welcome to the right hon. Person he resides with, to whom I sent Your Eminence's character of him and His Lordship finds it fulfilled in him.

I must most humbly thank you Eminence for the honour of a letter received at his arrival, but most for the declaration therein made of Your Eminence's readiness to do all good offices, and therefore since there can be none better to us than what we supplicate for, I will remain with firm hopes it cannot be long before we may have the satisfaction of styling Your Eminence our Father, whom as yet we can only glory in as our Protector. At present I shall not be longer tedious, but beg the continuation of the honour of being esteemed,

>May it please etc.,
>Your Eminence's most faithful and
>most humble servant.
>J[ohn] P[errot][25]

## Howard replied on 13 January 1685:

I received by the last post two letters, one from yourself in particular, the other in the name of your brethren, both bearing the same date of Nov. 16, and because their principal contents relate to the same subject, I shall endeavour to satisfy both with this one answer.

In the first place I must render you thanks for the expressions I find in them of your affection, and for the confidence your profess in my readiness to do all good offices within my power. As I am fully persuaded of your sincerity in the former, so I shall never give occasion to any diminution of the latter. I am no less convinced than yourselves of the necessity there is to have episcopal government restored and settled in our country. It is what I have ever desired, and what upon your present application to me, I shall endeavour to procure. Your desire of having the authority and character placed in my person is an obliging mark of the kindness and confidence which I have already acknowledged with my thankfulness for them. But upon mature consideration of this proposal I do not perceive the consequences or advantages that might be expected from a compliance with your desire to be such as may sufficiently induce me to it, or merit your farther insisting upon it.

I should esteem myself happy (if circumstances were proper for it) not only to cooperate with you all this distance, but to be fellow labourer amongst you, and bear my part of the burden which is so cheerfully and profitably undergone by you.

The second paragraph of your common letter doth not a little trouble me, for you seem by it to insist upon a point which according to my judgement hath more of nicety than substance in it, and which nevertheless, as it hath upon former applications obstructed the way by which we were to arrive at the principal end, so unless you depart from it in that you are now upon, I can hardly promise myself or you any better than a like success. The power which is necessary and which will not be refused, if any be granted, is ordinary; the same in substance by which other bishops govern their dioceses. This is thankfully accepted and managed with much fruits in other places where the condition is the same with yours. That this power doth not make the person who hath and acts by it 'ordinary' is not so much a defect of the power itself, as the misfortune of your circumstances, which according to the regular and received discipline of the church do not render you capable of having it in the manner you desire, without incurring greater inconveniences and dangers than those which you are afraid of. I desire you to make serious reflection upon this point, and not hazard the remaining deprived of a power which you judge necessary, because you cannot have it with the formalities and advantages which are rather to be wished than hoped.

The last part of your said common letter, by which you recommend to me the care of your Chapter is next to be considered. It hath ever been my opinion that a Chapter is very requisite both for assistance of a bishop, whilst you have one amongst you, and for preservation of episcopal authority in times of vacancies, and accordingly you may rest assured that I shall not be wanting in this point also to produce you what satisfaction is in my power. But since you know already by a long experience and by the ill success of several applications, and some very powerful ones, made in order thereunto, you must not wonder if what you recommend to me be not obtained in the manner which you desire and propose to yourselves. I have had concerning this particular, several discourses with persons whose influence is strong upon deliberation of this kind, and from them I find reason to conclude that your Chapter, upon the grounds it hath hitherto stood and doth at present stand, will not be allowed. It is here looked upon as illegal in its erection for want of authority in the erector, and no less illegal in its continuation. Of this substantial defect they remain so persuaded that nothing allegeable in your behalf can be capable to remove the persuasion. It is not a Chapter they except against, but a Chapter standing upon such grounds as yours doth stand, so that to procure one in virtue of a new erection, and with some few limitations and reservations is a thing which peradventure might be obtained without much difficulty. This is all I have to represent in answer to what your write concerning *that* point, and I likewise commend it to the serious consideration of yourself and brethren.

There remains nothing more but to take notice the persons who have been judged fit to undergo the burden which you desire should be layed upon one of them. I am well assured of the abilities of some by the knowledge I have of them, and I will not doubt of a like capacity in the rest, since they have your approbation with that of their brethren. I wish it were in my power to serve every one of them in particular according to his merit, but since this for the present is neither desired nor pretended I will at least endeavour to satisfy all by procuring that the lot may fall upon someone amongst them; in which if I do not succeed, it shall not be my fault.

When you have communicated the contents of this letter to the rest of your brethren and together with them made those due reflections which the subject deserves, I hope God will inspire you to resolve on such measures as may encourage me to use my best endeavours for procuring what shall most conduce to his divine glory, to the good of English Catholics in general, and of your body in particular, which is the sole aim and desire of, Sir,

Your most affectionate friend
CARD. OF NORFOLK.[26]

There is an updated and apparently unfinished draft of a reply, and the Chapter shall have the last word:

May it please your Eminence,
*Leves loquuntur dolores ingentes stupent* [Small sorrows are vocal, great sorrows are dumb], and so have ours ever since the 26th of April last when, after the miscarriage of your Em's letter of Jan 23, we received a copy thereof from Dr Smith. But now at length with all humility we beg leave of Your Eminence to give those sorrows a vent, which hitherto have been so oppressingly silent.

In the first place, therefore, we are to express our grief that Your Eminence pleased not to vouchsafe us that near relation of Father and Pastor, which we so much ambitioned and petitioned for, as a common and illustrious good to religion, as well as a private emolument and satisfaction to ourselves; but Your Eminence appearing inexorable on the matter, we must forcibly sit down with patience and bear that great one with other concomitant misfortunes.

Our next sorrow is that Your Eminence judges our insisting upon having a bishop who shall jointly be an ordinary in respect of all Catholics in England, to be only a nicety, and suppose it sufficient that he have ordinary power given him, whereas we humbly beg you Eminence to consider that both our late bishops had this power given them in as ample manner as was possible, yet the world is a scandalized witness of what contests both of them had, and particularly the last, my Lord Richard [Smith] with adversaries of several ranks and orders, only because they were not, as was pretended, ordinaries, but only had faculties of ordinaries over and above the archpriest's faculties—contests, I say my Lord, too irreligious and tedious to be here mentioned, and therefore by all means for the future to be avoided. And yet will they forcibly be resuscitated if ever any bishop be constituted over us with other title than that of ordinary. Nor can the title of ordinary over the Catholics of England, in our judgements and others we have conferred with, throw us upon any inconvenience which will leave any proportion to the mischiefs of dissention which will otherwise follow, or the odium, suspicions and calumnies which will arise from the title of apostolical vicar in a heterodox kingdom.

Our third, and that a very piercing sorrow, is that whereas in ours of the 26 November last we beseeched Your Eminence that nothing might be done inconsistent with the *esse* and *bene esse* of our Chapter, which under our late most reverend bishops and *sede vacante* since their decease had flourished about sixty years, Your Eminence answer we must not wonder if what we recommended to Your Eminence be not obtained in the manner we desire and propose to ourselves, adding our Chapter is looked upon as illegal in its creation for want of authority in the erector, and no less illegal in its constitution, and that of this substantial defect they remain so persuaded that nothing allegeable in our behalf can be capable to remove the persuasion. My Lord, we must confess this clause was read by us with amazement, and we are infinitely obliged to Your Eminence descending so low as to give us this candid relation of the sentiments of others, though we hope Your Eminence, as formerly, is still of a different opinion, and we shall strive to confirm this Your Eminence's favourable opinion by more reasons than the dispatch of this letter will permit.

This we must assure Your Eminence that his present Majesty very graciously received a memorial he was presented with, in which amongst other things His Majesty was most humbly supplicated to admit of no bishop but in quality of ordinary, and to support our Chapter, and make use thereof in such ecclesiastical emergencies as might require their duty and be for His Majesty's service, to which His Majesty graciously said he would, it being then represented to His Majesty how my

Lord Aubigny dispensed with and married our late sovereign and Queen Catherine now dowager by faculties had only from our Chapter, as appears in our archives.

The erector of this Chapter, Dr William Bishop, acted nothing without the advice of learned bishops beyond the sea and eminent canon-lawyers, amongst the rest Hermannus Ottenbergius formerly *Auditor Rotae* at Rome, and other famous men both at Paris, Brussels and elsewhere, who judged the erection necessary and valid; and surely had His Holiness judged it otherwise from the beginning, the erector, esteemed both holy and learned, would have been scrupulous in its continuance, and been reprehended proportionably to the fault by His Holiness or ministers, and the Chapter accordingly declared invalid and substantially defective, nor would afterwards have been approved, ratified and confirmed by the succeeding Lord Bishop Richard, who governed with it till his decease. This Chapter afterwards by its agent presented six worthy persons to His Holiness Alexander VII out of which he might choose one to succeed, who judging it then unseasonable, insinuated the dean and Chapter might supply any present inconvenience in government till a bishop, which he promised within some months, should be granted, though by the power of our adversaries (notwithstanding several agents since sent, of which Mr Alexander Holt was the last) hitherto a bishop could never be obtained. But this is not an argument against but strongly for the validity of the Chapter, it being not without horror to be thought that His Holiness would permit a Chapter to exercise all capitular jurisdiction for such a large tract of time, to wit under the two bishops, and since their decease no less than threescore years and better, and that notwithstanding, this Chapter should be substantially defective for lack of authority in the erector, and nothing be allegeable in our behalf that can remove this persuasion from those most eminent persons Your Eminence hath discussed with: whereas if it be not removed there can nothing imaginable fall with a heavier reflection both on His Holiness and the Roman court, nor more ignominious to us and the whole Catholic clergy of England, and lastly also in consideration of the infinite absolutions and dispensations which must be void and invalid, as also contracts. My Lord, both our bishops were confirmed by His Holiness and empowered not only with all faculties, *quibus Episcopi in suis Diaecesibus utuntur, fruuntur et gaudent* [which bishops in their dioceses use, enjoy and rejoice in], but also *quibus uti frui vel gaudere possint* [which they might use, enjoy and rejoice in], no exception in this plenitude of ordinary power being made against the erecting of a Chapter, and 'tis manifest that a bishop can by his ordinary power, unless restrained by His Holiness, as here it is not nor anywhere in the Canons, erect a Chapter... My Lord Bishop William [Bishop] therefore very validly erected the Chapter and his successor confirmed it, and so accordingly it stands confirmed nor needs further confirmation from His Holiness. The exercise of ecclesiastical and capitular jurisdiction for threescore years not only *vidente et tacente summo pontifice* [with the knowledge and tacit consent of the Supreme Pontiff], but also thus far *approbante* [with his (explicit) approval] that six Agents at several times have been received at Rome by several popes, and still we have been kept in hopes of a bishop, and by several popes (as hath been attested to us by such as were our agents) our government by a Chapter, *vivae vocis oraculo* [by verbal decision] was allowed, and protectors have writ letters to superiors of the Chapter, giving them their titles, which we have in our archives.[27]

II

Other references to Howard at this time do not concern him as protector but are here given for the sake of completeness. In 1679 he changed his titular church from S. Cecilia to the Dominican church of the Minerva. Hence it is not unusual to find him singing the Mass there on its two great feast-days, St Thomas Aquinas and 25 March for that annual distribution of dowries already described. In addition it is recorded that he sang midnight Mass in the Sistine chapel at Christmas 1683 and presided at Vespers on the last day of that year.[28]

He had been placed on the newly formed Congregation of Relics, and signs the certificates which accompanied the relics of the martyrs Liberatus and Victoria taken from the cemetery of St Callistus, which in January 1681 were sent to Baron Widdrington, with permission to keep them, or to give them away, and to expose them for veneration in any church or chapel.[29] One wonders whether they are still in existence. More interesting than the relics sent by him to England, is a relic sent him from England. In 1683 the body of his old friend Oliver Plunkett was exhumed and transported to the monastery of Lambspring in Bavaria, but the head was sent to him in Rome. It was exposed for veneration in a Dominican church in Rome (perhaps SS John and Paul) till 1708 when it was carried back to Ireland, where it long remained in the custody of the Dominican nuns founded by the martyr's relative, Catherine Plunkett. She is said to have been for a time with Howard's English nuns in Brussels, but there is no mention of her in their records.

In March 1683 Howard was laid low by a 'double tertian with a great catarrh which hath obliged him ever since to keep his bed. This day (writes Leyburn on 28 March), he takes physic which I hope will carry away the peccant humour that hitherto hath nourished his disease.'[30] As this book is not over-rich in improving details we must make the most of the following report of 20 March:

> The Cardinal of Norfolk is better today, with so much relief of his pains that it is to be hoped that he will soon be well again. Such is his goodness that he is not only observing all the rigours of Lent, but the other day when he was bathed in sweat and was brought a silk vest to change into, he refused to put it on, saying that the sons of St Dominic wore only wool.[31]

As soon as he was convalescent he moved to Castel Gandolfo, where he remained till November; not, however, in the pope's palace but in a villa of his own. It was in the midst of his convalescence that Antoine Arnauld, the celebrated Jansenist writer, approached him for information concerning the Oates plot, that was to be used in the third part of his *Apologie pour les Catholiques*, then on the stocks. Arnauld complains in a letter of 2 July that Howard was not helpful, and doubtless the double tertian was the reason.[32] Howard's relations with this Jansenist are somewhat obscure. Arnauld more than once speaks of him as a friend and an ally,* but it would seem that, like the English Chapter, Arnauld interpreted Howard's civility and kindness as approval of all that he stood for. There does not appear to be any evidence that Howard had leanings to Jansenism, though he was more than once charged

---

\* 'Cardinalis de Noordfolkia admodum nobis favet; tum ab ipso tum ab eius Auditore litteras iterum accepi quae summum ipsorum erga me spirant amorem', Neercassel to Arnauld, 8 Sept. 1684 (A. Arnauld, *Œrvres*, iv, 178). There is a considerable correspondence between Howard and Johannes van Neercassel, the Dutch Jansenist that I have not seen. cf. J. Bruggeman, *Inventaris van de Archieven bij het Metropolitaan Kapittel van Utrecht van de Roomsch Katholieke Kerk der Oud Bisschoppelijke Clerezie*, 's-Gravenhage, 1928, 188, 221. Howard also befriended François van Vianen, a professor at Louvain, who was strongly suspected of Jansenism (*Bulletin de l'Institut historique belge de Rome*, 30 (1957–8), 194).

with it. The same misunderstanding of Howard's courtesy is evident in his relations with the French historian Noël Alexandre. This learned Dominican sent Howard a complimentary copy of each of his works as it appeared, and Howard punctiliously acknowledged it with words of thanks and praise and encouragement, though he more than once admits he had not had time to read much more than the title-page. Then in 1684 Alexandre fell foul of the Holy Office for his views on the extent of papal authority, and his book was condemned. Arnauld's correspondent in Rome reported on 9 September 1684:

> I understand that Cardinal Howard must be displeased with this condemnation of an author who after all has never till now caused dishonour to the order of St Dominic. It cannot be doubted that the Jesuits will make the most of this condemnation.[33]

Howard's letter to Alexandre shows that he was more displeased with the author, and may be cited as an indication of how limited was the freedom of a church historian of those days. History was then the handmaid of theology and not a queen in her own right:

> I have only this week received your gracious letter of 15 July, together with the gift of three volumes containing chapters and commentary on the ecclesiastical history of the 13th and 14th centuries. I am vehemently displeased, both because of the duty and love I owe to our order, and also because of the singular love I bear towards you, that something in the earlier parts of this work should have been seized upon by the cardinals of the Inquisition and considered worthy of censure. For I desire that our writers should be free, not only from all blemish of error, but as far as possible, from all suspicion. I confess indeed that in previous letters I pointed out how difficult was the matter you had in hand; matter in which it is admitted that one cannot even state the truth without causing offence to many. It would perhaps have been wiser, certainly safer, to abstain altogether from treating of those controversies in which it is evident that great authorities are at variance; where the close connection of subjects makes it impossible to avoid controversies, then it is the part of an historian to record opinions rather than to make a judgment. I hope to find this approach, which I am glad to see you approve of, in the three volumes that have just arrived, and in the others that are still wanted for the completion of the work. I cannot praise too highly the veneration and devotion of your paternity towards the Apostolic See, nor your obedience

in submitting your work to its judgment: conduct becoming
in a Catholic teacher and a master of the Dominican order.[34]

Soon after his return from his convalescence at Castel Gandolfo he was entrusted by Innocent XI with the oversight of a convent of Ursuline nuns from Brussels designed for the education of Roman girls and founded by Laura Duchess of Modena, the mother of the Duchess of York. The brief of foundation is dated 24 December 1683 and in it Laura is informed that she will learn the pope's mind in greater detail from Cardinal Howard.[35] He took a great interest in this convent and remembered it in his will by a bequest of 500 scudi and a further 1000 scudi for a Mass to be said daily in perpetuity in their church for the repose of his soul.[36]

Two events in England at this time were of particular concern to Howard. On the night of 26 March 1682 the queen's chapel at Somerset House and the convent of her Portuguese Franciscans were burnt to the ground. Such valuables as survived the fire were carried off by the mob.[37] The queen moved back to her former chapel at St James's, and in the reshuffle demanded by economy Howard lost his office of grand almoner and the salary that went with it. It is doubtful whether he lost much financially, as his salary was rarely paid. In 1684 his brother Henry, 6th Duke of Norfolk died. Evidently Cardinal Howard had been receiving some assistance from him for in July the Duke of York writes to the pope, pointing out that Howard had lost all solid means of support by the death of his brother and the reform of the queen's chapel, and asks that a benefice may be conferred upon him.[38]

As though to compensate for the loss of the royal chapel at Somerset House there was founded during these years another Catholic chapel in London. The agent, or resident as he was called, of Cosimo III, Grand Duke of Tuscany wrote in 1681 to say that he would acquire much prestige if he followed the other foreign ambassadors and opened a public chapel. He would also be able to protect a priest from the operation of the penal laws. He asked that just one room in his house next to the Chirugions' Arms in Haymarket might be set aside for this purpose, with an English-speaking priest as chaplain.[39] It seems strange that the Tuscan agents, who had been continuously in London since the time of James I, had never thought of it before. Permission was given and the room soon proved inadequate. He next obtained authority to knock two rooms into one, as the Catholics were having to hear Mass on the stairs.[40] Soon there were four resident chaplains. They were all Dominicans and apparently all Irish. The only one mentioned by name is Fr Dominic Langton, who received £2 per quarter for preaching, in addition to the 7/– per week paid to each of them.[41] One of them departed at very short notice on the eve of Advent Sunday, and in a bitter letter the resident says that they could all go if they liked, as there was no difficulty of picking up friars in London to replace them. He does, however, admit that a shilling a day was rather less than the other ambassadors paid, and suggests an increase.[42] It is possible that members of the English province were associated with this chapel, for the address of Fr Dominic Gwillim in 1681 is given as 'St Alban's St, next door to the Chirugions' Arms'.[43]

The general impression one forms of Howard at this time, from surviving documents such as they are, is of a conscientious and kindly prelate, coping to the best of his ability with a thankless and well-nigh impossible task. Of his kindheartedness there is considerable evidence. English visitors to Rome, whatever their religion, found him ready to help them. There was for instance Lady Theophila Lucy, a daughter of George Earl Berkeley and widow of Sir Kingsmill Lucy of Broxbourne (Herts). She later became Lady Nelson. Howard had the happiness of receiving her into the church in 1681.[44] There was a Lord Grey of Ruthin, who writes that the cardinal 'hath been very civil to me and hath given me letters to most of the princes of Italy who have regaled me considerably'.[45] There were Charles Wigmore of Herefordshire and William Rixon of Worcestershire, two young Catholics who had suffered persecution in the Oates plot, and who in December 1679 were befriended by Howard. The former was admitted into his service; the latter became a papal guard.[46] There was Gilbert Burnet, later Bishop of Salisbury, who, in a letter of 8 December 1685, pays him the following tribute:

> Cardinal Howard is too well known in England to need any character from me. The elevation of his present condition hath not in the least changed him; he hath all the sweetness and gentleness of temper that we saw in him in England, and he retains the unaffected simplicity and humility of a friar amidst all the dignity of the purple; and as he sheweth all the generous care and concern for his countrymen that they can expect from him, so I met with so much of it, in so many obliging marks of

his goodness for myself, as went far beyond a common civility, that I cannot enough acknowledge it.[47]

Above all there is his correspondence with Cosimo III, whose friendship, begun in London, he retained to the end. There are ninety-seven letters from Howard to the grand duke between 1676 and 1694.[48] All but two are on behalf of people who had solicited his help. There are impecunious soldier-adventurers who want a place in the grand duke's bodyguard; obscure Italians looking for a job as minor officials in some town of Tuscany; a galley-slave, whose health has not improved after twenty-eight years of rowing; English sailors and merchants at Leghorn who have fallen foul of the local authorities; priests wanting preferment; English noblemen wanting to kiss his hand on their way home; French Flemish and Spanish visitors in some sort of trouble or other. Eighteen are on behalf of members of his own order, but only one is on behalf of an English Dominican. Howard begged from Cosimo a piece of land for the foundation of the Dominican convent at Leghorn, and later intercedes for certain young Irish Dominicans there who had not shown sufficient deference to the local council. He asks permission for the Dominicans to consult a manuscript of Albert the Great in the library of S. Lorenzo, when they were preparing a new edition of his works, and recommends Florentine Dominicans for lectorships in his schools. Occasionally the boot is on the other foot, as when Cosimo solicits Howard to obtain a dispensation for the brethren at S. Marco in Florence to pursue their studies at home, and not in the *studium generale* at Perugia, where there was a danger of their losing their simplicity of life. These details suggest a vast compassionate correspondence, for few were as business-like as Cosimo III in preserving papers and keeping copies of out-going letters.

If the office of cardinal protector had involved no more than the relief of needy English Catholic exiles, then Howard was fully adequate for the task. Obviously much more was expected and one can understand the disappointment of Fr Warner and the Chapter that no firm action was taken to ameliorate affairs at home. But surely the reason is not far to seek. There was nothing that Howard could do that would satisfy Warner *and* the Chapter. Any decision that pleased the one would automatically have antagonized the other. The times were not propitious. The recent martyrs and the

*Protector of England*

popular panic were all too fresh in everyone's memory. There was a good time coming and the only thing to do was to wait patiently. Charles II had no legitimate offspring and would be succeeded by his Catholic brother James, Duke of York. Then would be the time for action and the cardinal protector would come into his own.

## Notes

1. SB, 1643, ff. 1, 13, 3.
2. AVCAU, lib. 198.
3. Arch.Municip. Louvain, Carton 4318.
4. Dodd, *The Church History of England*, III, 385.
5. Arch. Municip. Louvain, Carton 4318.
6. *The Tryals and Condemnation of Lionel Anderson alias Munson ... for High Treason as Romish Priests, Upon the Statute of 27 Eliz. Cap. 2*, London, 1680, 13.
7. AAW, A36, no. 27 (20 Jan. 1693).
8. *Ibid.* no. 45 (Jan. 1694)
9. AVCAU, Scrit. 20, no. 22.
10. B, 2606.
11. G. Burnet, *History of his own Time*, London, 1714, I, 661.
12. P. M. Domaneschio, *De rebus Coenobii Cremonensis*, Cremonae, 1767, 327.
13. AP, t.502, f. 352 (5 Oct. 1688).
14. *Catalogus librorum qui ex typograhio S.C. de Prop. Fide variis linguis prodierunt et in eo adhuc asservantur*, Romae, 1793, 4, 13.
15. J. P. L. Gaduel, *La perfection secerdotale ou la vie et l'esprit du serviteur de Dieu B. H.*, Paris, 1861.
16. AAW, A34, no. 202.
17. *Synopsis Instituti Clericorum in commune viventium*, Romae, 1688 (BV, Stampa Barb. D. I, 61).
18. AV, Fondo Pio, 270; Misc. Arm. III, 16, f. 248; NI, 20, f. 138.
19. AAW, A34, nos.215, 216; BV, Ottoboni 2499, f. 385; AV, Misc. Arm. I. t.17, 411.
20. Camb. Univ. Lib., Ll, I, 19 (Letter-book of J. Warner, SJ), f. 62 (6 June 1681).
21. *Synopsis Instituti Clericorum in commune viventium*, Romae, 1688. (BV, Stampa Barb. D. I, 31.
22. J. Kirk, *Biographies of English Catholics*, London, 1909, 50.
23. OB, Gen. Assemblies 1667–1755, 84.
24. OB, Order of Consults 1667–93, 194 (13 Aug. 1684).
25. AAW, A34, no. 222 (another copy no. 223).
26. *Ibid.* no. 231. Printed in *Dominicana*, 79, though with many misreadings.
27. *Ibid.* no. 255.
28. BV, Vat. Lat. 12340, f. 286.
29. Ushaw MSS, III, no. 22.
30. AAW, A34, no. 205.

31 Avvisi 46, f. 518.
32 A. Arnauld, *Œuvres*, Paris, 1775–83, xii, lxix.
33 *Ibid.* II, 453.
34 BL, Add. 23720, f. 29.
35 *Innocentii Papae XI Epistolae ad Principes*, ed. J. Berthier, Romae, 1895, II, 152.
36 *Dominicana*, 91.
37 Avvisi 45, f. 116.
38 NF, 66A, f. 74.
39 Med. 4243, no. 462.
40 Med. 4245, no. 497.
41 *Ibid.* no. 132.
42 *Ibid.* no. 497.
43 *Dominicana*, 137.
44 T. Birch, *Life of Dr John Tillotson*, London, 1752, 128; BL, Birch 4274, f. 173.
45 BL, Add. 29560, f. 454.
46 AVCAU, Pilgrim Book 1654–1732, 32.
47 G. Burnet, *Some Letters containing an Account of what seemed most remarkable in Switzerland, Italy &c*, Amsterdam, 1686, 231.
48 Med. 3827–47.

# 9

# *The King's Servant*

I

CARDINAL HOWARD sent his greetings to Charles for the new year 1685 and the king replied on the 26 January, assuring the cardinal of his continued affection.[1] Before this letter reached Rome Charles was dead, reconciled to the church at the end by his old friend John Huddleston, OSB. James II succeeded without any immediate opposition, and on Sunday 25 February publicly assisted at Mass with Queen Mary in the chapel of the now dowager queen at St James's.[2] The Catholic lords who had been in the Tower since 1680 were released. In April the king and queen again attended Mass at St James's and walked in the procession of the Blessed Sacrament round the cloisters of the former Portuguese friars, now inhabited by the English Benedictines. The baldachino was carried by four Catholic peers, including Howard's nephew Thomas. Lord Powis (one of those recently released) carried the king's sword.[3] There was talk of calling over the Dominican Archbishop of Armagh to perform the coronation but finally James (though refusing communion) submitted to be anointed by Canterbury; an act for which Howard procured him absolution in the following December.[4] The question of holy oils raised a difficulty. They had been swept out of the Anglican church with the other popish superstitions but their use was still prescribed for the coronation service. Any oils surviving from Catholic times must have been destroyed with the other regalia in Cromwell's time. Charles II had ordered Canterbury to get some from the Bishop of Ghent. The bishop replied that either His Grace was a valid bishop and could consecrate his own, or he wasn't and had no business with them. However, he enclosed a copy of the *ritus consecrandi* and presumably this was used to provide oils for Charles II and James II.[5]

## Philip Howard

The news of the death of the king and his brother's peaceful succession reached Rome on 15 March and was conveyed personally by Howard to the pope, to Laura Duchess of Modena (the new queen's mother) and to the cardinals and grandees. There was the usual elaborate exchange of condolences and congratulations.[6] The news of the succession of a Catholic king was received in Rome with transports of joy. On 25 March Howard gave a banquet at SS John and Paul's for the English nobility, Catholic and Protestant, drank the health of James II and afterwards led them to a private audience with Innocent XI.[7] Early in April he moved his palace to a building adjoining the English College and part of its property.[*] In May a crowd of students (doubtless of the said college), with drums and tambourines and other musical instruments, and supported by a number of prelates, affixed the arms of England over the main door of Howard's palace.[8] There was to have been a solemn Mass and *Te Deum* in the college chapel on Sunday 27 May (which was also the anniversary of Howard's promotion). The principal guest was to be Madama Martinozzi, mother of Laura Duchess of Modena and grandmother of the new queen. She was over eighty. Alas, as few days before, she went to visit Howard's Flemish Ursulines and, convent floors being what they are, she fell from the top of the stairs to the bottom and was in no mood for a *Te Deum*.[9] The celebrations were postponed till the following Sunday and were attended by Howard and some thirty other prelates. For three days a fountain in front of Howard's palace flowed with wine and for three nights every window was illuminated with torches and flares. The old lady Marinozzi had rallied sufficiently to attend the High Mass; she now took to her bed and died.[10]

For a few days Howard's palace was the centre of attraction, and particularly the arms of England over the door. Perhaps the college funds did not run to a lion or a unicorn, for the royal arms

---

[*] This move had been determined upon as early as 1682, but the extensive alterations, including a new staircase and the raising of the ceiling of his state rooms, were not completed till the spring of 1685. Howard began paying rent to the college as from 17 April of that year. The alterations cost him 10,000 scudi. Much of the college was renovated at the same time. Howard lent the rector 1000 scudi for this purpose, but the cost was borne by the college. Howard's apartments, with their decorated ceilings are still to be seen and are still the property of the college (AVCAU, lib.XI, ff. 188, 271, and Scrit.7, no. 13).

were displayed without their supporters. However the professor of humanities at the Collegio Urbano, Julianus Blancarius, came to the rescue. What need had James of lions, he wrote in poetic verse, when he was supported by the herculean shoulders of Howard?[*] But not everyone was pleased. The French ambassador noticed that the arms quartered those of France and off he went to the Dominican master of the sacred palace to lodge a protest. The Dominican was equal to the occasion. He was able to find a precedent. In the time of Alexander VII (1655–67) a Dominican, who unfortunately is not named, had printed his public theses and dedicated them to Queen Catherine of Braganza, giving her the title of Queen of France.[11]

Towards the end of July came news of the rebellion of the Duke of Monmouth and of its speedy suppression. This time it was Laura's turn to celebrate. There were lavish quantities of free wine for all, and a happy day concluded with throwing plates and glasses out of the windows till the *sbirri* had to be called to put a stop to the fun.[12]

The accession of a Catholic king was a tremendous opportunity for English Catholics, but one that needed the utmost circumspection. For more than a century the government had been in the hands of Protestants. The simple people had been nourished on the crudest anti-Catholic propaganda, and recent events had shown how little it required to raise their credulity to fever-pitch.

---

[*] 'To some who look for supporting lions in the arms of the King of England recently displayed at the palace of His Eminence Cardinal Howard.

> Cur non Stemma Leo Regis de more Britanni
> Sustinet? a populo non semel ipse rogor;
> Huic ego: An herculeos humeros non cernis? Howardus
> Supplet, in hoc Regis stemma Domusque sedet.
> Casuris innixa feris, casum ipsa timeret,
> Hac virtute Domus fulta timere nequit.
> Utque ferae multam referunt a stemmate famam,
> Perpetuam nostro ex Hercule Stemma refert.

[Why does a lion not hold up the shield of the British King in the customary way? I am asked this by the people from time to time. To them I say: Do you not perceive the Herculean shoulders? Howard stands in, on him the shield and House of the King sits. Resting upon wild beasts liable to fall, it [the House] might itself fear falling, but a house supported by this strength cannot fear [falling]. And as wild animals proclaim from a shield great renown, this shield proclaims the perpetual renown of our Hercules.]

Julianus Blancarius.' (AV, Borghese 481, f. 140)

From press and pulpit had flowed a steady stream of abuse and misrepresentation; Catholicism had come to be generally regarded as a foreign tyranny that burnt true believers, stifled knowledge and destroyed liberty.

Those who had profited from the spoils of the church were apprehensive. Only with the greatest prudence and tact could a Catholic king hope to survive in the face of so many powerful vested interests.

Howard was fully alive to these hopes and dangers. He wrote for advice to Cardinal Francesco Buonvisi, who was then nuncio at Vienna. The reply is dated 8 April 1685. It is so enlightened and in advance of his time that it deserves to be translated in full.

> The obligations which I owe to Your Eminence for past favours and for those which I have just received in such profusion are so great that I only wish I could find words adequate to express them and worthy to match the great confidence that you repose in me. Pray have the goodness to supply what is lacking in this regard and be assured that I wish my capacity to help were as great as is my joy at the happy turn of events in England. However, my small capacity I find superfluous when I see that God is disposing all things *fortiter et suaviter* [firmly and gently] for the greater good of those kingdoms. For he sweetly instilled in King Charles a sweet disposition for the help of the Catholics and then the strength to declare himself a Catholic at the end of his life. In King James was first the strength to profess our holy religion and now the sweetness to propagate it in due season. I see also among the happy auguries the good fortune of having Your Eminence as protector of those kingdoms so that you may cooperate with these manifest dispositions of God, who has determined this fullness of time when the ancient piety will be seen to bourgeon in these nations, which before the schism were second to none in their devotion to God.
>
> Your Eminence has been good enough to seek my poor advice in this important matter, and I will do my best to obey. And I will say that we must not depart from *fortiter et suaviter*. The *fortiter* is already accomplished by the king's public profession of Catholicism; hence there remains the *suaviter*, because by this means the establishment of religion in the state will be assured. His Majesty has already begun to practise it, with so much applause not only of his own people but of all Europe, that it only remains to desire its continuance. Let me remind Your Eminence that Christ our Lord did not make use of his absolute power for the foundation of his church lest faith should

be deprived of all merit. He propagated the church by the blood of the martyrs and the prudence of the confessors, and then the conversion of the Emperor Constantine. In England there has been the constancy of the martyrs and the prudence of the confessors: now we have a new Constantine. But since the authority of the King of England is more limited by law than was the absolute power of the Roman emperor, in my opinion he must use greater caution. On this principle he should not permit the opening of public churches for Catholic services, for this would annoy the dissidents. It is enough that the late king and the present one have raised the standard of the Cross, leaving those who have the grace of God to follow it, and making it clear that he will not use force, save only the force of example. It would therefore be wise that His Majesty should protest in the first session of parliament, as he has already done before the privy council, that he wishes to identify himself completely with the interests of his people, and to procure not only their safety but their aggrandizement; and that in matters of religion, just as he will not be forced, so he will not use force against anyone. Once the fear of violent measures has been removed, and once assured of his will to promote their good and to remain totally united with them, they will be ready to give him unqualified obedience. After that it may be hoped that by God's grace and their love for their king they will in time conform to his religion.

In my poor judgment the worst danger to be avoided is from the priests. They must not boast of their triumph at his accession; they must not run all over the country expecting a sudden conversion of the whole kingdom; they must not expect more than they had in the previous reign. If they behave otherwise they will destroy first the king and then religion; excessive zeal causes only chaos. Some perhaps will urge the pope to send a nuncio both to congratulate the king and to further the cultivation of the vineyard. On this point I do not know what would be best. Certainly it should not be done before the dissolution of parliament, in order to avoid any demonstrations that might cause resentment. Even then the question would remain open to dispute. However it might not be a bad thing if he were sent on an extraordinary mission simply of felicitation, and to render due homage to so worthy a king; not with an ordinary mission, to start exercising jurisdiction. Even so to obviate all danger it would be necessary that such a nuncio should be endowed with great discretion and should treat with all without distinction, inviting them to his table and going to theirs, and never disputing about religion. He should give out that there is no question of reclaiming church lands from those who have usurped them.

Granted always these precautions, somebody should be sent with the acknowledged character of apostolic-minister, and therefore I consider it more appropriate that after the end of parliament His Holiness should send Your Eminence, without any public character and simply as a private act of courtesy, in order to make it clear that there is no intention of using any extraordinary diligence in matters of religion, and that there is no thought whatever of claiming church property.

His Majesty already knows what are the true interests of his kingdom to which he should conform. Hence I will only add that, who goes with the stream goes far and who goes against it strives without profit and even with peril. For the rest, in addition to the renewed thanks which I render to Your Eminence for the trust you have reposed in me, I beg you to forgive my ineptitude and to do me the favour of asking of His Majesty a kindly thought for the felicitations which I send and for the desire that I entertain of receiving his revered commands in this court, that I may render my hereditary service. I refer you to Sanders,* who speaks of Antonio Buonvisi and makes mention of the letter written to him by Thomas More with charcoal on the night before his martyrdom. From that account, so gratifying to my family, Your Eminence may infer the depths of my attachment to your nation (and particularly to the reverend person of Your Eminence, who so favours me) and the greatness of my desire to be of service.[13]

Carinal Buonvisi enclosed a letter of congratulation for the king, in which he again proudly mentions his ancestor Antonio with the additional claim that he did much for the English refugees in Flanders.[14]

Howard appears to have listened to this wise and statesmanlike counsel. It was a time for action, after so many years of waiting, but for action that would allay the Protestants' fears of vindictiveness and retaliation for all the injustices of the past. He had a long audience with the pope on 26 April and another on 28 May.[15] Things were really beginning to move at last. It was at this time†

---

\* Nicolai Sanderi, *De origine ac progressu Schismatis Anglicani*, 2nd edn. Rome, 1586, 306.

† The exact date of this important event is nowhere recorded. On 29 March 1685 Antoninus Cloche, as *socius* to the Master General (whom he succeeded in 1686) was instituted titular provincial of England but on 12 May he exchanged this office for titular provincial of Dacia (AGOP, Registers of the Masters-General OP, series IV, 159, last page). This was evidently done to provide England with an actual provincial.

that on Howard's petition the English Dominicans were restored to the full status of a province with Vincent Torre nominated provincial,[16] a sure sign of growing confidence that a brighter day was dawning. Now was the time to give England a bishop. The king wrote direct to the pope asking for one and on 8 August Innocent replied: 'We have promptly and most willingly decided to accede to Your Majesty's wishes, and we will appoint for that office our beloved son John Leyburn, whom we judge worthy of your acceptance.' Doubtless Howard was responsible for the appointment of his own auditor. James accepted this choice, but was impatient for more than one bishop. There is a report on 1 September that:

> This court is very pleased that the English king has nominated three Catholic subjects for the churches of England, of whom are the auditor of Cardinal Howard and another, a Dominican father, both English. There is talk of sending London a vicar general with pontifical authority, but the difficulty remains as to his jurisdiction.[17]

On 3 September Howard had an audience lasting two hours and on the 5th Leyburn was declared vicar apostolic in England. He was obliged to promise under oath not to recognize the English Chapter.[18] There were rumours that Howard was also to go to England as nuncio extraordinary, but it was eventually decided to send Ferdinando d'Adda, an Italian cleric, on this delicate embassy. He set out with Leyburn on 6 October carrying a letter from Howard to Queen Catherine, in which the cardinal expresses his readiness to obey her commands, having 'the honour to be one of Your Majesty's oldest servants'.[19]

The Roman court had acted with promptitude and it is clear that Howard was the prime mover. He was even accused of being in too much of a hurry. There is a report of 13 October that the Vatican was displeased with the public announcement of the consecration of a bishop for England, as such resolutions ought to remain secret till parliament had approved the coming of a resident minister from the Holy See. 'The publication of this news is attributed to Cardinal Howard, who, with the zeal of a true religious, wants to see the conversion of all these kingdoms in a single day.'[20]

James on his side determined to send an ambassador to Rome. His choice of Lord Castlemaine was not felicitous. Castlemaine was chiefly known as the husband of Charles II's favourite mistress, and was unlikely for this reason, to be welcome at the court of the austere Innocent XI. Barillon, the French ambassador in London voiced the popular criticism in a despatch of 29 October.

> I have not pressed the King of England to tell me the name of the ambassador he is sending to Rome ... but I knew from other sources that it was the Earl of Castlemaine, husband of the Duchess of Cleveland. I have no doubt that Your Majesty will make the same reflection as I know has been made by those who have learnt of the choice. It seems rather ridiculous to send a man who is so little known for his own sake and so well known for Madame of Cleveland's. The King of England is not put off by that, and has chosen him because the Catholics have great confidence in him, because he has paid several visits to Italy, and because he is believed to be very clever and a very zealous Catholic.[21]

d'Adda and Leyburn reached London in November. The former came ostensibly as a private envoy from the pope, with no more extensive mission than to carry the papal felicitations to the new king. This did not satisfy James, who insisted on receiving him as an official papal nuncio. d'Adda had to make a public entry, with all the elaborate ceremonial, though some prudence was shown in staging this event at Windsor and not in the metropolis. John Leyburn was appointed grand almoner to the new queen and occupied the apartments at St James's formerly used by Howard. He wished to appear in public in the non-descript garb that persecution had imposed on the priests, but James insisted on his dressing like a bishop and displaying a pectoral cross. There is a report of 5 November from the agent for Cosimo III, that the queen was not very pleased with having Leyburn thrust upon her as she wished the office of grand almoner to remain with her confessor, a certain Padre Galli, a Jesuit from Modena. He also informs us that there had been a rumour that the Jesuits and Benedictines were unwilling to acknowledge the authority of Leyburn, but had now thought better of it.[22]

Leyburn's episcopal garb caused some comment, but such as has survived is not particularly unfriendly:

> Nov. 29 [1685]
> Dr John Leyburn, Bishop of Atrumetum in *partibus infideliem*, goes in a long cassock and cloak, with a golden cross hanging to a black ribbon about his neck; goes in a chair or sedan, but his train is not held up—so Mr [Obediah] Walker. Dr Leyburn,

secretary lately to the Cardinal of Norfolk and now Bishop of Atrumetum, came as nuncio from the pope to King James II about the middle of this month, and took up his lodging in Lincoln's Inn Fields. His train *is* bore up. He confers popish orders.[23]

Barillon reports that his wearing episcopal dress 'causes some astonishment at court and in London but the King of England believes that it would be beneath his dignity if a bishop dare not appear in his true character'. He adds the first disturbing feature of the new religious regime at court. He states that the chief officers are bound to accompany the king as far as the chapel door, but most of them reluctantly go further. One Protestant peer went on Christmas night to carry the king's offertory. With great repugnancy, but fearful of doing otherwise, he actually knelt down.[24]

The queen wrote to Howard on 4 January to express her approval of d'Adda and Leyburn,[25] and in the same month d'Adda opened his own chapel in London. He chose as his principal chaplain the superior of the Irish Dominicans, who were in charge of the chapel of the Tuscan agent. This provoked another angry letter to Cosimo III. The agent complains that this priest had been taken without any reference to him, and that he was not accustomed to such discourtesy from ecclesiastics. The priest himself (whose name is not given) pleaded that he was carrying out instructions received from Cardinal Howard.[26] In August 1686 the agent appointed as his principal chaplain Fr Cornelius O'Heyn,[27] an aged Irish Dominican who had been affiliated to the English province. He died on 17 October (new style) and the agent, only two months later, informs the grand duke that all the Dominicans in London had gathered in his house on 18 October for his obsequies. He was buried the same day in the cemetery attached to the queen's chapel at St James's.[28]

There is not much evidence that, up to the end of 1685, King James had been guilty of conduct liable to cause fear and despondency in Protestant hearts. There does not appear to have been any outcry against the public appearance of d'Adda and Leyburn in the dress proper to their office. Howard had himself gone about London in the full dress of a French abbé, and had pooh-poohed the apprehensions of those who said that the presence of a Catholic bishop in full pontificals would be more than a nine days' wonder. It seems unlikely that he was perturbed by the ceremonial dress being publicly worn by these prelates. Yet there is evidence that he was already concerned by the precipitous conduct of certain

## Philip Howard

Catholics in England. In December 1685 Gilbert Burnet visited Rome and saw much of Howard. He thus refers to his interview:

> Cardinal Howard showed me all his letters from England, by which I saw that those who wrote to him reckoned that their designs were so well laid that they could not miscarry. They thought they should certainly carry everything at the next session of parliament. There was a high strain of insolence in their letters, and they reckoned they were so sure of the king that they seemed to have no doubt left of their succeeding in the reduction of England.* ... The cardinal told me that all the advices writ over from thence to England were for slow, calm and moderate courses. He said he wished he was at liberty to show me copies of them. But he saw that violent courses were more acceptable and would probably be followed, and he added that these were the production of England, far different from the counsels of Rome.[29]

This account is repeated by Macaulay[30] and has been given a wide publicity. It is difficult to assess its value. What were the 'violent courses' contemplated as early as 1685, and where are the cautious advices from Rome? It can hardly refer to the Bloody Assize, which was purely a political matter, and not unprecedented. There is nothing in the correspondence to d'Adda from the papal secretary that could be interpreted as a counsel of moderation, or any suggestion that the Roman court, was apprehensive. As for Howard's letters, there is only one belonging to this time. It alludes to opposition to Leyburn, but this is evidently the queen's opposition to having him as grand almoner. There is no hint Howard was afraid of violent courses. It is addressed to Lord Caryll, who had been recently appointed secretary to the queen, and is dated 22 December 1685:

> Sir, This post only I receive yours of the 5 November together with its cover the following post, being particularly favoured by it in many respects, not only the particular service you did our master [the king] at your arrival for the immediate admission of our Adrimat [Leyburn], who some unquiet spirits would have otherwise hindered as I doubt not but our master, when well informed by yourself and what I can say with the

---

* 'The popish party was so confident that I saw by some long letters writ to Cardinal Howard and which he showed me, for I was then at Rome, that they reckoned the matter sure' (H. C. Foxcroft, *A Supplement to Burnet's History of My Own Times*, Oxford, 1902, 172).

truth and justice, will clearly see that Bp Adrimat and I never desired or endeavoured anything but what was truly for the good of his person and honour as for those of his religion and servants. Wherefore one of the best news you could give me was of the offer His Majesty made you, to be the queen's secretary, as I hope you are, being it imports very much for the good of Catholics and its religion, for which I know you will willingly sacrifice your own quiet, lest the refusal of that high place might afterwards unquiet your mind much more in the sin of omission, when you may be so great an instrument for its religious good, and I myself (although the worse member of it) should lose so much by the absence of so good a friend from so good a mistress, who in all respects deserveth the best of our faithful services. Wherefore, as I hope you will not omit your part therein, so you will not incapacitate yourself in not assisting her, and consequently me, with the best instructions and commands for me how to serve Her Majesty, her religion and yourself to the best of my poor capacity at this distance, until it please God I may be yet able (before my few remaining days pass) to sense all personally. And what I cannot perform at this distance as I ought, I hope both their Majesties will of their goodness think none more proper to supply than our good Bp Adrimat, of whom I know I need say no more unto you who knoweth and esteemeth him so well, as the like I might say (if it were not superfluous) to him of you. But since I must also add your good brother and our young fishmonger herein I will add no more, lest the weight of all might drownd me.[31]

The insolent letters that Howard is said to have shown to Burnet were doubtless from individuals. There does not appear to be any other evidence that Howard or the Roman court in any way disapproved of the policy of King James as it was unfolding itself at the close of 1685.

II

In January 1686 news reached Rome that the Earl of Castlemaine was coming as the king's envoy. This posed a grave diplomatic question. The quality of royal and papal envoys was reciprocal. James had received d'Adda with all the marks of honour accorded to a nuncio, and he expected Castlemaine to be received with the corresponding rank of ambassador. Rome had sent d'Adda in a purely private capacity without the normal powers of a nuncio. To receive an English ambassador, in the full sense of the term, without acknowledging d'Adda as a complete nuncio was unthinkable, and the time was not ripe for a nuncio in London. There is a report of 12 January which shows how serious Howard considered this question:

> Cardinal Howard, having let it be known that he had matters of the gravest importance and for the service of the church which he wished to submit to His Holiness by order of the English King his master, was told to deal with Cardinal Cybo. He replied that he would have done so but that he did not wish to transgress the commands of the king his patron, who insisted that he must communicate this great business only to His Holiness. Nevertheless he could not obtain an audience.[32]

A week later there is a more detailed report:

> Last Saturday evening was held a congregation of State, and Cardinal Howard attended, because the matter under discussion was the mode of treating the ambassador of his Britannic Majesty, who wanted to know before sending him, how he was to be received. In the meantime all public functions of Mons. d'Adda, the nuncio-apostolic in that realm, have been suspended, and that, after he had been sent to London at the king's request. It is said that the king had asked the Holy See to allow something in favour of English Protestants in order to draw them sweetly and little by little to the holy faith, though without doing anything contrary to his conscience, for he is fully aware of his duty to suffer martyrdom if necessary for the faith of Jesus Christ. It is not yet known what has been decided.[33]

The precise status of Castlemaine seems to have been still undecided when he set out from England about 20 February. By this date all that is made public is that 'no accommodation will be prepared for him as he wishes to choose his own palace, and that till he has found one he will lodge in the house of the Cardinal of Norfolk'.[34]

On 26 March after four months of trying, Howard was received in audience, and immediately afterwards went to Castel Gandolfo to confer with the Duchess of Modena. He returned to Rome the same day and sent off his coach and servants to meet Castlemaine at Genoa, where he was expected to land from Marseilles.[35] Some of Castlemaine's servants arrived in Rome soon after, and the ambassador himself on 13 April. Howard met him beyond the city and escorted him to his palace at the English College. He remained incognito till the vexed question of his status should be settled.[36] He remained Howard's guest only four days and then moved to the palace of Cardinal Pamphili in the Piazza Navona, which that Cardinal had put at his disposal fully furnished. Perhaps his departure from the English College was accelerated by an incident that is recorded with some gusto by an anonymous writer, who had no great love for the Jesuits:

> It was but the other day that Father Morgan did so meddle with what concerned the lord ambassador as nothing might be proposed that was not first advised by him, who was earnest to have Fr Peters named a cardinal amongst the first things were offered to the pope's consideration. Albeit the ambassador lodged in the Cardinal Howard's palace, yet His Eminence was shut out from the knowledge of what he was proposing, and at the same time Fr Morgan in his slippers and night-gown was frequently with his excellency my Lord Castlemaine. In particular one evening my lord cardinal was obliged to wait at my lord ambassador's chamber door till Fr Morgan did perform his advice, and in coming out the cardinal, seeing him in his night-dress, told him that if for the future he should see him there, he with his own hands should break his neck over the stairs; which expression from so meek a gentleman and clothed with the purple was not without very great provocation. His meddling in every concern obliged the pope to give orders to Fr Noyelle the general to send him out of Rome, which was done accordingly as you know, for he was sent home to England and good Fr Charles was made rector in his place.[37]

On 17 April Howard accompanied Castlemaine for his first audience, and introduced him to the pope. The first question to be settled was the precise status of the new ambassador. The question of his making a solemn entry into Rome, with the cavalcade and paraphernalia that belonged to an ambassador of a country that professed obedience to the pope was discussed, but not settled. The concession was frowned upon by the punctilious masters-of-ceremony as an innovation and a dangerous precedent.[38] That evening Castlemaine was lavishly entertained by the majordomo of the apostolic palace.[39] Howard also introduced him to various cardinals and only after that to the Duchess of Modena, a procedure that eventually brought a stern reprimand from his outraged king and master:

> Having received an account of what happened between the Duchess of Modena and my Lord Castlemaine concerning his visits to her and the cardinals, I was much surprised to find that instead of assisting my ambassador in ordering matters so that he might pay the respect to the mother of the queen my wife, which he ought and was by his promise engaged to have done, you did rather join in making difficulties about it. This proceeding of yours I cannot but be dissatisfied with, as I am with my Lord Castemaine in this affair, which I have let him know and commanded him to ask her pardon for it, and have also enjoined him (which I likewise expect from you) that upon all occasions and in all places he should pay the Duchess of Modena the respect due to her person and quality and to the near relation she has to the queen.[40]

The principal object of Castlemaine's embassy was not to establish his claim to full ambassadorial status. He came on a matter of great personal interest to the king and queen but of no interest whatever to England or the English Catholics. As this matter was to affect Howard more closely than any other event in the reign it must be treated in some detail.

From the very moment that Beatrice Maria d'Este became Duchess of York in 1673 she had set her heart on seeing her uncle, Rinaldo d'Este, made a cardinal. He had accompanied her to England and there was no secret about their joint ambition. Only a few days after their arrival the Venetian ambassador reports 'that the prince [Rinaldo] wants the cardinal's hat without depending either on Spain or France, and is trying to get himself nominated by the Queen of England, a step for which the present moment seems very ill-chosen'.[41] It was certainly not a propitious moment to choose, as the marriage at Modena in defiance of canon law, was still a sore point at Rome. Perhaps that is why we hear no more of the project till after the brief of March 1675, which restored friendly relations. Then on 15 April 1676, the new French ambassador-extraordinary, on the point of setting out for England, received the following information:

> The only interest that the Duchess of York has manifested up to the present has been in favour of Prince Rinaldo d'Este her uncle. The thought of all her house is to see him raised to the cardinalate, and this princess took the opportunity of the resignation of his hat that Cardinal de Retz wished to tender, to solicit the king's influence to have it transferred to the prince.

Quite apart from the fact that this resignation never took effect, His Majesty does not deem it opportune to intervene in this matter, as it might lead to a further request to nominate him in the next promotion.[42]

There were, however, plenty of other strings to pull. There was Cardinal Barberini, a connection by marriage, and above all there was the English Cardinal in Rome, who was constantly expressing his desire to serve the duke and duchess. Far from opposing the scheme, Howard promoted it for all he was worth. There are constant references to it in his letters to the duchess's secretary, beginning with a letter of 16 May 1676:

> As to Prince Rinaldo's affair, Cardinal Norfolk hath twice (although nobody ever spoke to him of it) spoken earnestly about, but as affairs stand, nothing can at present be done for many reasons, and you may be sure that Cardinal Barberini, who hath so long endeavoured it, and the duchess's mother now at Rome, and Cardinal Norfolk will do their best when a fitting time and occasion will be, without others, foolish busybodies.[43]

When in September 1676 Innocent XI succeeded Clement X petitions became more frequent. The duchess wrote herself to the pope on 18 November 1677, 'with sentiments of most devout resignation' saying how much consolation it would bring her and all her house.[44] The pope replied on 20 December that he would be happy to oblige her 'were it not that the state of the times persuades us to wait for other occasions'.[45]

At the time of the Oates plot, when the duke and duchess were forced into exile and their plight had aroused much sympathy in Rome, another attempt was made. They each wrote separately to the pope from Brussels on 8 April 1679.[46] The pope replied on the 13 May, doing little more than referring them to his previous letter.[47] The next attempt was in 1682 when more tranquil times had returned. This elicited the following from Innocent:

> With reference to our honouring the prince whom you so diligently commend to us, when the state of the times should open a way for us, we shall remember your wishes with an attentive mind, and we will ask the Father of lights to inspire in us such counsels as he should know will be useful for his church.[48]

After he succeeded to the throne in February 1685 James increased the pressure on the pope, and Howard was his principal intermediary. In the newsletters of this year, from April onwards there are frequent references to Howard having audience with the pope and it is surmised that the promotion of Rinaldo is part of his business.[49] Nor were the king and queen backward in renewing their requests by letters direct to the pope. They both wrote in July 1685 and the pope answered on 4 August that the matter 'is so grave in itself that it calls for a certain special consideration by us. We shall not omit to ponder deeply upon it, asking the Lord most earnestly to grant us the beams of his light.'[50]

In none of his replies does the pope even hint at the main reason why he cannot grant their request. It was because Francesco II, the young Duke of Modena, was without a son, and his uncle Rinaldo was heir presumptive. It would be unbecoming for a cardinal, supposing the duke to die childless, to resign his cardinalate in order to marry. This argument nowhere appears in letters from Rome, but it must have been conveyed to the king by word of mouth. On 5 October he writes once more to the pope at great length, and his tone is more imperious:

> So grave are the causes that impel us to desire that our beloved cousin Prince Rinaldo d'Este should be raised to the cardinalate, that, though we have asked Your Holiness already in other letters, we cannot ask anything for ourselves without reiterating our very same petition, and commending it to Your Holiness with new and more urgent prayers. We have no doubt that you will deign to give a ready ear to our so-often repeated wishes, especially as this prince, whose dignity is now our care, is so outstanding for his integrity of life and conduct that he lacks nothing that is normally required in a good and perfect ecclesiastic. He scarcely needs an advocate before Your Holiness, when his own virtues are his best plea, and merit the grace which we ask for him, although neither we nor the prince himself have any other thought than to acknowledge that this grace is received solely from your supreme benevolence.
>
> As for the question of the relationship of this prince with our dear brother the Duke of Modena, and the possibility of his succeeding to that territory, this should place no obstacle in the way of your granting our wish. The youth of the duke and his lusty health do not allow us to doubt that, with God's favour, there will be a numerous and happy progeny. We hardly need mention here the example of other princes belonging to Italian families in exactly the same circumstances and yet they have been promoted to the cardinalate. In any

event we wish to guarantee to Your Holiness that if this prince, by your munificence is honoured with the sacred purple, he would never after entertain the slightest desire to renounce it, unless the greatest necessity and the public good (which are of such concern of the Holy See also) should demand it. Even in this extreme case, we further promise that this prince would never do anything that derogated in the slightest degree from his veneration for the Holy See and the dignity of the sacred college.

Consider further, Holy Father, how much detriment must needs be caused to our efforts to spread the Catholic faith in our domains, if it should be openly seen, especially by our subjects, who for the most part are not affected with due reverence to the Apostolic See, that we are unable after so many and so earnest prayers to obtain this grace from Your Holiness, which is regularly conceded to other sovereigns even though they may not be able to give the help that we have already given and are ready to give in the future for the well-being and the progress of the church.

When Your Holiness has carefully pondered these and other like reasons, we do not doubt that we shall receive a reply in keeping with the paternal love of Your Holiness and with our own filial piety.[51]

This petition was followed inevitably by one from the queen, dated 8 October, only three days after the above. With it went a new request from James. He now asked that his confessor be made a bishop *in partibus*, with jurisdiction only in the royal palace.[52] This was reasonable enough, as a king's confessor normally bore that rank. James's confessor, however, was a Jesuit, Edward Petre, and Protestant England cherished a special hatred of Jesuits. In his reply of 24 November the pope does not use this as an argument for refusing a mitre for Petre. It was enough to explain that Jesuits were not allowed to accept such honours except by special command of the pope, and that it was not customary for popes to be influenced in this matter by the representation of princes. He makes no mention of the other petition on behalf of Rinaldo, unless the last sentence of his letter means that he has passed on the unpleasant task to Howard. 'Your Majesty will learn the rest from our beloved son Thomas Cardinal of Norfolk.'[53]

By this time it should have been clear even to James that the pope was not enamoured of the prospect of having Rinaldo in the sacred college. But the royal couple would not take no for an answer, and Castlemaine was sent to press both these petitions at the papal court.

Castlemaine's second audience was on 3 May. After it he sent his secretary to inform James that he would not be allowed the cavalcade reserved for ambassadors of Catholic countries, and that the pope considered it impossible to confer a red hat on Rinaldo because in the event of there being no heir to the Duke of Modena, he would be compelled to renounce the cardinalate, which would be 'scarcely decent'.[54]

> The English ambassador [runs a report of 25 May] too impatient to await the return of his secretary with the reply from London from his king, and finding himself short of money has decided to leave at once. To colour his departure with a more decorous pretext, he tells everybody that he has taken this resolution because he cannot stay here without the loss of face as long as the pontiff refuses the graces he asks for, and in particular that of the cardinalate for Prince Rinaldo.[55]

There was more in it than that. Castlemaine finding that courtesy failed to move the pope, tried to hector and bully him and threatened to leave Rome if his requests were not granted. The pope calmly reminded him that May was a cooler month than June for travel. On the same day the cardinal secretary wrote to d'Adda.

> In the three audiences which the ambassador, Earl Castlemaine, has had with His Holiness, he has always striven, with extraordinary insistence, to renew the requests for the cardinalate for Prince Rinaldo d'Este and to obtain for Fr Petre, SJ, the title of bishop *in partibus*. As regards the former, His Holiness has given him the same answer as he gave to Mr Caryll the previous envoy. So with the latter. Whenever the Cardinal of Norfolk has had audience to discuss one or other of these petitions, His Holiness has put all the considerations and difficulties in the way of granting the cardinalate so greatly desired by His Majesty, but without ever saying absolutely that he would not promote Prince Rinaldo. As for the title of bishop he declared that he was unable to condescend to gratify His Majesty, principally out of regard for the good of the Society of Jesus, which depends in great measure on the observance of the vow never to accept ecclesiastical dignities. His Holiness believes that he ought not to dispense from it, lest it should open a wide road which would at once corrupt its best subjects by tempting them to obtain bishoprics and other dignities by means of the favour they enjoy

in the courts of princes. This would be a most grievous disaster to the Society to lose, together with its religious perfection, the men who are its chief glory and support.[56]

Howard had another audience on 15 June,

> stimulated with the desire to facilitate to promotion of Prince Rinaldo d'Este, at the instance of the King of England, but so far he has obtained nothing, as the pope wishes to wait for a reply from Mons' d'Adda to the letter [of 25 May] written after the last appeal made to His Holiness by Earl Castelmaine.

This report goes on to say that Castlemaine was embroiled in a dispute with the customs officers. They claimed the right to inspect his baggage though not to tax it; he refused to let them open it. Howard declared that Castlemaine was in the wrong, and in due course received another reprimand from the king, who supported his ambassador. A long disquisition on the rights and privileges of ambassadors was sent to London, and that is the last we hear of the dispute.[57]

On 17 August Howard had an audience that went on until sunset, and after it he visited first the Duchess of Modena and then Castlemaine.[58] What passed at this audience was not made public, but it would seem that the fateful decision was made. The pope remained adamant in his refusal of a mitre for Fr Petre, but at last succumbed to the pressure on behalf of Rinaldo. In September he created eight new cardinals, six of whom, including Rinaldo d'Este, were granted a dispensation because they were not in minor orders at the time. They were sent the biretta on 7 September, but it was not until more than two years later, on 6 December 1688, that Rinaldo was received to the kiss. The queen sent her thanks to Howard on 16 September 1686:

> His Holiness has been pleased to yield at last to those just requests which the king and I have made him in behalf of my uncle Prince Rinaldo. Less I could not have expected from so benign a father, who herein has no less done himself right and honoured the sacred college with so worthy a choice than he has obliged me and my family. As I should never have failed in my duty to His Holiness had he denied my request so in granting it (not withstanding all suggested difficulties) he has laid a stronger obligation upon me of increasing (if possible) that profound respect which is due and shall always be paid by me to His Holiness.[59]

James sent a suitable letter at the same time to Innocent himself, praising the high gifts and outstanding virtues of the uncle of his beloved wife and queen.[60]

It was now more than ten years since Howard had first espoused the cause of Rinaldo. What his own feelings were is nowhere recorded. It was James's wish and to a loyal Jacobite that was reason enough. He had done all he could to bring about the marriage with Mary of Modena, and it was but natural, in those days, that she should expect the pope to honour her family. Nor was it unreasonable, when cardinals were regularly nominated by Catholic kings, that James expected his first nomination to be accepted at Rome. Howard could not foresee that the promotion of this harmless non-entity was to prove so painful and injurious to himself.

## Notes

1. Stuart, I, 3.
2. Arnauld, Œuvres, II, 516.
3. NF, 75, f. 231.
4. Avvisi 48, f. 369.
5. NF, 75, f. 180.
6. Avvisi 48, f. 85.
7. Ibid. 101.
8. Ibid. f. 151.
9. Ibid. f. 167.
10. Ibid. f. 175. She died 9 June.
11. Avvisi 48, f. 168.
12. Ibid. ff. 215, 232.
13. Arch. Di Stato di Lucca, Buonvisi II, t.25, no. 77; printed in T. Trenta, *Memorie alla storia politica del Card. F. Buonvisi*, Lucca, 1818, II, 205.
14. T. Trenta, *Memorie alla storia politica del Card. F. Buonvisi*, Lucca, 1818, II, 332.
15. Avvisi 48, ff. 133, 167.
16. AFOP, XXIX (1959), 183.
17. Avvisi 48, f. 256.
18. Ibid. ff. 263–4; AP, Anglia Misc. IV, 5 Sept. 1685.
19. Original at Wardour Castle.
20. Avvisi 48, f. 298.
21. C. J. Fox, *History of the Early Part of the Reign of James II*, London, 1808, cxxix.
22. Med. 4245, nos. 90, 104.
23. A. Clark, *Life and Times of Anthony Wood*, Oxford Hist. Soc., 1894, III, 171.
24. TNA 31/3/163, f. 237.

25 Stuart, I, 11.
26 Med. 4245, no. 145 (27 May).
27 *Ibid.* no. 497 (7 June).
28 *Ibid.* no. 534.
29 Burnet, *History of his own Time*, I, 661.
30 *History of England*, ch. IV.
31 BL, Add. 28226, f. 11.
32 Avvisi 49, f. 9.
33 *Ibid.* f. 17.
34 *Ibid.* f. 42.
35 *Ibid.* f. 75.
36 *Ibid.* f. 92.
37 BL, Egerton 2260, f. 251.
38 AV, Carpegna 39, ff. 77 et seq. Relatio in forma di Diario di quanto e seguito in Roma dalli 9 di Aprile 1686 per tutto li 22 Maggio del detto anno. Another copy in BV, Vat. Lat. 10856, f. 132. Partly printed in *Arch. storico Lombardo*, Ser. II, VI, 39.
39 Avvisi 49, f. 100.
40 Marchioness de Cavelli Campana, *Les derniers Stuarts à Saint-Germain en Laye*, Paris, Genève, 1871, II, 100.
41 Cal.SP Venice, XXXVIII, 185.
42 TNA 31/3/132, f. 140.
43 Treby, *Letters*, 89.
44 AV, Prin. 104, f. 338.
45 Berthier, *Epistolae*, I, 142.
46 AV, Prin. 106, f. 113.
47 Berthier, *Epistolae*, I, 258.
48 *Ibid.* II, 43.
49 Especially Avvisi 48.
50 Berthier, *Epistolae*, II, 244.
51 AV, Prin. 114, f. 424.
52 *Ibid.* ff. 434–5.
53 Berthier, *Epistolae*, II, 260.
54 Avvisi 49, f. 115.
55 *Ibid.* f. 142.
56 NI, 16, f. 12.
57 Avvisi 49, f. 166; NI, 16, f. 18.
58 Avvisi 49, f. 271.
59 Stuart, I, 19.
60 BV, Vat. Lat. 10855, f. 384.

# 10

# *Eclipse*

## I

By the time James had satisfied the queen's ambition by extorting a cardinal's hat for her uncle, he had lost what popularity he had enjoyed in England when he came to the throne. Like the other Stuart kings James had a sense of tolerance that was quite out of keeping with his age. There seems no good reason to deny that he was actuated with the highest motives in working for religious toleration for the English Catholics. There was nothing particularly heinous in wishing to see Catholics in positions of trust, in the government and universities. They had shown their fidelity to the royal cause and it was a grave injustice to continue the disabilities for which there was no longer even a *prima facie* excuse. The Protestants did not, however, view the toleration of Catholics in this dispassionate and ideal fashion. For them it meant an immediate growth in numbers and influence. They knew there were still many Englishmen who in their hearts preferred the old religion and would openly profess it once the disabilities were removed. Toleration meant the growth of popery, and popery was the enemy of the established church. Once these papists were powerful enough they would get their revenge and persecute in their turn. Toleration as we understand it was an idea yet unborn. Protestants could point to events in Catholic France. In the autumn of 1685 Louis XIV had revoked the edict of Nantes that had guaranteed religious freedom to the Huguenots. A pathetic stream of Protestant refugees that soon numbered more than four thousand made their way to England. James, with all his leanings to France, disapproved of this new persecution and did all on his power to assist the unfortunate victims. They were the worst possible augury of what was to be expected from an

England in which Catholics were again in the seats of the mighty. Hence every move by James to alleviate the lot of the Catholics was viewed as another menace to the security of the constitution and the church. For a century the universities had been strongholds of Protestantism and closely associated with the established church. It was convenient to forget that they had been wrested from the Catholics, who had ever since been excluded, it was hoped for ever, by an oath that they could not conscientiously take. The vast monastic lands which had been parcelled and sold again and again were still technically stolen property, and sacrilege was still a word that gave their owners some anxious moments, if not an occasional twinge of conscience.[1] The works of Dugdale and Sir Henry Spelman had revived memories that many landed gentry would rather had been buried in oblivion.

Cardinal Buonvisi, far away in Vienna, was one of the few people who saw the situation as it really was, with a clarity of vision that was prophetic. The time had not come yet for the Catholics to emerge from the catacombs. The power of the new Constantine was inadequate to proclaim a universal peace.

The first clash between the king and the church came in the summer of 1686 when an ecclesiastical commission was empowered to stem the flood of abuse of Rome that flowed from Protestant pulpits. This was considered an unwarranted interference with their long-enjoyed privileges. How else were they to keep alive the hatred of idolatry in the hearts of simple illiterates? Next came a clash with the government when Sir Edward Hales, a Catholic, was admitted to office without taking the customary oath. A test case was staged and the king's action upheld by his judges. This was resented by the London populace and some rioting ensued. In February 1686 the papal agent d'Adda was solemnly consecrated Archbishop of Amasia at Whitehall by the Primate of Ireland. In May he made his public entry as a nuncio. In July the king's confessor, Fr Edward Petre, and four lay Catholics were nominated members of the Privy Council, and in December the king opened his new Catholic chapel at Whitehall. All these actions gave offence, though there does not seem to be any evidence that the English Catholics generally were using their new freedom otherwise than Buonvisi had counselled. John Leyburn, Howard's auditor, and now vicar apostolic, was behaving so circumspectly that he aroused the ire of M. Antoine Arnauld, the Jansenist writer who had always

## Eclipse

looked upon him as a friend. In a letter to his agent in Rome, dated 7 October 1686, Arnauld writes:

> You speak only of a hat *in petto*. If it is true that the pope has told the English ambassador what you pass on to me, this will presumably be for Fr Petre the Jesuit, who is all-powerful with the king. The secular priests and also the other well-disposed religious are very discontented with it, being convinced that this attachment of the king to the Jesuits can greatly harm the reunion of the Protestants. They complain that Dr Leyburn is nothing more than a cipher and that he has no power whatever, and they are rather alienated from him because they do not find him sufficiently firm or resolute. This is what one gathers from two Englishmen who are here at the moment; one provincial of the Recollects, and the other a Dominican, confessor to the English nuns here, who has just come from England and will return shortly. Could it not be impressed upon the Cardinal of Norfolk to write to Dr Leyburn and exhort him to have more courage? These two religious told me of a very bold action of a Dominican, who is Archbishop of Armagh and Primate of Ireland.* He went to call on the Earl of Clarendon, Viceroy of Ireland, and the earl sent a message asking him to wait a little as he was with the Primate of Ireland (meaning the Protestant Archbishop of Armagh). The Dominican asked the messenger to tell his master that it was he who was Primate of Ireland, that he came on behalf of the king, and that there was no other primate whatever in Ireland except himself. On hearing this the Earl of Clarendon caused the Protestant prelate to depart by another staircase.[2]

It was incidents such as this that Buonvisi had warned Howard to avoid, and it would appear that John Leyburn obeyed, at the risk of being considered a cipher. The English Catholics generally, clergy or laity, appear to have acted with commendable restraint and to have avoided incidents that might mortify or anger the Protestants. At least there are no complaints of clashes such as that between the rival Primates of Ireland. It was only in court circles that there were acts that could be interpreted as acts of papal aggression, and even here it was the fear of what they might lead to rather than any intrinsic evil in the acts themselves that united Anglican and Puritan in opposition to the king. This opposition had not yet reached its height. The more moderate Protestants

---

* Dominic Maguire, OP, who succeeded Oliver Plunkett in July 1683.

were prepared to bide their time. The queen had not provided an heir to the throne and on the death of the king the crown would go to his daughter Mary and to the Prince of Orange, who were free from all taint of popery.

Before the end of 1686 there was evidence that the Catholic church over which James was to preside was to be as Gallican as that of Louis XIV. There is a draft of a letter dated 15 October from Sunderland to Castlemaine, which shows the price that Rome was to pay for James's championing of the Catholic cause:

> The king being given to understand that some persons have been promoted to bishoprics in his dominion, and particularly in Ireland without his [knowledge *crossed out*] nomination. His Majesty commands me to tell Your Excellency that he would have you inform yourself of this matter, and if you shall find any such bishops to have been made since his accession to the crown, he thinks it fit you should complain of it to the pope, acquainting His Holiness that His Majesty expects to have all the power in nominating of bishops in his dominions that his royal ancestors have heretofore had, and which other princes have in their dominions. One of the articles of your instructions directs you to insist upon this right of His Majesty, and therefore I need say no more to you upon it.[3]

II

It was at this very time that James had succeeded in extorting from the pope a cardinal's hat for Prince Rinaldo D'Este. The brief is dated 7 September 1686, and it must have been nearly a month before the news reached England. The next step was to provide the new cardinal with a handsome salary out of the English exchequer. James's first thoughts were to send him to Rome as English ambassador with the customary salary of £5000. Archbishop d'Adda earnestly opposed this scheme, pointing out that such an arrangement would not be acceptable to the pope and would give great offence to France. James reluctantly complied, but by no means relinquished the idea of finding the queen's uncle a lucrative position. As early as 18 October d'Adda reports that Cardinal d'Este

> had pressed to have the protection of England, being unaware that Cardinal Norfolk had it. His Majesty would have had

much satisfaction in granting this, as he would undoubtedly do if Cardinal Norfolk were willing to resign. However he did not say that he intended to make any move to bring this about.[4]

Soon the king thought of a compromise. There is a draft of a letter of 8 November from Sunderland to Howard:

> His Majesty commands me to acquaint Your Eminence that he is pleased to appoint the Cardinal d'Este to be comprotector with you of the English, Scotch and Irish nations; that the nearness of the said cardinal's relation to the queen has induced His Majesty to it, and therefore His Majesty does not doubt but Your Eminence will be well satisfied that His Majesty does not hereby intend any diminution to you. My Lord Castlemaine will by this post receive his letters of revocation.[5]

Foreign observers in London were not slow to see the significance of this step. Barillon, the French ambassador, reported on 3 November.

> Those who have brought this about have done it to discredit the Cardinal of Norfolk, who (it is believed) has not acted as he ought to have done for Fr Petre. There was a cabal of Catholics here who had a design to bring the Cardinal of Norfolk here, but this plan has been wrecked. Those who are hand-in-glove with Fr Petre and Fr Warner, the confessor, have discouraged the journey of the Cardinal of Norfolk as being useless and liable to cause division amongst the Catholics, who are already far from united.[6]

Terriesi, the resident of the Grand Duke of Tuscany, writes on 9 December:

> Fr Petre the Jesuit dominates more than ever the mind of His Majesty, and therefore a great part is attributed to him in the conduct of ecclesiastical affairs, which the king carries out according to his direction. They desire that Cardinal Howard should no longer have at Rome that part in the management of His Majesty's affairs and those of the church in England, which otherwise it was believed he would have had.[7]

There the matter rested for a year during which nothing more is heard of the new comprotector. All through 1687 James continued to press for Fr Petre's promotion. At first it was for a bishopric but before the end of the year it was for the cardinal's hat. Castlemaine had been recalled in November 1686 but it was not until 8 January 1687 that he made his solemn entry into Rome as an ambassador, and he did not leave Rome till the following May. John Lidcott remained as the king's agent. In the last audience (in May) Castlemaine had asked the pope to appoint Petre to the then vacant See of York. This the pope refused, though there were rumours in Rome in July that the brief appointing him Archbishop of York had actually reached London.[8] Before he finally departed, Castlemaine was sumptuously feasted by Cardinal Barberini, with a host of English noblemen and three other cardinals including Howard. It does not appear, however, that Howard's relations with Castlemaine were the happiest. Lord Dartmouth has left it on record that Castlemaine made a poor impression on the Romans:

> One great reason for their dislike to Lord Castlemaine was the disrespect he showed to Cardinal Howard, who was much beloved in Rome upon the account of his strict life, great affability and high birth, which were as well known as Lord Castlemaine's incivility to him, of which don Guglielmo [William Leslie], who was one of the cardinal's chaplains told me several particulars that were extremely offensive: but he said it was thought the Jesuits put him upon it, the cardinal having had some disputes with them, though he had built part of the English College which he lived in. But they knew he could not carry it away with him, and that he had nothing more to give them.[9]

Of Howard's dispute with the Jesuits of the English College there remains only a letter in which the anti-Jesuit bias is too obvious to call for comment. It is dated Rome 7 May 1687, at the moment of Castlemaine's departure. There is a great deal about the wealth and iniquities of the regulars that makes it clear the author was a secular priest:

> Fr Cane living in the house [English College], but having no character except a Jesuit, proposed to the students, young English gentlemen of very good families, that they should abjure the oath of allegiance to their king, and that they then present nor none that were to succeed them in their studies in that house should be permitted to live there till they swear a solemn formal oath that they should never swear the oath of allegiance nor any other obligation binding them to be faithful subjects, because a time might come that the concerns of their religion would require some service not agreeable to such an oath. For this there was need of a form of an oath and that by public order from the

Rota Romana, which could not be obtained but by a memorial to that judicature. This memorial could not be presented, at least ought not, except by him who was protector-regent of the English nation; and this was my Lord Cardinal Howard, who is a person so loyal, and of better principles than to contribute to anything that could free subjects from that fidelity they owe their lawful prince. And therefore Fr Cane knew well the cardinal would never consent nor go alongst in prosecuting a concern of so black an aspect, and what might confirm what is often taught by the Jesuits, that to a heretic prince no loyalty nor fidelity is to be kept by the subjects.

Thus Fr Cane draws his memorial and boldly presents it himself, believing that the judges of the Rota would pass it *breve unum* [briefly as one], and that no more noise would be heard of it. But he found himself in a mistake when he found the thing was suspected when not given in by Cardinal Howard, and therefore was examined and sent to the pope, who called for the cardinal and asked if it was his purpose or design to oblige youth to do a thing which could have no good conscience. My Lord Cardinal [was] amazed at the design, but more at Fr Cane's impudence to meddle with what belonged to the college and youth without so much as once acquainting him, their protector. In a word, the memorial was cancelled and a heavy complaint made of Fr Cane to the general of the Jesuits, who thought himself obliged to revoke Fr Cane and send him from Rome. This gave ground of discourses amongst the priests themselves.[10]

Castlemaine's embassy had not been a success. His blustering, hectoring manner had antagonized everyone from the pope downwards. Upon his return to England, James, on 16 June, wrote to the pope apologizing for his conduct. 'We are sure that however much he has sinned, or rather erred, he was actuated by a burning endeavour to promote good relations (which we very much desire) between Your Holiness and us.' He goes on to press for a mitre for Fr Petre, or if that were not possible, a cardinal's hat.[11] On receipt of this letter the pope received Howard in audience on 15 August,[12] and next day replied to the king. He overlooked the conduct of Castlemaine, but regretfully refused the promotion of Petre.[13] In London this further refusal of a hat for a Jesuit was attributed to the influence of the Dominican cardinal. Terriesi informed his master on 22 September:

> The least ruffled by the pope's refusal of the hat for Fr Petre are the Catholics. They say openly and with laughter, as a thing

most certain, that the cause of it is Cardinal Howard, although he had protested quite the opposite.[14]

He writes again on 4 October to say the Jesuits are up in arms at the pope's refusal, and rumour has it that they are counselling the king not to be so indulgent in the future as he has been in the past. On 3 November he adds that they were advising the king to recall his ambassador from Rome, and to dismiss d'Adda, whom they considered the cause of all the refusals; that it had now been decided that the king should send a 'dry and compendious letter' making it clear that it was no longer a mitre but a cardinal's hat that he demanded for Petre, and pointing out 'that it was quite possible to be a Roman Catholic and do without the court of Rome'.[15]

The king had written on this subject to Howard himself, and on 23 August Howard had another audience, after which it was rumoured that he was to go to England as nuncio, but no word escaped concerning Petre.[16] James never gave in. It had taken him ten years to extort a hat for the queen's uncle, and there was nothing like trying. He wrote again to the pope on 24 September,[17] and the pope sent another refusal on 22 November, referring the king to d'Adda for further particulars.[18] But before this reply reached London the king had made a decision that very closely affected Howard. On 1 November d'Adda sends to the cardinal secretary a very long account of two interviews. The first was with the Earl of Sunderland, who informed him that the king had reluctantly agreed not to appoint Cardinal d'Este his ambassador at Rome and had therefore decided to make him cardinal protector. Then followed a long interview with the queen.

> Her Majesty began by saying that she wished to communicate to me, as an act of friendship, a matter of great moment. She had greatly desired that Cardinal d'Este, to whom the king had destined the management of his affairs in Rome, should stay there in the capacity of ambassador, but having learnt that this might incur in some way the disapproval of the Holy See, she had relinquished the idea altogether. Hence the king had resolved to give him the protectorship of England, and she could not persuade herself that there could be any difficulty about this, as it would serve to maintain ever more securely that perfect understanding between the Holy See and the king which he so infinitely desired, and that this cardinal would be the best instrument of all to bring this about. Besides his natural good parts he entertained such feelings of loyalty and devotion to the

## Eclipse

sacred person of His Holiness that he would always be ready to serve him in every way. He could have no other sentiments than those of His Majesty, which were to manifest in every way possible the reverent filial respect for the Holy See. She hoped that when the cardinal should have the good fortune to be at the feet of His Holiness, the pope would be even more completely satisfied of this sentiment than he could be at present.

After due words of respect I replied that Her Majesty could rest assured that the great esteem and the tenderness of paternal love for the king in the heart of His Holiness was in perfect harmony with her sentiments, and that he would hear with equal satisfaction and gratitude that His Majesty, always regulating his actions with supreme prudence, had relinquished the idea of an ambassadorship for the said cardinal. It was beyond doubt that this would incline His Holiness the more kindly towards the cardinal both for his own sake and because of his close association with His Majesty.

Nonetheless I could not refrain from pointing out that as there was already a Protector of England, the Cardinal of Norfolk, a man of such merit and virtue, there did not appear to be a vacancy for this office, which the cardinal exercised with such glory to himself and such benefit to this kingdom. Her Majesty replied that the said cardinal had never been declared protector by the king, and therefore there should be no question that His Eminence, to whom they did not wish to offer the least affront in the world, would rest contented. When it came to deciding the prior claims of one who was her own uncle she did not believe that there ought to be the slightest difficulty. On this basis she had already written yesterday to Cardinal d'Este, having refrained from doing so earlier, because for a long time there had been thoughts of his being ambassador. Although I said all I could do by way of answer, Her Majesty remained firm in the decision she had already taken, again telling me that she had wanted to communicate it to me in a friendly way and that the king would speak to me of it. I thought it good to go to Lord Sunderland afterwards to prevent if possible the adoption of an office which the Cardinal of Norfolk exercised so worthily, but he told me that their Majesties having relinquished the ambassadorship in consequence of the difficulties that had arisen in our discussions, were both determined on the protectorship, and that the king would be writing to the cardinal, that he should not take umbrage at this decision, but should endeavour to give every satisfaction. To have enumerated at this juncture all the objections to this scheme would have looked like wanting to oppose all the deliberations of their Majesties ...

## Philip Howard

> Yesterday evening, in the presence of Lord Sunderland, the king told me that the queen had already spoken to me concerning the matter of Cardinal d'Este, whom he had destined for Rome with the protectorship of England, although he would have preferred to have given him the office of ambassador, but had relinquished the idea when it was intimated that such a declaration would not be acceptable to His Holiness. I answered repeating to His Majesty all that I had already said to the queen and my lord there present, but His Majesty stood firm, saying that he had never had any hand in the appointment of the Cardinal of Norfolk as protector, and in any case, in competition with an uncle of the queen it seemed fitting that the latter should be given preference, though he would always regard the former with esteem and affection.[19]

The Earl of Sunderland wrote on 4 November to the king's agent in Rome:

> The king having resolved to put his own and his subjects' affairs at Rome into the hands of the Cardinal d'Este as protector of his dominions commands me to let you know it, and has writ to the Cardinal of Norfolk himself to acquaint him with the resolution. The letter goes enclosed, which you will take care to deliver. You are not to speak of this matter to any person till you hear further from me.[20]

The king's letter to Howard does not appear to be extant. Instead there is the draft of a reprimand, redolent of the headmaster's study, that once again shows the Gallican propensities of King James. It is dated Whitehall November 1687:

> The king being informed that Mr Michael Fitzhenry, Mr John Dempsey and Mr Edmund Dunne have been promoted by the pope to three benefices in Christchurch, Dublin, without his nomination or knowledge, and that Your Eminence was acquainted therewith; and His Majesty expecting that no person should be promoted to any benefice in his dominions but at his own nomination or the recommendation of some of his ministers in his name (which my Lord Castlemaine did let His Holiness and his ministers know), His Majesty has commanded me to signify the same to you that nothing of the like kind may happen for the time to come.[21]

Meanwhile the queen had caused her secretary Lord Caryll to notify Howard of the Royal will. Of this letter there exists only an undated draft:

## Eclipse

> I have a particular command from the queen to acquaint Your Eminence how much Her Majesty is concerned lest you should attribute to her any unkindness upon your account of transferring the protectorship of England to Cardinal d'Este. As it did not proceed originally from her, so when they would have made a compliment of it to her she would not take it as such, because it was a trouble to her that Your Eminence should be dispossessed of a charge which you had performed so well. Although she yielded to it for other reasons, I suppose not unknown to Your Eminence and which I believe have no less weight with you than they have with her, I can assure Your Eminence that Her Majesty at present has no less kindness for your person than ever formerly she had, and that she is ready to give you marks of upon any fit occasion that shall offer itself.[22]

The letter goes on to speak of the Flemish Ursuliness, whose convent in Rome, founded by the queen's mother, was one of Howard's special cares. Howard is to be removed from this office too, and it was to be entrusted to Monsignor Caprara, the Rome agent of the queen. As a consolation prize the king soon after appointed Howard his grand almoner,* though the salary of £500 a year was to be paid to Bishop Leyburn, who acted as his delegate, while d'Este received £5000 a year from the English exchequer as cardinal protector.[23]

The queen's letter of 28 November to Cardinal d'Este makes it clear that the grant of the protectorship of England was a way of circumventing the papal opposition to the title of ambassador:

> I have ordered the Marchese Cattaneo to inform you of the decision at last arrived at by the king to nominate you at once protector of these realms, and to give you with the responsibility of all his affairs in Rome the salary that is customarily given to his ambassadors, but not the title of ambassador for reasons that I do not mention now. This has given me the greater satisfaction

---

* I have not found this appointment on the patent roll. Francis Bishop of Ely was appointed grand almoner on 25 March 1684. There is a report of 2 December 1687 that 'Cardinal Howard is said to be made lord-almoner in the room of the Bishop of Ely, and Fr Petre is made subalmoner' (N. Luttrell, *A Brief Historical Relation of State Affairs from September 1678 to April 1714*, Oxford, 1857, I, 423). Fr Petre seems to be a mistake for Bishop Leyburn. There are letters patent of 4 January 1687/8 granting Howard, in augmentation of his salary as grand almoner, the goods and chattels of suicides, and a further clause allowing him to depute John, Bishop of Adrimet to act for him, because important affairs detain him abroad (TNA, C, 66/3300, n. 7).

and to me it seems like a thousand years till I see you actually employed in the service of the king. So I hope you will leave for Rome at once, and when you are there it will be absolutely essential to remove the arms of France immediately from the palace and substitute those of the king. Nobody must be left with the slightest suspicion that you could ever depend on any crown save this one.[24]

It seems beyond dispute that in the appointment of d'Este as protector the king was actuated principally by the desire to provide a place of honour and a comfortable income for the queen's uncle, rather than by any deep resentment at Howard's supposed lukewarmness in soliciting for Petre's red hat. This was certainly the view taken by d'Adda, who in several reports speaks of it as a way of circumventing the difficulties that had been raised against the title of ambassador. The English Jesuits were often reported to be hostile to Howard, but the more reliable witnesses do not associate this hostility with the alleged failure to press for Petre's cardinalate. An anonymous Italian report forwarded to Rome by d'Adda does not mention this among the enormities of the Jesuits:

> Fr Petre is under a great obligation to the cardinal of Norfolk for the continuous efforts that he makes to solicit the king's petition of his behalf. The said cardinal is much loved and esteemed by all. They desire and daily pray that he may be sent back to England, a course which they hope to God would be for the greater glory of God and of this country, if the good pope would deign to take the matter to heart and show his zeal by sending the cardinal home; or if he is not willing to send him, at least that he should move the king to ask for him. In doing this His Holiness would not only be assured of having a true friend in the court of England (by whose work a true understanding between His Holiness and the king might be hoped for) but the cardinal would be also a great help for the conversion of our kingdom, and what is more, a good means of frustrating the designs of those who are enemies of His Holiness and of the Eminence. These are uniquely the Black Mantels, and their name begins with G. [Gesuiti]. It is even to be hoped and prayed that the pope will so act that people like these will not dare to meddle in the political affairs of any state whatever, because if they cannot have from the pope all that they ask for, they urge princes to oppose and harass him. If our Protestants could but see such a

policy, nothing in the world would give them greater delight, seeing that the whole nation hates the Jesuits and the very name of Jesuit.[25]

Only once in all this official correspondence is there any suggestion that Howard opposed the promotion of Petre. On 19 December 1687, a month after the appointment of d'Este, d'Adda reports:

> Lord Sunderland, speaking of the affair of Fr Petre, told me in confidence that their agent had written that His Holiness had sent his confessor to the father-general of the Society to convey his views on this matter, the pope being persuaded that the said father-general was behind the king's petitions, and that the king was not acting on his own initiative, adding that the Cardinal of Norfolk was the one who had given this impression to His Holiness. Hence His Majesty was obliged, in order to defend the good name of Fr Petre, to clarify the situation and certify that the desire was his own, and that he would write to this effect. I tried to remove an idea so prejudicial to the cardinal from the mind of His Majesty, but I found the greatest difficulty, this belief being so deeply rooted.[26]

What Howard really thought of the promotion of Petre he has nowhere left on record. There is no reliable evidence that he opposed it. He appears, in this matter as in all that concerned the wishes of his king, to have been a faithful servant. Be the truth what it may, by the end of 1687 the king has lost confidence in him and had entrusted his affairs to the hands of one whose only recommendation was his kinship with the queen. From now on Howard was completely ignored. Successive agents were instructed to deal only with Cardinal d'Este. The queen still found Howard useful for gaining minor concessions, but in great matters such as red hats he was no longer the intermediary. It has always been assumed by English historians that by this high-handed action of the king and queen, Howard ceased to be Protector of England. This was far from being the case. The office was a papal life-appointment and Howard retained it till his death. He retained also his love and devotion for King James and his queen. He nowhere expresses the slightest resentment at the affront offered him. There were far greater matters to occupy his thoughts. The English fields were white with the harvest; the storm-clouds that were already gathering in England had not darkened the Roman skies.

## III

The general Chapter of the Dominicans that met in Rome in June 1686 restored the English Dominicans to the full status of a province with Vincent Torre as its first provincial. Something of the opinion that reigned in Rome is reflected in the letters that Torre wrote frequently to the king and queen, whose chaplain he had once been. On 20 July he informs the king of the election of the new Master General and sends him the patent of

> A perfect participation of all the prayers, Masses and other good works done by his whole order consisting of 45 provinces spread over the world. England for number being one of the least made a greater figure in this last general Chapter than the biggest, as well for number of vocals as for learning, lectures of divinity, public defence which were two, very solemn (other provinces had but one apiece) both dedicated to Your Majesty, His Eminence (Howard) assisting at them attended with a most numerous train of bishops, prelates, monsignors, provincials etc. Your Majesty's most dutiful subject presided over the defendant lectors, who acted their parts with great applause. *In fine* His Eminence and we his alumni used our best endeavour to raise Your Majesty's honour as high as we were able in outdoing (as is known we did) all other respective dedications to His Holiness, to the Emperor, to the kings of Spain, Poland, French king etc. My hope was to begin my journey immediately after the Chapter, the sooner to lay myself with the said dedications at Your Majesty's feet, but the heats were then increased to such intensity that it was thought too unseasonable for so long a journey.[27]

It was not, however, till another summer came round that Torre set out for England. In April 1687 he had a private audience with Innocent XI[28] and left soon after. On his way he was the guest of Cosimo III at Florence,[29] and thence travelled to Bornhem. He was destined never to reach England, for he was taken ill at Bornhem and died there on 24 August. He was succeeded by Dominic Gwillim, who, however, lasted less than a year, for he died in London in September 1688. He was succeeded by Thomas White alias Bianchi, who had been prominent in the king's marriage and for the past ten years had been a penitentiary at S. Maria Maggiore, save for the last few months when he had been prior of SS. John and Paul's. There are few signs of increased Dominican activity in England, but the following letter from Bishop Leyburn shows that

*Eclipse*

Howard was planning to establish his brethren in the West Indies. The letter is dated 9 December 1687.

> I omitted writing by the last two posts, as having nothing of importance to add unto what I had writ the week before. The patent of grand almoner which I mentioned in my last hath not yet passed the great seal but is in the way towards it. Mr Matthews* was with me yesterday and acquainted me with Your Eminence's desire that I should solicit my Lord Thomas Howard for payment of what is due to you from the duke his brother. I had not been failing to discharge that part of my duty before I undertook my northern voyage, and doubted not but an end would have been put to that business before my return. Upon occasion of my speaking to my Lord Thomas concerning it he ever shewed a readiness to serve Your Eminence so far as the matter in question depended on him. But he would frequently complain of his being hindered by the duke's disapplication to business, and the backwardness of those with whom he was jointly to act, from bringing it to so speedy an end as he intended and desired.
>
> A second thing which Mr Matthews acquainted me with was Your Eminence's pious design of sending into Jamaica a mission of St Dominic's order. This is a provision very necessary and much wanting both in that island and many others that are subject to the crown. His Majesty hath been pleased to speak of it as a thing which he had often in his thoughts. Now because Mr Churchill (whom Your Eminence may have often seen at Stafford House) hath for some years had a particular desire, and (as he persuaded himself) a vocation to employ his talent in service of that place. I named him to His Majesty above a year since as a person that might be useful therein. The execution of this good design was delayed many months, until at length, whilst I was in my northern visitation, the Duke of Albemarle going governor of the said island, the business was concluded. Mr Churchill had an allowance granted by His Majesty to serve the Catholics there, and was recommended to the duke, but in regard his churchstuff and other necessaries could not be in readiness for the time his grace began his journey, he was forced

---

\* Mr Matthew and Mr Jacob figure frequently in the letters of Vincent Torre preserved in the archives of the diocese of Hexham and Newcastle. The latter is Dominic Gwillim who succeeded Torre as provincial. The former has not been identified. There was an Anthony Matthews who in July 1688 received payments due to Howard (*Secret Services of Charles II and James II*, Camden Soc., London, 1851, 191).

to wait the opportunity of another ship, in which he departed not many days after my return home. He addressed himself to me for faculties, and by advice of such persons as I use to consult in matters of this nature, I granted him those which were judged necessary for the end he went thither. This I ventured to do partly upon my own authority, which in like circumstances hath been judged sufficient both by our learned men at home and able divines abroad, where judgements concerning it hath been formerly required, and partly upon the general grant received from Your Eminence of using your power when the exercise of my own might be disputable. Moreover though I had no prospect then, nor have yet, of any other priest that was to follow him, nevertheless to provide for what might happen and prevent such inconveniences as of late, not without scandal, have happened in the same island for want of some order and subordination, I judged it expedient to send him with title of superior in that mission. I was indeed informed of an Irish Dominican that was already there with ordinary faculties from Your Eminence, but without any special character. Whereupon Mr Jacobs the provincial being acquainted with what was done approved of it, not doubting of a good correspondence betwixt Mr Churchill and the said father, to whom he also wrote to that effect. I understood afterwards that the latter was empowered to act there in quality of vicar general to the Bishop of Cuba, or the Chapter in vacancy of that bishopric. Whereupon I ordered Mr Churchill not to enter into any dispute with the said bishop or Chapter concerning points of ordinary jurisdiction, though I concede that by having abandoned all care of Jamaica since it became subject to England, that bishop had forfeited any further claims thereunto. And indeed the king did not willingly hear that his Catholic subjects in Jamaica should be governed by a bishop subject to the crown of Spain.

This was the state of affairs relating to Jamaica when Mr Matthews acquainted me with the pious design of Your Eminence, who I hope will have the goodness to approve what I have done, as also to believe that on my part there shall be wanting no readiness to obey entirely Your Eminence's commands relating to this or any other concern. Had I received the least intimation of Your Eminence intending to send such a mission into Jamaica, as I am now acquainted with, t'would have been received by me, not only with submission but also with joy, my aim pointing no farther than that some reasonable assistance might be afforded to those distressed Catholics which were in great want of it. Mr Matthews stayed so short a time with me that he did not leave (at least I do not retain) a perfect account of what Your Eminence wrote to him and he represented to the king: but I will by the first occasion be informed by him more particularly, that I may be the better enabled to serve Your Eminence in seconding and promoting to my power your zealous design.

I have discovered upon some mention made to the king of foreigners who offered themselves to serve as missioners in some of his American plantations (as lately one did for Virginia) that His Majesty did not much esteem such offers fit to be accepted, which makes me fear lest some exception may be made against one of the fathers mentioned in Your Eminence's letter to Mr Matthews, who if I well remember is a subject of the King of Spain. I could also have wished that Your Eminence had made choice of an English father to superintend those who are natives of Ireland. For though many fit and able persons of that nation are to be found, yet the generality of them do lie under some prejudice as to the prudential part of their conduct, and errors committed at a great distance are not easily corrected. I take the liberty of hinting these particulars, which I submit entirely to Your Eminence.[30]

It would seem from this letter that the Dominicans to be sent by Howard belonged to the English and Irish provinces, with perhaps one Spaniard. Nothing more seems to be recorded of this venture. There were individual Irish Dominicans working in various West Indian islands from this time onwards, but it was to be two hundred years before their English brethren had a settled mission there.

Among the many converts of note during James's reign mention must be made of James Cecil, 4th Earl of Salisbury, a member of a family second to none in its hostility to the church. With his companion Charles Hales (brother of Sir Edward Hales) he was received by Howard at the Minerva at Easter 1687.[31] They stayed as Howard's guests till September, when they set out for England, taking as their chaplain Fr Thomas Cooper, OP, the Prior of SS. John and Paul.[32] Salisbury was again Howard's guest in December 1688.[33]

Another convert closely associated with Howard was Lord Perth, Grand Chancellor of Scotland. He was received in 1685 and Howard was at great trouble to obtain a dispensation for the marriage he had contracted with his first cousin Mary Gordon.[34] Macaulay and others assume that his conversion, and that of John Dryden, was mere political expediency, though both remained in the church and suffered for it under William and Mary. The following extracts from a long letter of Perth to Howard, dated 3 February

1688, shows the small minority of Scotch Catholics making hay while the sun shines under the benign rule of the new Constantine:

> Since my last letter one might have hoped a considerable progress would have been made in the advancement of the Catholic interest, but we have advanced little or nothing. We have indeed got the Abbey of Holyrood House Church (which joins the palace here, the nave is only up, for the quire fell under John Knox's fury) to be the chapel of the Order of St Andrew, and when we have got it we cannot find whom to give it to. It cost me a pull to take it from the parochin, but now all is quiet upon the point and I have made bold to ask as a favour from the trades of Aberdeen the church which belonged to the Trinitarians, and by methods I used have got it with their consent. It is to be put into the hands of a clergyman, to be equally for the use of the clergy and the regulars.
>
> The Jesuits are to set up their college in a house which formerly lodged the chancellors; it joins the palace too. Their schools will be opened next week or the week after. Some little jealousies have been working betwixt them and the clergy, but by some endeavours I employed, by which I lost some of the favour of both sides, things keep in a tolerably peaceable condition.
>
> Of late we have got over, six or seven monks from Germany, some of them very good men and like to prove able missionaries. They would fain be on the same foot as the others, but you know best how to order, for your zeal and pious care of these countries needs no solicitation for the good of the church here, and your prudence needs no insinuation to give you aim, nor am I so presumptuous as to offer anything of that kind save by way of information.
>
> There have been very few conversions of late. Some few ministers, exemplary men, have come in, many of the ordinary sort, but few in towns. The ministers and university men are so wild and furious and talk with that confidence in a very bad cause, that the people take their assertions for full proof of their veracity. Some debates have been amongst the people in the government. The Duke of Hamilton (who must still be complaining) has been exercising that querulous faculty on very frivolous occasions, but the truth is his business is to obstruct the Catholic interest, which I believe will very fully appear now very soon. Others here would have us believe they are friends, who really are our most dangerous enemies, especially some in the army, the hundredth man in which is not a Catholic, and we have scarce any officers of that persuasion; not that they are not to be had, but with all the art imaginable the king is diverted

from any such design as might bring in the army to us. This is the true state of our affairs.[35]

Meanwhile the development of the church in England was growing apace. On 30 January 1688 the pope sanctioned the appointment of three more vicars apostolic. They were consecrated publicly in London in the following summer, and the division of England into four vicariates was destined to survive until 1840.

One of the new vicars apostolic, Bonaventure Giffard had recently been the centre of a storm at Oxford. James had forced him on the Fellows of Magdalen College as their president in defiance of their statutes and privileges. James intended to turn this college into a Catholic seminary and as a nucleus three professors and a number of theological students were brought over from Douai.* It met with determined opposition and had to be abandoned.

Very soon after there was opposition from a more influential quarter. In April James had reissued his declaration of liberty of conscience and in May he ordered it to be read from every pulpit in the land. Seven bishops refused and on 8 June were sent to the Tower. James unwisely proceeded to their arraignment and they were triumphantly acquitted on 30 June amidst public jubilation.

On 10 June the queen had given birth to a prince, thus ensuring a Catholic successor. This more than anything else sealed the fate of the Stuarts. Many who would endure one Catholic king were not prepared to support a Catholic dynasty.

The news of the birth of an heir was sent to the pope by James himself and was received in Rome with far more joy than it caused in England. Howard sent his congratulations to the queen on 3 July:

> I wanted words to express the great joy and blessing which Your Majesty hath brought not only to our nations but the whole Catholic church, in the birth of our Prince of Wales, which is such an universal joy to all people here that it's inexplicable, and we knowing no better way of acknowledging our gratitude than by our humble thanks unto God almighty for so great a blessing, and prayers for many happy years unto Your Majesties and our prince. We hope Your Majesty will bring on many more princes and princesses.[36]

---

* One would hardly expect this to be done without recourse to Rome, but there is no reference to it in Propaganda till it had failed and the students had returned to Douai (AP, Collegi, IV).

Once more the bells of the Roman churches rang out and the palaces of those in any way concerned were a blaze of light. Once more the fountains flowed with wine and Howard marked the occasion in a very English way by roasting an ox whole in a public piazza. The celebrations at the Collegio Romano were more demure. A 'Genethliacon' extolling the spectacular virtues of the month-old Prince of Wales, composed by Carlo d'Aquino, SJ, and dedicated to the pope's brother was declaimed by three young Pamphili princes—presumably in relays, for these Latin hexameters in the printed edition[37] run to sixteen folio pages.

There were bonfires in England too, but they were to celebrate, not the birth of the prince but the acquittal of the seven bishops on 30 June. Once more the pope was burnt in effigy, and down in Somerset, which had felt the heavy hand of Judge Jeffreys, they added an effigy of the sickly little prince who had scarce begun to breathe.[38] On the very day the bishops were acquitted a secret deputation was sent to William of Orange inviting him to come and assume the crown of England. It must have been clear to almost everyone except James that this was the beginning of the end. James shows no sign of apprehension at the approaching doom. He was still obsessed with gaining a cardinal's hat for Fr Petre. In June he decided to despatch to Rome another ambassador to press for this, and he chose Lord Thomas Howard, brother of Henry, 7th Duke of Norfolk, and nephew to the cardinal. There is no record of any meeting between uncle and nephew, so perhaps the king had forbidden his envoy to have any dealings with the cardinal. Thomas Howard reports to Sir Richard Bellings on 2 August that in his first audience he delivered a letter from the queen,[39] but it is not till 28 October that there is any reply from the pope. On that day he wrote three letters to James as well as letters to the two English queens. Even at this late hour when his throne was tottering, James had offered his services as mediator between the Holy See and Louis XIV. The pope gratefully acknowledges his offer and refers him to Lord Howard and d'Adda for further particulars. A second letter concerns the cardinal's hat for Petre, and promises not to omit to ask the 'supreme giver of all good things' to lavish his treasures on the king. This was a gracious way of saying 'no'. The third letter concerns the new oath for privy counsellors, which was causing some apprehension in England. The pope praises the king's devotion to the Holy See and again refers him to Lord

*Eclipse*

Thomas.⁴⁰ It cannot be pretended that the new ambassador had been any more successful than Castlemaine, though he was much better tempered. It was perhaps from Lord Howard that the pope again heard of James's dissatisfaction with the Cardinal of Norfolk. Two days after these letters the cardinal secretary writes to d'Adda:

> It has come to the knowledge of His Holiness that it has been represented by His Majesty that Cardinal Howard here has opposed the advancement of Fr Petre and that Fr Carlo Noyelle, the general of the Society of Jesus, has said that His Holiness has expressly notified him that the petitions for it made by His Majesty are not his own. Neither of these suppositions has any foundation in truth. Not the first, because Cardinal Howard has never made any opposition to the advancement of the said father, but rather, with the special devotion and respect which he professes for His Majesty, has always striven to do all in his power for the entire satisfaction of His Majesty. Not the second, because it is incredible that Fr Noyelle, a man of such integrity and prudence could have said anything so far removed from the truth.⁴¹

This letter was entrusted to Thomas Howard, who was about to set out for England. He reached Paris towards the end of November and hearing of the state of affairs at home decided to press on at once. He later changed his mind. On 5 November, William of Orange had landed at Torbay and ever since there had been a steady stream of desertions. On 10 December the queen arrived in France with the baby prince, and on Christmas Day was joined by the king. Lord Thomas was waiting to receive them at Saint-Germain and remained their faithful servant to the end. He later accompanied the king to Ireland, was sent back to France on a special mission and was drowned off Brest on 9 November 1689. His elder brother, Henry Duke of Norfolk, did not emulate his loyalty, and the chalice of suffering that Cardinal Howard had now to drink was made even more bitter by the recollection that his older nephew, the head of the first family of the realm, had not only apostatized from the faith but had raised a large force of men in the eastern counties for the support of the Dutch usurper.

Archbishop d'Adda had been ordered by the king to lose no time in quitting the country. He left London the day after the queen in the company and in the livery of the Savoy ambassador.⁴² He saw the infuriated crowd on London Bridge throwing ordure and anything else that came to hand at the departing figure of Fr Petre, and was pursued down the river by their execrations and missiles. From Gravesend they took coach to Canterbury. Here the populace were waiting at the gate armed with every sort of weapon 'rustic and military'. There was some violence and looting. Their periwigs were torn off to discover which of them were tonsured. They arranged to take refuge at an inn and at great expense recovered most of their possessions. It was here that d'Adda met a man who had seen the king captured at Faversham, and who informed him that two of the vicars apostolic, Leyburn and Giffard, had been taken at the same time.[43] By now every Catholic chapel in London including the king's had ben wrecked by the mobs, no exception being made for those of foreign ambassadors. It was the end of an era.

## Notes

1. Hay, *The Jesuits*, 209.
2. *Œuvres*, II, 719.
3. Bod., Rawlinson A, 139B, f. 38.
4. Nunz. Diverse 231, f. 74.
5. Bod., Rawlinson A, 139B, f. 36.
6. Quoted in J. Lingard, *A History of England, from the First Invasion by the Romans*, London, 1849, X, 259.
7. Campana, *Les derniers Stuarts*, II, 127.
8. Avvisi 50, ff. 150, 243.
9. Note in Burnet's *History of his own Time*, ed. 1833, III, 171.
10. BL, Egerton 2260, f. 250.
11. BL, Add. 9341; B, 6337, no. 30.
12. Avvisi 50, f. 262.
13. Berthier, *Epistolae*, II, 359.
14. Med. 4245, no. 284.
15. Campana, *Les derniers Stuarts*, 147–8.
16. TNA 31/9/18, f. 80.
17. H. Ellis, *Original Letters*, 3rd ser. IV, London, 312; Foley, V, 279.
18. Berthier, *Epistolae*, II, 378.
19. NI, 12, f. 242.
20. Ellis (note 17), IV, 313.
21. Bod., Rawlinson A, 139B, f. 99.
22. Campana, *Les derniers Stuarts*, II, 158.
23. *Ibid.* 152, 154.

24 *Ibid*. 151.
25 NI, 15, f. 97.
26 *Ibid*.
27 Arch. of Eng. Province.
28 NI, 17, f. 139.
29 Med. 3833, f. 586; 4245, no. 243.
30 AAW, XXXV, no. 67.
31 Avvisi 50, f. 90; TNA 31/9/15, f. 72.
32 *Dominicana*, 83.
33 Avvisi 44, f. 50.
34 *Les grands écrivains de la France*, Bossuet Correspondence, III, Paris, 1910, 158.
35 Stuart, I, 30.
36 BL, Add. 28225, f. 308.
37 Bib. Corsini, 171-A-15 (no. 8a).
38 Med. 4246 (30 July/9 Aug. 1688).
39 Original at Wardour Castle.
40 Berthier, *Epistolae*, II, 416–18.
41 NI, 16, f. 135.
42 NI, 15, f. 154.
43 NI, 14, f. 58.

11

## Closing Years

I

THE NEWS OF THE FLIGHT OF KING JAMES and of his arrival in France reached Howard on 17 January 1689 and came apparently as a staggering surprise.¹ The last report that had arrived from London, dated 2 December 1688, gave no inkling of serious danger and made no mention of a hostile army firmly established in the west country. It spoke mostly of the universal wish of Catholics and Protestants alike (though not of the Jesuits) to see Howard in England.² The despatches of d'Adda are equally reticent about the impending disaster.

The news was received at the papal court with consternation. It was not a time to stand on niceties, and Innocent XI overlooked the affront that had been offered to his cardinal protector and accepted the one provided by the king. Cardinal d'Este received no brief of appointment and Howard still officially retained the office, but at this moment of supreme crisis in English Catholic affairs the pope chose to deal with the Italian, whose admission to the sacred college he had so long resisted. It was d'Este who was received in a long audience on the first Saturday of February, and after the audience a special courier was despatched to France with a letter of condolence to James and another to Louis XIV, thanking him for giving hospitality to the fugitives.³ At the consistory held on 7 February, after the pope had expressed his grief, three cardinals rose in turn to thank him for his allocution. The first was d'Estrées on behalf of France, the second was d'Este, who is called Protector of England, and the third was Howard, who is simply designated 'Anglus'.⁴

At both Versailles and Saint-Germain it was complained that Cardinal Howard had shown himself hostile to the interests of the king, and it was surmised that this was because the office of protector had been taken from him.⁵ The exiled queen, amidst her tears, had still a warm spot for uncle Rinaldo. She asked Louis XIV in April to be good enough to have him as Cardinal Protector of France, and received the characteristic reply that the king was in a position to offer protection, not to receive it.⁶ Sir James Porter, James's new ambassador to the papal court, had received his instructions on 4 February. After paying his respects to His Holiness he was to call on d'Este, deliver the king's letter and thank him for his care of the king's affairs. Even in this hour of tragedy the king could not restrain his Gallican meddling in matters ecclesiastical. Porter was to impress on d'Este that he must procure from the pope powers for the king to nominate Irish bishops and not merely to supplicate for them. Porter was further instructed to be nice to all the friendly cardinals, and in particular to Cardinal d'Estrées and the French ambassador. There is no mention whatsoever, in these instructions, of Cardinal Howard.⁷ Porter reached Rome about the middle of March and took up his lodgings in the palace of Cardinal d'Este, who accompanied him for his audience with the pope. Meanwhile the pope, who was suffering from catarrh, had refused an audience to Howard, who desired to speak with him of the affairs of England. On 2 April it is reported that Porter cannot obtain another audience and, like Castlemaine before him, he threatened to leave Rome. It was only with great difficulty that Cardinal d'Este prevailed upon him to stay.⁸ All through April, d'Este vainly pleaded for another audience and the pope, who was by now a very sick man, consistently refused.⁹

On 12 March James had landed in Ireland with a small army. He had the support of Louis XIV, who was at war with William of Orange in the Netherlands. The French king, however, regarded the Irish campaign as a diversion rather than a flank attack and his support was half-hearted and inadequate. It was continually stressed at the time and is now generally agreed that the crying need in Ireland was money. The Irish were faithful to their Catholic king and nobody doubted their bravery, but they were ill-clad, ill-equipped and unpaid. Many were bare-footed and armed with only makeshift weapons. Doubtless one of Porter's principal tasks was to beg a substantial subsidy from the papal exchequer. Howard's disgrace hardly affected events in England. James had never sought or desired advice from Rome as to how to conduct his affairs: he merely asked for red hats and mitres. But in Ireland the situation was different, and it may be that its history for the next two centuries might have been less tragic if Howard had retained the king's confidence and used his undoubted persuasive charms to obtain a timely subsidy from the pope. Neither d'Este nor Porter had much influence with the pope. The former had been reluctantly made a cardinal against all the pope's deepest desires and convictions: the latter manifested a pro-French bias that did not commend him to a pope who had been throughout his pontificate in bitter conflict with the French king.

At last on 2 May Innocent condescended to receive d'Este in an audience that lasted two hours.[10] On 8 May is a report that:

> The English envoy was with the pope and with many other cardinals, but carried no letter from the king, and showed himself more French than English. It is not known whether he has visited Cardinal Howard, with whom the king is said to be far from satisfied, as also with the nuncio d'Adda, declaring that the promoters of his expulsion from his kingdom are the Spanish ministers. These do not deny it, asserting that the close association of the King of England with France had caused great jealously in Spain.[11]

On 15 May Innocent wrote his last letter to James, expressing his gladness at the news of his safe arrival in Ireland, and referring him, for the other matters broached in the king's letter, to our beloved son Cardinal Rinaldo d'Este.[12] On 21 May Howard was given the important and fairly lucrative office of archpriest of S. Maria Maggiore, vacant by the death of Cardinal Rospigliosi. This caused considerable surprise because, in the ultra-conservative traditions of the papal court such an honour went normally to a cardinal of the reigning pope's own creation, and it is stated that Howard had not even petitioned for it.[13] Local gossip had a ready explanation:

> His Holiness has given the office of archpriest of S. M. Maggiore to Cardinal Howard. On this point there is infinite speculation, because they cannot discover the motives, seeing many of the creatures of His Holiness were asking for it. The wicked say it was done as a snub to d'Este and d'Estrées, and to mollify Howard, who declared pretty openly against the pope for not giving succour to King James.[14]

There may be something in this, for it would seem that about this time Innocent reacted violently against d'Este, who was notoriously scheming with d'Estrées, and once more smiled upon Howard: before the end of May Howard was received in audience several times and conferred at great length on the affairs of England.[15] But it was too late for any effective help. The pope was very ill and past caring about the kings of this world. He lingered through July and died on 12 August. For nearly two months, while James waited in Dublin for arms and for money, the two cardinal protectors were locked up in the Vatican, endeavouring to elect a worthy successor.

It is generally accepted by English historians that Blessed Innocent XI was unsympathetic to James and refused to aid him in his final struggle. May it not be that the pope was antagonized by a string of unpleasant and pro-French envoys that James forced upon him? And perhaps the final eclipse of the church and the centuries of oppression in Ireland owe more than is often realized to the vanity and family ambitions of the young lady from Modena, whose marriage Howard was so proud to have promoted.

II

On 6 October 1689 the cardinals elected Pietro Ottoboni, who took the name of Alexander VIII. He was already in his eightieth year and was destined to rule no more than sixteen months. For all his years he was a firm statesman and Louis XIV, whose political star was waning, was glad to make his peace with the pope on terms that were markedly in the church's favour. He combined a compassion for the poor with a scandalous liberality towards his own relatives, and revived much of the evil patronage that had been sternly suppressed by his saintly predecessors. James, still inactive in Dublin, thought it best to send a new envoy to replace Porter and he chose Lord Melfort, brother of Lord Perth and a convert like him. His instructions were to deal only with d'Este and not to acknowledge Howard as protector, but there is no longer any mention of Petre's red hat and the main purpose of the embassy was to obtain money and still more money for the Irish wars. The new pope much preferred to treat with Howard and from now on d'Este had less and less to do with the affairs of England. The following letter from Melfort to the queen dated from Rome 14 March 1690 shows the absurd situation created by having two protectors, and also the unwavering loyalty of Howard to the Stuart cause:

## Closing Years

I cannot deny that it was amongst the greatest surprises of my life that when I had been at the pains I had been at, and vested with such an entire trust from the king as that of ambassador, I wanted nothing but the honour, having all the power by the king's credentials and instructions, that yet that Cardinal Howard should have the first notice of the pope's intentions. Yet this should have gone well enough down if it had not been for my instructions by way of Mémoire from France, and the trouble I knew it would cause to the Cardinal d'Este, and the blame it might bring upon me. But all this was much heightened the day after when the cardinal brought me a brief from the pope to the king, in which, besides that it was directed to him by the secretary without taking notice of me, it had a clause in it of telling the pope's mind to Cardinal Howard and commending his care of the king's affairs.

This was so plain a setting of him up to be protector (a thing that I meddled not with so long as it lay asleep). Yet when it was so authentically produced into my hands, I could not be answerable to suffer it, knowing that the king had appointed another, and that till that was recalled, I was to look on none but him who was authorized by the king. And therefore notwithstanding of many considerations of friendship of relation etc., I was resolved to have all this remedied, and indeed it would have most justly afflicted the Cardinal d'Este if I had not. So I resolved to do it the softest way I could invent, and if possible shun giving the least offence even to Cardinal Howard, who is most zealous for the king and whom all the French here have vindicate to me in all his behaviours towards them, so that I have lived with all civility with him, but this was not my affair, and therefore I was not master of it.

He goes on to give a long account of his audience with the pope. The pope had promised 20,000 crowns, but it was made clear that this was not a war-subsidy but a gift to the poor Catholics, though it would be sent to the king. The pope said he was afraid of trouble with Spain and the Emperor if he gave money specifically to the king. Melfort asked that the money should be given in his (Melfort's) hands, 'but no argument would persuade him'. The letter continues:

Then I told him that I had reasons to desire it might not go by the Cardinal Howard it being all one to him, and begged it might go by Monsignor Caprara; that would save me a great deal of pains and be a greater favour to Your Majesty. His Holiness told me he was the Cardinal d'Este's agent, and that was as bad

> as to give it to me, pretending that in that case he could not so well defend himself against the Germans and Spain, but that he was content to give it to the rector of the English College for the ends he had mentioned. This I could not refuse being able to gain no more, having been refused likewise to give it to the Cardinal Altieri, Protector of Ireland where the king was, but that he smoked out immediately and told me the war was there and the case would be too plain that it was for the king. So I accepted the rector of the English College, but to show how apt His Holiness is to save his money, Your Majesty may consider that the Cardinal Howard had just pretences for money to himself and this he thought to stop his mouth. Next the English College has just right to expect his assistance, and thus their mouth is stopped though they be nothing the richer...
>
> He told me laughing he had read my last memorial and that there was something piquant in it. I told him there was so but I intended it against the king's enemies and not against him, and that if there was anything in it to offend him I retracted it with all my heart. He said 'our peace would be soon made, for we love and esteem you with our heart', and so he took me in his arms, embraced me and kissed me on the cheek, and said *pax tecum*, and so the matter was made up, though indeed I had no reason to regret that Mémoire, it having had better success than any of the smooth ones that went before it.
>
> I told His Holiness, for the same reasons I had mentioned before, I would beg of him to change the brief and not put the Cardinal Howard's name in it, seeing I know well no mortal had done more in that matter than the Cardinal d'Este had done, and yet he was not mentioned. That His Holiness approved of, and took back the brief and sent it to me this morning mended as Your Majesty will see by the two copies I send you here enclosed.[16]

On 9 May Melfort informs the queen that he has had another audience but that the pope had refused to give any more money.

> The occasion of this audience was mainly to accustumate the pope to hear this matter spoken of with patience, for Cardinal Howard, who thinks himself bound to do all he can for the king, having been since my last audience soliciting the pope for supplies, the pope told him flatly he neither could nor would give more, that he had given all he could and yet was not at rest. The cardinal desired him not to give him a positive denial but to take time to advise, and he refused even that, told he had thought on't already and could give no other answer. This the cardinal came and told me of, of which I admired, it being so

contrary to what he had formerly resolved, to regain the post which he had lost, and at least bring him back to consider, and having obtained that, I durst press no more lest I should be used as the cardinal had been, and meet with a flat denial.[17]

On 13 May Melfort sent a note to Howard enclosing a political pamphlet and telling him of his audience:

> The pope spoke something softlier to me than he did to Your Eminence and promised to do all that was in his power, but at the same time he said he had power to do nothing, yet I hope when he sees the good reason that there is for it he will not be so stubborn.[18]

On 30 June 1690 Catholic hopes in Ireland were dashed by the bloody battle of the Boyne, and on the following day James returned to France. The pressure on the pope appears to have ceased. In November Melfort complains to the queen that a portrait of the Prince of Wales she had promised to send him had never arrived, although Cardinal Howard had received his.[19] It is not known whether Howard, during these years of eclipse, had even sent his Christmas wishes to the king and queen, though he was so meticulous about these little courtesies that the presumption is that he did. There are no extant letters that had passed between them since the appointment of d'Este as cardinal protector. Then on 25 November Howard received a letter from the king.[20] Nothing is known of its contents. It was too early to be a Christmas greeting, and it would appear to have been a peace-offering. From now on their relations were more cordial and nothing more is heard of Cardinal d'Este in the king's affairs. Howard replied at once and on 15 January 1691 the king wrote a letter which makes it clear that Howard had been reinstated as agent, or at least as money-getter:

> Some days since I had yours of 25 November and do not at all doubt of you continuing doing your part in advancing my affairs where you are, and if they have not had the success I had reason to expect, I am sure 'twas not for want of your soliciting them, of which Lord Melfort has given me an account. The Prince of Orange is making great preparations for the next campaign, and, 'tis said by all the last letters from England, intends to head the confederate army in Flanders. He does all he can to advance the Protestant cause everywhere. Why should not His Holiness do the like on his side? The king my brother here does what he can, but he alone cannot do all, having so many enemies to

deal with. The Prince of Orange has sent arms into Savoy and Piedmont, and money is agoing now into Switzerland from him. Why should not His Holiness spare me some to buy arms here, to begin a magazine, that, for ought I know, I may have great need of before the summer shall be over, and then I suppose he would be sorry I should want them.[21]

His next letter, dated 14 February 1691, shows his reposing in Howard a trust that he had not expressed for years:

The last letters from Rome gave so bad an account of His Holiness's indisposition that 'tis believed, considering his great age, he will hardly recover, which has obliged this king to order all the cardinals in France, except the Cardinal of Furstenberg, to make what haste they can for Rome. The same reason makes me write so early to you upon that subject. I write also to Lord Melfort and send him such credentials and instructions as will be necessary for him on such an occasion. I shall order him to give you an account of his instructions that you may concur with him in doing your endeavours to get such a choice made as may be for the advantage of Holy Church and the good of all Christendom, which now is, in choosing such a one as may be for the effectual assisting me against the usurper, and doing his part to draw from him those Catholic princes who are now in league with him, the usurper, not only in my dominions, but even in the rest of Europe. All the world sees the sad effects the emperor's joining with the Prince of Orange has had in Hungary, and had not the King of Spain and Duchy of Savoy done the same, in all appearance before this I had been restored, and Catholic religion established again as it was in my time, in all my dominions.

I should think that these considerations should make all where you are, to join with you in the choice of such a pope as would bestir himself for the good of the church. The most Christian king's concerns and mine are now so united that all that wish me well must join with his there in the choice which is to be made, which I most earnestly recommend you to do, and that there may be a good understanding between you and the Cardinal d'Este for the better carrying on of my concerns there, which I am sure you will continue to do as you always have done.[22]

When this letter was written, Alexander VIII was already dead (1 February) and the cardinals already in conclave. There they stayed four months. The monotony this time was relieved by a furious fire near the cell of Altieri that necessitated opening the closely guarded doors to let in the firemen. It was the eve of Pentecost, and was a gift to the writers of pasquinades, who had much to say about the tongues of fire. But the great opportunity for pasquinades came on 12 July when Cardinal Pignatelli became Pope Innocent XII. Pignattello means a small earthen pot, and the new pontiff was represented wearing three pots as a tiara, with the caption: 'It took them four months to make three pots!' This was Howard's third and last conclave and when he emerged after these four months the cause of King James was as good as lost. Sporadic fighting had continued in Ireland since the battle of the Boyne a year before, but now the end was in sight. By the treaty of Limerick on 3 October 1691, the Irish laid down their brave but inadequate arms and agreed to conditions that showed moderation but were never honoured. There remained in England a faithful Jacobite minority, especially in the north, but it was never a serious threat. The Catholics went underground and for another century suffered and dwindled. At Saint-Germain James conducted his little court with faded gentility, issued his letters patent, created new peers, and continued to press the pope for powers to nominate Irish bishops, who could no longer function in Ireland.

It now all reads like an old nursery game of make-believe. At Rome, James was still honoured as King of England, Howard himself remaining the staunchest of Jacobites to the very end. There was little that the cardinal protector could do beyond succouring the English and Irish exiles and begging the pope for money that could no longer help restore the king to his throne. Innocent XII proved more generous than his two predecessors. There are receipts of 17 September and 23 November 1691, when the fighting had ceased in Ireland, for large sums given by the pope to James.[23] After that, however, Howard met with little success and is seldom in the news. There are reports of his singing High Mass at S. M. Maggiore when the pope made his solemn visit on the feast of the Assumption 1691, and of a cappella of cardinals assembled there on Christmas day to honour the archpriest.[24]

During all these years Howard spent much of his time with his English brethren at Ss John and Paul's. He was often also at St Sabina, where he joined in the choral office and dined in the refectory. Sometimes he celebrated Mass next door in the church of S. Alessio in honour of St Thomas of Canterbury, who is said to have stayed there when he visited Rome.*

Lord Melfort was recalled at the end of 1691 and was succeeded by Sir John Lidcott who had already served in Rome as agent on the departure of Castlemaine. Melfort's next letter to Howard is dated from Saint-Germain 17 March 1692. It is concerned with the status of Alessandro Caprara, a Modenese priest who was the Rome agent of the English queen. It is less than candid. There is extant a whole volume of letters from Melfort to Caprara for the years 1691-4 from which it is clear that Melfort was well aware that James had appointed Caprara his agent at the papal court; there is also a letter from the pope to the king acknowledging and accepting his appointment.[25] Caprara was also agent for Cardinal d'Este (who continued to live at Modena), and thus the pope was inveigled into treating with d'Este rather than Howard by having d'Este's agent thrust upon him under the pretence of being the agent of James. For the rest of Howard's lifetime it was Caprara who was entrusted with the more important and more confidential affairs of the king. But it was better that Howard should not know that he had been virtually supplanted: hence this disingenuous letter.

> I am informed that Monsignor Caprara has acted by some way as if he had a character from the king. When I was at Rome this was proposed to the French court, and that the king gave his consent to it. I did what I could to hinder it but in vain; the thing was too far advanced, so he had a letter sent him to deliver such letters as come to his hands, but to take on him no character, and it was thought he would have kept the secret. Now that it seems he has not, another shall be sent by me to take this name from him, though he who will be first sent is only for a short message which he is to carry, but it will put an end to this matter. Monsignor Caprara had never any secret of the king's affairs; we know his interest too well in the house of Austria, and he had only the ministry of delivering letters, as having been all along the queen's trusty, and it was thought it would save money. I was so far from approving of all this that I never would mention it. I well know that the ills I foretold from it would follow ... I hope ere long to send more news; in the meantime I beg you would be preparing the pope to do

---

* See J. J. Berthier, *Le couvent de S. Sabine*, Rome, 1912, 525–6. Berthier cites a manuscript, *Annales S. Sabinae*. He mentions two copies of this work, one in the archives of the order and another in Florence. Neither can now be found.

## Closing Years

something for the king, who deserves more from him than he can give.[26]

The news that Melfort hoped to send ere long was the news of James's landing in England. He had been preparing for invasion ever since the arrival of the Irish soldiers, who had been allowed by the treaty of Limerick to leave the country. Some nine thousand disembarked at Brest at the close of the year and there were about 20,000 already serving in the army of Louis XIV. By April 1692 James felt ready for the attempt and issued his famous declaration. He compared William to Nero, dismissed his claims as 'too vain and frivolous to deserve a confutation', forbade his subjects to pay taxes to William, and promised pardon to his rebellious subjects when he was restored to his kingdom. But there was a long list of exceptions that included not only nobles and divines, judges and juries that had convicted conspirators and all spies who had revealed Jacobite designs, but also the fishermen of Faversham, who had handled him roughly before his flight. He promised protection for the church of England, and liberty of conscience for all. It was hardly the sort of document to win him Protestant support and even ardent Jacobites strongly disapproved of it.

The next letter is from Lidcott and testifies to Howard's continued zeal. It is undated but belongs to the first half of May 1692, for there is a report dated 10 May to the effect that Howard had specially returned from his villa at Castel Gandolfo to expedite the business of the king's new envoy.[27] All proper names are in cipher, but the deciphered names are written over the numbers:

> I arrived, I thank God safely hither by Saturday the 3 instant, and immediately repaired to Cardinal Forbin from whose hands I received the packet relating to myself, and having forthwith perused it I signified all the contents proper to be imparted to him. The like to Cardinal d'Estrées the same night, but Cardinal Howard being at his country house I sent thither an express with what related to him, who upon receipt thereof came hither with all zeal and diligence.
>
> This morning Cardinal Howard was with the pope and did with a very good heart and his usual zeal press to the utmost for some addition for this present extraordinary exigence, but nothing it seems can yet be further done. Cardinal Forbin is scandalized at the little sum, and will speak home too on Thursday next. But every little must be welcome till it please God to send more ...

> I am lodged at Cardinal Howard, who is most generous and kind to me according to his usual temper. 'Tis now past 9 at night, and just now a messenger brings a note hither for the money, which amounts I reckon to above 5000 scudi more than the pope promised as yesterday, and Howard sends the said note under a letter of his own to the queen.[28]

The money was sent to the queen because James was with his army waiting for a favourable wind. It was acknowledged by her in a letter to Howard of 5 June, in which she says: 'I question not but your zeal and unwearied application for the king's service have contributed very much to these propitious inclinations and will cultivate them to a more considerable degree hereafter'.[29] There is no mention of her uncle, who does not appear to have lifted a finger to help her in her calamities. Evidently the queen, when she wrote this, had not heard of the calamity of the five previous days. The combined French and Jacobite fleet that was to carry the troops to England had been attacked in the channel by the English, decisively defeated and virtually destroyed. The invasion of England was very definitely off, and after this date became no more than a fond dream. Still, the news of Louis's campaign against the Dutch was more heartening. In June he captured the fortress of Namur that was believed to be impregnable. When the news reached Rome, Howard looked on the bright side. He writes to Melfort on 29 July:

> We being in continual hopes of the good consequences after the taking of Namur Castle, as we hope shortly to hear of the old rusty Tower of London and Edinburgh Castle, with all their appurtenances. In the interim I thank God for Her Majesty's recovery of her late indisposition of the gravel, and that our young prince is so well and so fine a child, it being a new comfort unto us all, being this addition doth the more strengthen the Catholic royal family. I did the other day again represent (*fortiter sed suaviter*) the last disappointment, which necessitates so much His Majesty's loyal subjects, and truly I think the pope hath a true sense of it, but Your Lordship knows how delicate and difficult money affairs are here, he having not long since told me that he hath in one year sent His Majesty five and fifty thousand scudi; however, I will hope better shortly, in which my dutiful endeavours shall never fail.[30]

Lidcott wrote by the same post, again praising Howard's kindness.

## Closing Years

> I need not tell you Your Lordship that Cardinal Howard's zeal and goodness is most important. He will, I doubt not, as I have begged him, get within a day or two one audience more before I part, so that if by staying about a week longer I may likely bring something along with me to make me more welcome, I should be most glad of the occasion. However I am ready to part by Friday or Saturday next, though indeed 'tis sultry frying weather.[31]

Lidcott delayed his departure still further for reasons that he states in a letter of 5 August:

> I reckoned ere this to have been in my return, but hopes, hot weather, and my Lord Cardinal's kindness easily induced me to defer a few days longer. I have resolved as soon as ever the next French letters come to be gone, though 'twill be frying weather indeed if I find no more fresco in the way than here. His Eminence bids me tell Your Lordship he would have answered yours, which he received last post, but that by multiplicity of feasts and holy days, with other business on the pope's side as well as his own, he has not yet had the audience which he asked six days ago, and truly that has been the chief cause too, that I am still here... Since the taking Namur 'tis a pleasure to see what a world of well-wishers Prince of Orange has lost even here, and when he is going once down the hill he will in all appearance precipitate more and more till he comes to the bottom.[32]

Howard explains in the next letter (23 December) how difficult it was to get more money from the pope, and why:

> Your last I suppose to be of about the 15 of November, it having in it His Majesty's of that date, but I answer it not now in hopes of a better time or a more grateful one, as I constantly play our good old man for, although he complaineth of not having wherewithal to finish and establish the 900 and odd beggars who rambled and importuned all mankind both in city, churches and everywhere in this city with scandal etc., as Your Lordship saw. He hath already spent above 30,000 scudi in repairing Saint John Lateran's palace to lodge them in and clothe them all from top to toe, besides their diet and all other necessities, *et nondum est finis* [and there is no end yet]; more are yet to be put in, and how to establish a fund for the future nobody knoweth, insomuch that although I thought not of it, His Holiness (at my return from Castel) ordered me to take a particular care of it, as I did unwillingly for some days, but when I saw a much greater number brought in than I thought needed to have been, *et quod*

*omnes quaerebant non quae Dei sed quae sua sunt* [and because all sought not what belongs to God, but what belongs to them], and would have other ways taken to keep them than that of Paris, Lyons and Holland, I withdrew my neck out of the collar, refusing my neck any longer to be in the collar which fitted me not, since which these who were joined in that beggarly care, find they must change measures, as they begin to do, and I wish them good success, although I do not much think it, until they change the whole system. Interim betwixt the new heat of this work and the cold of the weather, no grass will grow to feed our master's poor loyal necessitous subjects, but I hope by the lengthening of the new year's days, the sun's beams will so comfortly shine on us that new buds will produce us some sweet flowers, for which I will omit no pains in cultivating the Monte Cavallo garden, and all that liveth in it.[33]

In the beginning of 1693 Howard's health began to fail and he spent more time at his country villa. Apart from his gout he had some eye trouble that made letter-writing difficult, but there was no diminution of his optimism. Money was, however, difficult to come by:

> My gout and 'rhume' hath together of late been very troublesome unto me; however, they never have yet, nor I hope never shall hinder any part of my duty to His Majesty's concerns, and having limped of late to renew unto His Holiness His Majesty's faithful subjects' great indigence, which I am sure I have fully exposed, but yet can get nothing but good verbal hopes, which are now so old that I am so much ashamed of so often repeating them that I cannot with a good heart and hand send His Majesty such empty characters, until I feel the execution of them according unto my daily hopes. This, my Lord, maketh me ashamed (although due) to give His Majesty and yourself many humble thanks for the late favour bestowed on my nephew Bernard, whilst His Majesty hath been charitable unto him from top to toe, since his father having outrid the comestable hath nothing left behind him for what's to succeed.
>
> Finally, grateful thanks unto His Majesty and Your Lordship is that which should be the least part due, but I being now both by necessity as choice, a poor beggar, can only return, according unto my trade, a *Deo gratias*, for this and all other favours until it please God to enable me better to show my gratitude...
>
> I need not tell Your Lordship of the pope's borrowing and charging the Camera of 100,000 scudi towards a fund of future maintenance of the importune briganti (alias unruly beggars)

now enclosed in his repaired palace of S. Giovanni Laterano, nor of his taking away all future pensions which used to be layed on benefices which had care of souls; which good retrenchment is computed will diminish at least 200,000 crowns yearly unto the Dataria. Many other good things he hath in intention to do as soon as he can, if God grant him life, and amongst them our good king will considerably be one, if my poor endeavours can any ways prevail.[34]

He wrote again a few days later:

> I acknowledge at once the favour of Your Lordship's of the 12 January which mentioneth a monthly allowance for His Majesty's poor loyal subjects, but our good old man sayeth he is left so bare that he cannot get for the necessities of the streets' beggars, nor the future cardinals to be made, whilst several of these who are, were not yet provided for, which hath made some seek elsewhere, as he thinketh ought not to be; finally to tell you the many excuses will do you no good nor bring anything, although neither have nor will omit my best endeavours and I hope it will be better than that, for our good old man is endeavouring all he can to get a peace or at least a truce amongst Catholic princes, in either of which he will chiefly endeavour His Majesty's restoration, and I hope we shall soon see those who hitherto were so much against it, take better measures or else be forced into it.[35]

The Jacobite party in England were still convinced that James could be restored if only he would show himself more accommodating and forgiving. These 'compounders' drew up a declaration, which, after such searching of heart and many amendments, James signed on 17 April 1693. He had rejected a clause that promised that the Prince of Wales would be brought up a Protestant, but even in its final form the declaration was as alarming to Catholics as it was contemptible to Protestants. He promised that there should be no recriminations or revenge for past injuries: that a free parliament should redress all grievances, and that all laws passed since his abdication should be ratified. But it was the clauses concerning religion that filled Catholics with dismay. He promised 'an impartial liberty of conscience' and also that he would not use the dispensing power to nullify the penal laws. These two promises are virtually incompatible. He further promised to 'protect and defend the church of England as it is now established by law, and secure to the members of it all the churches, universities, colleges and schools, together with their immunities, rights and privileges'. This again was inconsistent with liberty of conscience, for many of the privileges claimed by the Protestants *ipso facto* deprived Catholics of their civil rights. Howard seems to have had some intimation of this second declaration before it was signed. He writes to Melfort on 14 April 1693:

> The defluxion which I had of late caused me sore eyes, which hindered my sooner acknowledgement of Your Lordship's letters, although I omitted no occasions of representing thoroughly unto His Holiness all the best reasons I could of His Majesty's faithful subjects' pressing necessities, but cannot yet get any effectual help more than a great compassion of his condition, with many kind words and good intentions, but that at present he is not able to do for him as he would, and Monsignor Caprara thinketh it yet not time to deliver His Majesty's letter, wherefore I do not yet answer His Majesty's and in this interim I pray God it may happen as Your Lordship mentions, that force (or at least the fear of it) may oblige His Majesty's subjects to a dutiful composition, although I hope it will not be such a one as might seem contrary unto Catholic religion, being I must ingenuously confess unto Your Lordship that I cannot well understand how such a composition can safely stand, but hope His Majesty will take first such secure advice in these matters as may not be censured as heretofore, and even in the late intended expedition, which was not well understood here, insomuch that the ill success of it was by some attributed to the forerunning declaration. This, in confidence, I thought good to give Your Lordship a hint of, not doubting but you will be very tender in so delicate matters.
>
> Your Lordship's last of the 18 March brings me their Majesties' commands in concurrence with their best (and indeed, as I may say, only powerful) friends, which I shall most willingly do as far as lieth in me, although I have been unhandsomely and unjustly censured for my plain-dealing good intentions, as Your Lordship knoweth. However I can say truthly that I have not omitted my endeavours when and where I thought best, according to my duty to my king and religion, although I cannot agree to all men's opinions who have in some things found to have taken such different measures to what with these circumstances and place, the business is not so soon ended therewith as might have been long since, if somebody else had been believed. However if I can contribute to a good understanding, Your Lordship may assure their Majesties I will not omit my endeavours, it importing

much, not only for their service, but also for the good and quiet of our religion, and therefore I hope their Majesties will also endeavour there, that at least something may be abated, which will be so from an abatement of his most Christian Majesty's true glory, that it will be much his greater glory in this world, and merit it in the next.[36]

When the text of this declaration eventually reached him, Howard sensed the unfavourable reactions of the papal court, and for once decided to disobey his royal master. Cardinal Forbin-Janson wrote to Louis XIV on 7 July 1693:

> The Cardinal of Norfolk has received orders from the king of England to speak to the pope on the subject of the declaration which he has caused to be published in England, but he has judged it prudent, just as I have done, not to have this matter discussed at all in this court. For, however great the zeal and good will of the pope for the reestablishment of the King of England, no approbation will ever be given (following the maxims of this court) to certain expressions in this declaration. Enough that the court should not challenge it, and when they want to discuss it, there will be no difficulty in making it clear to them that there is nothing in it against the rules. The Cardinal of Norfolk will speak with the pope on this subject, as I have done already, and no doubt the pope will tell him, as he told me, that all that is necessary at this conjuncture is that the English should reinstate their king as a Catholic; that they allow him the exercise of his Catholic religion; that the Prince of Wales be brought up in it, and that all Catholics have safeguards for their property and for their lives. He should stop at that, and not hazard a conflict with the cabal of our enemies; a cabal so strong that there are good grounds to fear it would gravely complicate this business.[37]

Howard himself wrote to Melfort on the next day in somewhat similar terms, and his letter shows the incorrigible optimism that still possessed the leading Jacobites:

> I answered not last post Your Lordship's of the 1 June, being I could not so soon confer with our old man, but having perused the heads of the declaration which Your Lordship sent me, and being you say it was already in the hands of some of His Majesty's friends in England, who are making good use of it, I think it will not be to purpose to mention anything of it here, for whatever the result would be, it cannot now but make a noise, which might do harm but no good, for here they will resolve

nothing on it without advising together with several, which although intended to be kept secret cannot probably be but some indiscreet person may let fall a word of it, which I leave to Your Lordship's consideration how prejudicial it may be in the present circumstances, insomuch that without His Majesty's and Your Lordship's order me to venture the examining of it, I should think (under correction) it would be now too late to mention anything of it. I have, however, acquainted the good old man of the appearance and great probability of His Majesty's restoration speedily, and that although he hath hard articles to agree unto, however he will never consent unto the breeding of our prince out of Catholic religion (as was proposed) or do anything that he thinketh can be contrary unto it; and when he will be restored he hath firm hopes of establishing a liberty of conscience, which will have a great influence throughout all Christendom and procure a peace, all which he heard with great joy, praying God to bless and prosper him.

This is all I could get at present, but I will not omit my endeavours for more, hoping we shall shortly hear from you the good effects of His Majesty's restoration, and then by little and little overcome all difficulties.[38]

The king's interest in the nomination of Irish bishops and others did not lessen but rather increased in his years of exile. There was so little else he could do that had even the semblance of reality. These Irish bishops were often unable to live in Ireland and there was no money for the upkeep of their rank, but James prized very highly the power to reward his friends with these almost empty titles. There is much in Howard's correspondence with Melfort on this perennial topic and a few extracts must suffice.

I have discoursed at long with Monsieur de Bru, who is the French expeditioner, and a very understanding and honest person, as the Bishop of Cork can well inform Your Lordship. He is absolutely of the opinion not to ask a bull confirmatory of His Majesty's nomination of bishops of Ireland, being the precedents of the new three popes granting them so, will be sufficient precedents to get the rest, so also from time to time, lest asking a confirmatory bull, we might put it in danger, or at least so "pussell" it in I know not what of their usual eternal difficulties commonly used here, that a remove and other inconvenience might happen. And for the deaneries, they will not grant them.

Finally, he sayeth it's best not to strive in these nice points until His Majesty be restored. Then we may hope to get as good a concordat made with his court as France, Spain or the Empire hath: and if I be alive I hope to do my best endeavour in that as in all other concerns of His Majesty and our religious services, although I was sorry to see that even few or none of our English churchmen have studied or had the practice of these things, much less lay people, both of whom so very wrongly informed His Majesty therein, and ordered them to write to blame me highly for having done only that which I ought for the service of both. But that imports no more than many other things for which I was blamed, although unheard. Yet I thank God I can clearly justify myself in all, *coram Deo et hominibus* [before God and men]. But to our purpose of deans, if His Majesty desires to have any, I hope to get such as will be the same as of his nomination. As for abbots, priors and some other titles, it's thought they may prejudice jealousy and other inconveniences, not only in Protestants, but several Catholics who are in possession of those lands etc. For there are many other honest and skilful expeditioners for the recurring affairs of His Majesty's subjects, as I told Bishop of Cork, who said he would carry a copy of the patent which Monsieur de Bru hath for France, that if His Majesty approve of it, such an other may be sent him for His Majesty's kingdoms, whether I pray God send him and Your Lordship speedily. (25 August 1693)[39]

The long and great pains I suffered above the two months permitted me not to write any letters... Unto what Your Lordship mentions of deaneries and other benefices not of His Majesty's nomination, they do not belong neither unto the ordinaries of Ireland; however, I will endeavour the best I can that they be such as His Majesty will like, but I must take the freedom to acquaint Your Lordship that all the nominated bishops cannot be dispatched here as soon as His Majesty's nomination arriveth here, informations *de vita et moribus* [on the life and character] being first necessary to be made on oath, and also a certainty that the person nominated will accept of the bishopric, being the Franciscan who came hither and went to Germany said that Fr John Dempsey at Dublin did absolutely refuse the bishopric unto which His Majesty named him, for that he is quiet now, and in that parish, which is better than the best bishopric in Ireland: wherefore if that be true, it's not fitting nor usual to make bishops (nowadays) against their wills, but as soon as we can be sure here of his consent to accept of it, that and the others will be accordingly dispatched, but some Irish busybodies here would, however, have persuaded Monsignor Caprara and de Bru to get them dispatched in post haste, putting the cart before the horse.

However I sent word to both, my reasons why that ought not to be done, being they might bring many inconveniences, and that I expected they should first have acquainted me, before proceeding farther in those affairs. (17 November 1693)[40]

### III

The flight of the king was followed by the voluntary exile of thousands of Irishmen including bishops and priests. Relatively few appear to have left England. Most of these exiles settled in France. Some found employment in the king's court at Saint-Germain and many more served in various foreign armies. So many Irish Dominicans arrived in France that the Master General had to issue orders forbidding any more to come as the French Dominicans were quite unable to support them.[41] Howard's correspondence is full of references to his vain efforts to obtain from the 'good old man' something towards support of all these thousands of needy, displaced persons.

Some of these exiles made their way to Rome, and Howard spent the few remaining months of his life in doing all he could for their relief. One of the first to turn to Howard for help was Philip Ellis, OSB, one of the four vicars apostolic. Howard writes to Melfort at the beginning of March 1693:

> Bishop Ellis came hither unexpectedly unto me; however, I do him what service I can, he having His Majesty's leave, and speaketh very honourable of Your Lordship, unto whom he tells me hath written. It's been commonly given out that he is, or is to be His Majesty's agent being another (who you know) pretendeth to be agent, although Your Lordship wrote me the contrary; however, he goeth to and fro very busily to all sorts of people, soliciting as if he were, which people ask me about, but I know not what else to say, but what Your Lordship wrote unto me, although I was always of the opinion that its fitting here should always be an agent for His Majesty provided he could live decently with esteem and without charges unto His Majesty, and ought to be a trusty subject, as (if Your Lordship judge it so) I think this bishop may be, he being already in good esteem with His Holiness and court, and hath gotten pretty well this country's language, whilst with what he hath from His Majesty already, and little addition of lodging, coach and what else I can help him, he liveth very honourably, and can better

## Closing Years

> help me in His Majesty's service than a stranger. This is also Cardinal Forbin's opinion as he tells me, which if their Majesties and Your Lordship approve of, I represent for their services.[42]

A few days later Howard refers to him again in one of the many letters which relate, with monotonous regularity, his failure to get any money from the pope:

> Not only because Your Lordship commends it to me, but also because of the personal merits of Lord Bishop Ellis, I will do him what little service layeth in me, especially of their Majesties and yourself judge him fitting for the employment I mentioned in my last unto Your Lordship. Yesterday I spoke again unto His Holiness of His Majesty's and his poor faithful subjects, but could get only very kind and compassionate words, renewing his own poor condition which renders him uncapable of sending any farther succours at present. I demanded likewise his benediction for Your Lordship and Lady, with yours, which is willingly granted, as also some *Agnus Dei's* which I will get and keep until I receive your commands how to send them. (10 March)[43]

Howard was able to do more than he promised. Ellis became his auditor while retaining the office of agent for the king.

There is mention of only one Dominican who sought and found relief from Howard. This was the Irishman Dominic Langton, who had served in the chapel of the London agent of Cosimo III. With the cooperation of Cosimo, Howard found him a final resting place for a time in the convent of St Maria Novella at Florence.[44] Cosimo also seems to have expended his generosity in assisting other Catholic exiles, who made their way to Florence, and they included Lady Theophila Nelson, who had been received into the church by Howard.[45]

Among the laymen who profited by the cardinal's generosity were the three sons of John Dryden. All three, still in their teens, had become Catholics with their father. The youngest Erasmus, after studies at Douai and Rome, entered the Dominicans, taking the name of Thomas. He made his novitiate at Fiesole and was professed there in 1692. He was ordained in Rome in 1693.[46] The two elder sons of the poet are the subject of the following letter from Howard to Melfort dated 30 June 1693:

> Now I have Your Lordship's of the 8 of June, being very glad to understand that you are recovered of your late indisposition, as I hope my good lady is also, for either of your sickness would

much prejudice His Majesty's service in this conjuncture of affairs, particularly now that we are in expectation of His Majesty's restoration, so many will petition for favour that I must also be one of these beforehand, begging of His Majesty (and Your Lordship's favour in it) that here being two brothers Catholic gentlemen called Mr Charles and John Drayton, sons to the famous poet laureate in London [*margin, in another hand*, a mistake of the old cardinal's for Dryden], one whereof I have in the interim got a place of *camerino di honore* with our old man, and the other liveth with me, but they always desiring to serve their natural king, and both their father and they having been always faithful, would have gone to serve him in France had it not been to put him to straits amongst many others for their maintenance; wherefore my humble request is that His Majesty will please to make them his gentlemen ushers, daily waiters in ordinary in his presence chamber, or grooms of his privy chamber, at his return into England, which honour I am confident they will both as faithfully and decently perform, their father being a convert and their mother a Catholic, sister of the Lord Berkshire. I having received a letter from my lord your brother trouble Your Lordship with its answer. The enclosed from the Irish Franciscan will acquaint Your Lordship how he hath begun his affairs as in the progress I will help him all I can, hoping we shall soon be in no more need of it. The two Irish Augustins are returned finding no possibility of getting a convent for them here.[47]

Meanwhile Queen Mary of Modena recommended to Howard's bounty three youths who had been her chapel-boys in England, asking him to find places for them in the English College at Rome. The first of these, commended by a letter of 14 November 1693 but not named, was probably Thomas Ragway, who was admitted to the college on 26 January following, and was ordained there in 1694. The others were George Collingwood and Christopher Piggot, who carried a letter of hers dated 30 November 1693.[48]

The king continued to busy himself with church affairs. Apart from his lavish nomination of Irish bishops he felt it incumbent upon him to write to Howard for the routine renewal of faculties. His letter is dated 19 October 1693:

> Being informed by Bishop Ellis that the faculties of the four Catholic bishops in England are expired, and that there is a necessity of renewing them, it is our desire they should be renewed as desired, provided they cannot continue to act as

## Closing Years

before without renewing them, in which case we should be glad to let all things stand as at present, lest anything relating to the Catholics should come to make a noise at this conjuncture. But if they cannot act without their faculties being renewed, we desire it may be done in the secretest manner imaginable, that the powers may be extended as far as other apostolical vicars have them in other missions, or as far as you shall find necessary for the good of the Catholic religion and that their powers be extended to all the islands adjacent to their districts belonging properly to England, with the exclusion of what belongs to the kingdoms of Scotland and Ireland.[49]

Howard answered this letter on 17 November 1693. He was by now a very sick man spending much of his time at his villa at Castel Gandolfo.

> Sire
> Were it not that necessity hath no law I ought to be ashamed to have at once two of Your Majesty's letters (of the 30 Sept and 19 Oct) to answer, if my late long fit of the gout together with a defluxion of my eyes had not hindered me from that double duty, whilst being on my recovery I made myself be brought to my country house where the good sir hath now so far recovered me that next week I intend to return to my former station in Rome to act the best I can with His Holiness in Your Majesty's concerns, and what else you was pleased to command me, all which hath suffered nothing by my sickness, I having sufficient powerful friends about His Holiness, who acquainted and acted as far as was hitherto requisite in my absence, whilst I ought not to trouble Your Majesty in the particular circumstances which I write to my Lord Melfort not only of the secrecy (which Your Majesty commands) but also of the right manner your affairs ought to be managed without such precipitation or knowledge to those who understand not the critical circumstances of rightly managing the affairs of Your Majesty's dominions.[50]

On the same day he wrote to Melfort stating that his health had improved in 'this good Castello air'. He warns Melfort of the danger of confiding His Majesty's affairs to Monsignor Caprara, the queen's trusty servant:

> I intend next week to return to Rome to get all His Majesty's commands performed the best I can; but to do them as I ought must acquaint Your Lordship that Bishop Ellis and myself having received His Majesty's and Your Lordship's letters this post of the 9 October, to keep the business of the bishops'

faculties secret, I find that as soon as you sent the like notice unto another he immediately told it to another who I am morally sure will not keep it secret, but tell it unto one or many more, and so the secret will go about the town as a common known secret. This I think requisite to acquaint Your Lordship that if such (or other) secrets be communicated to more than one, no one can well answer for the discovery of them, nor for the good success, especially when they are sent to one who doth not and is not to know of that affair as it was ordered expressly here, for although more than one may have good intentions, yet the untimely knowledge of several may spoil the execution, inasmuch that I think it requisite to send away immediately my Lord Bishop Ellis to Rome with the best instructions I can to hinder a farther vent and do evil, hoping next week to be there myself to conclude that and other affairs of which I will not at present give Your Lordship more trouble in, having been obliged (by the weakness of my eyes) to write this long letter on several days, whilst since towards the beginning of Sept. until now I could write no letter or but of late read my office, hoping this will be satisfactory unto Your Lordship and others also, being the persons recommended for the deaneries by the Bishop of Cork will be dispatched accordingly as I ordered Monsieur de Bru before I left Rome, and sent word to the said bishop at Brussels. In the interim I am very glad Your Lordship's good brother is safe as far as Holland, and if thence hither be not too far, will be bold to offer him an ill lodging in my house at Rome and here, together with my humble service, as with yourself and my good lady and family.[51]

The improvement in his health that Howard expected was destined never to come. He returned to his palace at the English College, but nothing is heard of him during the winter. On 11 March 1694 he made his will. He desired to be buried under a plain stone in his titular church of the Minerva, where his first Dominican friend Fr Hacket already lay. He ordered 2000 requiem Masses for the repose of his soul. The first charge on his estate was the sum of 8000 scudi to be paid to George Howard in satisfaction of a debt of £2000 that the cardinal had borrowed from his brother Henry. He gave a year's salary to all servants in his employ at the time of his death. 2000 scudi were to go to found places for a confessor and for a lay-brother in the convent of English Dominican nuns at Brussels. He stipulated that his life-long lay-brother servant Henry Peck should enjoy this place till death. He also left the nuns

## Closing Years

2000 scudi. The Flemish Ursuline nuns in Rome receive 500 scudi, and such of his effects as were in their custody, and a further 1000 to found a daily Mass in perpetuity. To the Oratorians of Chiesa Nuova, where he had passed part of his novitiate, he left the four great silver candlesticks and the crucifix that adorned his private chapel. One white vestment is left to the Minerva, a picture by Raphael to Innocent XII, and clocks are left to Cardinal Altieri and three other cardinals who had received the red hat with him; these four are appointed his executors. He left 100 scudi to Bishop Ellis, and in a codicil of 10 June added his coach and horses. The rest of his estate was to be used to satisfy one of his life-long desires, viz. to purchase from the Flemish Dominicans their convent in Douai. Legacies of 100 scudi go to Charles Hill and Francis Clayton, and fifty scudi each to Charles and George Dryden. George Hill receives his cupboard of provisions. To the English College he left the stables under his palace in satisfaction of one year's rent that was owing. Everything else was left to the English Dominican provincial, Fr Thomas Bianchi, and to his successors.[52]

On 30 April Howard was received in audience for the last time.[53] No details of what was said have been preserved, and it can only be surmised that they spoke of the affairs of the exiled king. On 28 May the general Chapter of the order met in Rome. The cardinal was by now too ill for such further business and was confined to his bed. He would have been gratified to have known that the fathers paid a tribute to his zeal and charity that had produced many sons for the English province, distinguished for their learning and gifts. They asked the Master General to do all in his power to foster this province, to help its missionaries and to enflame others to join in its missionary work.[54] On the 7 June at the conclusion of the Chapter, the Dominicans, over four hundred in number, were led by the Master General for their customary audience with the pope.[55] Throughout these days Howard's condition caused grave anxiety, though his life was not despaired of. His auditor, Bishop Ellis, has left us a detailed account of these anxious weeks, in letters addressed to King James himself. On 25 May he writes:

> My lord cardinal received the honour of Your Majesty's letter and commands, in bed and in the country, having been lately very ill of an accidental distemper which is turned to the gout. But his zeal and passion for your service made him discard his sickness and be taken out of his bed in men's arms to be

carried to his coach. Yesterday he came to town, but is not able to offer his humble duty to Your Majesty with his own hand: he most humbly begs you will graciously please to accept it from mine with the greatest assurance that he will make it his whole business to fulfil your commands in every particular as soon as his health will permit.

But if upon this occasion I may presume to make use of the liberty Your Majesty has been pleased to grant me of laying my opinion at your royal feet, with all humility I affirm the cardinal will not be able to answer your just expectation in this weighty affair unless Your Majesty vouchsafe to give him a commission as may qualify him to appear as your minister, and as such go to ordinary and extraordinary audiences, as Cardinal Janson does for France, Cardinal Goess for the Empire, Cardinal Giudice for Spain, etc.; for cardinals, as cardinals, seldom go to audience unless in consistory (which is once a fortnight at the most) when they have no time to speak of public affairs, especially with this pope, who will dispatch 30 cardinals in 2 hours or 2 and a half, and never sets longer. At other times they never go to the pope without asking leave, and sometimes are deferred several days before they get an answer, and when they are there are often despatched before they are entered into their business, for when the pope gives his benediction they must retire.

But he treats these cardinals otherwise who are commissioned by princes to treat with him. They have regularly their audiences once a week and extraordinary as often as they demand them, and never are deferred above a day. He also allows them as much time as they will to discourse their affairs. All this is as little as is necessary for one that is to manage Your Majesty's interests in the midst of so many enemies, and to break so great opposition. Besides, Your Majesty giving such a commission will revive the dignity and honour of the management of your affairs in this court, which have not a little suffered by several people pretending to be employed by Your Majesty or from your court, and such as one either utterly unqualified to do any real service, or publicly and certainly known to be in a contrary interest: which makes it generally believed in this court that Your Majesty has never had truly layed before you the true character of this court, of the men you employ, nor the right way of managing in it: and *in fine* that you do not at all depend of anything that might be expected from it in your present circumstances.

Sire, I might presume to add that Your Majesty's commission could fall very naturally on a cardinal of that rank and distinction, a subject so devoted to your interest, so much esteemed and favoured by the pope and so universally loved by his brethren and all the foreign ministers: insomuch that if it should happen that your minister comes to treat with those of other crowns, this is such a man as you would desire, that is, not liable to be suspected on any side, having kept himself independent of all crowns besides that of his natural prince and sovereign.[56]

He writes at greater length on 1 June:

> Of what I have discovered I dare impart very little to His Eminence while he continues in this weak condition: for he lays Your Majesty's concerns so much to heart that what I have already talked to him of them afflicts him more than his distemper, which is very great and not without danger. Yesterday on coming to take leave of him he charged to present his most humble duty to Your Majesty and to the queen, at which names he burst into a violent weeping, and that we could understand of what he said was, that he loved both with all his heart and had never served both faithfully to the best of his power, which saying of his, at a time when he thought of nothing and desireth nothing but dying and expressed with so much tenderness, and accompanied with so many tears, which I never saw him shed before, is a sort of an authentic testimony what faithful service Your Majesty may expect from such a subject, if God almighty please to spare him for that end. He finds himself something better today, and not so much pain in his stomach and bowels, where the goutish humour is at present lodged. His Holiness is in great concern for him, sends his chief physician every day, and indeed the whole college of cardinals and the whole town is in affliction by reason of the apprehension they have of him.
>
> I am always attending of him as well to assist him as to be assisted by him in his advice and instruction. The occasion makes me write to Your Majesty with less circumspection than I ought to do, and I hope will obtain my pardon ...
>
> Tho' I have been excessive tedious I cannot omit to add that the cardinal is continually talking of your concerns and shews that he suffers less from his pain than he does by keeping himself disabled to serve you at present. He sends me whither he cannot go in person, and the little time I am from him I employ in what I shall presume to give Your Majesty account of as soon as it shall come to maturity. The cardinal communicated to me Your Majesty's gracious letter to him, and My Lordship Melfort, which enlarged upon it extremely well. All these arguments and what else occurs, adapted to the genius of the pope, shall be made use of and set in the best light I and my friends can give them till such time as the cardinal recover to enforce them.

On the same day he was able to add a more hopeful postscript:

> Sire, since I wrote what is above, it has pleased God, as we hope, to hear the many prayers that have been offered through all the town, for the cardinal's recovery, and to give the usual efficacy to St Philippi Nerius's Cap, for soon after it was applied to my Lord, he voided several stones, when he had not the least suspicion of that distemper. The doctors say this is the best indication that could be, and bid us not doubt of his speedy recovery.[57]

A report of 5 June states that Cardinal Howard was *in extremis*, and on 7 June, the day the Dominicans were received in audience, his life was despaired of by the doctors. On 8 June Ellis informs the king:

> At present he is very weak and not without fever, which is no good symptom with the stone or gravel. Otherwise he is not in so much pain as he was, so that we have subject to hope as well as to fear.[58]

On 14 June Howard dictated his last letter to his old friend Cosimo III. The distorted signature is evidence of his pain and weakness. The letter itself is one more testimony to his kindness of heart:

> This will be the last grace that I ask of Your Highness, while a few moments of life remain. I implore you on behalf of my confessor Fr Thomas Fitzjames, who on my death will have nowhere to lay his head save under Your Highness's esteemed protection which he has already enjoyed in the past. I therefore commend him to you, that you may favour him with the customary generosity that has always bound me to you. Finally I commend myself to your holy prayers.[59]

Next day Bishop Ellis wrote at great length to King James:

> May it please Your Majesty.
> Since the last which I presumed to lay at Your Highness's feet we have lived or rather died every moment with fears it would have been my lord cardinal's last. He has been many days despaired of by all the physicians, and has been kept alive not with nourishment (for he takes not enough to sustain nature) but with the prayers of this whole town, which is all in tears, penance and vows for his recovery; for we can give no other account how it is that he lives. At present he has neither gout nor gravel, which hitherto have tormented him with all the violence imaginable, the matter having consumed itself. What remains is a swelling near his throat and a thrush in it, accompanied

## Closing Years

with a very small fever, all which would not give us so great apprehensions, had not his brother the late Duke of Norfolk died of the same distemper and with the same circumstances and indications. Soon after he had received his viaticum, to show what is dearest to him after his own soul, he thought fit to write a letter to the pope, of which I judge it my duty to send Your Majesty a copy,\* believing you would not be displeased to see the last action and desire of that heart which was full of nothing all its life but of God and you. This letter he ordered me to give unto our Holy Father's own hand when I went to tender his obedience and demand the apostolic benediction which is a thing of course when a cardinal or prelate is at the point of death.

Then he was believed on Corpus Christi so to be, and accordingly I was at the pope's feet for him, who expressed all the resentment imaginable, mixed with the greatest demonstration of affection and esteem, and would needs hope divine providence would preserve him for the service of the church, the Holy See, his king and his country. His Holiness was pleased to read the letter to me, and bade me assure the cardinal that nothing should be wanting on his part towards Your Majesty's restoration. When he was warm in expressions of this nature, to which I raised him by degrees, I thought it my time to tell him that there was something upon His Eminence's heart that afflicted him more than his sharp distemper or the sight of death before him, and that I did not doubt but it affected His Holiness too so far as to give him many unquiet thoughts, viz: that the princes on all hands had a design to strike up a peace without comprehending the King of England. The pope replied he believed so too, but I answered that could never be, because His Holiness would never consent to a thing so much against the law of God and nature; that would be the highest and most shameful breach of justice that was ever committed; that would be downright scandal to Christianity, a stain upon the Holy See, and take from that vast reputation that this pontificate would transmit to posterity etc., and a great deal of that nature that the occasion and my zeal for Your Majesty's service, duty and equity suggested to me. The pope allowed all this to be very true, but how can I help it, adds he, if they will do these things without or against my advice? I endeavoured to prove they would not on one side and dared not on the other do either, with the arguments I touched in my

---

\* This letter was to ask the pope to constitute a congregation of cardinals for the affairs of the English king. Printed in *Dominicana*, 92. The third line should read *gl' affari del Re d'Inghilterra*.

last, which I set off and enforced with all the vigour I could, because I knew endeavours had been used to make the pope despond and stand off, for fear they should not have due respect to his interposition. Not to be more tedious to Your Majesty, I won of him a promise to do all that should become a bishop and vicar of Christ in a matter of this weight, and that he would give his blood to have you restored if it were requisite. Here I told him that Your Majesty had committed the pursuance of His Holiness's good intentions and paternal affection for you to Cardinal Norfolk, to whom Your Majesty had been pleased to write to that effect just at the time he fell sick: that Your Majesty had also been graciously pleased to condescend so far as to lay your commands on me in your own royal hand, to be assisting to the cardinal, which I suppose gave the cardinal occasion to recommend me in that manner to His Holiness. He showed himself well pleased with it, and bade me come at any time very freely when I had anything to offer from Your Majesty or for your service, which nevertheless I shall not presume till such time as Your Majesty shall please to signify your royal pleasure concerning it. The meantime I shall lay all my measures to dispose the cardinals more and more that are judged the most likely to espouse your interests upon the account of honour or conscience. This thought of His Eminence to get a congregation established for Your Majesty's affairs is the most happy and promising that can be, for nothing has so much weight with the pope and binds him so fast, as the congregation: and in it we will be sure to have such men as otherwise have the greatest credit with him. I have already broke with Altieri upon it, whom I find as I desired, but dare not tire Your Majesty more at this time, no not with humbling myself before your feet for pardon of what I have already done, for Your Majesty is so discerning as to see my good will through my folly.

There is a postscript to this letter:

Sire, I cannot be at peace with myself till I have given Your Majesty the additional trouble of my profoundest gratitude for a fresh instance of your royal and unwearied goodness. Cardinal Spada came from the pope to visit His Eminence, to know what he would desire for his family or friends: but he would ask nor think of nothing but recommending Your Majesty's cause and begging our Holy Father would be firm to you. The cardinal promised the pope's and his own favour and protections to me, and that upon a new title, that the nuncio had acquainted the pope how gracious and condescending Your Majesty and the queen had been in ordering him to thank His Holiness for the marks of favour he had bestowed on me, and desire him to continue them. The cardinal added that the pope was very pleased that Your Majesty took notice of it... While I write this my lord cardinal is upon the utmost verge of life, and cannot continue there longer than this evening. I bewail the loss Your Majesty will have in such a subject in so critical a juncture. I cannot bewail my own (though very great in many respects) while I flatter myself that I am happy in Your Majesty's favour, and enjoy that blessing which comprehends and surpasses all the rest.[60]

Cardinal Howard died in his palace about the sixth hour of the night of 16 June. As the Roman day began at sunset this means that he died in the small hours of Thursday 17 June.[61] Later that day a post-mortem, carried out in the presence of some of his brethren, confirmed that he died of the stone or gravel.[62] His body was embalmed and lay in state in his titular church of the Minerva. On Friday the 18th all the cardinals resident in Rome attended his obsequies and he was buried in the choir behind the high altar, where lies the body of St Catherine of Siena. His monument is, as he wished, a flat stone with a plain inscription without adornment and without a word of praise. There he sleeps with so many of his brethren, including Fra Angelico and Fr John Baptist Hacket, the Irish regent of studies, who nearly forty years before had fired young Philip Howard with a love of his order.

The news of his death was conveyed to the king in another long letter from Ellis, dated 22 June:

> I would not be the first, and yet ought not to be the last, that should presume to mention the decease of so great a subject, or one so favoured by Your Majesty as the Cardinal of Norfolk. But it is only a necessary consequence of what I said in my last, that it might serve as preparation to abate the impression that the sudden news might have made upon the tenderness of your princely heart. Your Majesty's usual submission to the divine will, as to the sovereign rule of all things even those which we untruly call human contingencies, will enable you to bear this loss. I do not question but he will be more assisting to Your Majesty where he is, and that his prayers will put an end to those sufferings of his king and country which his heart could no longer bear, but broke, to make way for the soul and to take its flight towards heaven and be your agent there. It is certain,

grief was the principal cause of his death, and he had no other cause for it besides what relates to Your Majesty. From the time he heard how forward some proposals and negotiations were, that seemed to want a due regard for Your Majesty, he never held up his head. He suffered much from the gout and stone, but yet got the better of them, and there remained no indication on his body that either of them has taken away his life; for all the noble parts were perfectly sound and able to resist thirty years longer, according to the course of nature or any appearance to the contrary, in the opinion of the greatest artists that were employed in that enquiry. One of the principal having given me his opinion in writing, I send it to my brother to be presented to Your Majesty in case you are inclined to see it, which perhaps you may have from a better hand, for I sent a copy to Monsignor Caprara.

In fine, Sire, I am persuaded his holy soul is already acting with that blessed Spirit that put it into his mind to send that letter to the pope, to give it success. His Holiness has already spoken of it and showed it to some cardinals, declaring his resolution to appoint such a congregation as is there requested. Both your friends and enemies agree that nothing could have expressed so well the cardinal's duty and affection to Your Majesty, nothing so wisely invented to fix and determine the pope, and engage the dignity and credit of the Holy See to adhere to your interests. For besides that a congregation of cardinals is a most binding thing that can be done with the pope, and the only one that keeps him steady, it will also lay a necessity on the cardinals that compose it (who will be the principal) to be clear and sincere. For amongst our greatest politicians there are many who partake of the property of a certain bird that is not given for their emblem, for if it can but hide its head and not see, believes it is not seen. When these gentlemen find the means to work underboard and out of sight their measures are very different from those they take when they are in the eye of the world.

If I might presume, Sire, to add anything to this long discourse, I should do it to know your royal will and pleasure concerning myself; in what manner or posture it would please you I should live, for I must now live upon myself and stand upon my own legs: and am like a man that is going to set up hours after he had lost his estate. The cardinal, who had little to leave, yet as a mark of affection and to show he desired by establishment here, has left me a very good coach and horses and wherewithal to keep it. But the want of his shelter and protection will be a greater loss to me on other sides than this is an accession. Yet it obliges me to mourn him in a decent figure, with the addition that he having no relation here, the ceremony belongs to me to represent them, as the more dignified person of the country.[63]

The following letter from Caryll to Caprara was written (as will be seen) very shortly before the news of Howard's death reached Saint Germain. After acknowledging the news that his life was despaired of he continues:

> The king my master commands me to inform you of his wishes regarding the disposal of the part of the protectorship of England that becomes vacant on the death of the said cardinal. His Majesty wishes that all should be united in the person of Cardinal d'Este, in conformity with ancient usage and as it was united in Cardinal Howard until the part regarding temporals was transferred to Cardinal d'Este. For this purpose he has written the enclosed letter to the pope and sends it unsealed so that you may see it and be better able to further the king's demand when you present it at the feet of His Holiness. Cardinal d'Este can easily substitute some friendly cardinal resident in Rome to do the business of the protector in his absence, as has been done in similar circumstances, and there is no doubt he would nominate one fitted for the task. If it should occur to him to nominate his uncle, Cardinal Carlo Barberini, it would be very acceptable to His Majesty, as he is the nephew of the former Cardinal Francesco Barberini, whose memory is dear to the royal family, he having for so many years and so worthily exercised the office of Protector of England.

In a postrcript Caryll adds that the news of Howard's death has just arrived in a letter from Cardinal Altieri to the king. The enclosed letter from James was written before he had heard of Howard's death; it is dated 11 July:

> Since we have been afflicted by the very sad news of Cardinal Norfolk, it has seemed good to us, on the occasion of the loss, to us and to your beatitude, of so outstanding a man, to give expression to our mutual sorrow. Nevertheless our sorrow has at least this alleviation, that our servant has so well merited the many offices entrusted to him by the Holy See, and especially his assiduous labours and unremitting zeal in carrying out the duties that belonged to the dignity of a cardinal. He has left to posterity by his integrity of life, the highest approbation, and to the Purple a more than ordinary splendour. As we are naturally afflicted with the greatest grief at such a sad event, so we trust to the paternal affection and goodness of your beatitude

towards us to do everything possible to compensate us for this loss. Nothing could be more efficacious for the common good of the Catholic religion than that a distinguished man eminently worthy of such a burden, should succeed to the place of the deceased. It seems to us that nobody is more suited for this office than Cardinal d'Este, who for a long time has, at least in part, been protector of the English people. His great splendour of birth, his singular gifts of mind, his outstanding piety and his zeal both for the universal church and for the Catholics of England in particular make him such an obvious choice that no other seems conceivable. Therefore we trust that Your Holiness, with that paternal love for us that we have experienced on so many occasions, will accede to our wishes by granting this office to him.[64]

Innocent XII's paternal love for King James did not move him to appoint Rinaldo d'Este in the place of Howard. Ellis was able to inform the king on 10 August 1694 that 'the pope told me he had granted us a protector according to Your Majesty's desire, and I humbly thanked him for giving us a person so acceptable to Your Majesty and the nation'.[65] The pope evidently had second thoughts. He left the office vacant, and for the rest of the king's lifetime there was no Cardinal Protector of England.* It was just as well that he resisted James's importunity, for only a few months later Innocent XI's worst fears were realized. The Duke of Modena died without an heir and Cardinal d'Este succeeded. He surrendered his hat in order to marry and perpetuate his name.

* The rest of the struggle between pope and king for the right to nominate the protector is beyond the limits of this book. The queen's agent, Alessandro Caprara, continued to handle that business normally done by the protector. On 17 May 1706 he was made a cardinal and then, by a brief of 2 September, was appointed protector of England. On his death in 1711 James III (the Old Pretender) nominated Cardinal Gualterio, but it is clear that the moving spirit was the queen mother, Mary of Modena. In a letter of 2 August 1711 she thanks Gualterio for looking after the affairs of England since Caprara's death and assures him that he is best suited to succeed. She then embarks on a spirited defence of the king's right to nominate his own protector. She cites Howard's case as a precedent. She implies that Innocent XI accepted her uncle as protector as soon as he was made a cardinal, 'notwithstanding that the Cardinal of Norfolk was already in possession of that office in the time of King Charles my brother-in-law (who being a Protestant did not lay claim to these nominations). Even supposing the nomination belonged to the pope, he would never publicly insult the king my son by appointing anyone but the king's nominee' (BL, Add. 31254, f. 9). Gualterio duly received a brief of appointment, but not till three years later.

## Closing Years

### IV

After payment of his debts and certain small bequests Howard made Thomas Bianchi, the English provincial, his residuary legatee. The money was to be used to buy the convent at Douai from the Flemish Dominicans, and if this proved impossible, then to found a convent at Antwerp or Louvain. This would give the province three formal convents, all of them due to the zeal and generosity of Howard himself. Bianchi entered into possession of his palace and a very full inventory was made of his effects, an inventory that would make it possible to furnish his apartments room by room. In various Roman banks it was found he had deposited nearly 40,000 scudi, or about £10,000.[66] The cardinal's will involved Bianchi in two protracted lawsuits. The first was with the English College. It was claimed that the 10,000 scudi provided by Howard for rebuilding was a loan and not a gift. The rector on the other hand contended that they had lost all the rents on the shops that Howard had turned into his stables, and that the 10,000 scudi had been spent mostly on building his palace, which it was agreed was to be incorporated into the college on his death. Only the papers concerning the case for the college are extent and there is no indication of the judgement.[67] The other lawsuit was with the English Benedictines for the recovery of 500 scudi being half of a loan made to them by Howard.[68] It is not known whether this debt has yet been paid!

Of Howard's vast collection of papers very little remains, and that little is scattered in various collections. The following letter from Ellis to King James, dated 10 August 1694, tells us all that is known about them, and will be read by historians with dismay:

> Monsignor Caprara has sent to the provincial of the Dominicans, the cardinal's heirs, to have all the cardinal's papers relating to business. I presume to mention this to Your Majesty to obviate all subject of complaint. The cardinal for six months before his death (which he certainly foresaw) was continually burning his papers, and left none of public affairs that concern Your Majesty, but what he had either given me or communicated to me, which he had never done to anybody else, nor to me freely, till Your Majesty sent me order to serve under him, after which he had no secret for me. The papers concern managements wards and persons into which that monsignor has no insight, and so can be of no use to him (should Your Majesty commit your affairs

to him, which I am persuaded you will well consider) and may
be of much prejudice to others. But in this as in all other things
I perfectly acquiesce to Your Majesty's royal will and pleasure.[69]

Howard's lifelong desire of having, like the English Benedictines and Franciscans, a house at Douai where students at the English College might be attracted to the order, was never realized. The Flemish Dominicans were unwilling to sell. The money was therefore used to found a college at Louvain, which was opened in 1696. It would appear that Howard was prepared to sacrifice the Roman foundation for this new venture. His will makes no mention of Ss John and Paul and the annual income he had granted it ceased at his death. With no other means of support the students were withdrawn to Bornhem and only a skeleton staff left in Rome. Later the brethren made strenuous efforts to retain the Roman house, but it was too late. It was granted by Innocent XII to the Lazarists and later attempts to regain it proved fruitless.[70]

Howard's closing years had been darkened by the expulsion of King James and all that it foreboded for the Catholics in England and Ireland. His early hopes of toleration for Catholics, of a flood of conversions and of a Catholic dynasty, had all been cruelly dashed. The Catholics were about to enter the most depressing century in their annals. All that he had worked for seemed to have ended in failure and chaos. On the credit side, however, there was the lasting establishment of episcopal government in England, after the anarchy that had so distressed him. Once there was plurality of bishops the Chapter's claims evaporated and the Chapter became the Old Brotherhood. There remained the legacy of mutual bitterness that only time could heal, but there was never again to be the unedifying spectacle of open warfare between seculars and regulars. Nor was Tyburn to claim another martyr. The Catholic minority, crushed, disheartened, treated with contempt and ousted from public life, was still to survive.

If Howard's work for the church in England appears to have largely failed, his work for his order was destined to last. He had joined the order when the English province was no more than a handful of homeless men. He lived to see them a fully constituted province, with two convents and the promise of a third. In addition, there was the convent of nuns at Brussels that continued amid incredible hardships, and now flourishes with an unbroken tradition at Carisbrooke and Headington. If their growth was disheartengly slow their future was assured. A century later their convents were to be suppressed by the French revolutionaries, and they were to be all but homeless again. But their status of a province and the title of provincial were never to be taken from them, and they were destined to survive a further century of oppression. The story of their struggles in poverty and obscurity can never be fully told. Like the rest of the English clergy their lives were passed in ministering unobtrusively to dwindling congregations, and such records as they dared preserve in their convents abroad were largely destroyed in the French Revolution. But at least they had these convents in their darkest hour, houses for training the young and havens of rest for the old. They owed them to Cardinal Howard.

## Notes

[1] *Dominicana*, 85.
[2] NI, 20, f. 244.
[3] Avvisi, 51, f. 21.
[4] L. von Pastor, *Geschichte der Papste*, Freiburg, XIV, 2, 1035.
[5] Campana, *Les derniers Stuarts*, II, 505.
[6] Nunz.Fr., 179, f. 139.
[7] Carte 209, ff. 11–16.
[8] Avvisi 51, ff. 65, 67, 79, 110.
[9] *Ibid*. f. 162.
[10] *Ibid*. f. 173.
[11] *Ibid*. f. 175.
[12] Berthier, *Epistolae*, II, 445.
[13] Avvisi 51, ff. 228, 230.
[14] *Ibid*. f. 231.
[15] *Ibid*. f. 236.
[16] BL, Lamsd. 1163, I, 22.
[17] *Ibid*. f. 109.
[18] *Ibid*. f. 115.
[19] *Ibid*. III, f. 98.
[20] *Dominicana*, 86.
[21] Stuart, I, 60.
[22] *Ibid*. 63.
[23] Nunz.Fr., 180, ff. 318, 554.
[24] G.-R. Canpello, *Diario*, Roma, 1893, 11, 16.

25 BL, Add. 31246; the pope's letter is AV, ad Princ. 80, f. 131.
26 Stuart, I, 70.
27 Avvisi 52 (10 May 1692).
28 Carte 208, f. 5.
29 Stuart, I, 73.
30 Carte 209, f. 70.
31 *Ibid.* f. 24.
32 *Ibid.* f. 25.
33 *Ibid.* f. 52.
34 *Ibid.* f. 56.
35 *Ibid.* f. 58.
36 *Ibid.* f. 62.
37 *Les grands écrivains de la France*, Bossuet Correspondence V, Paris, 1911, 534.
38 Carte 209, f. 74.
39 *Ibid.* f. 66.
40 *Ibid.* f. 82.
41 Reg. 175, f. 187.
42 Carte 209, f. 58.
43 *Ibid.* f. 60.
44 Med. 3839, 9 and 24 Dec. 1689 and Feb. 1690.
45 *Ibid.* 3840, 24 May 1690.
46 AFOP, XXIX (1959), 187.
47 Carte 209, f. 74.
48 Stuart, I, 82; CRS. 40, 115, 116.
49 Stuart, I, 81.
50 Carte 209, f. 82.
51 *Ibid.* f. 84.
52 Oscott MSS, E.6.19; BL, Add. 38652; *Dominicana*, 89.
53 Campello, *Diario*, 65.
54 *MOPH*, XIII, 304.
55 Campello, 67.
56 Carte 208, f. 28.
57 *Ibid.* f. 44.
58 *Ibid.* f. 35.
59 Med. 3847 (14 June).
60 Carte 208, f. 37.
61 BV, Urb. Lat. 1701, f. 243; Avvisi 57, f. 214.
62 Carte 208, f. 219.
63 *Ibid.* f. 46.
64 BL, Add. 31245, f. 7.
65 Carte 209, f. 59.
66 BL, Add. 38652.
67 AVCAU, Scritt, 7, 13.

## Closing Years

[68] BL, Add. 38652.
[69] Carte 209, f. 121.
[70] AFOP, XXIX (1959), 168–77.

# Index

Aberdeen 248
Act of Emancipation (1829) 32
Act of Indemnity (1660) 28
Africa 74
Agretti, Claudio, Abbot 79, 82–7, 91, 93, 98, 102, 144
Airoldi, Carlo Francesco, Abbot (later Archbishop) 81, 98–100, 119
Albemarle, Christopher Monck, 2nd Duke of 245
Albert the Great, Saint 206
Alberizzi, Mario, Cardinal 142, 153
Albi 161
Aldobrandini, Donna Olimpia 5, 8
Alexander, Noël 203
Altieri, Emilio, Cardinal, *see* Pope Clement X
Altieri, Giambattista, Cardinal 87
Altieri, Laura 87
Altieri (Paluzzi-Altieri degli Albertoni), Paluzzo, Cardinal 88, 96, 98, 101, 102, 111, 112, 114, 124–5, 127, 135, 137, 143–5, 147, 149, 151–2, 154, 159, 162, 165, 171, 260, 262, 279, 287
Amsterdam 15
Andalusia 6
Anderson, Lionel 177, 186
Anderton, Christopher 181
Andover, Charles Howard, Viscount (later 2nd Earl of Berkshire) 30
Angelico, Fra 285
Antwerp 3, 8–9, 12, 15, 16, 119, 144–5, 149–50, 289
Aquinas, Thomas, Saint 4, 201
Aragon 6
Arlington, Henry Bennet, 1st Earl 98, 107, 108, 113, 117–20
Armagh, Archbishop of
  Maguire, Dominic 177, 209, 232–3

Plunkett, Oliver, Saint 52, 80, 91, 105, 108, 169–70, 177, 201–2, 232
Church of Ireland
  Boyle, Michael 233
Armstrong, Robert 15
Armstrong, Thomas 15
Arnauld, Antoine 202–3, 232–3
Ashley, Anthony Ashley Cooper, The Lord (1st Earl of Shaftesbury from 23 April 1672) 113
Asia Minor 66, 74
Atrumetum, Bishop of *see* Leyburn, John
Atwood, Peter 177
Augustinians 90, 233, 276
Avignon 145
Azzolini, Decio, Cardinal 37

Babington plot 175
Bacon, Francis, 1st Viscount St Alban 1
Baily 25
Baldeshi, Federico Colonna, Archbishop (Cardinal from 1673) 78, 88, 92–101, 110–12, 114, 116–20, 130
Baltimore, Cecil Calvert, 2nd Baron 30
Bangor 176
Barberini, Antonio, Cardinal 4, 5, 7, 8, 10–13, 110
Barberini, Carlo, Cardinal 287
Barberini, Francesco, Cardinal 3–13, 16, 23, 29, 33–4, 37, 52, 60–1, 63, 68, 88, 90, 110, 120, 122–3, 125, 128–9, 135, 144, 147, 149, 154–5, 158–9, 169, 171, 175–6, 178, 181, 186–7, 287
Barberini, Francesco (younger), Cardinal 188, 223, 236
Barberini, Taddeo 5, 11

Barrilon d'Amoncourt, Paul, Marquis de Branges 216–17, 235
Basle (Basel) 190–1
Bath 176
Battista, Giovanni 100
Baylie, Richard 2
Beaumont, Francis 1
Bede, the Venerable 67
Bedford 113
Bedloe, William 178
Bellings, Sir Richard 36, 250
Benedictine Order 34, 36, 40, 48, 53, 63, 74, 75, 85, 118, 128, 135, 151, 170–1, 177, 209, 216, 289–90
Berkeley, George, 1st Earl of 205
Berkeley, John, 1st Baron Berkeley of Stratton 108
Berlaymont, Louis Floride de, Archbishop 144
Bernardine, Thomas 12
Berwick 25
Bethaeus, Thomas 17
Bethan, John 194
Bética 6
Bianchi, Thomas *see* White, Charles
Bing, Edward 176
Bingen 192
Bishop, William, Bishop of Chalcedon 58, 91, 98, 114, 116, 118, 200–1
Blancarius, Julianus 211
Blood, Thomas, Colonel 106
Bloody Assizes 218
Bohemia 6
Bologna 105, 125, 152–3, 167
Borghese, Paolo 5
Booth, George, General (2nd Baronet, later 1st Lord Delamer) 25
Bornhem 19–26, 39–41, 119, 134, 136–7, 144–5, 150, 176, 244, 290
Bouillon, Emmanuel-Théodose de La Tour d'Auvergne de, Cardinal 162–4
Boyne, Battle of 261, 263
Breda, Declaration of 26, 28
Bremen 111

Brest 251, 265
Bristol 43, 176
*Britannia*, brief 58
Brouncker, William, 2nd Viscount 51
Browne, Thomas 1
Brudenell, Thomas, The Lord (later 1st Earl of Cardigan) 30, 31
Bruges 24
Brussels 9, 16, 19, 20–2, 24–5, 27, 38, 41, 66, 69, 70, 82–3, 87, 107, 116–17, 124 133, 136, 143–5, 150–1, 200, 202, 204, 223, 278, 290
Buckingham, George Villiers, 2nd Duke of 113, 117, 120
Bulgaria 66
Bunyan, John 113
Buonvisi, Antonio 214
Buonvisi, Francesco, Cardinal 212–14, 232–3
Burbury, John 3, 42
Burnet, Gilbert (later Bishop of Salisbury) 205, 218–19
Byrd, William 1

Calais 25
Calvinists 19, 190
Cambridge 56
  St John's College 2
Campion, Charles (alias Wigmore) 205, 221
Campion, Edmund 1
Canaries, the 50
Cane, Father 236–7
Canons Regular of the Lateran 5
Canterbury 54, 74, 131, 252
Canterbury, Archbishop of
  Thomas, Saint 54–5, 264
  Grindal, Edmund 62
  Juxon, William (Charles II) 209
  Sancroft, William (James II) 209
Capello, Marius Ambrosius, Bishop 144, 149–50
Capponi, Luigi, Cardinal 11
Caprara, Alessandro (later Cardinal) 241, 259, 264, 273, 277–8, 286–9

*Index*

Capuchin Order 36, 38, 43, 48, 49, 53, 63, 89, 90, 103
Carisbrooke 291
Carlos II, King of Spain 162, 244, 247, 262
Carmelite Order 36
Carrington, Charles Smyth, 1st Viscount 30
Carthusian Order 24, 152
Caryll, John, Lord 218, 226, 240, 287
Castel Gandolfo 167, 202–3, 220, 265, 267–8, 277
Castlemaine, Roger Palmer, Earl of 215–16, 219–22, 226–7, 234–7, 240, 251, 256, 264
Cataloni 102
Catchmay, George 15, 16, 41
Catherine of Siena, Saint 285
Cattaneo, Marchesse 241
Cecil, James, 3rd Earl of Salisbury 31
Cecil, James, 4th Earl of Salisbury 247
Cecil, Robert, 1st Earl of Salisbury 1
Cerri, Urbano 117
Chailot 125
Chalcedon, Bishop of 97 *see* Bishop, William & Smith, Richard
Chamberlayne, Edward 47
Chapter of the English Church (London Chapter, later Old Brotherhood) 58–9, 66–7, 70, 73–82, 84, 85, 91–3, 95–101, 103, 109–11, 114–20, 129, 146–7, 149, 174–5, 177–8, 193–201, 206, 215, 290
Charles I, King 2, 26, 28, 55, 191
Charles II 12, 24, 25–31, 33–8, 42, 49–50, 52, 56, 59, 64, 67, 75, 83–6, 90–1, 98, 100, 102, 105–6, 108, 113, 115, 117–24, 126, 130, 133–5, 137, 148–50, 159, 161, 163–4, 168–9, 173–5, 183–4, 191–3, 207, 209, 212–13, 215

Chester 25
Chigi, Flavio, Cardinal 37, 111, 165
China 74
Chirugion's Arms 204–5
Churchill, Father 245–6
Cianti, Ignazio 6, 7
Cistercian Order 20, 22
Civita Vecchia 107–8, 129, 131, 151
Clarendon, Henry Hyde, 2nd Earl of 233
Clayton, Francis 279
Cleveland, Barbara Palmer (Countess of Castlemaine), 1st Duchess of 215–16
Catherine of Braganza, Queen Consort 33–9, 42–3, 48–9, 52–6, 59, 61–4, 67, 81–2, 83–7, 89–91, 95, 98, 102, 105–9, 119, 121, 124, 126, 133–7, 147–9, 154, 163, 168–9, 175, 200, 204, 209, 211, 215, 250
Clifford, Thomas, (from 22 April 1672 1st Baron Clifford of Chudleigh) 113, 119
Cloche, Antonius 214
Codrington, Thomas 193
Coke, Edward 1
Coleman, Edward, Blessed 127, 161, 167–8, 177
Collingwood, George 276
Collins, William 21, 22, 176
Cologne 24
Coloma, Peter, Baron of Bornhem 19
Coloma, Peter (son of above) 20
Coloma, John Francis 21
Colonna, Egidio 112
Conclave
  (1669–70) 87
  (1676) 160–5
  (1689) 258
  (1691) 262–3
Congregation of Relics 201
Conn, Patrick 29, 34, 36, 110, 120, 128, 149, 154–5, 167, 169, 175
Constantine the Great 213, 248
Constantinople 42

297

Constantinople, Patriarch of 66
Coomans, Hyacinth 144
Cooper, Samuel 50
Cooper, Thomas 247
Cooper, Vincent 175
Corboniana, Prince 112
Cork, John Sleyne, Bishop of 272–3, 278
Coniuxdorp 21
Cosimo III, Prince of Tuscany 48–51, 56, 91, 134–5, 146, 151–3, 204, 206, 216–17, 244, 275, 282
Crescenzi, Alessandro, Cardinal 142
Cromwell, Oliver 15, 24, 31, 48, 209
Cuba, Diego Evelino Hurtado de Compostela, Bishop of 246
Cremona 3, 4, 8, 9, 88
Cunningham, James 14, 17
Cybo, Alderano, Cardinal 158, 220

d'Adda, Ferdinando (from 1686 Archbishop, from 1690 Cardinal) 215–20, 226–7, 232, 234, 238, 242–3, 250–2, 255, 257
Daggitt, George 21
Dangerfield, Thomas 178
D'Aquino, Carlo 250
D'Arcy, Arthur 12
Darcy, Oliver, Bishop 54
Darnley, Henry Stuart, Lord, King Consort of Scotland 2
Dartmouth, George Legge, 1st Baron 236
d'Aubigny, Esmé Stuart, 1st Duke of Lennox 2
d'Aubigny, Esmé Stuart, 3rd Duke of Lennox 2
d'Aubigny, Ludovic Stuart, 10th Seigneur 17, 29, 30, 33, 35, 37, 38, 41, 43, 51, 59, 101, 170
d'Avaux, M. 122
Davis, John 134
de Almeida, Paulo de 48
de Bru, Monsieur 273, 278
de Cabanes, Peter Dominic Joseph

de Gereuse 145
Declaration of Indulgence 117, 121, 133–4
Deepdene 35
del Rosario, Cristoval 36, 48
de Marinis, Domenico 6–8, 12
de Marinis, Giovanbattista 7, 13, 94
de Medici, Marie, Queen 2–3
de Mello, Francisco 33
de Montespan, Françoise Athénaïs de Rochechouart de Mortemart, Marquise 174
Dempsey, John 240, 273
Denmark 66
de Retz, Jean François Paul de Gondi, Cardinal 29, 37, 222
de Rocaberti, John Thomas 94
d'Este, Alfonso IV, Duke of Modena 121
d'Este, Eleanora 121–2, 126, 128, 130
d'Este, Laura 121–2, 125, 130, 204, 210–11, 221–2, 227, 241
d'Este, Maria Beatrice *see* Mary of Modena
d'Este, Rinaldo, Cardinal 131, 222–8, 234, 238–43, 255–62, 264, 287
D'Estrées, César, Cardinal 141–3, 159–60, 164, 166, 256–8, 265
Descartes, René 1
de Vecchii, Girolamo 38
Dieppe 41
Digby, George, 2nd Earl of Bristol 30
Digby, John 8, 10
Digby, Sir Kenelm 8, 30, 31
Domaneschio, Petro Maria 190
Dominic, Saint 152
Dominic of the Rosary (Dominic O'Daly) 14
Dominican Nuns 20, 26, 39, 40, 136, 150, 202, 278, 290
Donne, John 1
Douai 40–1, 59–60, 81, 93, 144, 149, 151, 170, 190–1, 249, 275, 279, 289–90

*Index*

Dover 25, 27, 43, 135
Dover, Treaty of 113
Downside Abbey 55
Drayton [Dryden], Charles 275–6, 279
Drayton [Dryden], John (son) 275–6, 279
Drayton [Dryden], John 247, 275–6
Drayton, Michael 1
Drewe, Ambrosius 20
Dryden, Erasmus (Thomas) 275
Dryden, John *see* Drayton, John
Dublin 134, 240, 258, 273
Dugdale, William 232
Dunkirk 35
Dunne, Edmund 240

Edinburgh 25, 56
  Castle 266
  Holyrood 248
Ellis, Humphrey 59, 147, 178
Ellis, Philip, Bishop 274–9, 282–9
Elizabeth I, Queen 1, 19, 56, 62, 117, 169, 177
Ely 176
Emperor Leopold I 259
Erasmus 54
Evelyn, John 42, 55
Evelyn, John (son of above) 42

Faenza 153
Falconieri, 144
Falkner, John 59
Farnese, Odoardo, Cardinal 66
Faversham 252, 265
Felton, John, Blessed 134
Fernandez, Antonio 48, 52
Ferrara 152, 157
Fidden, Thomas 176
Fifth Monarchists 36
Filipponi 143–5
Fitzhenry, Michael 240
Fitzjames, Thomas 282
Florence 50, 152–3, 264
  S. Lorenzo 206
  S. Marco 153, 206
  S. Maria Novella 153, 275

Flume, Ignazio 12
Forbes, Thomas 77, 92, 95–6, 98, 100, 101, 106, 109–10, 111, 114–17, 129
Forbin-Janson, Toussaint de, Cardinal 265, 271, 275, 280
Forli 153
Fowler, William 15
Fra Angelico 285
Francesco II, Duke of Modena 224, 226
Franciscan Order 3, 19, 20, 34–5, 38, 40, 49, 51, 169, 177, 191, 204, 209, 273, 276, 290
Fulton, William 78
Fürstenberg, Wilhelm Egon von, Cardinal 262

Gage, Francis 77, 149, 174
Galli, Padre 216
Gallicanism 57, 73, 129, 141, 165, 234, 256
Garimberti, Andrea 121, 123, 125, 128, 130
Gastaldi, Girolamo, Cardinal 167
Genethliacon 250
Geneva 190
Genoa 6, 220
Gerard, John 1
Germany 6, 150, 248, 273
Ghent 21, 23, 52, 184, 209
Gibello 190
Giffard, Bonaventure, Bishop 194, 249, 252
Gifford, Maurice 176
Ginn, Patrick 48, 86
Giudice, Francesco del, Cardinal 280
Gloucester 176
Godden, Thomas 48, 59, 73
Godden, John 194
Goderington 195
Goess (Goës), Johann von, Cardinal 280
Gonsalvo of Amarante, Blessed 56
Gordon, Mary 247
Gravesend 252

Great Fire of London 56
Greece 66
Green, John (Raymund) 50, 134
Grenville, Sir John 26
Grey, Lord 16
Grey, Henry Yelverton, 15th Baron de (from 1690 1st Viscount de Longueville) 205
Grimaldi - Cavalleroni, Girolamo, Cardinal 142–3, 164
Gualterio, Filippo Antonio, Cardinal 288
Gunpowder plot 175
Gwillim, Dominic ('Mr Jacob') 205, 244–6

Hackett, John Baptist 3, 9, 42, 88, 94–6, 98, 165, 278, 285
Hales, Charles 247
Hales, Sir Edward, 3rd Baronet 232, 247
Halifax, George Saville, 1st Viscount (later 1st Earl then 1st Marquess of) 117, 120
Hamilton, Sir James 16
Hamilton, William, Duke of 248
Harvey, William 1
Harwich 49
Hayes, Mr 161, 168
Headington 291
Helenopolis, Bishop of 116–21
Henrietta, Duchess of Orleans 41
Henrietta Maria, Queen Consort 2, 8, 14, 16, 30–3, 38, 43, 56, 61, 89, 90, 109, 146
Henry VIII, King 27, 160, 169
Hertogh, Louisa 39
Hexham 15
Hill, Charles 279
Hill, George 279
Hitchcock, William 170
Hodgson, George 77
Holden, Henry 185
Holland 1, 26, 67, 93, 101, 268, 278
Holt, Alexander 78–82, 92, 93, 95, 98, 106, 109, 115, 117, 147, 182, 200

Holy Office 75, 102, 103, 112, 117, 203
Holzhauser, Batholomäus 191–2
Horace 189
Howard, Antonia (Catherine) 39–40
Howard, Bernard 42, 50
Howard, Bernard (son of above) 268
Howard, Charles 35, 42
Howard, Edward 42
Howard, Elizabeth (mother of Cardinal) 2, 149
Howard, Elizabeth (niece of Cardinal) 169
Howard, George 278
Howard, Henry, 7th Duke of Norfolk 250
Howard, Henry, 1st Earl of Norwich (then 6th Duke of Norfolk) 2, 3, 9–11, 30–1, 42, 60–1, 106–7, 133, 146–9, 158, 169, 204, 251, 278, 283
Howard, Henry Frederick, 15th Earl of Arundel 2–3
Howard, John Stafford 149
Howard, Philip, 13th Earl of Arundel (attainted 1589), Saint 2
Howard, Thomas, 14th Earl of Arundel (restored 1604) 2–3, 5, 8–12, 42
Howard, Thomas, 16th Earl of Arundel (restored as 5th Duke of Norfolk in 1660) 2, 3, 51, 75
Howard, Thomas, Lord (nephew of Cardinal) 146, 149, 209, 245, 250–1
Howard, Thomas, 1st Earl of Berkshire 30
Howard, Thomas, 3rd Earl of Berkshire 276
Howard, William, Viscount Stafford, Blessed 2, 13, 30, 87, 149, 177
Huddleston, John 34, 134, 209
Huguenots 30, 163, 231
Hungary 6, 262

# Index

Huntly, George Gordon, 4th Marquess of (later 1st Duke of Gordon) 169
Hussoni, Giovan Battista 122–3, 130
Hyde, Anne, Duchess of York and Albany 17, 66
Hyde, Edward, Baron (later 1st Earl of Clarendon) 29

Imola 153
Inquisition *see* Holy Office
Institute of Clerics Living in Common 192–3
Ireland 6, 22, 48, 50, 54, 60, 66, 68, 80, 108, 114, 168, 184, 190–1, 202, 232–4, 247, 251, 256–8, 260–1, 263, 272–3, 277, 290

Jamaica 75, 246
James I, King 54, 204
James II, King 14, 28, 66, 98, 121–4, 126–8, 132–3, 148–9, 168–75, 207, 209–28, 231–5, 237–44, 246–52, 255–61, 263–6, 269, 271–2, 174, 276–7, 279, 282–90
James Francis Edward Stuart (Prince of Wales, King James III, 'The Old Pretender') 28, 249–51, 261, 269, 271, 288
Jansenism 35, 57, 77, 202–3
Jeffreys, George, 1st Baron, (Judge) 250
Jenkins, John 25
Jennings, Sir William, Captain 107
Jesuits 32, 40, 54, 73, 75, 77, 81–2, 84–5, 94, 96, 101, 105–6, 112, 118, 127–8, 134, 148, 169, 174, 177–8, 184–7, 193, 203, 216, 221, 225–7, 236–8, 242–3, 248, 251, 255
Jews and Judaism 55, 60
John of God, Saint 158
Jonson, Ben 1, 109

Kemys, Joseph 147, 149, 176
Knox, John 248

Lambspring 201

Langton, Dominic 205, 275
Lauderdale, John Maitland, 2nd Earl of (from 2 May 1672 1st Duke of) 113
Lazarists 290
Leghorn (Livorno) 50, 130, 151, 206
Leopold I, Emperor 259
Leslie, William 60, 63–5, 68, 69, 89, 95, 161, 168, 236
Lely, Sir Peter 50
Leyburn, George 60, 81–2, 93, 108, 109, 174
Leyburn, John, from 1685 Bishop 73, 75–7, 94, 96, 108, 149, 161, 166, 168, 170, 178, 195, 202, 215–19, 232–3, 241, 244–7, 252
Liberatus, Saint 201
Lidcott, Sir John 236, 264–7
Lierre 145
Lille 151
Limerick, Treaty of 263, 265
Lisbon, English College 59
London
  Hampton Court 42, 49
  Haymarket 204
  Islington 49
  London Bridge 251
  Somerset House 30, 49, 108–9, 204
    Chapel 30, 32, 38, 43, 47, 62, 65, 89–90, 109, 124, 134–5, 174–5, 204
  Southwark 125
  St James, palace 48–9, 51, 53, 133, 216
    Chapels 34–6, 38, 43, 47–9, 51–6, 62–7, 70, 72, 85–6, 89–90, 98, 105, 109, 133, 204, 209, 217, 252, 276
  Thames 49–50, 125
  Tower of London 2, 54, 109, 249, 266
  Tyburn 15, 177, 290
  Whitehall, palace 38, 47–9, 51–3, 55, 105, 184, 232, 240
    Chapel 52, 55, 62, 65; new chapel 232, 252

Louis XIV, King of France 11, 100–1, 121–2, 125–6, 130, 141–3, 149–51, 162–5, 231, 234, 250, 255–6, 258, 265, 271
Louvain (Leuven) 41, 202, 289–90
Lovel, James 21
Lucy, Kingsmill, 2nd Baronet 205
Lucy, Theophila, Lady (later Lady Nelson) 205, 275
Lumsden, Alexander 177
Lyons 151

Macaulay, Thomas Babington 218, 247
Maccioni, Valerio, Bishop 111
Madrid 62, 67, 142, 145, 153
Maguire, Dominic *see* Archbishop of Armagh
Maidalchini, Donna Olimpia 4, 8, 11
Mainz, Johann Philipp von Schönborn, Archbishop of 191
Malines, Archbishop of
  Creusen, André 39
  de Berghes, Alphonse 149
Marcin, Count 29
Marescotti, Galeazzo, Cardinal 142, 151, 153–4, 157, 279
Marseilles 151, 220
Martinozzi, Laura, Duchess of Modena 210
Mary I, Queen 146
Mary II, Queen 173, 234, 247
Mary of Modena, Queen Consort, Maria Beatrice d'Este, 33, 121–8, 131–3, 149, 167, 170, 175, 204, 209, 216–19, 222–5, 227–8, 231, 234–5, 236, 240–4, 249–51, 256, 258, 260–1, 264, 266, 276, 285, 288
Mary Queen of Scots 2
Matthias, Saint 65, 69
'Matthew', Mr (possibly Anthony Matthews) 245–6
Mazarin, Jules, Cardinal 11
Mazarin, Michaele 6
Melfort, John Drummond, 1st Earl of 258–62, 264–5, 270–8, 281
Middleton, George 77
Middleton, Thomas 15, 16
Milan 3, 8, 165
  S. Eustorgio 3
  S. Maria delle Grazie 9
Milton, John 1, 50
Modena 122–4, 128, 130, 132, 216, 264
Modena, Francis II, Duke of 121
Molloy, Francis 191
Monk, George, General (from 1660 1st Duke of Albemarle) 25
Monmouth, James Scott, 1st Duke of 211
Montacute, Viscount 30
Montagu, Edward, 2nd Earl of Manchester 108
Montagu, Walter 30, 89, 110
Monti, Cesare, Cardinal 8–10
Mordant, Henry, 2nd Earl of Peterborough 122–4, 128, 131–2
More, Sir Thomas, Saint 214
Morgan, William 221
Morlaix 14

Nantes, Edict of 231
Naples, S. Maria della Sanità 12, 13, 87
Neercassel, Johannes van, Archbishop 202
Nelson, Lady Theophila 205, 275. *See also* Lucy, Lady Theophila
Nepi 166
Neri, Philip, Saint 282
Nero 265
Nieuport 24
Norway 66
Norwich 42, 106–7
Noyelle, Carlo 251

Oates, Titus 32, 56, 118, 126–7, 167, 174–8, 184, 186, 193, 203, 205, 223
Oath of allegiance (1606) 27, 182–6, 236–7
Oath of Supremacy 27

# Index

Odescalchi, Benedetto, Cardinal (later Pope) *see* Pope Innocent XI
O'Flynn, Patrick 190
O'Heyn, Cornelius 217
Oratorians 9, 10, 279
Order of St Andrew 248
Ormond, James Butler, 1st Marquess (later 1st Duke) of 29
Orsini, Vincenzo Maria (later Cardinal) *see* Pope Benedict XIII
Orsini, Virginio, Cardinal 37
Ostend 108
Ottenbergius, Hermannus 200
Ottoboni, Pietro, Cardinal *see* Pope Alexander VIII
Oudenarde 20
Oxford, Magdalen College 134, 249

Padua 146
Pamphili, Camillo, Cardinal 8, 11, 221
Pamphili, Giovanni Battista, Cardinal *see* Pope Innocent X
Panzani, Gregorio 54
Paris 14, 16, 29–30, 34, 43, 58, 62, 66–7, 78, 82, 89–90, 117, 128–9, 142, 144–5, 151, 153, 162, 164, 169, 175, 178, 182, 185, 200, 251, 268
Parma 152
Paston, Sir Robert, 2nd Baronet of Oxnead (later 1st Viscount then Earl of Yarmouth) 106
Peck, Henry 136, 278
Pepys, Samuel 51, 56, 106
Pereira, Manoel 48
Perrot, John 193–6
Persons, Robert 1
Perth, James Drummond, 4th Earl of 247–9, 258
Perugia 206
Peterborough 176
Petre, Edward 174, 225–7, 232–3, 235, 237–8, 242–3, 250–2
Petre, William, 4th Baron 50
Piacenza 3, 10, 152
Piedmont 262

Piggot, Christopher 276
Pignatelli, Antonio, Cardinal *see* Pope Innocent XII
Pipi, Bernardino 188
Piracy 113, 153–4, 191
Pisa 129
Plague 21, 42
Plunkett, Oliver, Saint, *see* Archbishop of Armagh,
Plunkett, Catherine 202
Poland 244
Poli, Fausto, Cardinal 7
Popes
  Alexander VII 33, 200, 211
  Alexander VIII 258, 262
  Benedict XIII 113
  Clement VIII 116
  Clement IX 33, 87, 89
  Clement X 13, 87–8, 122, 126, 142, 147, 158–61, 223
  Gregory the Great, Saint 67
  Gregory XIII 62
  Gregory XV 114
  Innocent X 4, 8, 10
  Innocent XI, Blessed 75, 117, 162, 165, 167, 173, 190, 192, 204, 210, 216, 223, 244, 255, 257–8, 288
  Innocent XII 263, 279, 288, 290
  Paul V 116
  Pius V, Saint 55–6, 31, 115, 134, 157
  Urban VIII 5–8, 11, 16, 24, 114
Portalegre, Bishop of *see* Russell, Richard
Portocarrero, Luis Manuel Fernández de, Cardinal 162
Porter, Sir James 256–8
Portland, Jerome Weston, 2nd Earl of 129
Portsmouth 35
Portugal 35, 54, 166
Powis, William Herbert, 1st Earl (later 1st Marquess) of 209
Presbyterians and Presbyterianism 28, 36, 81
Primrose, Peter 16

303

Propaganda Fide, Sacred Congregation of 10–11, 15–16, 58–9, 61, 63, 66, 68–70, 74, 78–83, 88–9, 91–103, 108, 110–18, 130, 134–5, 158, 186, 191, 193, 249
Pugh, Robert 118
Pulton 80, 115
Puritanism 1, 15, 37, 233

Quakers and Quakerism 36, 60

Ragway, Thomas 276
Raleigh, Sir Walter 1
Raphael, Raffaello Sanzio da Urbino 279
Ravenna 152
Reeve, Richard 151
Rennes 14, 15
Richelieu, Armand Jean du Plessis, Cardinal 6
Ridolfi, Nicolo 4–8, 13
Ridsal, Baron 16
Ringrave 195
Rixon, William 205
Rocci, Cardinal Bernardino 142–3
Rome 3, 6, 51
  Chiesa Nuova 10, 279
  Collegio Urbano 211
  English College 59, 75, 129, 181, 188–9, 192, 210, 221, 236, 260, 276, 278–9, 289–90
  Irish College 75
  Minerva, the (S. Maria sopra Minerva) 5, 131, 154–5, 157–8, 165, 167, 201, 247, 278–9, 285
  Propaganda Fide, Collegio 129
  Quirinal Palace, 5, 10, 154, 157–8, 167
  S. Alessio 264
  S. Calistus, catacomb 201
  S. Cecilia 157, 165, 201
  S. Clemente 12, 41, 94, 95
  SS. Giovanni e Paulo 130, 166, 201, 210, 244, 247, 263, 290
  S. John Lateran 75, 129, 267, 269
  S. Maria Maggiore 244, 257, 263
  St Peter's Basilica 154, 165
  St Peter in Chains 5, 7
  S. Sabina 7, 56, 263
  S. Sisto 5, 11, 12, 41, 94, 95
  Scots College 75, 181
  Sistine Chapel 165, 201
Roncagli, Andrea 131
Rookwood, Robert 24, 25
Roper, William 30
Rose of Lima, Blessed (later Saint) 56
Rospigliosi, Felice, Cardinal 257
Rospigliosi, Giacomo, Cardinal 69, 102, 130, 165
Rota 200, 237
Rubens, Sir Peter Paul 50
Rump Parliament 25
Rushworth, John 50
Russell, Martin 21
Russell, Richard, Bishop of Portalegre 33, 48, 54, 115
Russia 66

Saint-Germain 251, 255, 263–4, 274, 287
Saint-Omer 40, 181, 184
Salisbury 42
Sanderi, Nicolai 214
Savoy, Duchy of 251, 262
Scotland 14, 66, 181, 184, 187–8, 190, 247, 277
Sedway 176
Sergeant, John 178, 185–6
Seville 187
Shakespeare, William 1
Sheldon, Edward 128, 170–2
Shrewsbury, Anna Maria Talbot, Countess of 178
Siena 153, 285
Smith, James, Bishop 85, 195, 198
Smith, Richard, Bishop of Chalcedon 58–9, 98, 102, 110, 114, 116, 118, 193, 200
Somerset 250
Sorbonne 82, 116
Southwell, Robert, Saint 1
Southwell, Sir Robert 107
Southworth, John, Saint 15

*Index*

Spada, Fabrizio, Cardinal 142, 144, 150–1, 153, 279
Spain 6, 8, 13, 19–20, 25–6, 33, 39–40, 63, 68, 84, 90, 98, 116, 136, 141, 145, 151, 159, 161, 163, 176–7, 122, 150, 187, 206, 246, 257, 259–60, 273, 280
Spanish Netherlands, the 17, 19, 26, 145, 256
Spelman, Sir Henry 232
Spragg, Sir Edward, Admiral 108
Stafford 15
Stafford, William Howard, 1st Viscount, Blessed, *see* Howard, William
St Albans, Henry Jermyn, 1st Earl of 109
Stoupe, Captain 49
Stuart, Charles, Prince ('the young pretender') 28
Sunderland, Robert Spencer, 2nd Earl of 234–5, 238, 240, 243
Sweden, Christina, Queen of 160
Switzerland 262

Talbot, Alethia, Countess of Arundel 2
Talbot, Peter, Archbishop of Dublin 68, 80–1, 105, 108, 169–72, 178
Tanara, Sebastiano Antonio (later Archbishop then Cardinal) 145
Tangiers 107
Tempsche 39
Termonde 20
Terriesi, Francesco 235, 237
Terzago, Monsignor 10
Test Act 121, 131, 174
Teynham, Christopher Roper, 4th Baron 30
Thimelby, Sir John 30, 31
Thomas of Canterbury *see* Canterbury, Archbishop of
Thornton 50
Thursby, Lewis 154
Torbay 251
Torre, Christopher (Vincent) 14, 127–8, 170, 215, 244–5

Torquemada, Juan de, Cardinal 157
Toulouse 16
Townsend, Horatio, 1st Viscount 107
treason 27, 31, 75, 127, 168, 184, 186
Trent, Council of 131
Trinitarians 248
Tuke, Samuel, Colonel 30, 31
Turbeville, Henry 190
Turco, Tomaso 4, 7, 13
Turin 151
Turner, Francis, Bishop 241

'unicorn horn' 54–5
Urbino 152
Ursuline Order 204, 210, 241, 279
Utrecht 3

Valladolid 59
van den Berghe, Peter 21
van Dyck, Sir Anthony 50
van Vianen, François 202
Venice 3, 190
  ambassadors 63, 80, 83, 98, 147, 222
Vergil 189
Verjuyse, John Baptist 21
Versailles 255
Victoria, Saint 201
Vienna 100, 142, 145, 153, 212, 232
Vilanova, Duke of 149
Vilvorde 21, 39, 40, 136, 150
Virginia 247
Viterbo 129

Waldegrave, Sir Charles, 3rd Baronet 30
Walker, Obediah 216
Walsh, Peter 169, 178
Ward, Humble, 1st Baron 30, 31
Warner, John 178, 181, 183, 186, 193, 206, 235
Wells 176
West Indies 50, 74, 75, 113, 245–7
Weston, Catherine 129

Whitehair, Anthony 59
White, Charles (Bianchi, Tommaso) 128–30, 132–3, 154, 244, 279, 289
White, Frances 131
White, George 129, 131
White, Jerome 129, 131
White, Richard 129
White, Thomas (Blacklow) 57, 73, 82, 99, 129, 178, 184
Widrington, William 3rd Baron 201
Wigmore, Charles *see* Campion, Charles
William III, King (William of Orange) 173, 234, 247, 250–1, 256, 261–2, 265, 267
Williamite Order 20
Williams, Dominic 13
Williams, Francis 77
Winchester, John Paulet, 5th Marquess of 30
Windsor 50, 134, 216
Winter, Sir John 30–1
Worcester, Battle of 34
Worcester, Edward Somerset, 2nd Marquess of 30
Worthington, Thomas 13

Zeeland 24

www.ingramcontent.com/pod-product-compliance
Lightning Source LLC
Chambersburg PA
CBHW032018230426
43671CB00005B/124